THE LIFE OF WISDOM IN ROUSSEAU'S
REVERIES OF THE SOLITARY WALKER

THE LIFE OF WISDOM IN ROUSSEAU'S *REVERIES OF THE SOLITARY WALKER*

Thomas L. Pangle

CORNELL UNIVERSITY PRESS
Ithaca and London

Copyright © 2023 by Cornell University

All rights reserved. Except for brief quotations in a review, this book, or parts thereof, must not be reproduced in any form without permission in writing from the publisher. For information, address Cornell University Press, Sage House, 512 East State Street, Ithaca, New York 14850. Visit our website at cornellpress.cornell.edu.

First published 2023 by Cornell University Press

Library of Congress Cataloging-in-Publication Data

Names: Pangle, Thomas L., author.
Title: The life of wisdom in Rousseau's Reveries of the solitary walker / Thomas L. Pangle.
Description: Ithaca : Cornell University Press, 2023. | Includes bibliographical references and index.
Identifiers: LCCN 2022023453 (print) | LCCN 2022023454 (ebook) | ISBN 9781501769221 (hardcover) | ISBN 9781501769238 (paperback) | ISBN 9781501769245 (epub) | ISBN 9781501769252 (pdf)
Subjects: LCSH: Rousseau, Jean-Jacques, 1712–1778. Rêveries du promeneur solitaire. | Rousseau, Jean-Jacques, 1712–1778—Criticism and interpretation. | Wisdom in literature. | Philosophy in literature.
Classification: LCC PQ2040.R53 P36 2023 (print) | LCC PQ2040.R53 (ebook) | DDC 194—dc23/eng/20221107
LC record available at https://lccn.loc.gov/2022023453
LC ebook record available at https://lccn.loc.gov/2022023454

For the classical view, in which the Epicureans to *some* extent share, the object of contemplation is the truth; and *the* truth is *the* most common good. The most common good, which doesn't mean that it is *actually* shared by all men, but in itself it is the most common good. It is something radically non-private; it cannot possibly belong to any individual, to any nation, or so. It is the common good. Now Rousseau's common good is emphatically private; namely, the sentiment of existence, which is rooted in *my* feeling of my existence. It is radically private, and that is the deepest reason for Rousseau's so-called individualism. In the highest respect, the highest good is a private good, whereas in the traditional view the highest good is in itself the common good.
—Leo Strauss, transcript of 16th class on Rousseau, course of 1962, University of Chicago

The quarrel between the ancients and the moderns concerns eventually, and perhaps even from the beginning, the status of "individuality."
—Leo Strauss, *Natural Right and History*

Contents

Preface ix
Author's Note xiii

Introduction 1

1. "First Walk"—Rousseau's Introduction 18
2. "Second Walk"—Nature, Mortality, God 35
3. "Third Walk"—A Spiritual-Religious Autobiography 47
4. "Fourth Walk"—The Virtue of Truthfulness 73
5. "Fifth Walk"—Happiness 95
6. "Sixth Walk"—Goodness versus Virtue 113
7. "Seventh Walk"—Botany as Consuming "Amusement" 125
8. "8"—Renewed Self-exploration 137
9. "9" and "10"—The Solitary Walker's "Truly Loving Heart" 148

Appendix: The Meaning of the Word Reverie *before Rousseau* 157

Notes 161

Works Cited 211

Index 225

Preface

What is the good life? What is human flourishing? Do these questions have answers? If so, are the answers singular or plural? What human wisdom, what life of wisdom, most adequately comes to grips with the vast range of our knowledge, and the equal or perhaps greater range of our ignorance, about ourselves? Socrates and his students, from Plato and Xenophon through Aristotle and then the Stoics and Cicero, made the study of the life and soul of the exemplary, independent sage as possessor of "human wisdom," led by knowledge of one's own ignorance, *the supreme* theme and source of norms for political philosophy and for humanity's moral as well as civic existence. In medieval political and moral philosophy, from Alfarabi on, the phenomena of the prophets and of the saints forced this normative cynosure to the background; and on the peaks of the political and moral philosophy of the modern Enlightenment, from Machiavelli to Montesquieu, the life of the sage remained in eclipse[1]—until Jean-Jacques Rousseau. He restored the classical centrality of the life and soul of the sagacious individual, as supremely normative for political philosophy. This restoration begins in Rousseau's opening work of political philosophy, the *First Discourse*, with its vivid portrait of the "sage" Socrates and then its celebration of "those who feel within themselves the strength to walk alone, in their own tracks."[2] In Rousseau's subsequent writings, starting with the polemics over the *First Discourse*, the life of the sage takes on an ever more personal dimension that becomes elaborated in *The Confessions of J. J. Rousseau* and then in *Rousseau Judge of/Judges Jean Jacques: Dialogues*. The culmination is *The Reveries of the Solitary Walker*, where we find Rousseau's most profound exploration and articulation of his own life, personality, soul, and thought as "the human being of nature enlightened by reason"—presented as a model for all modern humanity. In this sense it may even be argued that this is the dimension of Rousseau's political philosophy that is intended to be the most practical, as offering guidance to individuals seeking inner liberation while living in the unfree world of late modernity:[3]

> I have penetrated the secret of governments, I have revealed it to the peoples—not so that they would shake off the yoke, which is not possible

for them, but so that they would become again humans in their slavery, and that, enslaved to their masters, they would no longer be enslaved to their vices. If they can no longer be Citizens, they can still be sages.[4]

Rousseau as "the Solitary Walker" is the embodiment of the peak of experience and of wisdom from which flows and to which points Rousseau's political and moral philosophy, his theology, and his musical and literary art (cf. Newell 2022, chap. 1).

Of that literary art, *The Reveries* is widely acknowledged to be an acme. Yet, this aesthetic appreciation has not been accompanied by an adequate interpretation of this writing's complex and multileveled intended *teaching*, about the normatively best way of life. This hermeneutic failure is no doubt due in great part to the initially bewildering form of the work, in its unprecedented and never again replicated character. The leitmotif of most scholarship was expressed by the scholar of French literature Lionel Gossman writing in *Daedalus* (1978, 69): in *The Reveries*, "anything is now possible and no order seems natural or proper." As for Rousseau's "attempt to make order," that "has only aggravated disorder." Or as Huntington Williams put it (1983, 166), "The *Reveries* in no sense develop." In "the work as a whole," there is "little thematic or logical progression discernible." For Pierre Saint-Amand, "the examination of the subject" in *The Reveries* "is concerned only with the ephemeral, the day-to-day." *The Reveries* "are written in the lightness of inconsequence" (2010, 248). Others go further. For the biographer Leo Damrosch (2005, 100, 471), we have here a "release from conscious thought" and "an openness to experience that bypasses conscious thought." For the editor of a recent critical edition, *The Reveries* represents "a plunge into the meanderings of the unconscious" (Eigeldinger 2010, 29). Such conceptions of *The Reveries* have been a contributing factor in encouraging studies that treat the work as a sort of quarry into which excavation equipment may be wheeled in order to carve out blocks in which the commentator can sculpt his or her own creative reading or inspired reaction. As early as 1964, Michel Launay protested "the tendency of many French studiers" to "make pseudo-mystic commentaries on the *Reveries*—in brief, reveries on the *Reveries*" (86). Surveying the previous literature, Raymond Trousson (1992, 489) asked, "So ought one to be astonished to encounter analyses in which the author deploys treasuries of ingenuity in order to force the text to produce" or "perilous acrobatics in order to impose, from the exterior, a prefabrication?" A leading twenty-first century study avows, "through Rousseau's *Reveries* I fantasize what it would be like for Wittgenstein to write the book for which he chose the title 'The World as I Found It.' . . . I seek in the future of the *Reveries* (that is, in our present) the possibility of bringing its meaning to an end"—"all of which makes the revelation of truth of this text independent of reaching an understanding with its author" (Friedlander 2004, 7, 114–15). Other interpreters have imposed on Rousseau's text, sometimes against its plain meanings, their own images of "philosophic eros" and of "the philosophic life"—drawing on and inserting their own spiritual autobiographies. This is not to deny that the scholarly literature affords many instructive insights into the text, nor is it to deny that some helpful steps have been taken in discerning Rousseau's overall, artfully sequential design of *The Reveries*—and I have tried conscientiously to acknowledge the aid that I have received in these regards from previous studies.

What has been missing, however, and is very much needed and is my goal in the interpretation that follows, is to bring fully to light the unfolding (if not always perfectly sequential or coherent) order and plan that governs and helps explain both the design and the intended teaching of the work, as an ultimately integrated if highly complex whole, whose artful unity emerges only for the painstaking reader who follows the text chapter after chapter, paragraph after paragraph, sentence after sentence, even word after word, while constantly conducting a detective-like philosophically and psychologically reflective, self-reflective, and circumspect interrogation—a dialogue with the author—in the light of Rousseau's oeuvre in its entirety.[5] What is needed and missing is meticulous textual exegesis that scrupulously abstains from textual eisegesis: interpretation that resists every temptation to read into the text what we assume must be what Rousseau as "the philosopher"—or as "unphilosophic"—meant to convey. But this is not enough. To fully appreciate, and to come to terms with, the education that Rousseau offers in *The Reveries* requires that one constantly confront Rousseau's teaching in this work with the profound alternative teaching of that exemplary sage to whom Rousseau throughout his writings points back in gratitude and in contestation: Socrates, as presented not only by Plato but also by Xenophon and by Plutarch. As Pierre Hadot has passionately contended, even by the title of his book *Philosophy as a Way of Life: Spiritual Exercises from Socrates to Foucault* (1995), we need to become much more intimately aware of those philosophical texts that have been written not so much with a view to studying and explaining systems and doctrines but rather in order to illuminate and to revivify, as vibrant models or guides, what Hadot calls "spiritual exercises" leading toward and constituting deliberately paradigmatic ways of living that philosophers have enacted and promoted, in deed and in word. It is, Hadot justly insists, "the figure of Socrates" that "causes" such exemplary spiritual exercises "to emerge into Western consciousness" (89, 91). "The point" of Socratic dialogue "is not to set forth a doctrine, but rather to guide the interlocutor" (and indirectly, the reader) "towards a determinate mental attitude"; it is "a combat, amicable but real." In an artfully written text of this character, as Laurent Pernot (2021, 49) has put it, readers "are not limited to a passive role as recipients"; they "cooperate in developing the meaning, are secretly flattered to assist, and, through a phenomenon of self-confidence joined to self-regard, cling more firmly to what has been *suggested* to them." Such, I contend, is the character of Rousseau's *Reveries of the Solitary Walker* (consider esp. *Confessions*, OC 1:408–9). I mean to engage in and to attract others into the "amicable combat" to which this unique writing invites us all.

Author's Note

All translations are my own unless otherwise noted. Citations from primary sources are by standard pagination and line, or section and subsection, of standard critical editions. Specific editions of primary sources are listed below for cases where references have made peculiarities or page numbers of the editions significant.

Abbreviations for Works Frequently Cited

CC: *Correspondance complète de Jean Jacques Rousseau*. 52 vols. Edited by Ralph Alexander Leigh. Geneva: Institut et Musée Voltaire, 1965–98. Vol. 52, Index, by Janet Laming.

CW: *The Collected Writings of Rousseau*. 13 vols. Edited by Roger Masters and Christopher Kelly. Hanover, NH: University Press of New England, 1990–2010. Contains the highly accurate Butterworth translation of *The Reveries* (see Butterworth 1979). Running page heads show correlated page numbers in OC.

OC: *Jean-Jacques Rousseau, oeuvres complètes*. 5 vols. Edited by Bernard Gagnebin and Marcel Raymond. Paris: Gallimard, Bibliothèque de la Pléiade, 1959–95.

Clear photos of Rousseau's polished manuscript of the first seven walks of *The Reveries* (Neuchâtel library, 7882.MsR78) are available for viewing at https://www.e-codices.unifr.ch/en/bpun/R0078/3/0/Sequence-211.

Clear photos of Rousseau's somewhat rough manuscript of the last three walks (Neuchâtel library, 7883.MsR79) are available for viewing at https://www.e-codices.unifr.ch/en/bpun/R0079.

For descriptions of the preceding manuscript materials, see Butterworth 1979, Appendix A and Spink 1948, which has in footnotes a careful presentation of Rousseau's alterations, interpolations, and marginalia.

In Eigeldinger's (2010) critical edition are reproduced photos of the notes that Rousseau wrote on the backs of playing cards around the time of his writing of *The Reveries* (Neuchâtel library, 7872 bis).

Introduction

Jean-Jacques Rousseau's last work, written from autumn 1776 to April 1778 and first published in 1782, is deeply enigmatic regarding both its subject matter and its (labyrinthian) form.[1] And unlike his penultimate major work—*Rousseau Judge of/Judges Jean-Jacques: Dialogues*, written 1772–75—this swan song begins with no helpful preface titled "On the Subject and on the Form of This Writing."

The first paragraph does afford a glimpse of authorial purpose: "But me [*moi*], detached from them and from everything, what am I myself [*moi-même*]? There, that is what remains for me to seek." Readers of Rousseau's previous works may well be reminded of the famous imperative inscribed on the temple of Apollo at Delphi: "Know thyself!" (*gnōthi sauton!*). Rousseau made this inscription the launching pad for his *Second Discourse* (OC 3:122). Here in *The Reveries*, we soon (4:1)[2] hear Rousseau declare that he has become "well confirmed in the opinion" that the "knowest-thou thy-self [*connois-toi toi-même*] of the Temple of Delphi was not a maxim as easy to follow as I had believed it in my *Confessions*."[3]

But comparing the evocation of the Delphic command in the opening of the *Second Discourse* with that in *The Reveries* brings home the fact that at the end of his life, Rousseau's response to the ancient Greek injunction has undergone a momentous change.

For when he invoked the Delphic precept at the start of the preface to his *Second Discourse*, he did so as part of his call on philosophy to bring to light the human soul, and human existence, "as Nature formed it," in "its original constitution" (OC 3:122). He proceeded to a recovery of the original state(s) of nature, in an analysis that paid no attention to any divergent uniqueness(es) of natural human individuals. Since his "subject interested mankind in general," he supposed himself in the Lyceum of Athens, with Platos and Xenocrateses for judges: "Oh Human, of whatever country thou art, whatever may be thy opinions, listen; here is thy history such as I have believed it to read!" (OC 3:133). Rousseau's project in the *Second Discourse* was the presentation of a wholly new version of the perennial philosophical project: understanding and teaching the original, and still universally underlying, nature of mankind as a species.

Starting in *The Confessions of J. J. Rousseau*, however, he has become preoccupied with a quest for, and a presentation of, deeply personal self-knowledge—of me, of me alone—an "enterprise which has had no example and whose execution will have no imitator whatsoever." Thereby, and only thereby, Rousseau declares, will he reveal "a human in all the truth of nature"—despite or because of the fact that nature "broke the mold in which she cast me." His *Confessions* is "the only portrait of a human painted exactly after nature, and in all its truth, which exists, or which probably will ever exist." As such, "it can serve as the premier piece of comparison for the study of humans, which certainly is still to begin." Imploring the innumerable crowd of his fellow humans, Rousseau asks that after they have heard his confessions, "each of them uncover, in his turn, his heart," with the same sincerity (OC 1:3–5; cf. Friedlander 2004, 20–22).

The Reveries may be understood to take a step still further in the same direction, if we spotlight the fact that here the question is not "Who am I myself?" but "What am I myself?" (Manent 2019, 220–21). Rousseau has come to focus on the following proposition: that what has become, over time or history (including prehistory), fully natural for humans is the realizing of the perfectibility that contains the potentiality for radically divergent individualizations of the primordially universal sameness of human nature.

The Reveries thus completes Rousseau's profoundly un-Socratic, because radically solitary, and often intensely anguished, quest for knowledge of his own-most, individual, unique me—a quest completed by way of a primary focus on reveries.[4] Socrates, in contrast, interpreted the Delphic injunction to mean above all a thorough, dialogical-refutational analysis and purification of one's own, along with others', treasured opinions about (universal) justice and nobility.[5] The Socratic quest for self-knowledge sought not so much an understanding of Socrates's unique, own-most subjectivity (his "me alone") but rather an understanding that confirmed the philosopher's sharable self-consciousness as a morally opining member of the human species (*eidos*), viewed in relation to other crucial species or kinds (*eidē*) in the accessible universe. Plato's[6] *Phaedo* depicts

Socrates continuing even on the very last day of his life an unusually humane version of this dialogical and didactic activity, together with friends;[7] and Plato portrays Socrates's days and weeks immediately prior to his death as times of intense, if often comically playful, dialectical engagement (see Plato's *Theaetetus*, *Cratylus*, *Euthyphro*, *Apology of Socrates*, and *Crito*, and also the implicit, deeply thought-provoking critique of the peculiarly Socratic dialectics delivered by the Eleatic Stranger, in the presence of Socrates, in Plato's *Sophist*).

The title chosen by Rousseau, *Les rêveries du Promeneur Solitaire*,[8] when considered along with the titles he chose for the first seven chapters, each of which is titled a sequentially numbered "Walk" (*Promenade*), seems to announce a collection and/or a discussion of the pensive musings that the author has experienced on long walks that he has taken by himself.[9] These solitary walks have apparently become so defining of him that Rousseau now designates himself no longer—as he did on previous title pages—a citizen of Geneva or J. J. Rousseau—or even Jean-Jacques but, for the first and only time, the Solitary Walker.[10] The word for "walker"—*promeneur*—is Rousseau's neologism (Mercier 1801, s.v.; cf. Spink 1948, 235). No previous thinker or writer felt a need for such a word. When Plato gives his striking and famous depictions of Socrates engaged in deep private thinking, Socrates is said to do so habitually while standing stock still, for lengths of time that seem nigh superhuman (*Symposium* 175a–c and 220c–d). On the one occasion when Plato presents Socrates on a long walk, he is conversing with a young friend, and both agree that such a walk is highly uncharacteristic of the life of the philosopher (*Phaedrus* 227–30). Xenophon presents Socrates telling of his habit of dancing alone indoors (*Symposium* 2:17–19): Xenophon's Socrates is a solitary indoor dancer rather than a solitary walker. A kind of walking was so characteristic of Aristotle that his school takes its name—Peripatetic—from those walks; but they were circular strolls, in a stoa, with Aristotle discoursing to and with his students. Rousseau is the first solitary walker.

Yet, we soon start to realize that the initial impression that Rousseau has created—that we will find his work's chapters to comprise subsequently written recollections of musings of his that took place on a number of successive solitary walks—is deceptive.[11]

The First Walk begins our disabusal. Rather than a recollection of musings that took place during a walk, what we are given is a seemingly spontaneous outpouring of an anguished self-expression that segues into a stream of sinuous and cascading reasonings, all dealing with the Solitary Walker's idiosyncratic present, past, and (prospected) future life. In this way, he presents the autobiographical justification for, and the explanatory introduction to, this extremely (outrageously?) self-centered writing.

Now, but if, or since, the title of this first chapter—"First Walk"—suggests that it somehow counts as a walk even though no walking is ever evidenced, does the chapter's content also somehow count as reverie, or at least as recollection of reverie (Martin 2008, 245)? An affirmative answer seems implied when Rousseau says near the end of this First Walk, "I am writing my reveries" (para. 14); and at the start of the Seventh Walk, he seems to refer to the entire first seven chapters as "the collection of my long dreams" (*rêves*); moreover, at the end of the eighth chapter, he apparently refers back to the fifth chapter as "one of my reveries."

We are obviously provoked to wonder, what exactly does Rousseau mean by, and include in, the category of dream or reverie? (For the usage of the French term prior to Rousseau, see the appendix.)

Rousseau's Entire Life as a Long Reverie?

There is evidence that when he started writing *The Reveries*, Rousseau was at least strongly tempted to convey the impression that he conceived his entire life's thinking, or consciousness, as being chiefly if not entirely reverie. After his death, there were found among his possessions twenty-seven playing cards on the plain backs of which (cards so constructed were common at the time) Rousseau had written notes, "all of which have a relation to the autobiographical works, and of which only the first eight have been numbered by Rousseau, the others having been by Th. Dufour" (Eigeldinger 2010, 171). The playing card numbered "1" has as its first sentence, "In order to fulfill well the title of this collection I would have had to begin more than [*sic*] sixty years ago: for my entire life has scarcely been anything except a long reverie divided into chapters by my walks of each day."

How seriously ought we to take this extraordinary jotting? Are we to include in the category reverie Rousseau's intense, sustained, and rigorous philosophical reasonings and studies—his intellect's building of his "sad and grand system,"[12] the achievement that, in the eyes of Kant,[13] is the equivalent, as regards the understanding of humanity, of what Newton achieved as regards the understanding of subhuman nature? But would this not be stretching the category reverie to a point where it begins to lose any distinctive meaning?[14] So, then, is Rousseau now eclipsing his genuinely philosophical thinking? Or, still again, is he shoehorning his past philosophical achievements into the category reverie in order to obscure the hard, rigorous reasoning that was at the core of his being as a philosopher? Or is he indicating that he has found rigorous philosophizing to be ultimately valuable as something like a ladder for ascending or descending to a trans—or subphilosophical, spontaneously rambling musing and sometimes enraptured consciousness? Or all of the above?

Reverie in *The Confessions*

We are soon informed that *The Reveries* is the sequel or even an appendix to "my confessions."[15] If we look then to Rousseau's book *The Confessions* for help in trying to understand what Rousseau means by reverie, what do we find?

Rousseau certainly does not refer to *The Confessions* as consisting of reveries. By far, most of the references to reverie occur in the first part of the work—books 1–6, finished in late 1767 and dealing with his life until 1743, or age thirty-one. There, Rousseau applies the word *rêverie*, and the allied words *rêve* (dream), *rêveur* (dreamer), and *rêver* (the verb "to dream"), to a thinking or consciousness engaged in sometimes gay, sometimes melancholy daydreaming or light rumination or fantasizing (not least, erotic).[16] One receives the distinct impression that in writing the first part of his *Confessions*, Rousseau did not yet assign to the term *reverie* anything like its later great importance (Tripet 1979, 28), which begins to emerge only in some of the rare usages of the term in the second part of *The Confessions* (bks. 7–12, which Rousseau started writing in late 1769).

Meditative Walks

In the second part of *The Confessions*, we hear of solitary walks on which Rousseau engaged in sustained and deep intellectual activity that he designates not reveries but the work (*travail*) of philosophical and poetic writing. Describing his stay in Geneva in 1754 soon after completing the dedication to the *Second Discourse*, Rousseau reports (OC 1:394), "I did not lose either the taste for, or the habit of, my solitary walks [*mes promenades solitaires*], and I often made rather long ones" during which "my head, accustomed to work, did not remain idle." On those walks, he says, he formed the plan of the work that resulted in *Of the Social Contract*; he planned a history of Valaise, he planned his (never finished) prose tragedy *Lucretia*, and he pondered a translation of Tacitus (later started and broken off after the first book). A year earlier (OC 1:388), he thought out the thesis of the *Second Discourse* by spending seven or eight days at St. Germain where, "without a care in the world," he came in at mealtimes, while "all the rest of the day, immersed in the forest, I sought there, I found there, the image of the first times whose history I proudly traced; I made a clean sweep of the petty falsehoods of men, I dared to strip naked their nature," and "comparing the human [made by] human with the natural human, to show them" in the former's "pretended perfection the genuine source of his miseries." Rousseau says his "soul was exalted by these sublime contemplations" to the point where it "raised itself to the divinity." But he does not characterize these "meditations from which resulted the *Discourse on Inequality*" as reveries.

In an instructive passage describing the momentous start (April 9, 1756) of his residence outside Paris at the Hermitage,[17] Rousseau draws a sharp distinction between (a) the countryside delirium (*délire champêtre*) of his first few days' walks, which "transported me in idea to the end of the world" (these sound like reveries, though Rousseau does not use that term); and (b) subsequent walks, when, "provided with my little white notebook and with my pencil," he made "the forest of Montmorency henceforth my office for working" (n.b., not for dreaming or reverie)—"having been never able to write and to think at my ease except outdoors." He adds with some manifest pride, "If one counts and measures the writings that I have executed in the six years that I passed" there, "one will find, I assure myself, that if I lost my time during that interval, this was not at least on account of laziness" (OC 1:403–4).

There is only a single passage, unique in the entire *Confessions*, in which Rousseau explicitly associates dreaming (*rêver*) with serious philosophical thought.[18] He reports that not long after the publication of his first philosophical work, the *First Discourse* (1751), and prior to the writing of the *Second Discourse* (begun 1753), whenever possible "I went walking alone by myself [*j'allois me promener seul*], I dreamed [*rêvois*] about my great system, I threw some of it onto paper with the aid of a blank booklet and a pencil which I always had in my pocket" (OC 1:368). Here, dreaming would seem to have been profoundly philosophical and in some sense systematic.

But this dreaming about the great system required the very extensive and intensive supplement, once Rousseau returned home, of sustained, hard, rigorous, self-critical reasoning—a mental discipline that would seem to be at the opposite pole from any dreaming or reverie. We are afforded by *The Confessions* (OC 1:352) a vivid glimpse of Rousseau's typical manner of engaging in philosophical writing, starting with his *First Discourse*: "I worked on this discourse in a very singular manner," but "one which I have almost always followed in my other works. I dedicated the insomnia of my nights to it. I meditated in my bed with my eyes closed" and "shaped and reshaped my passages in my head with unbelievable pains"; then, "when I had succeeded in being satisfied with them, I deposited them in my memory." Upon his secretary's assigned arrival each morning, "I dictated from my bed [not walking or pacing, n.b.] my work of the night," and "this practice, which I followed for a long time, has saved me from forgetting many things."

There is here no hint of reverie or dreaming or promenade. It appears that Rousseau did much of his most important thinking not in rambling musings on daytime walks but, on the contrary, prone, immobile, in bed at night, excogitating, designing, and redesigning.

And as Christopher Kelly (1987, 157) has pointed out, Rousseau never characterizes as times of reveries the several years that he reports having spent studying the works of Locke, Malebranche, Leibniz, Descartes, and so on, following the law that he gave himself to "adopt and to follow each author's ideas without mixing in my own or those of anyone else, and without ever disputing with him," thereby acquiring the needed apprentice's foundation for "thinking without anyone else's help" and eventually, "sometimes judging my masters" (*Confessions* OC 1:237).

As Heinrich Meier has observed, "in the philosophic writings he published during his lifetime, Rousseau had always used the term *rêveries* in a pejorative or ironically defensive sense" (Meier 2016, 17–18).[19]

In an earlier passage in the first part of *The Confessions* (OC 1:114), Rousseau describes more generally the "slowness in thinking, joined to vivacity of feeling" that he experiences when he is alone and "when I work" and which explains "the extreme difficulty that I find in writing." His ideas, he says, typically circulate dumbly in his head, fermenting there and "moving me, heating me, giving me palpitations," in the midst of which "I see nothing clearly." Only after "a long and confused agitation" does this chaos insensibly sort itself out: slowly, "each thing comes to put itself in its place," and this requires in part a process of writing and rewriting, resulting in manuscripts that are "crossed out, blotted, mixed up, indecipherable." Even before writing down anything, he says, "there are some of my passages" that "during my insomnias" have been "turned over and over for five or six nights in my head before they were in a state to be put on paper." Does this not apply also to the writing of *The Reveries of the Solitary Walker*?

Walks of Self-Expansive, Drunken Rapture

Two striking passages in the first part of *The Confessions* present Rousseau's recollection of the flowering of his imaginative experiences on solitary travels by foot in his late teens (the very last of these occurred, he says, when he was nineteen [OC 1:171]).[20] On one especially happy trip, at the age of sixteen, "my sweet chimeras kept me company, and never did the heat of my imagination give birth to more magnificent ones": for "this time my ideas were martial"; "I was going to become a military man"; "my heart swelled at this noble idea." And yet, when "I passed agreeable countryside," then "I felt in the midst of my glory that my heart was not made for such," and soon, without knowing how, he found himself plunged back into his more usual fantasizing, about being a shepherd, and he "renounced forever the works of Mars" (OC 1:158; but cf. 256).

We are at first inclined not to take too seriously this recollection of teenage fantasizing on long walks; but a few pages later, Rousseau all of a sudden exclaims (OC 1:162–63), "never have I thought so much, existed so much, lived so much, been me so much—if I dare speak thus—as on those travels that I made alone and on foot." Then he shifts to the present tense, to describe his walks now, in his maturity, and he judges the latter to be inferior versions of those long ago, teenage travels and fantasizings, when "I buried myself at my whim in the land of chimeras." Nowadays, in contrast, his walks in the countryside have an element of escapism: they bring about "a distancing from all that makes me feel my dependence, from all that reminds me of my situation."

But all at once, these escapist walks of his maturity explode in significance: they "disengage my soul, give me a greater audacity of thinking, cast me somehow into the immensity of beings in order to combine them, to make a choice among them, to appropriate them to me as I please, without impediment and without fear." Going still further, he writes, "I dispose, as master [*en maître*], of nature, in its entirety"; "my heart wandering from object to object, unites, identifies with those that gratify it, surrounds itself with charming images, makes itself drunk [*s'inivre*] with delicious feelings."[21] When he chooses, he sometimes amuses himself by describing the charming images, in order to fix them, and he succeeds in portraying them vividly; and "that has all, it is said, been found in my works, although written in my declining years." But "oh, if one had seen those of my first youth, those I made during my travels, those that I composed and that I never wrote down!" Then "I soared in Heaven"; "I felt that a new paradise awaited me." He explains that in those greater teenage ecstasies, he did not foresee his ideas; "they came when it pleased them, not when it pleased me." Either "they did not come at all," or else "they came in crowds, they overwhelmed" with "their number and their force." The images themselves were experienced in a heightened consciousness, but they surged into the consciousness—to a degree that he finds has been lost in his maturity.

Reverie in Awe of Nature

The preceding chimerical and drunken but mastering experience of, and posture toward nature contrasts with the awed and pious, more self-forgetting, explicit reverie experienced by the mature Rousseau and described near the end of *The Confessions* (OC 1:642): "I have always loved the water passionately, and its sight throws me into a delicious reverie, though often without a determined object." Recalling in particular his sojourn on the island of St. Pierre in the middle of Lake Bienne (1765), when he let his eyes "sweep over the horizon of that beautiful lake, whose banks, and the mountains which bordered it, enchanted my sight," he is led to exclaim, "I find nothing more worthy of homage to the divinity than that mute admiration excited by the contemplation of his works." He then reflects that "for me, it is above all when I wake up, worn down by my fits of insomnia, that a long habitude carries me to those exaltations of the heart that *do not at all impose the fatigue of thinking*" (my italics). In order for such exaltations of the heart to occur, however, "it is necessary that my eyes be struck by a ravishing spectacle of nature." "In my room," he confesses, "I pray more rarely and more drily," but "at the aspect of a beautiful countryside, I feel myself moved without being able to say by what."[22]

Years earlier, in his novel *Julie, or the New Heloise*, we find the first passage in Rousseau's published writings that expresses enchantment with nature. The novel's hero (nicknamed St. Preux) experiences a less prayerful and less pious version of the preceding—a version that, in St. Preux's case, prevented reverie or dreaming (about his beloved Julie). St. Preux writes to Julie, "I wanted to dream [*rêver*], and I was always *distracted from doing so* by some unexpected vista," all of which, taken together, "has something, I do not know how, of magic, of the supernatural, which ravishes the spirit and the senses; one forgets everything, *one forgets oneself*, one no longer knows where one is"; "and I felt *contempt for philosophy* in is having less power over the soul than a sequence of inanimate objects."[23]

Reverie Creating Celestial Friends and Lovers

> To make a prairie it takes a clover and one bee
> One clover, and a bee,
> And revery.
> The revery alone will do,
> If bees are few.
>
> —Emily Dickinson

A longer passage in the second part of *The Confessions* (OC 1:425–29; see also 489) describes Rousseau's very different, escapist creations of sweet chimeras of societies of true friends and lovers. The time described is the latter part of the crucial year 1756, after he moved into the Hermitage. Having "friends of both sexes to whom" he "was attached by the most pure friendship," he found that sadly, "this friendship was more tormenting than sweet" on account of these friends' obstinacy in contradicting all his "tastes, inclinations, and manner of living." In addition, though his residence was "isolated, in a charming solitude," his homelife "imposed duties—sweet to fulfill, but indispensable," making "all my liberty only precarious, more enslaved than if under commands." Worst of all, he felt plagued daily by numerous idle visitors. Falling back on recollections of the "unclouded days of his youth" and thus experiencing acutely his aging as a grim trajectory toward death, he fell into depression: "devoured by the need to love without ever having been able to satisfy it well, I saw myself attaining the gates of old age, and dying without having lived." What started to disperse this morbid cloud of mortal finitude was a move to a moral claim on life: "destiny owed me something that it had not given me." The "sentiment of my internal deserving, in giving me this sense of injustice, compensated me in a way and made me shed tears that I loved to let flow." (Were not the tears so lovable because they expressed the emotion of hope for some kind of supernatural salvation from, or compensation for, his just soul's mortal finitude—a hope whose fulfillment was made plausible by the conviction of being morally owed?)

Then these "sad but touching meditations," along with the influence of the lovely countryside, somehow led him into recollections that soon surrounded him with "a seraglio of Houris from my old acquaintances," with the result that his "blood caught fire and sparkled." But this erotic "drunkenness, however far it was carried, nevertheless did not reach the point" of flattering himself "with still being able to inspire love, of trying to communicate this devouring but sterile fire."

This "impossibility of attaining real beings threw me," he says, "into the land of chimeras"—into "my sweet and mad reverie" (*ma douce et folle rêverie*): "seeing nothing existing that was worthy of my delirium, I nourished it in an ideal world that my creative imagination had soon peopled with beings according to my heart." In "continual ecstasies I made my self drunk in torrents with the most delicious sentiments that could ever enter the heart of a human." "Forgetting completely the human race," he made for himself "societies of perfect creatures as celestial by their virtues as by their beauties—friends who were sure, tender, faithful, such as I never found here below." In this empyrean he soared for "hours, for days without counting," "losing the memory of everything else."

A fuller account of his reveries creating these perfect creatures, dwelling in a heavenly realm beyond all earthly and mortal limits, is provided in the *Dialogues'* report (by the invented character "Rousseau"[24]) of the society of imaginary friends among whom "J. J." lives during the hours each day when he is left alone (now late in life): "delightful societies, composed of men just, true, gay, lovable, simple with great enlightenment, sweet with grand virtues"; and "women charming and wise, full of feelings and graces, modest without grimaces, droll without silliness, using the ascendency of their sex and the empire of their charms only for nourishing among men emulation over great things and zeal for virtue"; among them "he finds for his choosing sure male friends, faithful mistresses, and tender and solid female friends who are perhaps worth still more."[25] These polyamorous reveries, creating an imaginary heavenly society of friends and lovers, bulk very large in the *Dialogues'* account by the character "Rousseau" of the life and the nature of "J. J.," while the lighter daydreaming reveries that, as we have noted, pervaded the first part of *The Confessions* are almost absent (the exception is at OC 1:846 and perhaps 1:849).

The most substantial product of Rousseau's creative-erotic reveries was of course his novel *Heloise* (begun at the Hermitage in the summer of the crucial year 1756 and completed autumn 1758). As he reports in *The Confessions* (OC 1:434–35), "everywhere I saw only the two charming friends, their friendship, their liaisons, the land they inhabited, the objects created or embellished for them by my imagination. I no longer for a moment belonged to myself, the delirium no longer left me." Once committed to the writing, "I threw myself into my reveries up to my neck." A bit later, Rousseau tells us, "it is certain that I wrote the novel in the most burning ecstasies"; "one cannot conceive to what point I am able to enflame myself for imaginary beings!" (OC 1:548).

As regards the much more didactic and philosophical novel *Emile or On Education*, Rousseau recalls in *The Confessions* that he composed the fifth book—about the love of Emile and Sophie—"in a continual ecstasy" (OC 1:521; this would have been in May 1759). In the text at one point near the end of that fifth book, he characterizes himself, the author, as a dreamer (*rêveur*).[26] And in a letter,[27] he refers ironically to *Emile* as "my reveries on education." In the preface to *Emile*, however, he predicts with some asperity that "what will be called the systematic part," which in fact shows "nothing other than the march of nature," will be especially attacked in the belief that it is "less a Treatise on education than the reveries of a visionary on education."[28] He later speaks in the same vein, predicting that the resistant reader will protest: "this dreamer [*rêveur*] always pursues his chimera!" while "he believes he is always following nature!" (OC 4:638); and Rousseau has his spokesman contrast the profession of faith of the Savoyard vicar with contemporary refined religious beliefs, referring to the latter as "our ridiculous reveries" (OC 4:560). Above all, in a footnote, speaking in his own name, Rousseau characterizes "the science fashionable in our century" in the following critical terms: "one no longer studies, one no longer observes, one dreams [*on rêve*], and one seriously gives us, for philosophy, the dreams [*rêves*] of a few nights. One will say that I dream also; I agree; but I present my dreams as dreams, which the others are not careful to do; I leave it to the reader to figure out if the dreams have something useful for people who are awake."[29] Here, we note, Rousseau treats genuine philosophizing and dreaming as quite separate and distinct mental activities.

The escapist character of Rousseau's creative reveries is further highlighted when he shares with us what it can feel like when he lacks the capacity for such reverie. Explaining why, on "the last pedestrian trip I have made in my life" (at age nineteen), filled with the pleasing anticipation of seeing his beloved Mme de Warens, he "did not at all have those delightful reveries" that he described on an earlier trip by foot, Rousseau steps back to observe of himself that "it is a very singular thing that my imagination never manifests itself more agreeably than when my state is the least agreeable, and that, on the contrary, it is less smiling when everything smiles around it." My unruly head, he says, "cannot subject itself"; it "doesn't know how to embellish—it wants to create." And so, on this particular trip, enjoying the prospect of meeting his beloved, he had a serene heart, without drunkenness: "my ideas were peaceful and sweet, not celestial and ravishing"; "in a word, I was no longer in the empyrean"; "the real happiness which awaited me dispensed with searching for it in my visions" (*Confessions* OC 1:171–72).

An Evolution from Creative to Awed Reverie

In the third autobiographical letter to Malesherbes (January 26, 1762, OC 1:1139–42), we find a revealing account of Rousseau's having undergone an evolution, from the reverie that is creative to a reverie about nature and its beings, culminating in an awed adoration of what transcends nature and all its beings. Telling of his enchantment with the spectacle of the forest on his solitary walks in his mature years, Rousseau writes that "my imagination did not for long leave the earth, adorned this way, deserted." "I soon peopled it with beings in accordance with my heart." From them, "I formed a charming society." Yet, "in the midst of all that, I admit, the nothingness of my chimeras came sometimes to sadden, in a stroke." Even "if all my dreams [*rêves*] had turned themselves into realities, they would not have sufficed for me; I would have imagined, dreamed [*rêvé*], desired still." He found in himself "an inexplicable void that nothing could fill"—a "certain yearning of the heart for another sort of joy, the idea of which I did not have and for which nevertheless I felt the need."[30] But "that itself was an enjoyment, since by it I was penetrated with a very lively sentiment and an entrancing sadness that I would not have wished not to have."[31] Then soon, he reports, "from the surface of the earth I elevated my ideas" to "all the beings of nature, to the universal system of things, to the incomprehensible being who embraces all." With "the spirit lost in that immensity, I did not think, I did not reason, I did not philosophize"; instead, "I felt myself, with a sort of voluptuousness, weighed down by the heft of this universe; I surrendered with rapture to the confusion of these grand ideas." More than that, "my heart, confined within the limits of the beings, found that too narrow; I was smothering in the universe, I wanted to cast myself into the infinite." Rousseau goes so far as to say, in a profoundly unphilosophical formulation, "I believe that if I had unveiled all the mysteries of nature, I would have felt myself in a situation less delicious than that stupefying ecstasy to which my spirit surrendered itself without reserve, and which, in the agitation of my transports, made me sometimes cry out, 'Oh grand being! Oh grand being!'—unable to say or to think anything more." Thus, Rousseau says, "there unfolded in a continuous delirium the most charming days that a human creature has ever passed"; "these are the days that have made *the true happiness* of my life" (my italics)—and he dares to add the wish, "may similar days fill for me eternity, I ask for none other, and do not imagine that I would be much less happy in these ravishing contemplations than are the celestial intelligences."[32] Apt here is a contrast with the unqualifiedly philosophical Hegel (2021, 21):

> The naive mind [*der unbefangene Geist*], when it intuits vital Nature, as we find made vivid especially by Goethe in a sensory way, feels the life and the universal connectedness in Nature; it divines that the universe is an organic whole and a rational totality, even as it feels in single life-forms an inner oneness with itself; . . . And so, in the Philosophy of Nature, people have fallen back on intuition [*Anschauung*] and set it above reflective thought; but this is a mistake, for one cannot philosophize out of intuition. The intuition must also be thought; every particular must be brought back in thinking to simple universality. . . . The determinations of philosophical universality are not indifferent; it is the universality which fulfills itself, and which, in its diamantine identity, also contains the difference in itself.

Noteworthy among the many characteristics of Rousseau's stupefying ecstasy that mark it as profoundly unphilosophic is the absence of any concern to look for or to analyze manifestations of final causality, either within the constitution of distinct organic species or in the system of nature as a whole. In contrast, when Rousseau in *The Confessions* (OC 1:392) tells of the time he lived among the philosophers, he says that "the study of man and of the universe had shown me everywhere final causes and the intelligence that directs them," and on this basis, "the frequentation of the Encyclopedists, far from shaking my faith, had strengthened it." Equally revealing is the contrast with the unpublished and untitled fragment describing the reveries of "the first man who tried to philosophize": "abandoned to a profound and delicious reverie, and guided by that involuntary enthusiasm that sometimes transports the soul out of its dwelling and makes it, so to speak, embrace all the universe," he was led, having become "the philosopher," to focus on "the idea of order and the relation of intention and of end that I notice among all the parts of the Universe." But at this point, Rousseau has his first philosopher enter into critical and analytic thinking about the pros and cons of mechanism versus teleology in nature; and this genuinely philosophical wrestling turns the reverie into an experience that is no longer pleasant: "the indiscrete philosopher was forcing himself vainly to penetrate into the mysteries of nature" and hence "its spectacle that had *at first enchanted* was *no longer* for him anything but a subject of *unease*, and the fantasy of *explaining* it had taken from him *all the pleasure of enjoying it*" (OC 4:1044–47; my italics). Penetrating, critical philosophical analysis terminates enchantment and replaces pleasure with unease.

Reverie in Rousseau's Penultimate Work, *Dialogues*

In the *Dialogues* the illusion-filled and creatively escapist unphilosophical character of the reveries of "J. J." is insisted on by the character "Rousseau," after he has met "J. J." in person and spent time with him in close observation. "An active heart and a natural laziness ought to inspire the taste for reverie." And "this taste comes out and becomes a very lively passion" as soon as it is "seconded by the imagination," which is "what has happened to J. J." Since he is "too subjected to his senses to be able, in the playing of his imagination, to throw off the yoke, he would not without difficulty elevate himself to purely abstract meditations, and he would not remain there long." But "this feebleness of understanding is perhaps more advantageous to him than would be a head that was more philosophical." This "renders his meditations less dry, more sweet, more illusory, more entirely appropriate for him." For after all, "which is the more consoling in misfortune"—"profound conceptions that are tiring," or "smiling fictions that are ravishing, and that transport the one who surrenders to them into the bosom of felicity? He reasons less, it is true, but he enjoys more."[33]

The character "Rousseau" asks his interlocutor, "The Frenchman," to set aside for a moment all the personal events of "J. J.'s" life and to focus only on "natural causes drawn from his constitution": imagine another person with the same nature but different life circumstances (*Dialogues* OC 1:820–22). What suits such a nature?—A contemplative life in which "there is no attraction more seductive than that of the fictions of a loving and tender heart, which, in the universe that it creates for itself at its pleasure, dilates itself and extends itself at its ease, delivered from the hard obstacles that confine it in this world." "Rousseau" goes even further, saying that he considers this "the key to the other singularities of this man" (i.e., of "J. J.")—or of any human with the same natural constitution: "from this inclination to sweet reveries I have seen derived all the tastes, all the penchants, all the habits of J. J., even his vices, and the virtues that can be seen" (OC 1:817). "J. J. is indolent, lazy like all the contemplatives: but this laziness is only in his head. He thinks only with effort, he tires himself in thinking." But "he is lively, laboring in his own manner"; "it is necessary" that "his body be exercising" while "his head remains in repose"—"that's where his passion for the walking comes from" (*sa passion pour la promenade*); then "he is in movement without being obliged to think." In "the reverie one is not at all active"; "the images trace themselves in the brain, they combine themselves as in sleep without the cooperation of the will." But "as soon as reasoning and reflection mix themselves in, the meditation is no longer a repose" and becomes a very painful action—"and that is the pain that is the terror of J. J., and the very thought of which weighs him down." "I never found" him thus weighed down, "except in all work where it is necessary that the mind be active, however little this might be" (OC 1:845). "Rousseau" quotes the following words as uttered by "J. J." to him in private: "to think is for me very painful work that tires me, torments me and displeases me"; "if I like sometimes to think, it is freely and without impediment in letting my ideas go as they wish without subjecting them to anything" (OC 1:839). Jean-Jacques "thinks only with lots of slowness and effort, in fear of the fatigue, and often not understanding the most common things except in dreaming [*rêvant*] at his ease and alone" (OC 1:798).

After the character "Rousseau" has succeeded in persuading "The Frenchman" to study with an open mind the system laid out in the books of "J. J.," and not least in the *Second Discourse*, with its account of the original, radically solitary, prelinguistic true state of Nature (*veritable état de Nature*),[34] "The Frenchman" declares that he has come to understand what led "Jean-Jacques" to so radical an insight into "those original traits so novel for us and so true once they are traced": deep reflection on his own personal life experience—"a life retired and solitary, a lively taste for reverie and contemplation, the habit of returning into oneself and seeking there, in the calm of the passions, those original traits that have disappeared in the multitude"; that alone was what could make him rediscover those original traits of solitary human nature. Or in the words of the character "Rousseau," "given by taste to his sweet reveries, thinking profoundly sometimes, but always with more fatigue than pleasure, and loving to let himself go, governed by a smiling imagination, rather than governing with effort his head by reason"—as such, "J. J." is "the man of nature enlightened by reason."[35]

We find the author himself ratifying this judgment (made by his character "Rousseau") when, speaking in a footnote in his own name, he assimilates his own nature to "the primitive nature of the human" (*la nature primitive de l'homme*).[36] And in *Emile*, when arguing for Emile's following the order of nature and adducing as supporting evidence those who are more and those who are less far from nature, Rousseau quotes as authoritative the following observations of Claude Le Beau: "during the childhood of savages, one sees them always active," but "as soon as they have attained the age of adolescence" they "become tranquil, dreamers" (*rêveurs*).[37] The entire difference (Rousseau himself adds), in the case of Emile, is that "he has in his work and in his play learned to think."

But against all this, the character "Rousseau," within the fictional *Dialogues*, is convinced that he knows that "an absolute solitude is a sad state and contrary to nature" (he seems in his reading to have taken what is designated the true state of nature in the *Second Discourse* less seriously than did "The Frenchman"); the character "Rousseau" is convinced that he knows that "our most sweet existence is relative and collective, and our true me is not entirely within us" and that "such is the constitution of the human being, in this life, that one never arrives at enjoying well oneself without the cooperation of another." On the basis of this presumed knowledge of his, the character "Rousseau" was of course deeply perplexed by "Jean-Jacques's" apparently unqualified love of solitude; and the character "Rousseau" saw the need "to unravel its precise cause, or else to give up understanding well the man." Observing firsthand "J. J.'s" gaiety and serenity on the latter's return from his solitary walks or after being left alone and tranquil, the character "Rousseau" hypothesized that the reason solitude does not make "J. J." "somber, taciturn, and always unhappy in life" must be that his solitude is filled with his visions of imaginary societies of friends.[38] This hypothesis was, however, never tested by suggesting it to "J. J." and by then listening to how "J. J." reacted to the hypothesis. Whether the character "Rousseau" is presented as entirely understanding "J. J.," and above all the latter's delight in solitude, is obviously very doubtful (consider also what "Rousseau" dubiously claims about "J. J.'s" reveries at OC 1:816–17).

In a remarkable passage late in the novel *Heloise*, Rousseau has his hero lover St. Preux write to a male friend about an experience of reverie that he underwent immediately after he for the first time sadly imagined his beloved Julie in her actual real condition—as married to another man and as the happy mother of that husband's children. For two hours, "to which I *would not prefer any time of my life*" (my italics: not even the hours spent with, or dreaming about, his beloved Julie as his own!), he "found that there is in the meditation of honest thoughts a sort of well-being that the wicked have never known: this is that of being pleased with oneself. If one dreamed on it without preconception, I do not know what other pleasure one could compare as equal to that."[39]

The first paragraph of *The Reveries*, in its brief adumbration of the work's primary purpose—"What am I myself? That is what *remains* [*reste*] for me to seek" (my italics)—indicates that somehow, all of Rousseau's previous, extensive autobiographical reflections and writings remain decisively incomplete (see also 6:3).

Chapter 1

"First Walk"—Rousseau's Introduction

Before proceeding in his proclaimed quest for full self-knowledge, the Solitary Walker says that "unhappily, this quest must be preceded by a glance at my situation," and he plunges into a staggering tale of woe and angst that has been foreshadowed in his tortured opening words: "Here I am, then, alone on the earth [*Me voici donc seul sur la terre*], no longer having brother, neighbor, friend, society except myself" (characteristically leaving out of account his devoted wife, whose caring company he begins to acknowledge, though only incidentally, in the Second Walk).[1]

Mental Derangement

The Solitary Walker's condition is far worse than that of lonely isolation. He proceeds to describe an experience of feeling, as if in a kind of dream (*rêve*, not quite a nightmare[2]) that "for fifteen years and more"[3] he has been the victim, for reasons he has never been able to understand,[4] of a fiendishly cruel and unjust psychological torture carried out on a daily basis by a historically unprecedented deliberate cooperation of all other living humans—"an entire generation, by a unanimous agreement"—treating him as a monster (a poisoner, an assassin),[5] as "the horror of the human race"; and all this directed by a cunning conspiratorial cabal, employing "those spies they keep constantly on my trail" (1:2–3, 5, 9–10; see also 8:6, 12–14; 9:8).

At the outset of *The Reveries*, we thus witness our author pathetically convulsed by a frantically paranoid sense of his own victimization, at the hands of a plot participated in by the entire rest of the human species.[6] Expressions of this mental illness[7] will burst out repeatedly in the course of *The Reveries* in forms sometimes less severe (3:2, 4:1, 6:11, 7.24–26, 9:8, 20), sometimes more (2:14–end, 3:19, 8:3, 6–8, 12).[8]

There is no doubt that Jean-Jacques Rousseau was in fact viciously conspired against by Voltaire and other powerful luminaries, that he was betrayed by close friends, and in part through those erstwhile friends' machinations, was subjected to severe public persecution, official as well as unofficial, which (as he says) covered him with "defamation, depression, derision, and disgrace."[9] But it is also indubitable that these genuine sufferings unhinged or contributed to unhinging Rousseau's mind to some degree—driving him into feverish overreactions, starting at least in the autumn of 1761,[10] and leading to a recurring hysteria that sometimes blighted his last years and that sporadically interrupts and disfigures his last writings.

It must be added that contrary to the strong impression Rousseau gives, it is by no means the case that he was universally scorned and persecuted in his later years. On the contrary, when in November 1765 he fled Paris and Switzerland and came to Strasbourg, he was feted and celebrated for a month by civic dignitaries and the public—not least, with a fine and elaborate production of his popular opera, *The Village Soothsayer*.[11] In the summer of 1770, Rousseau spent two months being warmly welcomed in Lyon, where his plays were performed in his honor, with *Pygmalion* performed for the first time as set to music by Horace Coignet (with whom Rousseau contracted a warm and daily renewed friendship);[12] in the same year, he was highly honored by Polish noblemen inviting him to write what became *The Government of Poland* (1771).

Moreover, Rousseau was not the only one of his distinguished associates who suffered persecution and betrayal by close friends during this time: as Maurice Cranston points out regarding Denis Diderot and his great *Encyclopédie*, "the achievement cost Diderot years of many bitter struggles against the hostility of the Church and Sorbonne authorities and against the unreliability, the pusillanimity and occasional treachery of his friends."[13] But of course, Diderot was not driven by these sufferings into paranoia. Diderot never spoke of all mankind as his enemy. And we cannot help but be reminded of the Platonic Socrates's assessment of misanthropy (*Phaedo* 89d–90a): a condition of "holding no one to be sound in any way at all," resulting from a person's experience of being very often betrayed by close kin and intimate companions who have turned out to be wicked; this resulting misanthropy is a shameful condition, the worldly-wise Socrates avers, because it is a manifestation of one's having "undertaken to deal with humans while lacking the art regarding the human things."

Rousseau's Paranoia as Expressed Prior to *The Reveries*

Paranoia first erupts in Rousseau's published writing[14] in his introduction to the second part of *The Confessions* (begun November 1769): "the ceilings under which I live have eyes, the walls that surround me have ears; surrounded by spies and malevolent and vigilant monitors, anxious and distraught, I hastily throw onto the paper some interrupted words that I scarcely have time to read, still less to correct."[15] As the second part of *The Confessions* proceeds, Rousseau explains what he understands to be the origin (in December 1757), and then the growth, of his erstwhile friends' conspiracy against him.[16] He does so with only a mercifully few bursts of outright paranoia (OC 1:491–93, 587–88, 611–12) and occasional hysteria ("the most black, the most dreadful plot that has ever been schemed against the memory of a human being" [OC 1:568])—and with some indications of awareness of his own proclivities to madness (*folie*) caused by "my cruel imagination."[17] But in the closing pages of *The Confessions*, and then in the footnotes that he added later, Rousseau becomes more frenzied.[18]

The *Dialogues* give a complex presentation. Near the end of the First Dialogue, the character "Rousseau," prior to having met Jean-Jacques in person, is depicted as himself hysterically embracing the idea of "an entire generation conspiring against a single, totally isolated man" whose position is "unique in the history of the human race"—as the victim of a plot that treats him "a hundred times worse than the Spanish Inquisition" and is carried on by "intelligent impostors, and led by some adroit and powerful intriguer" whose tentacles stretch from "the two opposite ends of Europe" (OC 1:764–67).

Early in the Second Dialogue, however, after having met and spent time alone with Jean-Jacques, the character "Rousseau" is depicted as taking a certain distance: "I don't pretend to give you as realities all the disquieting ideas that are furnished to J. J. by the profound darkness with which they work to surround him"—mysteries having "an appearance so black that it is not surprising that they affect with the same coloring his frightened imagination." Still, "among the bizarre and fantastic ideas that this can give him, there are some that, considering the extraordinary manner in which he is treated, merit a serious examination before being rejected." After summarizing a story that he has heard from Jean-

Jacques of how a conspiracy has made it so that a certain portrait of him has painted him in the worst light, the character "Rousseau" concludes, "These have the air of being chimerical conjectures—rather natural fruits of an imagination beaten by so many mysteries and such unhappiness" (OC 1:780–82). Moreover, both speaking characters in the *Dialogues* are presented as expressing doubts about the universality of the plot (OC 1:876, 895, 969).

So Rousseau as author of the *Dialogues* definitely exhibits and expresses some recognition of his own paranoid mental imbalance, or at least of how delusional he must appear to some sober and well-disposed readers.

But the Third Dialogue slips back into the atrabilious regions of insanity (*Dialogues* OC 1:940–44, 963). Rousseau as author has his character "The Frenchman" become converted to the idea that there is indeed a "plot, such as there never has been and never will be another like it," unfolding step by step over more than fifteen years, whose ultimate aim includes driving Jean-Jacques to suicide out of despair. If Jean-Jacques "understands his situation, he ought to comprehend, however little he reflects on it, that every proposition that anyone makes to him under whatever color is given it, has always a goal that is hidden and that would prevent him from agreeing if the goal were known to him." The facts and details of this plot the Frenchman claims (sounding rather hysterical himself) he has ferreted out better than has his interlocutor "Rousseau": "I know so many facts concerning it that you don't know!"; "all is so well organized in regards to J. J., that an angel could descend from Heaven to defend him without being able to!" At this point, the real Rousseau, speaking in his own name as author, intervenes with a footnote, responding to readers whom he anticipates will suggest that this is a megalomaniacal exaggeration of his own importance; Rousseau responds by insisting on his own gigantic political significance: he claims that the French invasion of Corsica in 1765 was carried out in order to prevent him from moving there to find refuge![19]

The Recovery from the Delirium of Indignation

If we return now to the First Walk of *The Reveries*, we find that in the third paragraph the Solitary Walker reflects that initially, "indignation plunged me into a delirium which has taken no less than ten years to calm itself." So his deliriousness, as he now recalls it, was more one of victimized moral outrage than of fear.[20] And although his indignation is no longer delirious, this does not mean that he has ceased to be subject to indignation. Late in *The Reveries*, he affirms that "the spectacle of injustice and of wickedness still make my blood boil with rage" (6:16; see also 6:12), and he declares that he is "forced to try to forget humans, who overwhelm me with ignominy and insults, for fear lest the indignation might finally embitter me against them" (7:17). In fact, he still remains, he confesses, "as easy to render indignant as before" (8:19 end; also 9:18).[21] He does, to be sure, portray his own vengefulness as of a passive-aggressive sort (Pagani 2014): on the playing card #17 we find, "Do I wish to take vengeance on them in as cruel a way as possible? For that I have only to live happily and content; this is a sure way to render them miserable." Similarly, the Solitary Walker writes in the Seventh Walk (7:3), "This is to take vengeance on my persecutors in my own way; I know no way to punish them more cruelly than to be happy despite them."

The Solitary Walker does not give any sign that his recovery from delirium was achieved by his sharing or his recalling a Socratic or Aristotelian critique of the incoherence of the commonsense opinions at the core of righteous indignation—and of what is inextricably connected, guilt and forgiveness. Indeed, nothing more profoundly separates Rousseau's presentation of himself as a moral-political thinker from the presentation of the moral and political philosopher in Plato and Xenophon and Aristotle than the treatment of moral indignation and guilt. Nowhere in the Socratic writings of Plato or Xenophon, or in the writings of Aristotle, is the philosophical soul ever portrayed as in the grip of any righteous indignation whatsoever; and Aristotle in his *Nicomachean Ethics* notably excludes righteous indignation (nemesis) from the moral virtues, even treating it as tantamount to a moral vice (*Nicomachean Ethics* 1108b1–8; see Bolotin 1999). As Plato's Socrates repeatedly emphasizes, the truly rational soul is profoundly and entirely and permanently governed by the insight that all vice is a manifestation of pitiable[22] ignorance, about what is truly most choice-worthy, noble, advantageous, and beneficial.[23] Rousseau presents himself as far from being so governed. He judges of his persecutors: "even if they mistake themselves on my account, they cannot be ignorant of their own iniquity. They are unjust and wicked toward me not by error but by will: they are such because they willed to be such."[24] He proclaims that "justice consists in measuring the punishment exactly to the fault," and this great principle dictates that "murderers ought to be punished by death, thieves, by the loss of their property, or, if they lack that, of their liberty" (*Letters Written from the Mountain* OC 3:755, 779). For Rousseau, crime and punishment are governed by retributive justice thought of as coherent (see also 3:16); for the Socratic outlook, if punishment is to avoid incoherent thinking, it cannot be retributive but only rehabilitative, deterrent, restorative, and preventative or impeding of further harm (see above all the complex discussion and articulation of the penal code in Plato's *Laws* bks. 9–10 and L. Pangle 2009).

Eventually (8:12–13), we hear the Solitary Walker go still further away from Socrates by claiming that he calmed his righteous indignation only by coming to view his fellow humans as "automatons who acted only on impulse and whose action I could calculate only from the laws of motion"—lacking intention and "destitute of all morality with respect to me"; the Solitary Walker will eventually make the extreme anti-Socratic (or pre-Socratic) claim that the wise man escapes indignation by "seeing only the blows of blind necessity in all the misfortunes that befall him." (The most explicit Socratic attacks on the pre-Socratics' determinism of this sort as applied to human agency are at Plato *Phaedo* 98d–99b and *Laws* 892a–99c.)

Alternatively, the Solitary Walker will testify that his passion for revenge is tied to his lack of power to wreak vengeance and that "in order to extinguish within me any desire for vengeance, it would have sufficed for me to have the power to avenge myself" (6:7). He comes closest to a Socratic perspective when he imaginatively plays with the question of how he would behave if he had a godlike judicial power, "reading easily to the depths of men's hearts": he says that, finding only a few "odious enough to deserve all of my hatred," their "very wickedness would have disposed me to feel sorry for them, by the certain understanding of the evil that they do to themselves in wishing to do it to others." But he adds that his consequent "thousand acts of clemency and equity" would be accompanied by "some acts of severe justice" (6:18; see also *Dialogues* OC 1:670t—and clemency of course presupposes guilt and the deserving of retributive punishment, all contrary to the Socratic understanding).

So far as I am aware, the nearest that Rousseau ever comes in his published writings to expressing recognition of what are the first foci of the Socratic analysis of the incoherence of the opinions at the heart of moral indignation are two statements of the Savoyard vicar in *Emile*. The first is the very brief and unelaborated remark (OC 4:595), "If moral goodness is in conformity with our nature, the human being would not be healthy in soul nor well constituted except to the extent that he is good." The second is the anti-determinist passage that Rousseau decided to add to what he put into the mouth of the Savoyard vicar:[25]

> When one asks me what is the cause which determines my will, I ask in return what is the cause that determines my judgment: because it is clear that these two causes make only one, and if one comprehends well that the human is active in his judgments, that his understanding is only the power of comparing and of judging, one will see that his liberty is only a similar power that derives from that one;[26] he chooses the good as he has judged the true; if he judges falsely he chooses badly.

> What is then the cause that determines his will? It is his judgment. And what is the cause that determines his judgment? It is his faculty of intelligence, it is his power of judgment: the determining cause is within himself. Beyond that, I understand nothing.
>
> Doubtless I am not free to not will/want [*vouloir*] my own good, I am not free to will/want my evil; but my liberty consists in this very thing—that I can will/want only that which is suitable [*convenable*] for me or that I esteem to be such, without anything external to me determining me.

There is no sign, however, that Rousseau (or his Savoyard vicar) truly defined his existence—as did Socrates—by the full thinking through of all that is here necessarily implied, morally and theologically. There is no sign that Rousseau underwent what Plato's Socrates calls the turning around of the soul (*Republic* 518c–19a) that finally results from such thorough analysis of moral indignation. In the very next paragraph after the preceding passage that I have just quoted, Rousseau's vicar blatantly contradicts the above and returns to an anti-Socratic outlook: "the principle of every action is in the will of a free being. One cannot go back beyond that."[27]

The Solitary Walker certainly does not attribute the calming of his deliriousness of righteous indignation to his having laughed at this passion, or having laughed at himself, on account of having allowed himself, a philosopher, to be overcome by absurd righteous indignation. Commenting on Aristophanes, Leo Strauss observes that "comedy would be powerless against righteous indignation if righteous indignation were not always on the verge of turning into boastfulness."[28] Rousseau, in contrast, insists that "nothing is less funny or laughable than virtue's indignation."[29]

The other side of the moral passion of indignation is the weeping that expresses the tragic hope that virtue will receive the compensatory recognition that it is thought to deserve.[30] In *The Confessions*, Rousseau reports himself weeping almost forty times and repeatedly speaks of his love of weeping: "few humans have shed as many tears in their life" (OC 1:103). His weeping is often deeply moralistic: "he weeps in thinking of his innocence and of the reward that his heart deserved" (*Dialogues* OC 1:825; see also 803, the character "Rousseau" speaking of "J. J."). Later in *The Reveries* (6:16), the Solitary Walker will declare, "The acts of virtue in which I see neither boastfulness nor ostentation always make me quiver with joy and still wring from me sweet tears."

In this as in some other crucial respects, Rousseau appears much closer to Jesus as presented in the Gospels than to Socrates, who is never reported as having wept a single tear (see also Plato, *Laws* 732c). Socrates's dislike of weeping, especially moralistic weeping, in those around him is made plain in the closing scenes of Xenophon's *Apology* and of Plato's *Phaedo*.[31] Socrates is portrayed as almost always subtly comical, engaging in irony of the classic Greek kind—*eirōneia*. As a wise commentator has put it, the "irony of the Socratic question," which is "historically the origin of the term," is "the device of a philosophical genius" in an "intellectual situation in which the knower of his ignorance requests enlightenment from the pretended knowledge of an ignorance unknown to itself." Yet, "the situation is not unique—it accompanies man throughout his history, though he is seldom aware of it. For this reason Socrates became an eternal figure."[32] Plato presents Socrates disapproving of the outburst of laughter (*Republic* 388–89a), and it is only on the day of his death that Socrates is portrayed by Plato as laughing, gently (*Phaedo* 84d, 115c; "smiling" at 86d and 102d). To quote again the wise Kurt Riezler (1975, 177) on Socrates: "Though we smile at the successful irony, we do not laugh at it. It aims at a seriousness behind all laughter." Rousseau is not, of course, given to irony, especially not through Socratic questioning.

If it was not by laughing at himself that the Solitary Walker achieved a calming of his delirious indignation nor through Socratic nor even semi-Socratic dialectical analysis of the opinions at the core of righteous indignation, what did bring about the calming?

A simple, exhausted impotence—still as a victim of injustice, still in the face of what Rousseau conceived to be morally outrageous assaults: "feeling finally that all my efforts were useless and that I was tormenting myself only with my own loss," he decided that he had no other option but to "submit to my destiny without any longer complaining against necessity."[33] In this submissive resignation to the destiny of unjust victimhood he found, however, "the compensation for all my evils by the tranquility that it procured" (1:4).

Yet, the Solitary Walker's tranquility depended also on the fact that his persecutors were not adroit enough to leave him any hope, by which they might still have had a hold on him, or any further fear, which his imagination might have inflated—for, while "real evils have little hold over me," in the case of those that "I dread" (the Solitary Walker realizes) my "alarmed imagination combines them, turns them over, extends them, and augments them." Since "my persecutors" have "used up prodigally all the shafts of their animosity," they "have deprived themselves of all empire over me, and I can henceforth mock them" (1:5–6; see similarly *Dialogues* OC 1:952).

The Solitary Walker's detachment begins to sound more misanthropic in the subsequent paragraphs. He first relates that once he "began to see into the plot in all its extent," he "lost forever the idea of winning the public back while I was alive." He then goes much further. He declares that even if the public were to return to him, he could no longer reciprocate: "humans would in vain come back to me, they would no longer find me"; given "the disdain they have inspired in me, relations with them would for me be insipid and even a burden"; still worse, they "have torn out of my heart all the sweetness of society," "which, at my age, cannot sprout anew" (1:8). What the Solitary Walker's feverish mind perceives as the public's unanimous malice has succeeded in disfiguring his very heart.

Nevertheless, until recently, he did not become a complete misanthrope. Up until almost two months previously,[34] he counted still on the future (1:9), and this was "a hold by which a thousand diverse passions did not cease to agitate me" (1:7). The Solitary Walker lived in the hope that his writings would prevail among posterity (see also *Confessions* OC 1:568). This is "the hope that made me write my dialogues[35] and suggested to me a thousand mad attempts [*mille folles tentatives*] to pass them on to posterity."[36] But "I deceived myself. Happily I sensed it soon enough to find still before my last hour an interval of complete calm and absolute repose" (1:9). The Solitary Walker tells himself that in the previous two months, he has finally(!) reached a point of serene, disdainful detachment from any interest in communicating, even by writing, with any other humans, in future generations as well as in the present.

And yet, "very few days pass without new reflections" on his relation to audiences in future generations (1:10; so "how absolute can his repose be?" [Davis 1999, 66]). These reflections confirm, to be sure, "how much I was in error to count on the return of the public, even in another era." For the public "is conducted, in what relates to me, by guides who are renewed ceaselessly in the groups that have taken an aversion to me." The "individuals die, but the collective bodies do not die," and "their ardent hatred" is "immortal like the demon who inspires" the plot.[37] The Solitary Walker names, as "groups that have taken an aversion to me," the medical doctors and, worst of all, the oratorians.[38]

The reader may well be provoked to a pitying smile by these expressions in their fantastic feverishness. Is it at all plausible that medical doctors and oratorians, or other groups, will have such a hold on the reading public in future centuries? And even if they were to secure such a hold, how does that exclude the possibility or likelihood of numerous individual readers who will escape the sway of a public opinion dominated by these dubious cohorts, individuals who will in centuries to come read Rousseau's writings with open or even iconoclastic minds? Or will the demon who inspires the plot prevent this? Is not our author's neurosis here reaching truly preposterous levels?[39]

Or could the preposterousness of this outburst signal a degree of deliberately histrionic, not to say theatrical, exaggeration in this purportedly spontaneous, unplanned outpouring of our author's hysteria? Is it not the case that Rousseau is not only aware of his own proclivity to mental illness but also capable, as an autobiographical genius, of strategically exploiting his own mental debility? At this point, if not earlier, we are provoked to suspect that the Solitary Walker's expression, supposedly written solely to himself, of his proclaimed renunciation of hope or of concern for any future readership expresses a performer's artfulness in some decisive degree.[40] Apart from the fact that Rousseau left the text of the first seven walks of *The Reveries* painstakingly prepared, by himself, for publication,[41] is not the entire First Walk a soliloquy in and by which the artist Rousseau has creatively brought himself before us in the role of the suffering, victimized, martyr-like Solitary Walker? As Lionel Gossman (1978, 67) puts it, "It is not, ostensibly, addressed to the reader, but overheard by him, as it were, in much the same way as Diderot's proposed realist plays were to be acted without reference to an audience, and as if the latter did not exist." Or in Jean Starobinski's (1971, 422; 1988, 358) words: "In the very act of announcing this speech without external auditor, he performs it before us, who constitute the audience denied."[42]

Certainly, we are presented with a speaker whose expression of serenity is wavering (Froidefond 1997, 116). He says that he is here tranquil but adds, "at the bottom of an abyss, a poor mortal [who is] unfortunate."[43] He claims to be impassive like God himself (the impassivity of God perhaps explains the Solitary Walker's quasi-Gnostic claim that a demon controls the entire human race). But in the next breath, the Solitary Walker admits that he is still gripped by indignation: "I cannot cast my eyes on what touches me and surrounds me without finding there some disdain that makes me indignant or some pain that afflicts me." Recoiling, he turns inward: "therefore, let us expel from my spirit all the troublesome objects with which I occupied myself as sadly as uselessly"; "since I find solely in myself consolation, hope, and peace, I ought not, nor do I wish, to occupy myself with anything except me" (1:12). At this point, the turn inward comes to sight as a retreat, not an advance.

Writing for No Readers except the Author

"It is in this spirit," the Solitary Walker continues, turning to explain the character of the present writing (Davis 1999, 62), "that I take up again the continuation/sequel [*la suite*] of the severe and sincere examination that I previously called my confessions."[44] The Second Walk will restate this as "the project [*le projet*] of writing the continuation/sequel of my confessions" (2:4); in the thirteenth paragraph of the First Walk, Rousseau indites that "these pages can therefore be regarded as an appendix [*un appendice*] to my confessions" (or, as he puts it in the fifteenth paragraph, to "my first confessions").[45] *The Confessions* was of course a book written for publication.

28 CHAPTER 1

As if anticipating the question, "So why not title this new work something like *Continuation/Sequel of My (First) Confessions*, or maybe even *Second Confessions*?" Rousseau immediately adds (1:13), "but I do not give to them anymore that title, not sensing anymore anything to be said that could merit it. My heart has purified itself in the smelting of adversity."

This purification that his heart has achieved in the time since his writing and publication of *The Confessions* is not presented as the result of further self-examination and still less of self-purgation. It is rather, as we have seen, presented as the outcome of his submission, after many struggles, to the horrible destiny of having become a victim of unjust persecution—and as victim, a totally isolated pariah. The "most sociable and most loving of humans" has been "proscribed by a unanimous agreement." Having "sought out, in the refinements of their cruelty, that torment which would be the most cruel for my sensitive soul," they have "violently broken all the bonds that attached me to them" (1:1). So "what would I have still to confess when all the earthly affections are torn from" my heart? "I no longer have anything for which to praise or to blame myself: I am henceforth nothing among humans," and "that is all I can be, no longer having any real relation with them, any veritable society" (1:13). The Solitary Walker's heart has purified itself in the peculiar sense that it has finally resigned itself, with tranquility, to the fact that his fellow humans have in their deliberate aggression rendered impossible any further active moral relationship between him and them. He repeatedly proclaims that he is speaking and writing to and for only himself, having utterly abandoned all hope or wish for dialogue with others, or for publication, or for being read by any other human at any future time. In the penultimate paragraph of this First Walk, the Solitary Walker imagines himself in his final days reading this writing in order to "double, so to speak my existence"—in order, that is, to bring back to life his earlier self—and thereby to create the charm of society for what will then be his decrepit old self. He thus underlines the undoubled, undialogical, strictly monological character of this opening chapter.[46]

The Reveries as Pious Self-Examination

The Solitary Walker immediately stresses, however, that his soul's "*moral* life seems still to have increased itself by the death of every temporal and terrestrial interest" (my italics). His "abstention" from involvement with others is a morally just abstention: given that he can "no longer do any good that does not turn into evil" nor "act without harming another or myself, for me to abstain has become my unique duty [*mon unique devoir*], and I fulfill it as much as is in me." This duty is pious as well as moral: in fulfilling it, he looks to the afterlife of his incorporeal soul: "for me, my body is no longer anything except an encumbrance, and I disengage myself from it in advance as much as I can."[47] The Solitary Walker has previously said that by his "severe and sincere self-examination" he consecrates his last days to "preparing in advance the account of myself that I will not be tardy in rendering": "if, by dint of reflecting on my interior dispositions I manage to put them in better order and to correct the evil that can remain there, my meditations will not be entirely useless" (1:12). The impassivity of God (His lack of indignation and of love) is not incompatible with His judgment in the afterlife. Indeed, God's impassivity is what renders Him the totally disinterested, fair Judge. The Solitary Walker's personal hope for that afterlife, and for the divine judgment there, makes his own, human, all-too-human, impassivity qualitatively different from that of God. (But we observe that in the penultimate sentence of the First Walk, the Solitary Walker speaks of the possibility of his soul's extinguishing itself [*s'éteindre*]; he is not totally confident in his hope for the afterlife.)

The first paragraph's very brief and sad statement of the purpose of this writing as being the lonely pursuit of self-knowledge for its own sake has now been eclipsed by, or has been transformed into, a moral and pious version of self-examination.

More generally, most of the First Walk up to this point (1:13) delivers what can serve as a kind of moral and pious apologia[48] for the radical self-centeredness of this entire writing, by showing that this self-absorption is not a product of selfishness, or of egoism, or of inhumanity, or of incapacity to love, or of impiety. No, the Solitary Walker has been driven to retreat within himself by what he experiences as the inhuman aggression of all the rest of mankind: "I would have loved humans, in spite of themselves. Only by ceasing to be such have they escaped my affection. So there they are, strangers, unknowns—nonentities, in short—for me, since they willed it" (*puis qu'ils l'ont voulu* [1:1]). The Solitary Walker here claims in effect to be the sole truly human being left on earth (see similarly 8:12). Accordingly, he says in the twelfth paragraph that it is as if he has fallen[49] onto an alien planet. And precisely since, or insofar as, readers are impelled to see in these words the marks of his mental derangement, they may be all the more moved to pity, rather than condemnation, of a thinker who has been thus driven by unjust persecution out of his naturally loving and sociable mind, into such atomized, agonizing inwardness.[50] Here, as in *The Confessions* and in his novel *Heloise*, Rousseau is deliberately founding a major dimension of that vast cultural revolution that he originated and that came to be known as Romanticism: in the words of Cranston (1994, 17), by depicting St. Preux and himself as another loser, Rousseau "establishes for such victims a place in romantic mythology as compelling as that of the hero." After "St-Preux comes the Werther of Goethe, the René of Chateaubriand and all the wounded and defeated warriors who figure in the paintings of Géricault." Rousseau inspired what is distinctive in Romanticism: "the 'anti-hero,' the victim, the man of sorrows like Rousseau himself." As was claimed by a later Romantic, Percy Bysshe Shelley, "poets are cradled into poetry by wrong; They learn in suffering what they teach in song."

Rousseau's self-presentations here and in the *Dialogues* move in a Christ-like direction,[51] away from the Platonic presentation of Socrates with whom Rousseau had in some sense identified or associated himself in the *First Discourse*.[52] In *Dialogues*, Rousseau dares to have his character "The Frenchman" conclude that "J. J.'s destiny is a perhaps unique example of all the possible humiliations, and of a patience almost invincible in enduring them" (OC 1:937). In *Emile*, Rousseau has his Savoyard vicar decry the pettiness of "the books of the philosophers with all their pomp" in contrast to the "majesty of the Scriptures" with their portrait of Jesus. The Scriptures' portrait of Jesus,[53] the vicar says, is appreciated by the philosophers in only a single text: "when Plato paints his imaginary just man (De. Rep. Dial. 2) covered with all the opprobrium of crime and deserving of all the prizes of virtue": then "he paints Jesus-Christ feature for feature" (also *Letter to Beaumont*, OC 4:992–93). The vicar is referring to the portrait drawn by the Platonic character Glaucon (Plato's brother), in his long speech laying down the challenge to Socrates to prove that justice is intrinsically choice-worthy: the test case, Glaucon submits, is the just man, "stripped of everything except justice": "doing nothing unjust, let him have the greatest reputation for injustice, so that his justice would be tested to see if it is softened by reputation for being evil and the consequences that come from that"; and "let him go unchanging until death, having the reputation of being unjust throughout life, while being just"; such "a just man will be whipped, he will be racked, he will be bound; he will have his eyes burned out, and at the end, having suffered all evils, he will be crucified" (*Republic* 361b–362a).

The Savoyard vicar further expostulates, "What prejudices, what blindness, must one not have, to dare to compare the son of Sophroniscus to the son of Mary? What a gulf between them!" On one side, we see "Socrates dying without pain, without ignominy, easily sustaining to the end his personage"; on the other side, "Jesus expiring in torments, insulted, jeered, cursed by an entire people." In his elaborate late letter to Franquières,[54] Rousseau expresses in his own name a less vehement version of this judgment of the inferiority of Socrates to Jesus. And Rousseau remarks, as one sign of the inferiority of Socrates, this philosopher's manner of arguing dialectically and ironically: "He stood up against the Sophists like Jesus against the priests, with this difference that Socrates imitated often his antagonists; and that if his beautiful and sweet death had not honored his life *he would have passed for a Sophist like them.*"[55] In contrast, "the sublime flight that Jesus's soul took elevated him always above all the mortals," and "from the age of twelve until the moment when he expired in the most cruel as well as the most shameful of all deaths, he never for a moment claimed to be what he was not" (Jesus was never ironic). Similarly, Rousseau's unpublished, untitled fragment on the reveries of "the first man who attempted to philosophize" concludes with the epiphany of an avatar of Jesus Christ, presented as clearly superior to the avatar of Socrates who also is featured, as *the* philosopher.[56]

Rousseau's massive foreground presentation of himself, the paradigmatic wise man, as a pitiful, and self-pitying, righteously indignant victim of injustice, overheard in moments when he is alone and speaking to and for himself, moves in exactly the opposite direction from that in which the Platonic Socrates urges artistic presentations of the life of the wise to move. Plato's Socrates emphatically admits that such a portrait as Rousseau gives is much more pleasing to and admired by—but deeply corrupting of!—the crowd or mass of mankind: see the severe critique of Homer and all tragic poetry in precisely these regards in *Republic* book 10.[57] That Rousseau was fully aware of, and indeed focused his attention on, this specific Platonic writing is manifest in Rousseau's published but coolly noncommittal representation of this precise Platonic text: "On Theatrical Imitation: An Essay Drawn from Plato's Dialogues."[58] The most remarkable difference between the Platonic original and Rousseau's representation is that whereas Plato in these pages of his *Republic* does not use the term *philosopher*, Rousseau introduces an explicit short digression (in the form of a response to an imagined reader who raises an objection) explaining how Plato's text applies to the philosopher, who is or ought to be, Rousseau declares, "the architect who draws up the plan" of which "the poet is the painter who makes the image" (OC 5:1204).

Rousseau is thus fully conscious of his break with Plato in this most important respect—in regard to the way in which the wise man should be dramatically portrayed.

The Reveries as a Sweet Conversing with His Soul

No sooner have we been directed to think that this writing has as its purpose the expected usefulness, with a view to the coming day of divine judgment in the afterlife, of his own soul's corrective self-examination, then the Solitary Walker abruptly, in the midst of the twelfth paragraph, again transforms his writing's stated purpose. He now speaks of this work as written to provide a future, all-consuming, spiritual pleasure of communion with his soul, to be enjoyed in what remains of his earthly life: "let us give ourselves up entirely [*tout entier*] to the sweetness of conversing with my soul, since that is the only thing that humans are unable to take away from me." The Solitary Walker attests that he has already enjoyed this sweetness, in the charming contemplations that have often filled his daily walks, the memory of which he regrets having lost. Now, he declares, he "will fix, by writing down, those that can still come to" him, and each time that he will reread them will bring back to him their enjoyment (1:12).

A tenuous link between this consuming, lighthearted earthly pleasure and the previously stressed usefulness of severe and corrective self-examination with a view to divine judgment in the afterlife comes to sight when the Solitary Walker adds that a crucial part of the pleasure of reading these recollections will be "forgetting my misfortunes, my persecutors, my disgraces, in dreaming [*songeant*] about the prize that my heart will have deserved."[59]

The Reveries as Self-Observational Diary

So we now have three divergent stated purposes of this writing. The next, thirteenth, paragraph seems at first to return to the very first stated aim: progress in self-knowledge for its own sake. But now, this goal is presented in a much less serious—in a sweeter, a less intense and focused—version; it is at this point that Rousseau introduces the word *reveries* for the very first time in the body of his text: "these pages will only be, properly speaking, an unformed diary of my reveries." The diary will contain much about "me, because a solitary who reflects[60] necessarily occupies himself with himself a great deal"; but "all the foreign ideas that pass through my head while I walk will find *equally* their place" (my italics). He goes on to promise that he will "say what I have thought, all as it came to me" and "with as little connection [*aussi peu de liaison*] as the ideas of the day before ordinarily have with those of the next day." From this written record of the spontaneous unconnected sequence of feelings (*sentimens*) as well as thoughts there "will always result a new understanding of my natural temperament and humors."

The Solitary Walker concedes that "a situation so singular merits, surely, to be examined," as well as described; and at first, he says that "it is to this examination that I consecrate my last leisure" (1:14), sounding like he is returning to the first stated purpose. But then, he immediately retracts this: a successful examination, he says, would require "proceeding with order and method," and "I am incapable of this work." Besides, such work would "take me away from my goal," which is "to give myself a report of [*me rendre compte de*] the modifications of my soul and their succession." He compares the report that he has in mind to meteorologists' recordings of daily barometric observations: his analogous reported observations, if they were "well directed and repeated for a long time could [*pourroient*] furnish me with results as certain" as those arrived at by the scientists; but (he insists) "I do not extend so far my enterprise."

At this point, it sounds as though the goal of a searching, severe, even corrective self-examination has given way to, or been eclipsed by, a new and different plan or idea (a fourth stated purpose of this writing): a simple observational record or diary, of rambling musings, the subsequent reading of which will result in something like a deepening, pleasing familiarity with the temperamental mutations of the Solitary Walker's own soul, as opposed to either a philosophical-scientific or a moral and pious searching analysis of his soul.

The Reveries as Consolation in Decrepit Old Age

But then, this easy or relaxed diary writing immediately becomes itself overlain or supplemented, by yet another, a fifth, stated purpose: namely, the prospect of a more passive, consoling, mild future pleasure that will suffuse the Solitary Walker's "most elderly days, as departure approaches," when he is decrepit. Assuming that when he is on the threshold of death he will in those future days remain, "as I hope, in the same disposition that I am in," then the reading of the record of "my reveries" (employing the word for the second time) will "recall to me the sweetness that I taste in writing them"; that will "thus make reborn for me the past time" and "will double, so to speak, my existence"; "in spite of humans, I will know how to taste again the charm of society, and while decrepit, I will live with myself at another age," "as if I were living with a less elderly friend" (1:14). The future Solitary Walker, when on the verge of death, will, by reading his former writing, live in society with himself as former writer: so writing, or at the least rereading and recollecting one's own writing, remains to the very end of life a very great Rousseauian joy.[61] Socrates, of course, refrained most deliberately from partaking in joy of this kind: see Plato's *Phaedrus* 274–end.

Questions Going Forward

Far from giving us "a program fixing the endeavor of the following introspections,"[62] this first chapter bewilders us by this cascade of pronouncements of five varying explicit purposes of this writing that is addressed to and purportedly only for the author. How do these five diverse aims fit together? It is easy to see a complementarity of the first two stated goals: #1, achieving greater self-knowledge for its own sake and #2, self-examination with a view to preparing for divine judgment in the afterlife. It is not so easy to see how these two goals, given their gravity, comport with the mutually reinforcing last three stated purposes, given their levity: #3, abandoning himself entirely to sweet conversing with his soul during his remaining days for the sake of sheer enjoyment in this earthly life; #4, writing an unformed and unanalytical diary of quasi-barometric observations of the ungoverned ramblings of his mind for the sake of gaining greater familiarity with his natural temperament (which may well include observation of the enjoyment mentioned in #3); and #5, making a written record of his reveries for the sake of having at the very end of life reading material that will allow converse with his earlier, writer's self and thus dispel the loneliness of his eventually decrepit final days. How will the subsequent chapters interweave this mixture of gravity and levity that characterizes these five stated diverse aims of this writing project?

Chapter 2

"Second Walk"—Nature, Mortality, God

The Second Walk is explicitly linked in sequence to the first by a beginning that is emphatically in the past tense, of conventional narrative: "Having, then, formed the project. . . ." The Solitary Walker thus conspicuously leaves behind, and thereby highlights, the First Walk's artfully soliloquized performance—which was of course all delivered in the present tense.

The project is here characterized (using the word *reveries* for the third time) in terms like those used when the First Walk (1:13) gave the fourth of its five distinct statements of the work's overall purpose: to keep a quasi-barometric, "unformed diary of my reveries." Now, on one hand, the Solitary Walker no longer makes any reference to "all the foreign ideas that pass through my head while I walk" as finding equally their place in his diary. On the other hand, he lays even greater stress on the unplanned, ungoverned, undirected character of the consciousness of which the record is to be kept: "I leave my head completely free, and my ideas follow their bent without resistance and without impediment." The freewheeling thinking that is to be recorded thus seems to be far from any serious, thematic, and discursively philosophical or moral investigation, entailing inner question and answer concerning the nature of things or even of oneself. And nothing whatsoever is said about the First Walk's second stated purpose: the proposed severe self-examination with a view to judgment day in the afterlife. Equally absent now is any repetition of the fifth or final purpose—the preparation of a consoling pleasure of reading for the Solitary Walker's enfeebled dying days. In fact, that fifth purpose will never again be referred to.

Nature's Goal

Switching to the present tense, from narrative to asseveration, or perhaps back to soliloquy, the Solitary Walker suddenly makes a momentous declaration: "these hours of solitude and of meditation are the only ones of the day when I am fully me (*moi*) and for me (*à moi*) without diversion, without obstacle, and when I can truly say that I am what nature wanted" (*ce que la nature a voulu*, 2:1).

This is the first mention in the work of nature—here presented as having volition (Davis 1999, 83n2). Nature wanted the Solitary Walker to be the completed subject and the exclusive object of his own consciousness, immersed in undirected, self-engrossed, sweet musings. With a view to the teaching of the *Second Discourse*—the work in which, of all Rousseau's writings, "my principles are manifested with the greatest boldness not to say audacity" (*Confessions* OC 1:407)—are we not provoked to surmise that this is the aim of human nature as such? Are we not given here a glimpse of the deepest meaning and meaningfulness of reverie for Rousseau? Does not the Solitary Walker embody a retrieval of the originally natural, integral, human consciousness? That consciousness was contentedly solitary and self-engrossed, on the basis of an existence that was subrational and unimaginative; it now can become contentedly solitary and self-engrossed on the radically new, historically developed basis of a truly enlightened, rational wisdom married to a harmoniously developed imagination, all unleashed to ramble "entirely free, following their bent without resistance and without impediment."[1]

Love of or even attachment to others seems to have no place in nature's directedness, so understood (see also 8:2); Rousseau has achieved this recovery of nature's aim only by dint of having been violently cast out of human society, into "the most strange position in which a mortal could ever find himself" (2:1).

We note that the statement of nature's objective also contains no reference to God or to the afterlife (which were also absent from the *Second Discourse*'s account of the original natural human condition).

The Subsiding of Creative Reverie

In the second paragraph, the Solitary Walker at first returns to his observational diary and to the narrative voice in the past tense, but the narration and diary takes a depressing downturn: "I soon felt that I had delayed too long to execute this project."

Then the Solitary Walker plunges back into sad soliloquy in the present tense, and the diary becomes lugubrious: "my imagination, already less lively, does not inflame itself as before in the contemplation of the object that animates it; I get myself less drunk with the delirium of reverie" (*je m'enivre moins du délire de la rêverie*—employing the word *reverie* for the fourth time); there "is more of reminiscence than of creation [*creation*] in what imagination produces henceforth"; "my soul no longer throws itself, except with difficulty, outside its obsolete envelope."

Thus, the opening paragraph's lightning-like glimpse of the deeply gratifying attainment of what nature wants, in aimless reveries of sweet self-immersion, is eclipsed by a gloomy recognition of the desuetude of the imagination's creative reverie, which in the Solitary Walker's earlier years projected his consciousness out from his "me," so as "to people my solitude with beings formed according to my heart" (as we are reminded by these words in paragraph six of this Second Walk). The Solitary Walker goes so far as to lament that were it not for the hope for the future "state to which I aspire because I sense that I have the right to it, I would no longer exist except by memories" (2:2). The observational diary reports that the blocking of nature's vector, by the dolorous awareness of the elderly loss of the capacity for creative social reverie, makes the afterlife with its just deserts once again loom as all important.

The reader is provoked to ask, what exactly is the relationship between these two very different sorts of this-worldly reverie: on the one hand, the creative-social reveries, that people his solitude with "beings formed according to his heart," and on the other hand, the totally and sweetly self-absorbed reveries that, as asocial, achieve "what nature wanted"? Is not the subsiding of the former a precondition of the latter?[2] Is this not part of what was missed by the character "Rousseau" in his attempt to understand "Jean-Jacques" in the *Dialogues*? But is not this achievement of what nature wanted—in the aimless reveries of sweet self-absorption—to a crucial degree deficient, because haunted by a sadness at the loss of the enchanting powers and delights of the ultimately less natural but more rapturous and ecstatic reveries of the creative-social imagination?[3]

Apparently continuing in the grip of his depressed sense of loss of his creative capacity, the Solitary Walker's soliloquy ignores or turns way from his present, now not-so-sweetly self-absorbed "hours of solitude and meditation."

He declares that "in order to contemplate myself before my decline, it is necessary for me to reascend [*remonte*] at least several years," back up to "the time when, losing all hope here below [*ici-bas*] and no longer finding any food for my heart here on earth," he accustomed himself, he says, "little by little, to feeding it with its own substance" (*le nourrir de sa propre substance*) and "to looking for all its food inside me" (2:2). He thus learned by his own experience that true happiness (*bonheur* is here mentioned for the first time) has its "source in us" (2:3). For four or five years, while he was being persecuted,[4] he "tasted habitually those internal delights that the loving and sweet souls [*les âmes aimantes et douces*] find in contemplation." He here refers to contemplative joys that were *not* unique or peculiar to him but that are shared by "loving and sweet souls" generally; he refers to delights that he enjoyed inasmuch as he too was "loving and sweet"—that is, far from totally self-absorbed. It was by participating in those imaginative social contemplations that the Solitary Walker experienced raptures and ecstasies, which he did not mention when he characterized his present self-engrossed rambling and more serene reveries that achieve nature's objective. Nevertheless, without the imaginatively social raptures and ecstasies, the Solitary Walker says, he "would never have found or known the treasures that I carried within myself." So which of the two, precisely, are these treasures? Are the treasures the raptures and ecstasies? Are those the true happiness? Or are the treasures (and the true happiness) rather the self-absorbed, nonrapturous and nonecstatic, drifting reveries—the door to which was somehow opened by the enjoyable solitude in which was experienced the rapturous and ecstatic, social-creative reveries?

In what immediately follows, it is these last that seem predominant.

For no sooner has the Solitary Walker introduced his past raptures and ecstasies than he indicates a major problem that they pose for his present project of writing an observational diary: when one is "in the midst of so many riches, how keep a faithful register of them?" Accordingly, when he "wished to recollect for myself so many sweet reveries," he fell back into them, instead of describing them (2:3).

It would seem that the diary project was short-circuited by the recollections of the rapturous reveries.[5] And this is what happened very much, he reports (2:4), on the walks that he took after he conceived this "project of writing the continuation of my confessions" (referring to the second of the five aims laid out in the first chapter). This happened above all on the walk that he is now going to relate, which was aborted, however, in shattering fashion.

Thus does Rousseau lead into this work's first account of an actual walk upon which there occurred an actual reverie.

An Actual Walk and Its Actual Reverie

But this lead-in turns out to be very misleading.[6]

It makes us expect an account of the Solitary Walker recollecting and then becoming reimmersed in a rapturous or ecstatic creative social reverie recalled from years before—a recollection whose enjoyment prevented him from keeping a faithful record of the experience.

But we get no such thing (Butterworth 1979, 162).

Instead, we are given what looks more like a well-executed chapter in the faithful observational diary—as a diary of an old man's present thoughts and reveries. In other words, we are back to what the first sentence of the Second Walk led us to expect as the project of this writing overall. We are back to the fourth of the five overall aims stated in the First Walk. Our author continues to challenge us to follow, somewhat breathlessly, his amazing divagations.

The Solitary Walker's report begins (2:5) with a meticulous diary-like register of exactly what path he took and precisely when ("after lunch, on Thursday, October 24, 1776") and of how he first enjoyed with interest "the cheerful countryside."

Then he records how in the second place he enjoyed discovering and contemplating several botanical specimens that he had previously seen only rarely around Paris—the *Picris hieracioides* and the *Bupleurum falcatum*; we suddenly begin to be made aware that learned contemplation of such specimens is a major source of pleasure in his life these days. This gladdening activity was never so much as hinted at in the First Walk's anguished account of his present situation (an account that we now see was in more than one way a rhetorical-dramatic exaggeration).

The diary-like report continues in a long paragraph (2:6) that first tells how these botanical observations were "left behind, little by little" in a "surrender to the impression, no less agreeable, but more touching," made by the countryside as a whole. But we find here nothing like the enchantment with nature that we found described in *The Confessions* and in the third letter to Malesherbes: countryside walks during which Rousseau's "heart makes itself drunk with delicious feelings" that "disengage my soul, give me a greater audacity of thinking, cast me somehow into the immensity of beings in order to combine them, to make a choice among them, to appropriate them to me as I please, without impediment and without fear." Here, in contrast, the Solitary Walker speaks of the aspect of the grape fields after the harvest, having been deserted by strollers from the city and even by most of the peasant workers; then of the countryside as "green and cheerful"—and yet, partly defoliated and thus "offering as a whole the image of solitude" and, indeed, "of the approach of winter" (the image of solitude was tinged with a chill); and this then resulted in the emergence of an impression "mixed of sweetness and sadness, that was all too analogous to my age and lot." Focusing on this analogy and turning inward, the Solitary Walker became downhearted. He saw himself "in the decline of an innocent and unfortunate life," with a "soul still full of vivacious feelings" and a "spirit still adorned with some flowers—but now wilted, by sadness, and desiccated by troubles."

The self-absorbed depression deepened: "alone and forsaken, I felt coming the cold," and "my flagging imagination no longer peopled my solitude with beings formed[7] according to my heart."

Under the shadow of gloom about life's approaching end, with his creative-social imagination incapacitated, he sank into anguished despondency: "I said to myself, sighing, 'What have I accomplished, here below? I was made to live, and I am dying without having lived.'"

This descent into despair at his looming demise without having lived was halted not by a reverie creating "sweet chimeras," as in the parallel instance in 1756 that we have seen described in *The Confessions*,[8] but by a moral-religious reflection on the coming day of divine judgment: "at least this has not been my fault; and I will carry to the author of my being, if not the offering of good works, which they did not let me do, at least a tribute of frustrated good intentions," and "a patience under the ordeal of the contempt of men."

Once again, the melancholy consciousness of the loss of the capacity for creative social reverie makes the afterlife and its just desserts loom as all important.

But at this point, "tenderly moved by these reflections" (that is, by reflections on his hope for just desert from God in an afterlife), he was propelled into a spiritual upclimb: he recollected with satisfaction, and even with pleasure, the whole course of his spiritual and emotional life, especially his love of others; he recollected his heart's affections, its "attachments so tender and yet so blind," and finally "the ideas less sad than consoling" (i.e., somewhat sad) on which his spirit "had been nourishing itself" in his more recent several years.

He reports how he prepared himself to recall all this in order to describe it in writing. The prospect of executing the writing (cf. Friedlander 2004, 16–17) made him start looking forward to "a pleasure almost equal to that which" he had in surrendering himself to these reveries (presumably, the latter uplifting ones?). The rest of his afternoon passed, he says, "in these peaceful meditations," which he was recalling with contentment as he returned homeward, still "in the thick of my reverie" (*au fort de ma rêverie*) when this all suffered a terrible termination.

This leading—and as it turns out, sole[9]—example in *The Reveries* of an account of an actual recent reverie of the Solitary Walker is conspicuously lacking (as is underlined by its misleading introduction) in actual or recalled ecstatic or inebriated raptures. There are here no recollected creations of consoling imaginary societies of friends, earthly and heavenly; no recollected dreaming on the great system or of dreaming on any other philosophical theme. There is no recollection of being led, by contemplation of the countryside, either to manipulative mastering of nature or to awed intimation of the divinity behind nature. In short, the mental and spiritual powers and achievements that distinguished Rousseau, especially in his prime, are entirely absent. On the other hand or by the same token, the reverie of the aged Solitary Walker is suffused with moral and pious hopefulness for the life to come, counteracting the depressing sense of his lonely old age and of the looming end of his unfulfilled life. The peak of the reverie is the Solitary Walker's uncomplaining and rather vague report of his synoptic recollection of his whole spiritual life, and especially his "so tender but blind attachments," and then "the less sad than consoling ideas" on which his spirit has nourished itself during the recent years; these years are here characterized in unprecedentedly gentle terms as the long retirement (*la longue retrait*) in which he has been "sequestered from the society of humans."

These last formulations make this reverie as a whole come close to sounding like an experience that very many other sensitive, sociable, lonely elderly people may well have. Rousseau's leading presentation of an actual reverie of the Solitary Walker is a consoling and enriching model that could be realized or aspired to by many readers in their retrospectively melancholy last years of retirement, living sequestered from the society of humans and perhaps consoled by keeping a diary, inspired by the example of the Solitary Walker. Is it not one major intention of our author to present such a model? Is not this work, *The Reveries*, in part animated, despite or even on the basis of its vigorous disclaimer, by a benevolently devious, public-spirited cultural project? Is not this work in part a gift to the sensitive and lonely elderly in generations to come?[10]

Here again, we note a striking contrast with Socrates, as presented by Plato and Xenophon. In Rousseau's *Reveries*, we hear as a constant refrain the Solitary Walker's compassion-arousing lamentations over the debilities and loss of his powers on account of his enfeebled old age. In the Socratic writings, we are given a philosopher who exhibits to the very last days of his seventy-year life a youthful beaming vigor of body and of mind, engaged in a ceaselessly seductive and passionate reaching out to and conversing with the young.

CHAPTER 2

Being "Born into Life"

What I am inclined to call the quasi-every-old-man's model reverie was explosively destroyed when, as the Solitary Walker reports, he was violently bowled over and knocked unconscious by a rushing Great Dane dog (2:7–8). We are given a detailed account of the accident, then of his recovery of his senses and of his finding his way home to his caring and nursing wife, and of his subsequent sufferings from the serious injuries he incurred. But what is most important in this incident, the Solitary Walker indicates, is the state that he found himself in at the moment when he regained consciousness: "it is too singular not to give the description of it here" (2:9).

It was nightfall. He perceived the sky, some stars, and a little greenery. What was radically singular was a deliciousness of the absence of his self-consciousness: "I had no distinct notion of my individuality" (*mon individu*). "Being totally in the present moment, I remembered nothing": "I did not sense myself anymore, except as by the over there" (*je ne me sentois encor que par là*)—that is, by the barest form of subjectivity in the perception of objects. We are at the opposite extreme from what the Solitary Walker will later speak of as his wish to extend his "existence over the whole universe" (6:14 end; contrast Grimsley 1972, 449) and equally far removed from reveries in which one feels identified with the universe as all (e.g., 7:9). The Solitary Walker felt no identification, no identity, whatsoever. He watched his blood flowing "as if I were watching a brook flow, without even dreaming that this blood belonged to me, in any way" (*en aucune sorte*). He felt "neither hurt, nor fear, nor worry"; instead, "I felt in all my being a rapturous calm to which, each time I recall it, I find *nothing comparable in all the activity of known pleasures*" (my italics). Amazingly, the Solitary Walker declares, "I was being born, in that instant, into life" (*not*, of course, into "*my*" life), "and it seemed to me that I filled with my weightless [*legère*] existence all the objects that I was perceiving." To our astonishment, he does not say a word of regret about the fact that his reverie, with its sustained individual self-consciousness, was permanently broken; nor does he give any indication that his subsequent memory of that loss of self and of reverie clouds or qualifies in any way the incomparable sweetness of the memory he now has of having been born into life, which seems to mean exiting self-consciousness (and exiting all reveries).

To be born into life is, it seems, to awaken into a rapturous calm of the disappearance of self-concern, of memory and of imagination, of pain, fear, and worry, of all but the most minimal subjectivity.[11] Contrary to what many commentators have asserted, this is by no means a recovery of the famous "sentiment of one's own existence"[12] experienced in the state of nature; that sentiment is neither mentioned nor alluded to in this passage, and we must not impose it on Rousseau's text. The sentiment of existence as described in the *Second Discourse* is a sentiment of the human's own self, and is closely joined to the care for the human's very own self-preservation: "the first sentiment of the human was that of his existence, his first care was for his preservation"—"his very own preservation [*sa propre conservation*] making up almost his only care" (OC 3:164 and 140; see also 3:144, "the sole sentiment of his very own present existence"); "the Savage lives in himself," finding there "the sentiment of his very own existence" (*le sentiment de sa propre existence*; OC 3:193); what's more, "nature alone does everything in the operations of the beast, whereas the human contributes to his, in the quality of a free agent." The "human experiences the same impression, but he recognizes himself as free to acquiesce, or to resist." To "will and to not will, to desire and to fear, will be the first, and almost the sole operations of his soul" (OC 3:141–43).

Rousseau obviously provokes us to compare and to contrast this strange birth into life that he experienced as he awoke with the immediately previous explicit reverie. That reverie, so sweetly elegiac, intensely autobiographical or self-centered, and religiously hopeful, was inspired by the specter of his impending end of life;[13] in contrast, the incomparably pleasant, self-erasing swoon left that lugubrious shadow entirely behind.[14] Is this succession and release not a major component in the swoon's amazingly[15] incomparable attractiveness for Rousseau, in retrospect? Does not Rousseau indicate here how heavy—and how constitutive of developed human self-conscious, and not least of reverie—is the burden of the awareness of one's own mortality?[16] This is a burden that was unknown to humans in and by their primal nature, according to the teaching of the *Second Discourse*: the only evils the human by and in nature fears are "pain and hunger; I say pain and not death—because the animal will not know what it is to die"; and "knowledge of death, and of its terrors, is one of the first acquisitions that the human has made in moving itself away from the animal condition."[17] In his self-losing swoon, the Solitary Walker did recover, if only temporarily, the "pure state of nature's" blissful freedom from consciousness of mortality. This is a freedom from, that the positively self-aware sentiment of existence lost forever when it departed the original, solitary state. And we add, this selfless life into which the Solitary Walker was temporarily born, like the life of "the primitive nature of man" in "the pure state of nature," contained no hint of experience of (or felt need for) God, either in or beyond nature.[18]

Despair in the Face of Life's End Inspires a Revised Theodicy

The Solitary Walker devotes most of the rest of the Second Walk to a diary-like account portraying his condition and his thoughts the day after his accident and then in the days and weeks following. The picture is not a pretty one. He describes a collapse back into a grotesque form of his paranoia of victimhood. Reverie disappeared from his life; his paranoia seems to render reverie out of the question.[19]

Rousseau pauses, at the start of this narrative of neurosis, to reflect on, and thus to reveal awareness of, his natural mental disorder: "I have always hated shadowy darkness [*ténébres*], they inspire in me naturally a horror—which the dark mysteries that they have surrounded me with, for so many years, ought not to have diminished" (2:13; see similarly *Confessions* OC 1:566).

It was when he was eventually brought face-to-face with the thought of his death and its aftermath that "these black shadows [*ces noires ténébres*], with which they relentlessly surrounded me, reanimated all the horror that dark shadows naturally inspire in me" (2:22). For when he recovered sufficiently to take walks again, he believed that he discovered that the public, including no less than the king and queen of France, had become convinced that his accident had been fatal, that he was dead and gone. Then things got even worse. Someone wrote to him that the newspaper *Avignon Courier* had greeted the happy news of his demise with a preview of "the tribute of outrages and indignities being prepared in my memory for the funeral oration after my death."[20] Then, still worse, he learned by chance of the announcement of a public subscription to raise money to publish manuscripts that would supposedly be found among his belongings after his death: "by that, I understood that they were holding ready a collection of writings fabricated for the express purpose of attributing them to me right after my death" (2:21).[21] "These observations, making blow after blow and followed by many others that were scarcely less astonishing, alarmed my imagination all over again when I believed it to have calmed." He reports that he became even more convinced than ever before that his gift to future generations after his death—the messages in his writings—would be blocked and distorted by his enemies: "it is completely impossible for me to transmit any bequest to other ages" (2:22).

But this time, he exclaims, "I went further" (2:23). In a kind of dialectical somersault from despair into hope, his frantically imaginative reason discovered a dark, radical new theodicy: an unprecedented doctrine of providence and of the divine judgment that will be passed on us all after death. The initially crushing empirical evidence of the all-encompassing, totally unqualified, completely successful but deeply mysterious character of the plot of persecution led the Solitary Walker to become henceforth convinced, he declares—switching from the narrative past tense to the persisting present tense—that all his persecution originates in and is directed by eternal decrees that as "secrets of heaven impenetrable by human reason" are to be "suffered without a murmur." The First Walk's demon behind all the persecution now gives way to a mysterious—and therefore paradoxically solacing—persecutorial omnipotence. That "the perfect being whom I adore" is responsible for all this persecution is an idea that, so "far from being cruel and rending to me, consoles me, tranquilizes me, and helps me to resign myself." For in this idea, based on the apparent empirical evidence, the Solitary Walker finds (he says), an unprecedentedly credible promise of eventual vindication and salvation. Explicitly disavowing St. Augustine's extreme of disinterested submission to divine will, the Solitary Walker proclaims, "God is just; he wishes that I suffer; and he knows that I am innocent"; "there, that is the motive of my confidence" (*voilà le motif de ma confiance*); "my heart and my reason cry out" that this confidence "will not deceive me"; "everything must at the end return to order, and my turn will come sooner or later."[22] For the first time in this writing, the Solitary Walker discloses his recovery of a faithful hope that his repute, and thus the messages in his writings, will, after all, in the long run shine forth somewhere and in some age that is indubitably going to come. From this point on—and thus, in point of fact, from the beginning of this book, leaving aside quasi-theatrical acting—our author is hoping with some confidence that through God's eventual vindication, *The Reveries* will be read with deep appreciation in a future age, somewhere, somehow: see 3:17. When one can interpret one's own terrible unjust suffering as imposed by a just God's providential plan that is impenetrable to human reason, then integral salvation and justification after death becomes morally certain. For even though, or precisely because, God's providential plan is unfathomable by human reason, the essence of retributive-corrective justice, in strict accord with deserving, is clear to human reason (Rousseau's Solitary Walker thinks). And justice and God are mutually entailing. Despair, in the face of one's demise, at the cruel and unjust suffering of the innocent, is transfigured into hope—nay, into confident expectation—of the immortal deserving that is essential to a just order. As Rousseau has his Savoyard vicar proclaim, "If I had no other proof of the immateriality of the soul except the triumph of the wicked and the oppression of the just in this world, that alone would prevent me from doubting of it" (*Emile* OC 4:589b). Here in *The Reveries*, the Solitary Walker portrays himself as having undergone an extreme version of the experiential path to God that may be traced through the hellish swamp of unjust victimhood.[23]

We see in the Solitary Walker's previous protracted relapse into paranoia, which eventually transfigures itself into this dark new theology, a kind of abysmal recoil: back to struggling with, and overcoming, the shadows of old age and mortality, from the rapturous calm's momentary liberation from all sense of aging and mortality and selfhood. Does this suggest that the creative reveries of Rousseau's earlier prime, in which he imaginatively constructed visionary societies of beloved beings both in a future heaven as well as on earth, may have been blissful not least insofar as those raptures afforded a more ecstatic (and hence, now seen to be more dubious) escape from awareness of aging, and mortal finitude? Consider again his account of his creative reveries in the third autobiographical letter to Malesherbes that we quoted previously: "the *nothingness* of my chimeras came sometimes to sadden, in a stroke"; "I found in me an inexplicable void that nothing could fill"—a "certain yearning of the heart for another sort of joy, the idea of which I did not have and for which nevertheless I felt the need"; then "soon, I elevated my ideas" to "the universal system of things, to the incomprehensible being who embraces all" (OC 1:1139–41). Now, in his less creative but more deeply receptive old age, those earlier flights of imagination are replaced by the seemingly more solid footing of a caliginous theology of hopeful confidence in righteous deserving, achieved in and through horribly unjust suffering.

Chapter 3

"Third Walk"—A Spiritual-Religious Autobiography

The stygian theological culmination of the Second Walk, following on an account of an actual walk's autobiographical reverie that was preoccupied with death and the afterlife, leads quite reasonably (Bonhôte 1992, 244; Manent 2019, 223) to the major theme of the Third Walk: a synoptic account of the evolution, over the Solitary Walker's entire lifetime, of his religiosity. The reasonable order of the chapters and of their train of thought remains clear.

Once again, as in the First Walk, we are allowed to eavesdrop, so to speak, on a soliloquy but this time, one that is more sequentially lucid. This would seem to be an example of the "sweet conversing" with his soul that was the third of the five aims laid out in the First Walk. Are we to take this Third Walk to be a written reproduction of a train of thought that occurred on an actual walk? Does this chapter count as the written recollection of an actual reverie? But apart from the title, in this chapter there is no mention of any walk or of any reverie.

The soliloquy begins (and ends) by taking issue with a famous line of autobiographical poetry "repeated often in his old age" by Solon, the (pagan) Athenian lawgiver who was one of the Seven Wise Men of Greece: "I become old while learning always."[1] The Solitary Walker, speaking not at all like either a great lawgiver or a famous wise man but apparently once again as a simple soul and *homme vulgaire* (recall the close of the *First Discourse*, OC 3:30), ruefully observes that in his own case, the "very sad knowledge" that experience has taught him as he grows old is that "ignorance is still preferable" to learning.

The second paragraph makes clear that in saying this, the Solitary Walker has in mind primarily his lugubrious learning about his own uniquely unhappy destiny (*destinée*) and "about the passions of others that shape it": "I have only learned to better understand humans so that I can better feel the misery into which they have plunged me." This latter knowledge, "though it discovered all their snares," did not enable an "escape from any of them."

The Solitary Walker laments the loss of his younger, "feeble-minded but sweet" trustfulness, even though that made him the dupe, the prey, the victim of the plots of his erstwhile seeming friends. For he did believe himself loved by the latter (even as they inspired in him love for them), and his heart rejoiced in those sweet illusions, which are now destroyed.[2] The Solitary Walker thus introduces his spiritual[3]-religious autobiography by speaking in a deeply unphilosophic, indeed anti-philosophical, vein.

He does concede that wisdom should be studied; but "youth is the time to study wisdom" (3:1). He starts off speaking as if for him, even as for most men, the fitness of youth was unfortunately wasted, and any wisdom that he has acquired has come only when he has become so very old, on the verge of death, that it is too late to be of any use: "we enter the lists at our birth, we leave them at death; what use is it to learn how to conduct one's chariot better when one is at the end of the race?" (3:3).

Rousseau here has the Solitary Walker erase from his life's picture the years he devoted to philosophical study and reflection and then to the writing and publishing of his great system. The Solitary Walker once again presents himself as a rather typically melancholy, even morbid, old man—distinguished by his unparalleled victimhood: "the study for an Old Man [*l'étude d'un Vieillard*], if there remains one for him to undertake, is solely to teach himself to die" (3:3).

The Solitary Walker's Distinctive Philosophizing

But then, the Solitary Walker adds, "And it's precisely that which one does the least at my age; one thinks about everything but that"; and in this last censorious phrase, the Solitary Walker's distinctiveness begins to peek out from behind the opening persona of tristful elderly averageness (Manent 2019, 223). Then he takes a more emphatically critical distance on all the old men (*tous les vieillards*). They "all hang on to life more than do the children and leave it with less grace than do the young people." The reason is, "all their works having been for the sake of this same life," and "they see, at the end, that they have wasted their labors." The aged Solitary Walker's criticism of all other old men intensifies when he adds, "they have not dreamed [*songé*] of acquiring anything during their life that they could carry away at their death" (3:3).

In the next paragraph, he takes us further up a path from average to rare, or to his unique, elderliness. He starts explaining how, when he looks back, he sees that from a very early age he was highly uncommon in his thinking and learning: "I did tell myself all that"; and "when it was time for me to tell it to myself"; and, what's more, in "well-digested reflections." Early in life he learned, he says, by his "experience of the whirlwind of the world," that he "was not made to live in it": that in it he "would never arrive at the state" for which his "heart felt the need." He "ceased therefore to seek among humans the happiness" that he "felt he could not find there"; his "ardent imagination leaped then above and beyond the space of my life, scarcely commenced"— "as if it were an alien terrain"—to "settle down in a tranquil resting place" (3:4).

The Solitary Walker does not explain what that tranquil resting place was, nor does he explain the curious and ambiguous phrase expressing the space that his imagination transcended (*l'espace de ma vie, à peine commencé*). The thematic context (this Third Walk's religious autobiography) prompts the assumption that these formulations refer to his expectant belief, even while young, in the afterlife believed to await us all.

But the Pléiade editor aptly reminds us at this point[4] of an important statement of the character "Rousseau" in the *Dialogues* (OC 1:858; see similarly 819 and 828), a statement claiming to give a key to the character of "Jean-Jacques": sometimes the latter "launches himself into the future for which he hopes, and that he feels is owed him" on account of "the evils he has been made to suffer unjustly in this world"; but more often, he "forms for himself beings in accordance with his heart, and, living among them in a society which he feels he deserves," he "wanders in the empyrean amid the charming and almost angelic objects with which he surrounds himself." Then, his "fictions become more sweet than the realities themselves"; he is "happier and richer by the possession of the imaginary goods he creates than he would be by that of goods that are more real, if you wish, but less desirable."

So there seem to have been two alternative avenues of imaginative expression of Rousseau's spiritually transcendent life: (a) imaginatively anticipating an afterlife such as he deserved versus (b) imagining an earthly life here and now, among angelic friends and lovers such as he deserved. This latter avenue of Rousseau's spiritual life is omitted here in the Third Walk's pious autobiographical account.

Still, what the Solitary Walker does go on to reveal is momentous. This sentiment of imaginative transcendence of mundane life, having been nourished by education from the time of "my childhood and reinforced during all my life," by a "long web of miseries and misfortunes," has "made me seek *at all times to know the nature and the destination of my being, with more interest and care than I have ever found in any other human*" (3:5; my italics). The Solitary Walker's imaginative flights of transcendence, so far from being a hindrance to the most intense quest for knowledge of the nature and the destination of his own being, have been the incentive to an unequaled thirst for such knowledge. Here, in "the only place in the *Reveries* where philosophy explicitly emerges as an issue" (Davis 1999, 85), the Solitary Walker defines his own distinctive or even unique way of participating in philosophizing, in contrast to the character of the philosophical activity he has seen in most participants:[5] "I have seen many who philosophized much more learnedly than me, but their philosophy was to them, so to speak, alien." Out of "wishing to be wiser than others," they "studied the universe in order to know how it was arranged, as they would have studied some machine that they might have perceived, through pure curiosity." But in point of fact, their curiosity was not so pure: they "studied human nature in order to be able to speak wisely, but not in order to know oneself." They "worked to teach others" but "not to clarify oneself within." As for him, the Solitary Walker avers, "when I have desired to learn, this was in order that I myself might know, and *not in order to teach*" (my italics). Going still further, he breaks unmistakably with Socratic, dialogical-theologico-political philosophizing: "as regards all the studies that I have tried to pursue in my life amid humans, there is scarcely any that I would not have carried out the same if alone, on a desert isle where I would have been confined for the rest of my life."[6]

The Solitary Walker's philosophizing, as here presented, appears to have no important connection with the direct experience of, and the crucial theologico-political evidence provided by, the Socratic dialectic of refuting treasured opinions about the just and the noble not only in oneself but then, ceaselessly, in others—through conversational argumentation on the basis of the premises of the interlocutors, and leading to conclusions that are agreed to by the interlocutors. In radically un-Socratic phrases, the Solitary Walker can declare that "I soon was consoled about my small aptitude for conducting myself skillfully in this world, by feeling that it was not necessary to seek in it" the true end of life (3:5). We hear repeatedly from Rousseau of his natural aversion for disputation: his distaste, not so much for written polemics, as for the give-and-take of immediate, interpersonal, somewhat competitive Socratic dialogue in which the very way of life of the interlocutors is at stake.[7] Socrates, in profound contrast, "dealt as he wished with all who conversed with him," as he "engaged in conversations always about the human things": "What is piety, what is impiety?" "What is noble, what is shameful?" "What is just, what is unjust?" "What is moderation, what is madness?" "What is courage, what is cowardice?" "What is a city, what is a statesman, what is rule of human beings, what is a skilled ruler of human beings?" (Xenophon, *Memorabilia* 1.1.16 and 1.2.14). The Platonic Socrates goes so far as to assert that it is the activity of conversational refutation that proves that the philosopher transcends humanity and becomes a god: *Sophist* 216a5–b6. Rousseau in the *First Discourse* (OC 3:13–14) spotlights Socrates in his refuting activity, paraphrasing Plato's *Apology* 21–22; but Rousseau drastically alters Plato's text to make the activity appear a defense of virtuous civic life against sophists and thus as anticipating Cato the Elder; Rousseau ignores and obscures the truly profound, critical, theologico-political goal that Plato's Socrates articulates: the refuting (*elenchōn*, 21c1) of the Delphic oracle through refutations primarily of the Athenian democratic statesmen (*politikoi*, 21b8–22a9).

The Purported Beginning of His Spiritual-Religious Journey

From this penetrating, if very brief and incomplete, glimpse into his uniquely intense, solitary, and self-centered philosophizing, the Solitary Walker turns abruptly to chronicle what he claims was the spiritual course of his early life (3:6). From the time of most tender childhood, he was imbued with "principles, maxims, which others would say were prejudices, which have never abandoned me totally" (so they have largely abandoned him). Making clear his Protestant sectarian stance, he reports having been, while still a child, enticed, seduced, lured, even forced, to convert to Roman Catholicism: nonetheless (he protests, with mordant irony [Crogiez 1997, 91]), "I remained always a Christian." In his own case, at least, conversion to Roman Catholicism became sincere. Under the instruction, and inspired by the example, of Mme de Warens,[8] and in the conducive situation of rural solitude, combined with the intense study of good books, he became devout: almost (not quite) in the manner of Fénelon—that is to say, verging on mysticism.[9] The Solitary Walker proceeds to elaborate what this means: "meditation in retreat, the study of nature, the contemplation of the universe, force a solitary to launch himself *incessantly* toward the author of things and to search with a sweet uneasiness the *end* of all that he sees and the *cause* of all that he feels" (my italics).[10]

This statement reminds of the accounts that we have quoted from Rousseau's third autobiographical letter to Malesherbes and from the end of *The Confessions* of the awed reveries induced in his mature years by his contemplation of nature. But *The Confessions* contains no account of any such reveries in his younger years; to repeat, the Solitary Walker erases from this pious spiritual autobiography the creative-social, this-worldly reveries that so delighted and transfigured Rousseau's youthful and prime years.

Reaching Middle Age, the Turning Point

The Solitary Walker proceeds to claim that from this youthful Roman Catholic piety, bordering on Fénelon's mysticism, his destiny (*destinée*) cast him back into the torrent of the world, where he "no longer found anything that could gratify his heart," even for a moment. A yearning for his lost sweet leisure followed him everywhere, making him indifferent to, even disgusted by everything he did that was "apt to lead to fortune or honors." He felt that even were he "to obtain everything that I believed that I was seeking, I would not at all have found this happiness for which my heart was avid—without knowing how to decipher its object." Thus everything, he says, contributed to detach his affections "from this world, even before the misfortunes" that were to render him completely alienated from it. In this condition, he claims, he reached the age of forty (the year 1752), "living according to chance, without principles well decided by my reason"[11] and careless about "my duties, without contemning them" but "often without understanding them well" (3:6).

Earlier in his young manhood, the Solitary Walker reports (3:7), he had decided that whatever he had achieved by the time he reached the age of forty would be "the end point of my efforts to arrive [*pour parvenir*] and of my pretensions of every sort" and that he would then abandon worldly ambition in order to live day by day without any more concern for the future; and so he did (he claims)—"not only without regret but with real pleasure." He "quit the world and its pomp":[12] "no more sword, no more watch, no more white stockings, gilding, or headdress" and instead "a very simple wig and a good coarse cloth garment." Nay, better than all that, he uprooted from his "heart the cupidities and the forms of covetousness which give the value to everything that" he was quitting. In releasing himself "from all those lures, from all those vain hopes," he succeeded in giving himself up, fully, to "carefreeness (*l'incurie*[13]) and to the spiritual repose which was always" his "most dominant taste and most durable inclination" (cf. *Confessions* OC 4:363–64).

Is it not strange, comments the ingenuously earnest Pléiade editor Marcel Raymond, "that Rousseau was able to affirm that he gave himself up 'fully to carefreeness'" when he was describing "the very moment when he began to write, to publish, at the moment of his premier 'glory'?" (OC 1:1781). For the fact is, "the year 1751 was the one in which Rousseau became a literary celebrity" (Cranston 1982, 244).[14] This was when Rousseau launched what was to become perhaps the greatest cultural revolution ever achieved by a philosopher in his own lifetime.[15] This is the time right after Rousseau exploded onto the scene with the inspired formulation and then publication of the Greco-Roman-republican *First Discourse* and its attendant polemics (including the preface to *Narcissus*), initiating Rousseau's elaboration of his great but sad system, accompanied almost immediately by the composition and premiere of his enormously popular and profoundly influential romantic opera *The Village Soothsayer*,[16] joined soon by the revolutionary *Letter on French Music*, and followed by his intervention in the great culture war that followed on the *Querelle des Bouffons*.[17] As Rousseau says in *The Confessions* (OC 1:369), "*The Village Soothsayer* completed my being in fashion, and soon there would not have been a man more sought after than me in Paris. . . . This piece is epoch making." This was almost simultaneous with the appearance of the first volume of the *Encyclopédie*, and "since Rousseau was not only an intimate friend of the two editors but the author of numerous articles on musical subjects, he shared in the glory of its success" (Cranston 1982, 246; see also 271). Four years later, Rousseau started to write the novel *Heloise*, which when published in 1761 became a universal best seller and "turned Rousseau from a celebrity into the object of a cult" (Cranston 1994, 11). As the character "Rousseau" says of "Jean-Jacques" in *Dialogues*, his life is divided into two parts, plus "the epoch that separates them, that is to say the time when he published books" (OC 1:676; the epoch would be about ten years: see 687, 827, 865–66, 871–72). All of this ten-year period and its world-historical literary activity goes unnoted by the Solitary Walker except for a very brief passing mention of "literary vainglory whose vapor had hardly touched me before I was already disgusted with it" (3:9). The truth will peep out only in the later Sixth Walk in passing, where we learn that Rousseau also became rather prosperous at this time and therefore the object of much financial importuning (6:5).

So immediately after having flashed a fulgurant glimpse of his uniquely solitary philosophizing, Rousseau portrays himself as if, when he arrived at his early forties, he resembled, and is still imitable by, sensitive and modestly talented, middle-aged, impoverished, socially disenchanted and disengaged loners (not to say, bohemian losers and misfits). Is not Rousseau in some measure concocting this fictive spiritual autobiography as a kind of spiritual oasis for such souls, who in their marginalized condition are thus potentially closest to nature of all those dwelling in universally corrupt bourgeois society?[18]

The Introduction to the Purported Reform of His Opinions

But no sooner has the Solitary Walker thus depicted himself as having become, at the age of forty, a sort of withdrawn free-spirited slacker, than his fictive narrative takes a new tack. He reports that he felt that this external and material reform (3:13 end) was such as to require another reform, in his opinions, or an intellectual and moral reform (3:13 end). This latter reform, he says, was "no doubt more burdensome but more necessary": "I undertook to submit my interior to a severe examination that would regulate it for the rest of my life, as I wished to find it at my death" (3:8). But he tantalizes us by at first saying nothing about the content of the opinions that he put under severe examination and regulation (Butterworth 1979, 173). Instead, he provides only a remarkably allusive list of what were his various motivations to this second reform, in his opinions and not just in his mœurs.

He says that he was spurred by the fact that "a great revolution had just carried itself out in me," but he does not explain what that revolution was beyond the previously indicated reform in his dress and vanities. He adds that "another moral world was unveiling itself to my vision," but he does not explain what that envisioned alternative moral world was. He tells of his beginning to feel the absurdity of people's senseless judgments without explaining in what the absurdity consists (3:9).[19]

Then he devotes a paragraph to informing us that the intensity of that taste for solitude that characterized all the rest of his life was first generated by the experience, at this time in his life, of his being forced into a solitary manner of living—because of "the task which I was undertaking": for that task, of severe examination of his opinions, could "not be executed except in an *absolute* retreat," a "*total* renunciation of the world" (3:10; my italics).

This portrait of a leap into an eremitic existence once again ignores and obfuscates both Rousseau's brilliantly fashionable revolution in romantic music at this point in his life, and the nigh-simultaneous *First Discourse*'s comprehensive and eloquently trumpeted critique of the Enlightenment in the name of a modernized, pagan, austere republican virtue and of a reconceived Socratic political philosophizing. Rousseau bends his efforts to having his Solitary Walker depict his moral-philosophical revolution as if it had been exclusively personal and private and entirely apolitical, anerotic, and amusical. One would never guess from reading this purported spiritual-religious autobiography that in fact at the time in question Rousseau was (in his own words from *Confessions* OC 1:356–57) "philosophizing about the duties of man," with his heart animated by a fermentation of "that first leaven of heroism and virtue" which his father and "fatherland and Plutarch had put there"; that he "no longer found anything great and beautiful but to be free and virtuous"; that he "looked at [him]self as a member of Plato's *Republic*"—and in that light interpreted not only the "laws of nature, justice, and reason" but also the laws of "that pure, holy religion" that is as "eternal as its author."

Nor would one ever guess from this purported spiritual-religious autobiography in *The Reveries* that when he arrived in Geneva, he "abandoned [him]self to the republican enthusiasm which brought [him] there," and (following the teaching of Thomas Hobbes and of Baruch Spinoza) "thought that since the morality of the Gospel was the same for all Christians and the basis of dogma was different only in things one got mixed up in explaining [and] that one did not understand," in "each country it was up to the sovereign alone to settle both the worship and this unintelligible dogma, and that consequently it was part of the citizen's duty to accept the dogma and to follow the worship prescribed by the law" (*Confessions* OC 1:392).

The Content of the Opinions That Were Purportedly Reformed

After speaking of the zeal with which he gave himself up to what he claims was his hermit's task—a zeal proportionate, he says, both to the task's intrinsic importance and to the need he felt in regard to it—the Solitary Walker finally indicates, but with remarkable indirection, the substance of the opinions that he claims were the ones that he critically examined and reformed at this period of his life (3:11).

He begins (3:11) by explaining that at the time being described, he was living (for reasons left entirely unexplained) with modern philosophers. We are suddenly reminded of his earlier (3:5) momentary lightning flash illuminating his unique kind of self-centered philosophizing, in contrast to the socially directed philosophizing of all others he has found or seen. Now, however, he does not focus on this difference, between his own and others' philosophizing. In fact, he now does not present himself as a philosopher at all or as at all philosophical. He speaks rather of the great difference between the ancient and the modern philosophers (among the latter of which he certainly does not include himself). For "the modern philosophers scarcely resemble the ancients" because the moderns are "ardent missionaries of atheism"[20] who, instead of relieving his personal doubts and fixing his resolutions, had "shaken [*ébranlé*] all the certitudes" that he believed that he had, "on the points that were most important" for him to know.[21] Thus does the Solitary Walker begin to disclose that it was his opinions about divinity—even about the very existence or nonexistence of divinity—that he claims he was compelled to examine and to reform. And he in passing makes it clear that in his view, the ancients were not at all ardent missionaries of atheism nor very imperious dogmatists, but instead relievers from religious doubts who reinforced the certitudes that are most important matters of faith for piously modest, unphilosophical folk (such as the Solitary Walker presents himself as having been at that time).

The modern, virulently atheistic philosophers had not, the Solitary Walker explains, "persuaded me, but they had worried me; their arguments had shaken [*ébranlé*] me without having ever convinced me" (3:12). He confesses that in dialogues with these philosophers, dialogues that occurred often, he defended his opinions feebly. This was due, he says, not only to his hatred for dispute but (he claims) his "little talent for sustaining it" (3:11). He was able to find no good reply to their arguments; he only felt there must be one: "my heart replied to them better than my reason" (3:12).

Instead of proceeding, as would a philosopher, to seek a good reply—instead of refuting, or even addressing, or even letting us hear the argumentation of his philosophical critics (contrast the dramatically different procedure of Plato's Athenian stranger when he conjures up and confronts philosophical atheists in *Laws* bk. 10)—the Solitary Walker says that he dismissed the modern philosophers' arguments as sophisms, and he proceeds to impugn their motives as well as their manner of arguing. They were, he insists, such intolerant men: a bunch of very imperious dogmatists, who "would not in any way put up with anyone daring to think other than they did, about any point whatsoever" (3:11). Even worse, he charges, they did not argue in good faith or as true rationalists. They were blinded by passions; they prostituted their philosophizing to subphilosophical interests. He finally said to himself in disgust (he claims), "their passions, which govern their doctrines" and "their interests to impose belief in this or that, renders impossible penetrating to what they believe themselves"; "can one look for good faith in chiefs of faction?"[22]

On this invidious, not to say slanderous, ad hominem basis, the Solitary Walker now revises and makes considerably weaker his previous striking account of how his own attitude toward philosophy differs from that of the (other) moderns (3:13): "their philosophy is for others; my requirement was for one for myself." In this condition of requiring (not yet possessing) a philosophy, he said to himself (he claims), "let's search for it, with all my strengths, while there is still time left." For, he claims, he conceived of himself at that time as mentally already at the beginning of decline (*déjà je touche au déclin*).

Striking an utterly unphilosophical tone, the Solitary Walker reports that he told himself that he needed to devise a fixed rule of conduct as regards thinking about divinity, a rule that he could then follow "for the rest of my days"—so that he would never have to think critically again![23] With a perhaps curious mixture of the plural and singular of the first person (could Rousseau have in mind his own religious faction?), the Solitary Walker reports that he said to himself, "Let us fix once and for all my opinions, my principles; and let us be, for the rest of my life, what I will have found I ought to be, after having thought well about it" (3:13).

The Solitary Walker gives no further explanation of what precisely were the certitudes and the most important points that he claims defined his religious faith prior to its being shaken by the modern philosophers. Nor does he ever relate what the critical and worrisome religious argumentation of the modern philosophers actually was.[24]

In sum, the Solitary Walker has now painted the following word picture of himself: he was a fellow of average or undistinguished mental abilities but of unrivaled sincerity and honesty, who reached middle age as a Christian loner, having lapsed somewhat from an earlier quasi-mystical devoutness akin to that of Fénelon; inexperienced in philosophizing and inept in argumentation, his persisting faith was troubled but not destroyed by a bullying den of colubrine atheist philosophers among whom he chanced to be living (for reasons never explained). The sophistic, bad faith arguing of those wicked philosophers drove our beleaguered unphilosophical believer to construct a so-called philosophy of dogmatic theological doctrine, never to be questioned by him again. He felt vividly, he says, that the mental repose[25] of "the remainder of my days, and my total lot [*sort*], depended on" achieving a fixed dogma (3:14). After "the most ardent and sincere researches that have perhaps ever been made by any mortal," he decided (he claims), for his entire life on "all the feelings [*sentiments*] that it was important to have"—"not at all doubting, it is true, that the prejudices of childhood and the secret wishes of the heart made the scale lean toward the side most consoling."[26]

The Solitary Walker makes crystal clear exactly what is most consoling or "what is desired with so much ardor": "who can doubt that the interest in admitting or rejecting the judgments on another life is determinative of the faith of the greater part of humans according to their hope or their fear?" What he says he had most to dread in the world, given "the disposition I felt in myself," was "to expose the eternal lot of my soul for the sake of the enjoyment of the goods of this world which have never appeared to me to be of a great value [*prix*]."[27] The Solitary Walker thus makes it sound as if the outcome of his researches was pretty much a foregone conclusion from the start, given his piously hopeful heart's tidal yearning for an afterlife. If these researches of his were unrivaled in sincerity and ardor, they contained (at least as he describes them) little of genuinely philosophical doubt and self-critical openness.

The Solitary Walker proceeds to confess yet again that he did not always remove, to his own satisfaction, all the difficulties that had troubled him and about which he had been browbeaten by the wicked modern philosophers (difficulties that he never shares with us). What is more, he admits that he found in these matters not only impenetrable mysteries but insoluble objections to every point. Despite all this, he decided to adopt in each question the feeling (*sentiment*) which seemed to him "the best established in a direct way, the most believable in itself"—"without pausing over[28] objections that" he "could not resolve but that are countered by other objections no less strong in the opposed system" (3.16). The Solitary Walker continues to refrain from specifying what might be these objections and counterobjections and their clashing systems.

At this point, the Solitary Walker, switching to the first-person plural, adds a consideration that has far-reaching implications for all of us readers. As regards this most grave matter, it is important, he solemnly counsels, "to have a feeling [*sentiment*] for oneself [*pour soi*]" and to choose that feeling "with all the maturity of judgment that one can put into the choice";[29] for if, "despite that, we fall into error, we would not understand ourselves to incur the punishment [*la peine*] in good justice because we will not have incurred the guilt/sin [*la coulpe*] for it." And there, he says, is "the unshakable principle that serves as the basis of my security" (3:16 end). So the Solitary Walker's foundation is in the rather intimidating principle of divine retributive justice: mistaken religious faith is punished as sinful but not for those of us who choose a religious feeling that is not only sincerely our own but that is also chosen only by, and after exercising, the maximum possible maturity of our judgment. The awesome premise, of course, is that humans are morally responsible, under threat of divine punishment, for how they choose to feel in religious matters. Rousseau will not let his readers overlook the absolute, existential stakes in the question of the existence and character of retributive divinity.

Evoking the Savoyard Vicar

Arrived at this juncture, the Solitary Walker abruptly declares (3.17), "the result of my arduous researches [he no longer calls them sincere] was quite nearly such as [*tel à peu près*: i.e., not quite the same as[30]] what I have since set down in the profession of faith of the Savoyard vicar."

The since (*depuis*) in the preceding statement is a significant hint for penetrating to the truth behind this fictive account of the Solitary Walker's purported spiritual life.[31] It was only in 1757, when he was forty-five years old, that Rousseau started to work on writing first Julie's,[32] and then later (1758) the Savoyard vicar's, professions of faith: that is to say, several years after the period in which the Solitary Walker indicates his religious views were settled in the wake of the completion of his arduous researches. In this period during which the Solitary Walker attests that his religious views were settled, after his completed research and reflection (his early forties) Rousseau in fact proceeded to write the *Second Discourse* (1753–54). The natural man as there depicted is an atheist: "in our primitive state, in the true state of nature, . . . each human in particular regards himself as the sole spectator who observes him, as the sole being in the universe who takes an interest in him, as the sole judge of his own merit."[33]

The Solitary Walker's purported spiritual-religious autobiography has abstracted entirely from Rousseau's career as an author. Now, however, our author feels compelled to add to this artfully doctored self-portrait emphatic reference to his single most famous and influential theological writing. He does so as briefly as he can and in words that misleadingly suggest that "The Profession of Faith of the Savoyard Vicar" is a stand-alone work (*ouvrage*)[34] rather than a small part of a long philosophical novel linked with, and integrated into, a corpus of writings conveying a philosophical system.

In its original context, Rousseau introduces this section of his novel *Emile or on Education* with an explicit address to his readers: "Readers, . . . instead of saying to you here what I think when I am my own boss [*de mon chef*], I will say what was thought by a person who would count for more than me" (OC 4:558). Having thus distanced himself from the thoughts being introduced (Plattner 1979, 43; Kelly 2012, 72–73), Rousseau then adds the following curious and striking statement: "I do guarantee the truth of the *facts* that are going to be reported. *They did really* happen to the author of the paper that I am going to transcribe" (OC 4:558; my italics). Rousseau as author thus underlines his failure to guarantee the truth of the theological opinions expressed in the paper. In the *Letters Written from the Mountain*, Rousseau says, it is important to note that the views of the vicar "in no way prove mine, especially after the very express declaration that I made."[35] At the conclusion of the vicar's profession, Rousseau as author says that he has transcribed this writing "not as a rule for the sentiments that one ought to follow in the matter of religion" but instead "as an example of the manner in which one can reason with one's *student* so as not to diverge at all from the method that I have tried to establish"; "this is what I *limit* myself to with my Emile" (OC 4:635–36; my italics). We may add that the Savoyard vicar never mentions reveries; they play no part whatsoever in his profession of faith (see also OC 4:560).

The author to whom Rousseau attributes the paper that contains the story and the profession of the vicar addresses "my dear fellow citizen" (OC 4:563): the paper containing the vicar's profession is thus explicitly a message from a citizen to a fellow citizen; it remains within the horizon of the citizen (Butterworth 1979, 176). Rousseau himself later characterizes the vicar's profession as "affirmative and demonstrative on all the fundamental points of the *civil* religion" (my italics).[36] As for how Rousseau (or "the author" whose paper Rousseau claims he is merely transcribing) presents the vicar himself viewing the addressee of his profession, the vicar opens and ends by apostrophizing his listener as "my child" (*mon enfant*; OC 4:565, 635).

Here in *The Reveries*, the Solitary Walker characterizes the vicar's profession as a statement "unworthily prostituted and profaned in the present generation, but that can one day effect a revolution among men if ever there is reborn among them good sense and good faith." The Solitary Walker thus makes it plain that he has squarely in mind the religious-cultural revolution that he dares to think and to hope may someday be the effect of the publication of "The Profession of Faith": the writing is conceived here by the Solitary Walker as having an emphatically popular or exoteric character and goal.[37] Is this not a major clue to the popular, exoteric aim and intention of this entire spiritual-religious autobiography in the Third Walk? Is *The Reveries* not a work that is meant to play a significant role in Rousseau's hoped for future religious-cultural revolution? For a vivid portrait of one major type of his envisaged readers whom Rousseau hopefully imagines, one needs to study the character "Rousseau" in *Dialogues*, starting especially with OC 1:727–29.

The Vicar's Profession of Faith

Let us now remind ourselves (as Rousseau prods us to do) of the culturally revolutionary articles of faith pronounced by the Savoyard vicar.

The profession of faith proper is introduced (OC 4:565) by the vicar reportedly declaring to his child addressee that he will not engage in profound reasonings since he is not a great philosopher and cares little to be one; he can claim only that he possesses sometimes some good sense and that he always loves the truth. In saying this last, the vicar affirms his moral virtue of truthfulness or sincerity—not the philosophical-intellectual virtue that consists in passionate striving to progress in unraveling the riddles of existence, by ceaseless self-critical requestioning and reexamination of all one's core convictions

"THIRD WALK"—A SPIRITUAL-RELIGIOUS AUTOBIOGRAPHY 61

(on this passion for truth, see again Rousseau's "On Theatrical Imitation: An Essay Drawn from Plato's Dialogues," OC 5:1204). Indeed, the vicar proceeds to launch a very harsh assault on not only the doctrines but the moral character of all philosophers, the ancient philosophers not excepted (OC 4:568–69; the philosopher singled out for denigration by name is Montaigne [4:598–99]). In striking contrast to Rousseau, the vicar stresses that he has no system at all to maintain.[38] A few pages earlier, however, the vicar has indicated that he is a partisan of Samuel Clarke's (1998) "new system so grand, so consoling, so sublime, so proper for elevating the soul, for giving a basis to virtue, and at the same time so striking, so luminous, so simple, and, as it seems to me, offering fewer incomprehensible things to the human spirit than it finds of absurdities in every other system!" (OC 4:570). From this vantage point, of Clarke's teleo-cosmological-theological system, the vicar attacks the foundation of none other than Rousseau's own system! The vicar targets specifically the concept of the state of nature as elaborated in the *Second Discourse*. Insisting that observation of nature shows that an intelligent and powerful will has created the human species with a fully developed intelligence and civilized power—and that the same will has appointed our species to be "the king of the earth"[39] as well as being the chief purpose of all the rest, the vicar scathingly condemns a philosopher who would attempt to understand human nature as comparable to that of beasts:[40] "you abject soul, this is your sad philosophy that renders you similar to them; or rather, you wish in vain to debase yourself; your genius testifies against your principles, your beneficent heart belies your doctrine, and the very abuse of your faculties proves their excellence in spite of yourself!" (OC 4:582). The good priest is convinced that one cannot doubt that "the human is sociable by his nature, or at least made to become so" (OC 4:600; but contrast OC 4:588, where the good priest trenches on self-contradiction in appealing to the superior naturalness of the primitive simplicity and the state in which humanity had neither memory nor foresight).

The body of the vicar's profession is divided into two main parts. The first, expressing feelings (*sentiments*) of whose truth the vicar says he is deeply persuaded (OC 4:606–7), elaborates a strictly natural theology, without any reliance on, or even mention of, revelation or Scripture.[41] The vicar cuts off his listener's one attempt at any questioning (OC 4:595). The vicar's leitmotif in this first part is an appeal to what the vicar asserts is the universal experience of the conscience and the virtues, and rules, and (above all) the hopes, that the conscience dictates.[42] The core of the theology thus produced is summed up as follows (OC 4:589–91): "God, it is said, owes nothing to his creatures"; but "I believe that he owes them everything that he promised them in giving them being." Now "this is to promise them a good—to give them the idea of it and to put into them the feeling of the need for it." The "more I return into myself the more I consult myself, and the more I read these words written in my soul: 'be just, and thou shalt be happy.'" But "this is not at all the case, considering the present state of things: the wicked one prospers, and the just remains oppressed." And "how indignation kindles itself within us when this expectation is frustrated!" The "conscience raises itself up and murmurs against its author; it cries out to him, moaning: 'thou hast deceived me!'" To which we may conceive God replying, "I have deceived thee, rash one? And who told thee that? . . . Why dost thou say: 'virtue is nothing,' when thou art going to enjoy the prize [*du prix*] for thine own? Thou art going to die, thinkest thou; no, thou art going to live, and that is how I will keep everything that I have promised thee." The vicar acerbically adds, "One would say, on the basis of the complaints of impatient mortals, that God owes them their recompense [*récompense*] before their deserving, and that he is obliged to pay [*payer*] their virtue in advance. Oh let us be good first, and then we will be happy. Don't require the prize before the victory nor the salary [*le salaire*] before the work!" For "if the soul is immaterial, it can survive the body, and if it survives it, providence is justified. If I had no other proof of the immateriality of the soul except the triumph of the wicked and the oppression of the just in this world, that alone would prevent me from doubting of it." The vicar declares that what he can "know well is that the identity of the me does not prolong itself except by the memory, and that in order to be the same in fact, it is necessary that I remember having been." Now "I could not recall after my death what I had been during my life unless I also recalled what I had felt, and consequently what I had done, and I do not doubt at all that this memory makes, someday, the felicity of the good and the torment of the wicked." It is "then that the pure pleasure which is born from the contentment with oneself and the bitter regret of having abased oneself will distinguish by inexhaustible feelings [*sentimens*] the lot which each has prepared for himself." The vicar admonishes, "Do not at all ask me, oh my good friend, if there will be other sources of happiness and of punishments; I don't know, and these that I imagine suffice to console me for this life and to make me hope for another." He then adds an important qualification: "I do not at all say that the good will be recompensed [*récompensés*]; because what other good can an excellent being attain than to exist according to its nature?[43] But I say that they will be happy"; that "they will then be compensated [*dédommagés*] in another [life]. This feeling is founded less on the deserving of the human than on the notion of goodness that seems to me inseparable from the divine essence."

We note that in contrast to the Solitary Walker's outpourings to which we have listened in the First and Second Walks, the vicar makes no reference to a demon who inspires terribly hateful plots (recall 1:10; and see 3:19). We note further that, again in contrast to the Solitary Walker, the vicar does not conceive of God as the designer of horrible persecutions for the just, as part of the mysterious, eternal decrees of His divine justice (recall 2:23–24).[44] This silence may go with the fact that the vicar exhibits no signs of anything like the mental derangement, the hysteria of victimized oppression, that we have seen exhibited by the Solitary Walker. By the same token, the vicar, unlike the Solitary Walker or Rousseau, is himself not at all a Christ-like figure, though he professes his admiration for such.

At the end of the first part of the vicar's profession, the author of the paper interjects to the reader, "I believed I was hearing the divine Orpheus singing the first hymns and teaching men the cult of the Gods."[45] This astonishing reaction—astonishing not least because the vicar has just previously condemned ancient paganism for having given birth to abominable Gods (OC 4:598)—is almost luridly highlighted and supported by Rousseau as author. For Rousseau supervised Charles Eisen in the latter's design of a complex engraving to face the title page of the original edition's third volume, which commences with the beginning of the paper containing the vicar's profession.[46] In the engraving, Orpheus is depicted before a forest audience of barely clothed men and women, all but one of whom (a striking exception, who seems to be falling on his face in panic) are looking up in awe or fear to the sky (in which no sidereal bodies are visible but only a bird in flight, from left to right, a bad omen in ancient Greek religion). The humans are joined by an attentive horse and cow and other animals, who are looking calmly, without fear or awe, straight at Orpheus. The latter is well coifed and clothed as a civilized Grecian and is looking off horizontally in a transfixed or dreamy stare (a reverie?), a lyre tucked under his left arm, his right arm raised to the sky, and his mouth closed, as if having completed a hymn and a sermon. The human audience in its childlike, awed or fearful, reaction to the music and homily is manifestly lacking in the least degree of critical thought.[47]

The author of the paper continues his interjection by declaring that in reaction to the vicar's profession of faith, he "saw crowds of objections to make to him." But he uttered none of them because moral persuasion was on the side of the vicar: "to the extent that he spoke to me according to his conscience, mine seemed to confirm to me what he had said." Still, the author of the paper says that he confessed to the vicar that he could not yet share the vicar's religious faith, though he promised that he would meditate on it most seriously (OC 4:606).

The author of the paper goes on to report that he next said, "You have told me only the half of what I need to know. Speak to me of revelation, of the scriptures, of those obscure dogmas through which I go wandering since my childhood without being able to conceive them nor to believe them, and without knowing whether to admit them or to reject them" (OC 4:606).

The vicar is reported as having responded by disclosing that as regards revelation and Scripture, "I see in it only problem [*embarras*], mystery, obscurity, to which I bring only uncertainty and distrust [*défiance*]." The vicar then confessed that if his interlocutor had more stable beliefs in revelation, then "I would hesitate to disclose to you my own," "but in the state that you are in, you will gain by thinking as I do." Rousseau as author appends to this a striking footnote: "This, I believe, is what the good vicar could say at the present time to the public." Rousseau through his vicar is self-consciously speaking, in a kind of rescue mission, to a public that Rousseau believes has largely lost its faith in religion as revealed in the Bible (OC 4:607 and see also in the same vein especially 4:630).

Rousseau certainly does not have his vicar restore faith in biblical revelation by anything that the vicar is reported to have said in the second part of his profession (in which the conscience is rarely mentioned). The vicar elaborates at least ten strong arguments against the reasonableness of any and all revelation, including the Christian in all its forms. To be sure, these arguments rather disgracefully commit the elementary logical fallacy of presuming what they are supposed to prove or what is at issue (the supreme authority of reason as the measure of what is real and true). The vicar barely mentions grace (OC 4:616–17) and does not even attempt to analyze, or to test, or even to listen to, witnesses (numerous of whom are sincere, completely sane, and sometimes highly intelligent) testifying to the experience of being graced with inspired insight.[48] Instead, the vicar creates an utterly un-Socratic dialogue between "The Reasoner" (who agrees that he speaks for philosophers) and "The Inspired"; the main thrust of this dialogue is to hold "The Inspired" up to dogmatic-rationalist mockery (OC 4:614–17).

Nevertheless, the vicar ends by reconciling himself, in practice at any rate, to his vocation as a Catholic priest and thus to the Christian revelation. In its final (and thus most exposed) pages, his reported profession of faith veers in a dramatically new direction that is much less critical of revelation. Out of the blue, the vicar concedes[49] that if he were "a better reasoner or better instructed," he would perhaps feel the truth of revelation[50] as well as its "utility for those who have the happiness to recognize it." He suddenly proclaims that "there are as many solid reasons in favor" as there are against (having shown us none of those solid reasons in favor). What is more, the vicar now avers that not only does "the majesty of the Scriptures astonish" him, but "the holiness of the Gospel speaks to my heart." He proceeds (as quoted in our commentary on the First Walk) to praise the vast superiority of the scriptural portrait of Jesus—not as divine but as a moral man unjustly tormented, victimized, persecuted, abandoned—over and against the Platonic portrait of the serene Socrates dying tranquilly amid his friends. In addition, the vicar proclaims that "the facts concerning Socrates which no one doubts are less well attested than those concerning Jesus Christ." He cannot refrain, however, from adding that "this same Gospel is full of unbelievable things, things that are repugnant to reason and that it is impossible for every sensible human to conceive or to admit" (OC 4:625–27). After completing his entire profession of faith, the vicar insists that he and his listener not carry on any dialogue of question and answer regarding what he has said (OC 4:630).

The Years since the Purported Reform of His Opinions

The Solitary Walker proceeds to a narrative of his spiritual life in the years since the purported settlement of his religious opinions (back in his early forties). He begins by reaffirming his claim to have made the principles that he then arrived at the immovable rule of his "conduct and faith, without further worrying" himself about objections which he "had not been able to resolve" or objections that he had not foreseen and which "from time to time presented themselves" to his spirit as new (3:18).

But then, he concedes that the latter objections did, in fact, sometimes disquiet his calm. Nevertheless, they never shook him (*elles ne m'ont jamais ébranlé*). For he always was able to tell himself that they were "all only metaphysical quibbles [*arguties*] and subtleties." They were never challenges to "the moral order, the system of which is the result of my researches." As merely metaphysical, the objections were totally outweighed by the "fundamental principles adopted by my reason, confirmed by my heart, and all carrying the seal of the interior assent in the silence of the passions," thus constituting "a body of doctrine so solid, so well integrated and formed with so much meditation and care" (3:18).

With these formulations, the Solitary Walker presents the fundamental principles as unshakably held because they were primarily based in a pure moral reasoning, seconded but not led by the heart, without interference from the passions. The Solitary Walker speaks like a true disciple of the Savoyard vicar (or like a Kantian avant la lettre).

But the Solitary Walker proceeds to add a further momentous consideration. These fundamental principles enable him, he says, to "perceive the congruity between my immortal[51] nature and the constitution of this world and the physical order[52] that I see reigning there." He thus finds in the corresponding moral order and the system that is "the result of my researches" the "props[53] of which *I have need* in order to bear the *miseries* of my life" (my italics). In fact, he admits, in any other system he "would die without hope" and thus "would be the most unhappy of creatures" (3:18; for "creatures," Rousseau originally wrote "beings," manuscript p. 61).

So an intense passion, of hope for his own personal immortality as essential to avoiding his own personal unhappiness—or, as he put it back in 3:16, concern for "the eternal lot of my soul"—admittedly fuels the Solitary Walker's theological-moral system.

The Savoyard vicar, in contrast, did not focus on the fate of his own personal soul, and he did not bemoan his own miseries. What is much more, even though the vicar certainly taught the soul's afterlife, the vicar hesitated to teach of the human soul's immortality or eternity: "I believe that the soul survives the body long enough to maintain the order; who knows if that is enough to endure always?" On the other hand, "not imagining how the thinking being can die, I presume that it doesn't die. Since this presumption consoles me and has nothing unreasonable, why would I fear to surrender myself to it?"[54]

The Solitary Walker takes an even bigger step away from the self-transcending and priestly pastoral composure exhibited by the Savoyard vicar's profession of faith. For the Solitary Walker asks himself whether he has not perhaps received a personal divine revelation (3.19): "this deliberation and the conclusion that I drew from it, don't they seem to have been dictated by Heaven itself in order to prepare me for the destiny [*destinée*] which awaited me, and to put me in a condition to endure it?" And then he precipitously plunges back into his persona as outraged[55] incarnation of the Platonic Glaucon's Christ-like just man. He expostulates on "the incredible situation to which I am reduced for the rest of my life, without a refuge where I might escape my implacable persecutors"—"delivered totally to the most horrible lot that any mortal has ever experienced on the face of the earth," by a betrayal plot that was "forged in the pit of Hell" (*forgés au fond des enfers*).[56] "What would I have become" (he cries) "without compensation [*dédommagement*] for the disgraces that they made me suffer in this world, and without hope of ever obtaining the justice that was due me?"

This indignant hysteria prepares us for the Solitary Walker's admission that the seemingly heaven-sent doctrine was not so effectively consoling after all.[57] It transpires that it is only after years of agitations, only after he finally recovered his spirits, that the Solitary Walker has come, very recently, to realize that "since this life is only a condition of ordeals," the precise character of those ordeals matters little so long as they result in "the effect for which they were destined." "Consequently, the greater were the ordeals, the more advantageous it was to know how to sustain them." And what is that sustaining knowledge? "All the most lively pains lose their force for whomever" can descry, through them, "the great and sure compensation [*dédommagement*]"; "the certainty of this compensation was the principal fruit" that the Solitary Walker says that he "reaped from his previous meditations" (3:20). We are returned, from the more irenic theology of the Savoyard vicar to an outlook closer to the grim theodicy elaborated in the final two paragraphs of the preceding Second Walk.

But this impassioned faith in compensation after death, guaranteed by the depth of misery suffered in earthly life, also turned out to be insufficiently sustaining. The indignant Solitary Walker confesses that because he was overwhelmed by outrages without number and indignities without measure, he experienced intervals in which his hope was profoundly shaken (*ébranler*). For the powerful objections that he had not been able to resolve presented themselves to his spirit with greater force. Moreover, new arguments reinforced those that already tormented him. He came to fear that his reason, destroying its own work, would lead him to suspect that the consolations which his reason had provided were nothing but chimeras, thus "reversing all the support of hope and confidence that it had provided." When he contemplated in addition the fact that he alone seemed to wish to believe otherwise—that everyone else in the present generation "finds the truth, the evidence, in the system contrary to mine," he had to admit that his own system "would seem illusory even to myself if my heart did not support my reason." He even arrived at the point of crying out to himself, "I believe myself wise and I am only dupe, victim, and martyr of a vain error!" (3:21; Rosenberg 1987, 96).

These terrible crises of faith were rather frequent, but they were always brief. At the present time of writing, the Solitary Walker is "still not completely delivered from them." But they have now become rare, and they pass so quickly and are of such feather-like weight that they "do not have the force to trouble my repose." He recalls and reaffirms his past refusal to rethink these matters and the reasons for that refusal to think. He adds that in the present, unlike in the past, he no longer experiences the calm of life that years ago allowed him "no other dominant interest except that of knowing the truth" (this last hardly accords with the autobiography that has been elaborated in the previous pages!). At the present time, he has "a heart constricted by distress, a soul weighed down by troubles, a frightened imagination, a head troubled by so many awful mysteries" and a declining reason. In fact, all his "faculties, enfeebled by old age and anguish, have entirely lost their spring." Besides, he has a compelling moral reason not to make himself unjustly unhappy by trusting to his declining reason rather than to his "reason, when it was full and vigorous"—when it formulated the system by which he will "gain the compensation for the evils that I suffer without having deserved them."

He is aware that some new difficulties may present themselves. But he is certain that they will be nothing but "the sophisms of a subtle metaphysic which does not know how to weigh the eternal truths admitted in all times by all the sages, recognized by all the nations, and engraved in the human heart in indelible characters."

Against metaphysical doubt the Solitary Walker appeals finally to the purported *consensus gentium et sapientium*.[58]

But after all this, to our astonishment the Solitary Walker abruptly (3:22 end) allows himself to entertain the possibility of going over to the side of his persecutors!—to "the ardent missionaries of atheism!" (recall 3:11). He is led to this shocking possibility, of a complete surrender to his enemies, by the self-serving question, "What profit might I find in abandoning it?" (i.e., in abandoning his own and the Savoyard vicar's theistic doctrine). As he considers the possibility of taking this shocking step and adopting his persecutors' atheistic doctrine, what seems to give him pause is not so much the ugliness or untruth of atheism itself as its moral consequences: "In adopting the doctrine of my persecutors, would I also adopt their morality?" He immediately makes it clear that this question is complicated. For the Solitary Walker now discloses that he is keenly aware that his persecutors have a morality or moral doctrine with two faces. There is a public face that has neither root nor fruit but that they "display pompously in books or in some striking scene in the theater" and thereby mask a secret and cruel but authentic morality of all their initiates, which "alone they follow in their conduct and which they have so skillfully practiced with regard to me." So the Solitary Walker now concedes that his persecutors are animated by a morality, albeit one that is cruel as well as secret. He does not further explain the tenets of that secret cruel morality. If pressed to explain, presumably Rousseau would refer to such genuinely philosophical, artfully exoteric/esoteric moral and religious writings as those of John Locke and Montesquieu, as well as some of their lesser acolytes in the French and European Enlightenment.[59] By his language, the Solitary Walker makes it clear that he is far from being attracted to either the exoteric or the esoteric moralities of his opponents.[60] Nevertheless, he does not therefore dismiss the possibility of his adopting their unattractive two-faced morality. Instead, he points out that their two-faced morality is purely offensive and good only for aggression (his opponents are carrying on a grandly aggressive moral-cultural warfare of which Rousseau is only one major target) and so does not serve for defense (which is what Rousseau and his Solitary Walker are conducting). "How would it serve me, in the situation to which they have reduced me?" In that situation, only his innocence, he says, sustains him in his miseries; and he would render himself still more unhappy if he took from himself "this unique but powerful resource" and substituted for it wickedness (*méchanceté*). He would lose his self-esteem (*ma propre estime*) and "would gain nothing in its place" (3:22 end).

It was by reasoning thus (*ainsi*) with himself, the Solitary Walker testifies, that he finally(!) arrived at the point of no longer allowing himself to be shaken (*ébranler*) in his theological principles (3:23 beginning).

That this was the final decisive reasoning is disconcerting, not least in that it shows the Solitary Walker open to and admitting the possibility that in some other situation, where he was less embattled and not on the defensive, where he needed and was enabled to engage offensively, he might discern some profit for himself that would serve his happiness to such an extent that it would lead him to choose to abandon his innocence and his self-esteem and to embrace wickedness like that of, but perhaps practiced against, his persecutors with their cruel morality. What seems most fundamentally decisive for the Solitary Walker is not his gentle morality nor even his self-esteem, in and by themselves, but rather whatever most conduces to his personal happiness—be that some degree of wickedness and loss of self-esteem or be that innocence and unqualified self-esteem. Yet, how could the Solitary Walker conceive of a situation in which becoming aggressively wicked would conduce to his happiness more than does his innocence and justice, given his confident belief in a sanctioning just deity in the life to come? The obvious answer is that the Solitary Walker is not entirely confident in that belief: "shaken hope [*l'espérance ébranlée*], discouraging doubts, come back again from time to time to trouble my soul and to fill it with sadness" (3:24).

The Solitary Walker closes this soliloquy that elaborates his purported spiritual-religious autobiography by reiterating his melancholy at his decline in capacity for theoretical reasoning: "fallen into spiritual languor and heaviness, I have forgotten even the reasonings on which I founded my belief and my maxims,"[61] "but I will never forget the conclusions." Upon the latter he "rests in the shelter of my conscience" (*ma conscience*, using that term for the first time in the work [3:23]). "Incapable of the operations of the spirit necessary in order to reassure myself, I have need of recalling my former resolutions" (3:24). "Thus confined within the narrow sphere of my former understanding, I do not have, like Solon, the happiness of being able to instruct myself each day as I grow old" (3:25).

But then, in a sudden volte-face, the Solitary Walker declares that his hopelessness as regards "acquisitions in the sense of useful enlightenment" (*acquisitions du côté des lumières utiles*) is outweighed by a confidence that he has "very important acquisitions to make as regards the virtues necessary for my situation." In that regard, "it would be time to enrich and to adorn my soul with an acquisition that it can carry with it, when liberated from this body that obfuscates and blinds it" (recall 1:13). Then his soul will finally see the truth without a veil. The Solitary Walker at the close of the Third Walk announces a return to a somewhat softened version of the second of the five aims he set forth in the First Walk—"continuation of the severe and sincere self-examination that I formerly called my confessions" by which he consecrates his last days to "preparing in advance the account of myself that I will not be tardy in rendering" (recall 1:12). The Solitary Walker concludes by professing his confidence that "patience, gentleness [*la douceur*], resignation, integrity, impartial justice are a good that one carries away with one, and from which one can enrich oneself ceaselessly, without fearing that death itself makes it lose its value [*prix*] for us." The Solitary Walker says that he will consecrate the rest of his old age to the study of these virtues (which are such as will remain actively enriching in the afterlife) and that he will be (provisionally) happy if by progressing he learns "to exit life not better—because that is not possible—but more virtuous" than when he entered (3:25).

These last words remind us that to be more virtuous, for Rousseau, is not the same as to be better; virtue is not the same as goodness (Grimsley 1972, 460–61). Goodness fully characterizes humans at their birth, and in the original state of nature continued to do so throughout mortal human life—prior to any virtue or any felt need for virtue, which emerged only in response to corruption of the original, self-sufficient life of happiness in goodness without virtue. And here, in the context of the close of his purported spiritual-religious autobiography, the great value (*prix*) of virtue is closely tied to its being believed to be that by which one enriches oneself not merely in this life but in another life, the life to come. Thus, the Solitary Walker finds not only immunization against death as extinction but also immunization against death as the beginning of endless penal servitude. Acquisition of virtue mainly with this end in view is now said to be the Solitary Walker's guiding goal and the source of his happiness in the short time on earth that remains to him. The second of the five aims of this writing that were set forth in the First Walk now eclipses the other aims.

The Third Walk as a whole vindicates the wisdom of the course that the Solitary Walker claims to have chosen as an old man nearing his death: to cease thinking about any doubts that might occur to him about his belief in an afterlife in which a just God will guarantee happiness to those who deserve it on account of their virtue. This presentation of himself as eschewing, in the shadow of death, critical thinking about the afterlife and the virtue it requires stands in striking contrast to Plato's presentation of Socrates devoting the very last day of his life to a searching, critical argumentation with young friends over, while contending for the plausibility of, the grounds for the possibility of a deserved immortality of the soul, in an afterlife that will be engaged in the intellectual virtues of theoretical philosophizing (*Phaedo*, esp. 84c, 91a–c).

On the other hand, the Solitary Walker maintains a complete silence about any experience of having communicated with divinity in prayer, or in worship, or in times of study of Scripture. This goes with his almost total silence on the possibility of having received communication from divinity through inspiration or grace, not to speak of dreams or visions; throughout this spiritual autobiography, there is an almost complete absence of testimony to any commanding divine presence in the Solitary Walker's life, even in his powerful experience of the conscience.[62] The Solitary Walker omits the fact that at the age of seventeen (on October 16, 1729), Rousseau believed that he had partaken in a major miracle under the guidance of Bishop de Bernex: the latter's prayers (in which Rousseau joined) seemed to be answered by an abrupt shift of the wind that saved the house of Mme de Warens as it was starting to be engulfed by flames from a raging fire next door. Twelve years later (in *The Confessions*, Rousseau falsely claims that it was only two years later), Rousseau sent to the biographer of the bishop a memorandum (dated April 19, 1742) attesting as eye witness to the genuineness of this miracle as an act of God; a Catholic critic found and published this memo in 1765, and in *The Confessions* Rousseau defensively says that although he no longer believes his memorandum's faith-based interpretation of the experience, "nonetheless, as far as I can recall my ideas, which were sincerely Catholic at that time, I was in good faith."[63] Rousseau never provides a rationalist-philosophical explanation, or disposal, of this momentous religious experience. He does not deal with its profound challenge. He simply excises it from his record of his spiritual evolution.

All this distances the Solitary Walker very far from traditional or typical believers and their self-understandings. Here again, the contrast with Socrates is vivid. The latter proclaims in his sole public speech that his way of life as a philosopher has been "commanded by the god, through prophecies and through dreams and in every other way in which anyone was ever commanded by divine dispensation to do anything whatsoever."[64] And through repeated and numerous references to his daimonion, Socrates in both Xenophon and Plato will not let the reader cease to be aware of the challenge of such powerful apparent experiences of direct divine communication or revelation. David Hume, in a letter of December 28, 1765, to his friend Hugh Blair (professor of philosophy at Edinburgh), gave a report about Rousseau after their first in-person meeting that included the following (Greig 1932, 1:297): "I am well assured, that at times he believes he has inspirations from an immediate communication with the divinity. He falls sometimes into ecstasies which retain him in the same posture for hours together. Does this example solve the difficulty of Socrates's genius and of his ecstasies? I think Rousseau in many things very much resembles Socrates." But the Solitary Walker gives no hint of resemblances of this kind.

Chapter 4

"Fourth Walk"—The Virtue of Truthfulness

Given that the Third Walk consisted of an artfully untruthful spiritual-religious autobiography, while it concluded with a resolve to pursue, with a view to the afterlife, the fullest possible acquisition of moral virtue, including specifically integrity (*l'intégrité*), it is altogether reasonable that the next walk is devoted to investigating the paradox of how deliberately deceptive communication is consistent with, and even a duty demanded by, dedicating one's life to truth.[1] The unfolding order of the chapters and of their train of thought continues to be clear.

This Fourth Walk begins in the present tense but quickly moves (for a while) to the narrative past tense: "The day before yesterday I was reading [etc.]." The opening paragraph introduces the theme of, and explains what occasioned, the intensely reasoned self-examination that the Solitary Walker will proceed to describe himself as having engaged in during and subsequent to his walk yesterday. So this chapter, unlike the previous, promises a record of a train of thought from an actual (previous day's) walk. But here, there is no diary-like description of the walk as there was in the Second Walk's example of an actual walk, with its actual reverie. And in this Fourth Walk, reverie is never mentioned. Moreover, here, unlike in the explicit reverie meticulously described in the Second Walk, the Solitary Walker certainly does not "leave his head entirely free and allow his ideas to follow their bent without resistance and without obstacle" (recall 2:1 and 2:5–6). The thinking that is reported in this chapter is by no means a spontaneous outpouring of thematically unsequential ideas, "with as little connection as the ideas of the day before ordinarily have with those of the following day" (recall 1:13). And so here again, as in the case of the immediately previous Third Walk, we have to wonder whether the thinking we will hear reported qualifies as a reverie. We are prompted again to wonder, as we did when we pondered the First Walk, whether Rousseau is not vastly ballooning the meaning of the category reverie—squeezing into that genus his sustained, intense, self-critical, and philosophical reflections. Certainly, the meditation we will now proceed to analyze seems to be an execution of the second of the five divergent aims that were set forth in the First Walk: "the continuation of the severe and sincere examination that I previously called my confessions" (1:12). Now, however, the Solitary Walker does not at first mention the afterlife, which was said to motivate his severe and sincere self-examination back in 1:12 and which he claimed at the end of the Third Walk was to be henceforth his guiding concern (a momentary reminder of that concern appears when the Solitary Walker speaks here of swearing before heaven [4:2]; see also 4:28 beginning). So what follows seems initially to fit better the first of the five purposes laid out in the First Walk.

Plutarch

Not the least of the links connecting this Fourth Walk with the immediately preceding Third Walk is Plutarch, despite the fact that Plutarch was not mentioned by name in the previous walk. For, as we noted, an unattributed quotation from Plutarch's life of Solon began and ended, and inspired, the Third Walk's soliloquy; and now the Fourth Walk (which will end by again invoking the very same quotation from Solon) begins by informing us of the Solitary Walker's lifelong attachment to and profit from reading this pagan philosopher: "among the small number of Books [capitalized] that I read sometimes still, Plutarch is the one who grips me and profits me the most." No doubt the Solitary Walker continues to read *the* Book—the Bible (which is cited only once in *The Reveries* and then in jest [7:12]); but that reading of his is evidently less gripping and less profitable than his reading of the many works of the pagan moralist, who is almost the sole author whom the Solitary Walker has "never read without taking from the reading some fruit." This disclosure constitutes a tacit (truthful) revision of the preceding chapter's quite untruthful, more biblically pious spiritual autobiography.[2]

The Solitary Walker reports that "the day before yesterday, I was reading in his [Plutarch's] moral works the treatise *How One Will Be Able to Draw Util-*

ity from One's Enemies."[3] Now, if we consult that short treatise, we find that Plutarch (86c–e) tells his readers that the work is inspired by the teaching of Socrates in Xenophon's *Economist*.[4] That teaching as a whole is utilitarian to a rather extraordinary degree. Moreover, this very same treatise of Plutarch's, explicitly inspired by Xenophon's Socrates, is the source from which Rousseau derived the idea for the frontispiece for his *First Discourse* (OC 3:15 and CW 2:207n34). In that *First Discourse*, the pagan Socrates is held up as *the* model philosopher, while *the* model civil society is exemplified partly by Xenophon's pagan Persia (as depicted in the first book of Xenophon's fictional *Education of Cyrus*)—along with the emphatically pagan Rome and Sparta (at the very heart of the *First Discourse* is the prosopopoeia of the Roman Fabricius that begins, "Gods!" [OC 1:14]). At the end of this opening paragraph of the Fourth Walk, the Solitary Walker makes it plain that the inquiry that will be reported in what follows continues his obedience to the commandment set forth by the pagan god Apollo at his Temple of Delphi. So this Fourth Walk takes us unmistakably and deeply into what one may call the classical-pagan orbit of Rousseau's spiritual life. That major dimension of Rousseau's thought and writing was completely excised from the purported spiritual-religious autobiography presented in the previous much more biblically inclined Third Walk.

The Solitary Walker proceeds to recount that soon after he had reread Plutarch's treatise, he happened to come across an inscribed issue of a journal that he had been sent from the journal's editor, the great botanist François Rosier with whom Rousseau had collegially conducted field studies of plants during his happy 1768 sojourn in Lyon. Abbé Rosier had inscribed the following words: "*vitam vero impendenti, Rosier*" ("to the one who dedicates life to truth, Rosier"— all underlined by Rousseau in the manuscript p. 70). The Solitary Walker seems to presume that we readers will know, without his having to tell us (see also 4:41), that Rousseau's chosen motto is *vitam impendere vero* (to dedicate / consecrate life to truth), a line from the pagan Roman poet Juvenal's *Satires* (4:91).[5] In his paranoia,[6] the Solitary Walker assumes that Rosier "had believed that under this air of politeness he would say to me a cruel sarcasm" (*une cruelle contreverité*— literally, "the opposite of truth"). Not surprisingly, the Solitary Walker could not or did not brush off what he imagined was the nasty imputation; but neither did he suffer his all-too-usual flare-up of moral indignation. Instead, under the influence of having just read the Socratic[7] recommendation of serenity (*gravité*, translating *hēsuchia*) and self-critical interrogation as the rational reaction to calumny from enemies, the Solitary Walker calmly asked himself, "what basis could I have given for" the accusation? And then he decided to profit from the teachings he had just read in the good Plutarch by resolving to spend the next day's walk "examining myself on the lie"—confirmed in the opinion that he says he had already formed, "that the knowest-thou thy-self of the Temple of Delphi [referred to by Plutarch on his p. 89] was not a maxim as easy to follow as I had believed it in my confessions."[8]

In other words, continuing but advancing beyond Rousseau's self-examination in *The Confessions*, the Solitary Walker took from Plutarch the Socratic inspiration to make use of what he perceived to be a malicious accusation from an enemy as the stimulus to examine whether there was not some hitherto unrecognized, valid basis for the enemy's charge. The specific accusation here is that of hypocrisy[9] and arrogance, detected in the Solitary Walker's claiming that he dedicates his life to truthfulness, given the fact of Rousseau's lifelong, not infrequently exhibited penchant for mendacity (an elaborate example of which we have been witnesses to in the preceding Third Walk).

A Youthful Lie

Commencing his narration of the self-examination that occupied yesterday's walk and that fulfilled the agenda he had set for himself the day before yesterday, the Solitary Walker reports that the first thought that came to him was of a dreadful lie he had told in his young adulthood. The memory of this deceit, he says, has troubled his entire life and still now continues to sadden his heart. This prevarication, in itself a great crime, was made even greater by its effects.

But then he immediately adds that as a matter of fact, he has never learned what those effects actually were; it is the remorse that has made him "suppose them to be as cruel as possible."

But then he declares that as a matter of fact, the offense was "very far from originating from an intention to injure her who was its victim"; instead, the lie was torn out of him by invincible shame. And he "can swear to heaven's face [*jurer à la face du ciel*] that at that moment" when he told the lie, he "with joy would have given all the blood" in him to turn the harmful effect "on myself alone." He committed the lie in a delirium that he now believes he feels can be "explained only in saying that at that instant" his "timid nature subjugated all the voices of my heart."

So the lying was violently forced out of him by irresistible psychological compulsion expressing something deep in his nature and temporarily deranging his psyche to such a degree as to drown out all the voices of his heart and to paralyze his joyfully self-sacrificial conscious will and intention (4:2).

Accordingly, he switches to characterizing the lie as an unhappy/unfortunate action (*malheureux acte*) instead of a great crime and switches to speaking of inextinguishable regrets instead of remorse (4:3). For otherwise, "that would be to punish an offense that could be involuntary, and one ought to punish in the evil only the will."[10]

It sounds as if the most certain and serious (spiritual) harm from the incident was suffered not by the young lady victim but rather by the young perpetrator Rousseau: he suffered first the grave, if temporary, psychological dementia and then the subsequent lifelong remorse (or, on rational reflection, regret).[11] Still, the incident proved to have some benefit for Rousseau: the memory of it inspired for the lie a horror (*pour le mensonge une horreur*) that guaranteed his "heart against the *vice*" (4:3; my italics).

But how does this make sense (cf. Manent 2019, 227)? How could anyone, or anyone's heart, be guaranteed against deliberately choosing to lie by the memory of such a wholly unchosen, violently compulsive, if temporary, psychological delirium, countermanding one's heartfelt intention (cf. *Confessions* OC 1:38–39)? How can such a memory do more than put one on guard against, and lead one to try to figure out how to practice combatting successfully, the threat of having one's heartfelt, deliberate intentions and choices once again overwhelmed by contrary, violent, quasi-epileptic fits of psychological compulsion? Or is not this last precisely what the mature Solitary Walker now has come to conceive the so-called vice to be? That is, not a deliberately chosen, intentional evildoing for which one appropriately feels guilt and remorse but rather, on the contrary, a totally involuntary, natural, guiltless, psychological debility that compels one to act contrary to what one's heart and rational consciousness and understanding indicate to be what is most truly choice-worthy? Do we not now see coming to the fore an incipient version of something reminding of the Socratic conception of vice—as the action of a conscious psyche whose practical-moral understanding and thus deliberation and choosing are involuntarily blinded to what the mind's unoccluded practical reason does or would dictate as most choice-worthy in the particular case and circumstances? Is the Solitary Walker's horror toward the lie a horror at the thought of how his psyche, and the human psyche as such, can become so violently disabled as thus to lose the capacity for rationally responsible choice and action and agency?

Yet in the fifth paragraph, the Solitary Walker goes back to saying, contradictorily and in un-Socratic fashion, that it is the *remorse* for a lie that has not ceased to afflict him (my italics; see also the twenty-fifth paragraph). He speaks thus while asserting, in un-Socratic language, that "the moral *instinct* has always conducted me well, my conscience has preserved its initial integrity" (conscience is linked to instinct rather than to reasoning or opining). Yet, he then immediately adds the confession that his conscience sometimes "*altered*, by *bending itself* to my *interests*" (my italics):[12] this seems, contradictorily, to entail that conscience, unlike instinct, can allow itself to be persuaded, and thus corrupted, by calculation of interest. Then, however, he veers back to saying that his conscience "preserved *all* its rectitude[13] on the occasions when the human, *forced* by his passions, can at least *excuse* himself on grounds of his *weakness*" (my italics): this formulation presents conscience as, like instinct, remaining unaltered while being dominated by the sheer forceful compulsion of passions.[14]

Does the Solitary Walker (does Rousseau) have a coherent conception of moral responsibility? Or is he profoundly confused? In *The Confessions* (OC 1:84–87), Rousseau tells the story of this lie at much greater length but with the same dubiously incoherent unfolding of his psychological analysis of his own moral responsibility.

Certainly, the Solitary Walker goes on to say that when he adopted his motto, he felt himself made to deserve it and that he continued to so regard himself as deserving when he began the present more serious self-examination—this despite, nay, because of, the horror-inspiring memory of his youthful lie (4:3).

The Solitary Walker's Puzzlement

Still, he was quite surprised when, upon scrutinizing himself more carefully, he counted the number of his inventions that he has falsely spoken as truths, at the very time when he was simultaneously proud of himself for his "love for the truth" (*amour pour le vérité*)—to which he would sacrifice his security, interests, and person "with an impartiality of which he knew no other example among humans."[15] We are reminded of his avowal in the Third Walk that he was "made to seek at all times to know the nature and the destiny of my being, with more interest and care than I have ever found in any other human" (3:5). This implies that the truth that the Solitary Walker has at all times loved is above all the truth about the nature and destiny of his own being. Impartiality in love for the truth in this sense does not at all mean lack of the most intense self-concern or self-love; paradoxically, it is that self-concern and self-love that insists on and absolutely requires the impartiality. This may give us some hint contributing to the solution of the obviously perplexing puzzle: how does this species of love for the truth go hand in hand with so much falsification in communicating with others?

But the Solitary Walker reports that for him at this time, the puzzle only deepened. What surprised him the most, he claims (4:5), was that "in recalling for myself these falsifications [*controuvées*], I felt in regard to them no true[16] repenting." By "what bizarre inconsequence," he wondered, does he "thus lie with gaiety of heart, without necessity, without profit"—he, "in whose heart horror at falsehood has no counterweight," who "would endure tortures if to avoid them would require a lie"? By "what inconceivable contradiction" does he "feel not the least *regret*" (my italics)?

The Solitary Walker ends the fifth paragraph by reporting that he "saw that on the solution to this problem depended the justice of the judgment [*la justesse du jugement*] that he had to pass on" himself in this point. And here, he says, "after having examined it well, is how I came to explain it to myself."

And with this, he switches to the present tense (4:6ff.), which he maintains for the rest of the chapter (the lengthiest of all the chapters in the book). He thus leaves behind his truncated, promised narration of the thinking that occurred on his walk. He presents instead a teaching that is a kind of permanent or timeless distillate, presented in the here and now, of the self-examination that occurred back then and there on the walk—whose actual train of thought he will never communicate to us, falsifying the deceptive expectation he built up. The walk giving the account of Rousseau's truthfulness begins with a massive deception of the readers.

The Philosophical Response

The Solitary Walker begins (4:6) by laying down a definition of lying that he says he remembers having read in a certain unnamed "Book of Philosophy":[17] "to lie is to conceal a truth that one ought to make manifest" (*mentir c'est cacher une vérité que l'on doit manifester*).[18]

From this definition, he immediately draws a pregnant entailment: "to remain silent about a truth that one is not obliged [*obligé*] to speak is not to lie."[19]

Then he poses a question, the answer to which is still more pregnant and radical: what if one is not satisfied with simply concealing the truth that one is not obliged to speak but instead communicates in such a way as to deliberately convince the addressee(s) of the contrary of that truth?

It follows from the definition, he submits, that this is also not to lie, though it is of course to carry out a deliberate and total deception. Indeed, the Solitary Walker would seem to have in mind a deception intended to spread through the public, as more and more people become successively dupes of the untruth, received from others who have previously been made dupes; that this is the drift of the Solitary Walker's thinking is indicated by his assimilating the deception he has in mind to the deliberate passing of counterfeit money to someone to whom one owes nothing. This analogy with passing counterfeit money opens the door to the conclusion, following from the definition taken from the "Book of Philosophy," that originating a deception that one knows will spread through the public might not be lying.

The Solitary Walker concedes that two very important questions present themselves here (4:7). The first question is "when and how one owes to another the truth"—given that "one does not always owe it" (and by the last, he makes explicit an important aspect of the philosophical premise). The second question is "whether there are cases where one can trick [*tromper*] innocently." Continuing to put the focus on the latter, he declares that he knows very well that this second question is very settled: the answer is emphatically *no* in the books in which "the most austere morality costs the author nothing"; but the answer is *yes* in "society, where the morality of the books passes for prating that is impossible to practice."

The books, with their authors' self-righteousness, obviously do not include the "Book of Philosophy" from which the Solitary Walker has taken his definitional premise. The Solitary Walker certainly does not show to the books, with their categorical imperative, any more respect than he shows to society with its moral pragmatism: "let us then leave behind these authorities that contradict one another, and let us seek to resolve for myself, by my own principles, these questions."

Regarding the first of the two questions, he lays down as his own a philosopher's premise, stated with remarkable forthrightness: "the general and abstract truth is the most precious of all the goods." Without it, "humanity [*l'homme*] is blind," for it is "the eye of reason" (this entails that any other eye or source of vision for mankind, be it conscience or moral instinct or sentiment or the heart or revelation or inspiration or intuition, absolutely depends for its validity on guidance by reason's grasp of general and abstract truth). This holds in practical matters as well as, or even more than, in theoretical pursuits: it is by the general and abstract truth that "humanity learns to conduct itself, to be that which it ought to be, to do that which it ought to do, to tend toward its true end" (4:8). The Solitary Walker does not, however, state here what is that general and abstract, true end of humanity. Evidently, he does not think that he owes it to us readers to tell us that truth. Instead, in his didactic benevolence he provokes us to wonder about, and to try to figure out by and for ourselves, what his understanding of this most important general and abstract truth may be.

In contrast, the particular and individual truth is "not always a good, it is sometimes an evil, very often a thing indifferent." For "the things that it is important for *a* person [*un homme*] to know, and understanding of which is necessary to *that person's* happiness, are perhaps not very numerous" (4:8; my italics). In other words, the expression "the particular and individual truth" signifies here, all truths—be they general and abstract or unique and concrete—considered with a view to whether knowledge of them is or is not necessary for the happiness of diverse, particular, and individual human beings. It may be that for many or most particular individuals, it does not conduce to their happiness; it may lead to their unhappiness to know many truths, including many that are general and abstract (perhaps including the very truth expressed in this sentence). "As for truths that have no sort of usefulness, either for instruction or for practice," they are not part of the moral order: "the truth owed is that which interests justice, and it is to profane this sacred name of truth to apply it to vain things whose existence is indifferent to all and knowledge of which is useless to all." As a "consequence, he who is silent about or disguises" useless truths does not lie at all.[20] Every individual has a right to claim as owed always and everywhere the communication of those (perhaps very few) truths the knowledge of which is truly necessary for that individual's happiness (cf. Neidleman 2013, 823, 830–31). To frustrate an individual's knowledge of such truth is "to commit the most iniquitous of all robberies, since" (the Solitary Walker suddenly adds a deeply complicating and controversial moral premise) such truth "is among those goods common to all, whose communication does not at all take it away from whoever gives it" (4:8). Could the Solitary Walker really be forgetting that there are circumstances in which it is essential to the happiness of a defined group that it be kept totally and deliberately deceived about a truth that entails deadly damage to another innocent group? To take a nearby and famous example—that is, from a text of Plutarch's now on Rousseau's mind: the massive fraud that the wise statesman Solon practiced on his own citizenry of Athens in order to stir them up to make war on Megara so as to acquire Salamis.[21]

When the Solitary Walker takes up the second of the two questions he tabled as needing to be answered in order to understand the philosophical position ("whether there are cases where one can trick innocently"), he shows that he is well aware that the knowledge of truth which is necessary for an individual's happiness is by no means always a common good: "*very often* the advantage of one is to another's prejudice"; still worse, "individual interest is *almost always* in *opposition* to the public interest" (my italics). As a consequence, the Solitary Walker declares, very difficult questions arise for practice: "is it necessary to keep silent about, or is it necessary to speak, the truth that, profiting one, harms another?" And "is it necessary to weigh everything that one ought to say only on the scale of the public good?"—or "on that of distributive justice?" (which is evidently not always congruent with the common good). And then, what about "the rules of equity?" (yet a third distinct moral standard, sometimes countering the two previous). Can I be "assured that I understand all the relationships in the matter well enough so as to apply the enlightenment of which I dispose" in a manner that accords with those rules of equity? And then, beyond all this, there is a more radical set of moral questions: "in examining what is owed to others have I examined sufficiently what is owed to oneself?"—and in addition, "what one owes to the truth for its own sake?" (Must one not protect some truths from vulgarization and others from being degraded by the manipulations of unscrupulous or overly sophisticated elites?)[22] Finally, and not the least of the perplexities, is one's "never being unjust sufficient, for being always innocent?" (4:12). True innocence, as regards deceiving and truth telling and hiding of the truth, requires a philosophically informed knowledge that correctly weighs, against one another, the vastly diverse, authentic, competing individual human goods, widely varying over times and places. True innocence requires a practical wisdom that combines profound psychological understanding of varying human needs with manifold, versatile, moral flexibility. This is the wisdom that Xenophon's Socrates insists on and teaches in the writing that inspired Plutarch. This is the wisdom that is seen at work throughout Rousseau's published writing, and not least in *The Reveries*, with their multiple levels of envisaged audiences and their strategic, multilayered exoteric and esoteric teachings.

Given these extremely high moral and intellectual demands imposed by the philosophically conceived virtue of truthfulness, or dedication of life to truth, it is easy to understand how powerful is the temptation to self-indulgent moral laziness: "what troubling discussions—from which it would be easy to extricate oneself in saying, 'let's always be true, at the risk of all that can be the consequences'"; "'the lie is always iniquitous'"; "'whatever effect results from the truth, one is always without culpability when one has uttered it'" (4:13).

But the Solitary Walker sternly rejoins, what is at issue is not ease but morality: not "if it would be good to say always the truth" but rather "if one is always equally obligated to do so"; and "supposing, on the basis of the definition which I was examining" that the answer is no, then what is at issue is to "distinguish the cases in which the truth is rigorously owed, from those cases in which one can keep silent about it without injustice, and disguise it without lying: since I have found that such cases do really exist."[23]

At this point, having set this very demanding agenda of reflection for his philosophically inclined reader, the Solitary Walker breaks off his teaching on the philosophical moral virtue of truthfulness in communication. He leaves behind the complex and flexible moral wisdom to which he has indelibly pointed as the necessary entailment of his philosophical premises. He at first substitutes "seeking for a sure rule for recognizing and determining well such cases" (4:14 end). But he immediately aborts that search and then explicitly interjects a pause: "But from where take that rule, and the proof of[24] its infallibility? . . ." (*sic*, 4:15 beginning; manuscript p. 77).

Conscience and Moral Instinct Replace Philosophical Reason

Having marked with his explicit pause a gap in his writing, the Solitary Walker turns to a radically unphilosophic approach and perspective—to "the dictate of my conscience, *rather than* the lights of my reasoning": that is, to the moral instinct, which he links with the thought of the severity with which "I shall be judged by the sovereign judge after this life" (4:15; my italics). Thus, the meditation now switches from the first to the second of the five aims of this writing outlined in the First Walk. In examining the doctrine of the "Book of Philosophy," the Solitary Walker never mentioned his heart, which he had repeatedly spoken of immediately before and to which he now returns (prior to this philosophical silence on the heart, it has been referred to about thirty-five times in *The Reveries*). We recall that before he took up the premise which he had read in "a Book of Philosophy," the Solitary Walker declared that "the moral instinct has always conducted me well, my conscience has preserved its initial integrity" (4:5); he here returns to that prephilosophical bedrock but now reinforced by the hopeful and fearful thought of the afterlife, presided over by a severely judgmental divinity—something that did not figure at all in the philosophical perspective.

The philosophical understanding of virtue stressed primarily what is owed to others, on account of the consequences for their happiness in this life—without losing sight of the need to weigh also in the balance what is owed to one's own, earthly happiness. Now, in following "the dictate of my conscience, rather than the lights of my reasoning" the Solitary Walker ceases to refer to his or to others' earthly happiness and focuses instead on the purity of his own heart, and on the consequences, for his own happiness, of the day of divine judgment in the afterlife. He criticizes the "judging of the discourses of men by the effects that they produce," on the grounds that the effects are "not always easy to understand" and vary infinitely with the circumstances. He now asserts that "it is solely the intention, of the one who discourses, that measures the worth of discourses and determines their degree of malice or of goodness" (in the philosophical perspective, there was no reference whatsoever to intention or to malice). He adds that the intention to trick (*l'intention de tromper*) can be innocent only if it is based on a "certitude that the error into which one throws one's audience cannot harm either them or anyone else, in any way whatsoever"; and "it is rare and difficult for one to have that certitude"; and "so it is difficult and rare that a lie would be perfectly innocent." The nonphilosophical moral perspective thus locates deliberate deception in a range of the more and less imperfectly innocent (the philosophical perspective, which did not demand certitude about the effects of deception, referred to no such range). Accordingly, the Solitary Walker now speaks as if "lying for one's own advantage," or "lying for the advantage of another," are only somewhat less wrongful species than "lying in order to harm"—which is identified with calumny, damage to another's reputation or amour-propre (there was no reference to concern for reputation or amour-propre in the philosophical perspective). He exempts from blame only "lying without profit or prejudice to oneself or to another"; such profitless and harmless deliberately deceptive communication is not lying but rather fiction (4:16), which now, unexpectedly, becomes his theme, especially fictive writing.

Deliberate Deception through Fictional Writing

The Solitary Walker first briefly disposes of morally instructive parables and fables in which "the de facto lie is only the garb of the truth," as the audience can be expected to be well aware: no real deception whatsoever is involved (4:17).

Then he turns to "purely idle fictions such as are the greater part of stories and novels which, containing no true instruction, have as object only amusement." Intention, now the intention of authors, continues to be the basis for judging the extent to which such playful writings express the virtue of truthfulness or the vice of lying: "stripped of all moral utility, they can indicate their worth only by the intention of him who invents them" (4:18).

But this leads, surprisingly, into a rather lengthy attack on the philosopher Montesquieu's notorious short prose poem *Le temple de Gnide*, a succès de scandale that has remained to this day a famous example of high-toned erotica.[25] The Solitary Walker's attitude toward this erotic writing sounds like that of a censorious citizen and shocked paterfamilias: "if there is any moral object in *The Temple of Cnidus*, that object is well obfuscated and spoiled by the voluptuous details and by the lascivious images." As for Montesquieu's playful pretension that "his work was the translation of a Greek manuscript," this arouses the Solitary Walker's heated indignation—in an outburst addressed directly and imploringly to his audience of readers (for a moment, Rousseau drops the lie of his claim that this book is not written with publication in view): "if this is not a very positive lie, then will someone tell me what it is to lie?" (4:18). "One will say in vain that this is only a pleasantry" and "that in fact no one was persuaded"; "I will reply that such a pleasantry, without any object, is nothing but a very stupid childishness [*un bien sot enfantillage*]" and "that a liar lies no less when he affirms although he doesn't persuade" (4:19).

Our initial bemusement at the humorless prudishness being exhibited by the Solitary Walker toward the risqué philosopher-artist Montesquieu gives way to greater understanding when the real gravamen of the Solitary Walker's complaint comes into view as he goes on to say, "it is necessary to separate from the learned public the multitude, of simple and credulous readers, who really have been deceived by the account of the manuscript, narrated by a serious author giving the impression of good faith" and "who have imbibed without fear, from a goblet of ancient appearance, the poison of which they would have been at least suspicious if it had been presented to them in a modern vessel."[26] It thus appears that this attack on Montesquieu's jeu d'esprit is of a piece with Rousseau's attack on modern, Enlightenment, philosophical rationalism in general for what Rousseau charges is its elite neglect and belittling of marriage and family as the sublimely fulfilling, if often tragic, object of heterosexual eros, through which ordinary people like Sophie and Emile—the epitome of a common soul (*un esprit commun*) or of vulgar people (*les hommes vulgaires*: Emile OC 4:266, 459, 537)—can find islands of spiritual redemption within modern, amour-propre-ridden, bourgeois society. The poison that the Solitary Walker sees the multitude drinking from Montesquieu's refined erotica is evidently the arousal, in a wide readership, of erotic fantasizing about nubile, orgiastic worship of Aphrodite/Venus in an imagined ancient Greek neverland of polyamorous lovers, which makes the realities of faithful parental-spousal sexual love seem humdrum. This is one of the sorts of poison for which Rousseau's great novels, *Heloise* and *Emile*, are an intended antidote. (We cannot avoid observing, however, that there is at least a family resemblance between Montesquieu's published erotic fantasy and the polyamorous erotic fantasies Rousseau reports he delighted himself with: "a seraglio of Houris from my old acquaintances," "my blood caught fire and became effervescent," "here is the grave Citizen of Geneva, here is the austere, almost-forty-year-old Jean Jaques [sic] becoming suddenly the extravagant shepherd" [*Confessions* OC 1:427; see also 1:88]; nor can one unqualifiedly defend Rousseau as having only spoken about his fantasies while Montesquieu portrayed his: see *Confessions* OC 1:445, not to mention the scandalous 1:15–18.) Yet, note the major respect in which the Solitary Walker refrains from any criticism of Montesquieu the philosopher-artist: he does not condemn the impiety and blasphemy of Montesquieu's having made sensual pagan divinity and orgiastic pagan worship appear so very attractive (Montesquieu has the temerity to write, "the temple of Venus: the universe has nothing more holy nor more sacred than this place" [*Le temple de Gnide*, chant premier; cf. Schaub 2009]). As he decries the effects of Montesquieu's erotica, the Solitary Walker does not speak as an indignant defender of the biblical God and of biblical morality

But has not the Solitary Walker insensibly moved back in the direction of judging this work of Montesquieu's to be a lie by the criterion of the philosophers (i.e., by the effect on readers' happiness that the writing produces), rather than by the criterion of the conscience or the moral instinct or the heart (solely the intention—in this case, the stupidly childish jesting—of the author)?

The Solitary Walker moves to a statement of the standard, for truthfulness and lying, that is to be found not in the books but "in the heart of every person of good faith with himself, who does not wish to permit himself anything for which his conscience could reproach him" (4:20). And now, deserved distributive justice is laid down as the criterion for whether a communication is or is not a lie: "to give an advantage to one who ought not to have it [*à qui ne doit pas l'avoir*], this is to disturb order and justice"; and "everything that, contrary to the truth, wounds justice in any fashion whatsoever, this is lying. There is the exact limit [*Voilà la limite exacte*]." This entails that engaging in deliberately deceptive communication that is to one's own undeserved advantage "is no less to lie than if one says it to the prejudice of another," "although the lie would be *less* criminal" (my italics). A key part of purity of heart, of avoiding criminality, is subordinating one's own advantage to a dedication to distributive justice, which is deeply concerned with whatever deservedly "results in praise or blame, inculpation or exoneration" (repute continues to be a preeminent concern of the nonphilosophical moral perspective of the heart or conscience).

But by the same token, this exact limit also entails that to blame oneself undeservedly and to one's own disadvantage is to do an unjust thing. And now the Solitary Walker reiterates, with still stronger emphasis, the corollary that "anything contrary to the truth that does not interest justice in any way is only fiction." He adds a notable confession of what distinguishes his own conscience from that of others: "and I confess, that whoever reproaches himself for a pure fiction as being like a lie has a conscience more delicate than I" (4:20). In point of fact, does not the logic of the exact limit entail the injustice of such self-reproach—the injustice, though perhaps not the criminality, of such a more delicate conscience?

However that may be, after this self-distinguishing confession, the Solitary Walker takes up in the next paragraph (4:21) another closely related point: the dictates of the conscience regarding "what one calls *mensonges officieux*." The last two words constitute a pregnant terminology, often used interchangeably with *mensonges pieux* and for which there is no adequate English equivalent. In its most general sense, the two-word phrase signifies, in Rousseau's time, lies told as useful means to what are opined to be good or noble ends (see especially the article "Mensonges officieux" by Diderot in the *Encyclopédie* 1751–72, 10:337). The single most important meaning and connotation of the expression in Rousseau's time is gestured at in a passage in Voltaire's comical *Candide, ou l'Optimisme* (chap. 13). The hero is asked a discomfiting question about the status of a young lady accompanying him: "Is she not your wife?" And Voltaire indites, "He didn't dare say that she was his wife, because in fact she wasn't at all; he didn't dare say that she was his sister, because she wasn't that either—and although the *mensonge officieux* was once quite à la mode among the ancients, and though it could be useful among the moderns, his soul was too pure to traduce the truth." Voltaire thus playfully indicates that this is a term that applies to, among other things, exoteric/esoteric communication, as understood to be practiced especially by the ancients but also by the moderns, most significantly as regards divinity or religion: for example, the famous noble lie in Plato's *Republic* and Rousseau's kindred account of the legislator in the *Social Contract* 2:7.[27] The Latin translation for the expression in this most weighty meaning is *pia fraus*.

The Solitary Walker at first issues what appears to be a blanket condemnation, labeling all such falsehoods true lies, on the grounds that "imposing, to the advantage either of another or of oneself, is no less unjust than imposing to one's detriment." Now this formulation omits or forgets the crucial qualification of desert, which lies at the heart of distributive justice. Nevertheless, the Solitary Walker persists in this crude oversimplification of the aforementioned exact limit: "whoever praises or blames contrary to the truth lies." The Solitary Walker's seemingly crude or morally obtuse pertinacity serves to highlight the great exception which he does immediately add, and which opens the floodgates to deliberately deceptive writing on a vast scale: the preceding holds only if the untruth concerns a real being. For, "if it concerns a being that is imaginary, one can say anything one wishes without lying"—"at least, if one does not judge falsely on the morality of the facts that one invents."[28] In writing deceptively about a being that the author conceives to be imaginary— a divinity, for example (such as, in the vivid case before us, Venus, about whom the philosopher Montesquieu wrote in the pretended voice of a believer and worshipper)—an author never truly lies so long as he refrains from praise or blame of any being he conceives to be nonimaginary and real and provided that he judges correctly the moral benefit and the distributive justice of his invented facts, including any deceitful claim on his own part to be a believer in and votary of the imaginary divinity about whom the author is deliberately deceiving his audience.[29] But of course, the imaginary beings created by writers include much more than divinities. In Rousseau's case, the imaginary beings whom he has created include most notably the Savoyard vicar, along with Emile and Sophie and Emile's tutor in *Emile*; Julie and St. Preux and Wolmar in *Heloise*; and not least, the characters designated "Rousseau," "A Frenchman," and even "Jean-Jacques" in the fictive *Dialogues*. Some readers might well ask, "To what extent is the Solitary Walker yet another such imaginary being whom Rousseau has created?" This much is certain: Rousseau as author has here made clear, through his Solitary Walker, the license he understands is granted to him and to every other author, by conscience and moral reason, as regards his deliberately deceptive writing about all imaginary beings.

At this point, we need to draw attention to a theological distinction that is highlighted in the confession of faith of the Savoyard vicar: the distinction between the divinity said to be discoverable by unassisted natural human reason and sentiment versus the divinity said to be revealed by supernatural revelation and grace and knowable through purportedly heaven-inspired scriptures. Divinity in either or both of these senses may or may not be imaginary or real; neither Rousseau nor his Solitary Walker have pronounced definitively on this grave matter.

"The Person Whom I Call Truthful"

The Solitary Walker proceeds next (4:22–23) to contrast "the person whom I call *truthful*" (*vrai*, underlined in the manuscript)[30] with "people who are called truthful in the world."

The latter people have a veracity that "exhausts itself in idle conversations" in which, when they are speaking of "anything that does not in any way touch their interests," they are "of the most inviolable fidelity," but whenever they communicate regarding their interests, they deploy rhetoric "to present things in the light most advantageous to themselves"; "and, if the lie is useful to them," though they may "abstain from saying it themselves, they adroitly promote it" and "manage so that it is adopted without it being imputable to them." The Solitary Walker need not mention justice in describing their presumed veracity (4:22).

The complete contrary is done by "the person whom I call *truthful*." In matters that are perfectly indifferent, this person has little scruple in deceiving his audience. But every discourse that, "contrary to justice and the truth, produces for someone profit or damage, esteem or contempt, praise or blame," is "a lie that will never approach his heart, nor his mouth, nor his pen." This person is "solidly *truthful* [*vrai*, again underlined in the manuscript], even against his interest"; "he never deceives for his advantage or to harm his enemy"; nay, he "never serves the truth so faithfully as when it is necessary to sacrifice himself for her" (*quand il faut s'immoler pour elle* [4:23]).

So this man's "ardent love for the truth,[31] for which" the Solitary Walker glorifies him (4:24) is not the philosopher's love of the truth (Meier 2016, 148–49). Rousseau as philosopher is propelled by his "heart's need for happiness" to transcend "the world among humans" and to "seek at all times to know the nature and the destiny of my being" (recall 3:4–5). In contrast, the person whom the Solitary Walker calls truthful has the love of truth that "is only an emanation of the love of justice"; "justice and truth are in his spirit two synonymous words that he uses interchangeably";[32] "the truth that his heart adores" is holy and "consists in rendering faithfully to each what is owed him in things that are truly his" (4:24). The Solitary Walker gives no indication that this person wrestles with the troubling discussions that flowed from reflection based on the premise taken from the Book of Philosophy—discussions about what is justly owed to diverse individuals, including oneself, in light of their vastly differing needs for happiness in vastly differing circumstances (recall 4:12–14). Does not the person whom the Solitary Walker calls truthful avoid thinking about this perplexing part of the truth and of true justice? The person called truthful is especially concerned to "render faithfully to each what is owed him in good or bad imputations, in retributions of honor or of blame, of praise or of disapproval." And it "is above all of his self-esteem that he is jealous; this is the good which he can least do without, and he would feel a real loss in acquiring others' esteem at the expense of this good" (4:24). The person called truthful is not said to regard this most indispensable good as essential to his happiness, nor is he presented as being mainly concerned with his happiness. After all, this good—his self-esteem—is based on his "never serving the truth so faithfully as when it is necessary to sacrifice himself for it." There is no reason to think that this person ever asks himself which of the two is more important to him: justice/truth as the adored object of his sacrificial service or the good, the very great benefit to himself, that is the self-perfecting virtue and self-esteem that he gains through and by such sacrificial service. But it is not clear whether Rousseau means to prod us to ponder this (Socratic) question.

At the very end of this account of the person whom he calls truthful, the Solitary Walker abruptly returns to the philosopher Montesquieu's erotica. To our surprise, the Solitary Walker does not suggest that Montesquieu's writing be condemned or judged by the standards embodied in the person whom he calls truthful. Instead, the Solitary Walker returns to the philosophical criterion for judging truthfulness and lying (recall 4:12, "the obligation to tell the truth is found solely on its usefulness"). Ceasing to judge Montesquieu's writing in the voice of a paterfamilias and citizen and instead speaking in what sounds like the voice of a philosopher, the Solitary Walker reopens, and leaves open, the question of Montesquieu's innocence or guilt: "If *The Temple of Cnidus* is a useful work, the story about the Greek manuscript is only a *very* innocent fiction; it is a very punishable lie if the work is dangerous" (4:24 end; my italics). The jury remains out. Clearly, in order to settle the question, Montesquieu's work would need to be reread with care and reconsidered with profound reflection on its effects (cf. Schaub 2009).

The Solitary Walker's Truthfulness

The next words are, "Such were my rules of conscience concerning the lie and concerning the truth" (4:28 beginning). Now to which of the two radically different sorts of rules of conscience does this refer: to the rules of philosophical, utilitarian morality, aimed at maximizing happiness for others as well as oneself, to which reference was made in the previous sentence? Or to the rules followed by the self-sacrificial person whom I call truthful, solidly truthful, who was characterized earlier in the preceding paragraph?

The elaboration that follows makes it appear that the Solitary Walker's truthfulness has not been that of the philosopher. His has rather been a truthfulness in which reason is subordinated to instinct or to the heart—now conceived, however, as mechanical in its operation: "my heart followed mechanically [*machinalement*; see similarly 4:30 end] these rules before my reason had adopted them, and the moral instinct alone [*seul*] applied them" (4:25). This formulation tables the possibility that the Solitary Walker, as he matured, eventually transformed or transfigured originally instinctive rules of the heart into rules or maxims of practical reason—in a proto-Kantian moral maturation.

But we are soon disabused of any such impression.

The Solitary Walker avows in the next paragraph that he has hardly adhered to any moral rules or maxims regarding any matter whatsoever: "I have scarcely acted by rules and have scarcely followed any other rule in any matter except the impulsions of my natural temperament" (4:26). What has made him forbid himself "all lies that could in any way whatsoever touch the interest and the reputation of another" has been his generalizing the effect of his ineradicable remorse for the "criminal lie of which the poor Marion was the victim" (4:25; recall 4:2–3. But again, are not the concepts of remorse and of criminality rooted in the idea of a nonmechanical free will and consequent moral responsibility?). He has thus been dispensed from the requirement of the philosophical understanding "to weigh exactly the advantage and the prejudice, and to mark the precise limits of harmful lying or of the *mensonge officieux*" (4:25).

In His Conversation

Nonetheless, while his thinking has never been even approached by a premeditated lie out of calculation of interest, he has often lied out of shame in order to get out of embarrassing situations in "matters of indifference, or which at least interest solely" himself. This has occurred when his slow-wittedness in conversation has compelled him "to have recourse to fictions" (4:26); and he provides an elaborate illustration, showing how it is "certain that neither my judgment nor my will dictated my response, and that it was the mechanical effect [*l'effet machinal*] of my embarrassment" (4:29–30). Nevertheless, in such cases, acting a bit like a rafter steering to avoid boulders in torrential rapids, he has kept enough of his wits about him to be as careful as he could be in the invention of these shame-compelled lies so as to avoid strict "lies, i.e., anything that harmed either justice or the truth owed." Otherwise, in these cases he has "almost always been forced to speak before thinking" and has often uttered stupidities and ineptitudes that not only his reason disapproved but that his heart disavowed the minute they escaped his mouth. These are "lies in which my will has no part at all," being "no less against my conscience and my principles than those that can influence the fate of another." He calls on Heaven as witness that he sincerely repents his fault and would retract the lie in each case, "with all his heart," if he were not prevented by the absolutely irresistible impulsion of shame (4:26–27). But what coherent meaning can sincere repentance have in such a mechanical psychology? And how, in such a psychology, can the mighty feelings of remorse and the attendant conception of Heaven's just retributive judgment not be centered on a deeply confused self-understanding? (We recall that in the philosophical perspective, mankind is simply blind when it is not guided by the eye of reason [4:8].)

In His Published Writing

The Solitary Walker proceeds to devote no less than eight paragraphs to an account of his truthfulness in writing *The Confessions*. (He says not a word about his truthfulness in writing his more strictly philosophical works.) He begins by declaring that in writing his confessions, he never felt better his natural aversion to lying—since "the temptations would have been frequent and strong" to keep silent about or to conceal that of which he could be accused.

But then he confesses that as a matter of fact, he did feel an urge to lie deliberately—an urge to which he may have succumbed: he felt an inclination to lie "in the contrary sense, of accusing" himself "with too much severity."

That he did succumb to this urge—that he deviated from the strictest justice and thus from the code of the person I call truthful—is suggested by his adding that his conscience assures him that "one day I will be judged less severely than I have judged myself" (does this mean, judged one day by future readers, or by God on the day of judgment?). He says he can scarcely explain to himself his morally excessive, self-condemning, deceptive turn of spirit. He speculates that it might be due to his distancing himself from imitation. But what he goes on to say provides a much more telling clue to a very different explanation of this seemingly perverse form of lying: "Yes, I say it and I feel it with a proud elevation of soul—I have carried, in this writing [i.e., *The Confessions*], good faith, veracity, frankness, as far, nay farther, at least so I believe, than any other person ever; feeling that the good surpassed the bad, *I had my interest in saying everything*, and I said everything" (4:31; my italics). So he went overboard because he sensed that he would attain, through the unprecedented extremes of his self-accusation in *The Confessions*, his own very great benefit, including a proud, soul-elevating preeminence above all other humans. But then, how can it be true that, as he claimed previously, "never have I lied for my interest" (4:26), "for any motive of interest of mine" (4:38)? Still more fundamentally, if or since telling the truth as self-accusation was his own great spiritual benefit and interest, how can it be true that, as he will seem to claim in conclusion "in all things I *sacrificed* for the truth my interest" (4:41; my italics)?[33] We have here more evidence suggesting a major moral contradiction of a sort that is a principal target of Socrates's searching refutations and Socrates's subsequent observations of the consequences (see, e.g., Xenophon, *Memorabilia* bk. 3). But does Rousseau have in mind such refutation and, above all, Socratic observation of its (especially theological) aftereffects? Does Rousseau at all share Socrates's focus on the contradiction and its enormous import?

Rousseau has the Solitary Walker proceed to an admission of a more superficial sort of lapse. Since in writing his confessions memory often failed him, he filled in the gaps by details that he imagined. But he insists that these deliberate falsehoods only supplemented, without ever being contrary to, what he remembered. What's more, they never consisted in putting a lie in the place of the truth so as to palliate his vices or to arrogate virtues to himself (4:32)—or at least, not deliberately. "If sometimes without thinking about it, by an involuntary movement," he hid his deformed side and depicted his good side, these "reticences were well compensated" by those through which he was "often more assiduously silent about the good than about the bad." Here, we are back to the more profound sort of deliberate deceptions, now in a more emphatic and unambiguous version, which the Solitary Walker characterizes as bizarre or even unbelievable: "I rarely spoke about the good in all that it had of what is amiable, and often" (over a hundred times, we soon hear [4:38]) "I remained altogether silent about it because it honored me too much, and in making my confessions I would have given the impression of making my eulogy" (4:33). He devotes the next four paragraphs (4:34–37) to elaborating two examples of youthful good deeds—exhibiting the happy qualities with which his heart was endowed—that he deliberately omitted from his confessions "solely for the reason of which I just spoke" (4:33). In both these vignettes, the young Rousseau's happy quality consists in his skillful, compassionate lying about matters of the greatest significance in order to protect friends from receiving just punishment for having injured him badly. His compassion trumped any concern for retributive justice. To the report of his second compassionate lie, the Solitary Walker exclaims, in the famous words of Tasso (*Jerusalem Delivered* 2:22), "Magnanimous lie! Now when is the true / So beautiful that it can be preferred to thee?"[34] These are certainly not stories depicting a youth who gave promise of becoming the person I call truthful.

No wonder the Solitary Walker concludes with a severe self-criticism, by the standard set by that imagined person who is the paragon of the virtue of truthfulness. What follows from all these reflections, the Solitary Walker confesses, is that "the profession of truthfulness that I made for myself [*la profession de véracité que je me suis faite*] has its foundation more in the feelings of right and equity [*de droiture et d'équité*] than in the reality of things." He makes no reference to, or allowance for, his feelings of compassion. He says only that what he has followed in practice is "more the moral dictates of my conscience than the abstract notions of the true and the false." It is "solely by that, it seems to me, that truth is a virtue [*c'est uniquement par là que la vérité est une vertu*]." He goes so far as to make the radically unphilosophical declaration that "in every other respect the truth is for us only a metaphysical being from which there results neither good nor bad" (4:39).

By this standard of virtue, he does not feel his heart sufficiently satisfied to believe himself entirely irreprehensible. As Pierre Manent puts it (2019, 228), "at the end of the Fourth Walk, written so to speak in the present, Rousseau is obliged to admit that his conscience and his heart are not enough, and that even his heart demands that he returns under rule. Goodness does not take the place of virtue." In Rousseau's words, by "weighing so carefully what I owed to others," he neglected what he owed by right and equity to himself and, more importantly, to the truth. He now judges that when in conversation he was overcome by shame forcing him to supply innocent fictions, he "was in the wrong [*j'avois tort*], because it is wrong to abase oneself in order to amuse another"; and when the pleasure of writing led him to add invented ornaments, he was even more in the wrong, because this was in effect to disfigure the truth. What renders him still more inexcusable is the motto chosen by him. Especially given that choice of motto, it was not enough for him to have in all things sacrificed to truthfulness his interest and inclinations. He ought also to have "sacrificed his weakness and his natural timidity." He "ought to have had the courage and the force" to do so. His weakness, given his awareness of that weakness, is not only a poor excuse but also a contributor to the inexcusability of his vice: "with a weak soul, one can at most guarantee oneself against vice, but it is arrogance and temerity to dare to profess great virtues" (4:41). The Solitary Walker confesses his newly discovered guilt—as a consequence of his choice of motto—for the moral wrongs, for the moral vices, of arrogance and temerity, perhaps even of hypocrisy, with which he now believes he was justly charged by Rosier.

But it is not too late, he insists, to "redress the error and to put my will back in line": "henceforth that is all that depends on me." This could hardly mean that he thinks he can and will in the short time remaining to him in life transform his character from being morally weak to being morally strong and thus capable of finally living up to his motto understood to entail an implicit standard of great virtue. So what does this mean? That he will discard the motto and thus finally put an end to the arrogance and temerity of his morally weak soul making such a profession of great virtue? This seems to be further suggested by his last word, in vindication of the maxim of Solon, delivered by Plutarch: "it is never too late to learn even from one's enemies to be wise (*sage*), true, modest, and *to presume less of oneself*" (4:42; my italics; cf. Meier 2016, 164). But there is no subsequent indication that Rousseau or his Solitary Walker abandoned the motto. So could he covertly mean that he will put an end to his arrogance and temerity by henceforth ceasing to interpret his motto in terms of the standard set by truth as a virtue, a great virtue, and instead will interpret his motto, or will return to interpreting it in terms of the alternative standard, that of the goodness of the philosopher's pursuit of happiness?[35] Such, we will find, is suggested by the next chapter.

Chapter 5

"Fifth Walk"—Happiness

This walk is related to the preceding as a kind of dialectical rebound, from virtue to happiness. In the preceding walk, the overriding concern for happiness shone forth briefly, as belonging to the philosophical perspective; but happiness was then eclipsed by the unphilosophical call of conscience evoking the self-sacrificing virtue of truthfulness intimately tied to justice. In this Fifth Walk, the eclipse of happiness has ended, though the eclipse of the philosophical perspective continues. We are abruptly ushered into an unphilosophical thinking illuminated by the glowing golden memory of a peak time of happiness, a dozen years previously (September–October 1765): "I count these two months as the most happy[1] times of my life." In this chapter, the Solitary Walker never mentions the conscience, nor moral virtue, nor truthfulness and justice as virtues.[2] Duty is referred to only near the end, as the life prescribed to most other people (para. 15). Hope for the afterlife continues to manifest itself but without mention of God's judgment of deserved reward for virtue and deserved punishment for vice (see the Pléiade editor's note 4, OC 1:1801). In stylistic contrast with the preceding chapter, this Fifth Walk is short, lyrical, and rhapsodic. It seems to be a peak execution of the central of the five aims laid out in the First Walk: "the sweetness of conversing with my soul" (1:12).

But there is a momentous difference from the First Walk: enchantingly, this walk now invites readers to aspire to share in, or at least to regard with envying admiration, some version of this very rare but nevertheless accessible, true happiness enjoyed by the author (recall 2:3). Decisively abandoned is the deceptive pretense of the First Walk—the Solitary Walker's claim that he is writing these pages only for himself. On the contrary, the Solitary Walker proclaims that in this fifth chapter "by the description of the life that I there led, I would endow all the human beings of this century with a divination of the happiness and in what its enjoyment consisted";[3] "for although I am perhaps the sole person in the world to whom destiny has made it a law" to enjoy "the happiness of a human who loves to circumscribe[4] oneself," still, "I am not able to believe that I am the sole person who has so natural a taste"—"though I have not until now found it in anyone else" (5:1). The explicit public aim of this fifth chapter thus transcends all five of the aims set forth for this book in the first chapter; the Solitary Walker now reaches out to give to "all human beings of this century" a writing that will allow a divinatory share in his sweet conversing with his soul.[5]

The Setting

The first five paragraphs set the stage by describing the very agreeable and singularly situated place—the island of St. Pierre in the lake of Bienne—which rendered the Solitary Walker so truly happy. The Solitary Walker makes clear at once that there have been other such charming places in which he recalls having been rendered truly happy. But none have rivaled or have left such tender regrets as the one now to be described (5:1 and also 5:11).

Before describing his island habitation, the Solitary Walker portrays, in more vivid colors, the shores of the lake. These are wilder and more romantic (*romantiques*)[6] but no less cheerful than those of the lake of Geneva; the shores of the lake of Bienne have less cultivated fields and vineyards and fewer towns and houses. These happy shores are "seldom frequented by travelers" and so, the Solitary Walker avers, are "interesting for solitary contemplators who love to make themselves drunk (*s'enivrer*) at leisure with the charms of nature, and to gather themselves (*se recueillir*), in a silence troubled by no noise other than" the cries of eagles, the chirping of other birds, and "rushing torrents that fall from the mountain" (5:2; see also 5:17 for "the distant romantic [*romanesques*] shores").

The island itself, although "solitary, naturally circumscribed and separated from the rest of the world" (5:17), was by no means without society;[7] and it is the human company on which the Solitary Walker focuses (much more than in the parallel description in *The Confessions*: OC 1:637–38). Not only did residents of Berne often pay him visits,[8] but the island was inhabited by a tax collector with his family and his servants, and they had a farmyard, a pigeon house, fish ponds, pastures, vineyards, and orchards, as well as "a pretty salon where the denizens of the neighboring shores gather and come to dance Sundays during harvest times," which was the season when the Solitary Walker sojourned there (5:3). Dining together with this household[9] and often taking walks together and working the harvest alongside them, the Solitary Walker found "the society of the small number of inhabitants convivial and sweet without being interesting to the point of occupying me incessantly" so that he could "give myself up all day without obstacle and without care to the occupations of my taste, or to the most soft idleness" (5:17; characteristically, he refers to his devoted wife as "my Housekeeper" [*ma Gouvernante*], 5:7; she figures more prominently in the description in *The Confessions* of this sojourn on the island [OC 1:639, 642, 644]).

Addressing Kindred Spirits

In describing the romantic shores, the Solitary Walker reaches out to solitary contemplators, whom, as readers, he all but urges to visit and to enjoy this lake (not the island itself) or to go and find for themselves some similarly romantic unpopulated countryside (cf. G.-A. Goldschmidt 1978). The gathering of self by these kindred spirits in such environs recalls what the Solitary Walker briefly referred to back in the Second Walk as his present "hours of solitude and of meditation" that "are the only ones of the day when I am fully me [*moi*] and for me [*à moi*] without diversion, without obstacle, and when I can truly say that I am what nature wanted" (recall 2:1). By the same token, these kindred spirits are said to have an experience of self-inebriation with romantic nature that sounds like a more serene, moderate, and self-possessed echo or version of the self-inebriation Rousseau described in his *Confessions* (OC 1:162–63). There, we recall, Rousseau reported that on countryside walks "my heart, wandering from object to object, unites, identifies with, those that gratify it, surrounds itself with charming images, makes itself drunk with delicious feelings."

Still, these kindred spirits to whom the Solitary Walker is now reaching out do *not* seem to experience the countryside in the melancholy and nostalgic mood, shadowed by the end of life and the weakening of his capacities, that the Solitary Walker described in the lead-in to his account of his own most recent, explicit old man's reverie (recall 2:6). And something of that melancholy and nostalgia suffuses this Fifth Walk's *present* time of recollection of the good old former time on the island (see especially the final two sentences of this Fifth Walk).

Shadows

But another sort of shadow, a moral and civic shadow, falls across the Solitary Walker's sweet recollection: in recalling how the smaller of the two islands in the center of the lake is slowly being deliberately destroyed by people in order to repair the larger, he is led to a momentary, gloomy animadversion on the world's ceaseless and universal injustice: "it is thus that the substance of the weak is always employed for the profit of the strong" (5:2).

Moreover, he recalls that "it is on this island that I took refuge after being stoned at Môtiers."[10] Indeed, he recollects that, given "the forebodings that worried" him then and the calming retreat he found on the island, he "resolved to finish his days there" and "would have wished" the authorities would "make this asylum a perpetual prison,"[11] and even forbid him "every kind of communication with the mainland so that ignorant of everything done in the world," he "might forget its existence," while his own existence became forgotten by the world (5:3, 5:17—he would have thus again "drawn utility from his enemies").

Still, he claims that all this does not mean that during his stay on the island, thoughts of the world's unjust persecution played any important role. As he will claim at the end of this chapter, the island was "where nothing offered itself to me except cheerful images," where "nothing reminded me of saddening memories." And there is no hint, in his recollection as given here in *The Reveries*, of his paranoia having troubled him while on the island.[12] On the other hand, he does repeatedly indicate that thoughts of his own death hung about him, especially on his arrival: "resolved to there end my days" (5:4), "hoping to there end my days" (5:7), "living in the habitation in which I counted on finishing my days as in an inn I would have to leave on the next day" (5:7), "so as to occupy myself for the rest of my days" (5:7). And thoughts of his death come to him now, as he reminisces in the present about that sojourn back then: "If I could only go end my days on this beloved island"; "alas, it is when one begins to leave one's carcass that it hinders one the most!" (5:17).

Idleness

"What, then, was this happiness and in what did its enjoyment consist?" The "precious *fa niente*" was not only the primary but the principal of these enjoyments; "and *everything* that I did during my sojourn was in effect *nothing but* the delicious and necessary occupation of a person who has *devoted himself* [*qui s'est dévoué*] to idleness [*oisiveté*]."[13] One is reminded of the "indolence of the primitive state" of nature, which involved, however, no need for any devoting of the natural human's self: the savage human "wishes only to live and to rest idle [*rester oisif*]" (*Second Discourse* OC 3:194).

Another major difference from the pure natural state concerns sleep: its pleasures, whether during the night or in daytime naps and dozing, including pleasant dreams (what one is inclined to characterize as the most natural form of reverie, a form shared with other mammals), figure not at all in the Solitary Walker's account of his island indolence. In contrast, "the savage human, solitary, idle, and always near danger, must love sleeping and be a light sleeper like the animals, who, thinking little, sleep, so to speak, all the time when they are not thinking."[14] In sharp contrast, the Solitary Walker's is a true happiness in idleness of daytime wakefulness.[15]

In harmony with Rousseau's statement in the *Second Discourse* that "if nature has destined us to be happy, I dare almost to be confident that the state of reflecting is a state contrary to nature, and that the person who meditates is a depraved animal" (OC 3:138), the Solitary Walker stresses his own joyful abandonment of study, reading, and writing: "one of my greatest delights was above all leaving my books permanently well packed up and having no writing table whatsoever. In place of these sad papers and of all that used bookstore [*bouquinerie*], I filled my room with flowers and dried plants"—for he was at that time in his "first fervor of botany" (5:7).

Botany as Amusement

He does not speak of or describe his botanical pursuit as reverie. But neither does he treat it as in any sense a serious scientific, let alone philosophical, preoccupation: "not wanting any more work of labor [*oeuvre de travail*], I required a work of amusement that pleased me and that gave me no pains except those that a lazy person likes to take."[16] So he set himself the noble project of spending two or three hours after the communal breakfast every morning walking around alone cataloging all the plant species on the little island and collecting samples as "provision for amusement after dinner in the lodging, in case of rain." He blithely imagined that he would execute (for publication, presumably) a *Flora Peninsularis* or catalog of plants growing on the big island that would be exhaustive and in a detail "sufficient to occupy me the rest of my days." Highlighting the lack of intellectual seriousness of this project, he compares it to a book that some German is said to have written about the lemon peel; he says that he could have written a similar book, about "each grass of the field, each moss of the woods, each lichen that carpets the rocks." Yet despite or because of the disconnection of his observations from any broad and deep scientific and philosophical questions and reflections about nature or life, "nothing is more singular" (he exclaims) "than the raptures, the ecstasies" that he "experienced with each observation" that he made of "plant structure and organization, and on the role of the sexual parts in the forming of spores," whose system was to him at that time completely new. He was enchanted to "distinguish generic features of which previously" he had had "not the slightest idea." He was filled with joy to observe for the first time a thousand little games of reproduction (5:7). The delight in *novelty* seems to have figured rather large in this first fervor of botany; one is provoked to wonder, was the amusement going to continue to produce raptures and ecstasies and enchantment as the novelty wore off?[17] As we will learn in the first paragraph of the Seventh Walk, when he reached his sixties, "given up to my music copying enough so as not to have need for another occupation, I had abandoned this amusement [of botany] which was no longer necessary to me." He sold his herbarium and books on the subject, and after a while, he reports, the "little that I knew had almost entirely effaced itself from my memory."

Enjoying Casual Society

His lighthearted botanical publication plan makes it clear that his delight in this botanizing hobby was by no means simply self-contained. What is more, in his excitement about his plant discoveries, he was propelled toward society. He went around asking everyone else on the island if they had noticed one or another of the details he was filled with joy to have discovered. He says that he acted like La Fontaine, who, struck with enthusiasm by being shown for the first time one of the biblical books of prophecy, is said to have buttonholed every acquaintance he encountered for a while, asking excitedly, "Have you read Habakkuk?" (5:7).

Another sort of enjoyment of society filled each late morning when, after his hours of solitary botanizing, he took pleasure in the company of his wife and the tax collector, along with the latter's spouse, by joining them in visiting the farm workers and usually lending a hand in the harvesting. This is where he was often found by "the residents of Bern who came to see me"—visitors he seems to have found pleasing. In the good humor produced by all this physical exercise in the company of fellows, the Solitary Walker found the communal midday dinner very agreeable. But when this prolonged itself too long and when, in addition, beautiful weather invited, he slipped away (*je m'esquivois*) to be by himself (5:7). Later, "after supper, when the evening was fine, we went again all together on a little walk on the terrace to breathe there the air of the lake and the freshness." Resting in the pavilion, they chatted, laughed (this is the first time in *The Reveries* that laughter has been mentioned, and in the manuscript, the word is inserted above the line, along with "chatted"), "and sang some old[18] song which was worth as much as the modern twisting and turning" (5:10). It is astounding that this is the sole mention in *The Reveries* of music having played any role in the Solitary Walker's happiness.[19]

We note also that serious, loving friendship, with an equal or with students, and the deep conversations that philosophical friendship entails, have absolutely no place in the social relationships that form part of the Solitary Walker's true happiness.[20] Here, we have a very wide gulf separating Rousseau from all the schools and sages of ancient philosophy—Socratic, pre-Socratic, and non-Socratic (see L. Pangle 1999, 2001, 2003).

The Solitary Reveries Described

So what exactly did the Solitary Walker enjoy in the afternoons when he went off by himself? He tells us first of the times when he would go throw himself into a boat that he would row to the middle of the lake if the water was calm. There, stretched out in the bottom of the boat, his eyes turned toward the heavens, he let himself be swayed back and forth with the water's movements (without watching or hearing the water), "sometimes for several hours,[21] plunged in a thousand confused but delicious reveries, and which, without having any object well determined or constant, did not fail to be, to my taste, a hundred times preferable to everything that I have found most sweet in what are called 'the pleasures of life'" (5:7). In contrast to his account of his botanizing, he does not speak of having experienced any raptures or ecstasies during these reveries. Nor does he specify or explain what were any of the thousand evanescent contents of these tranquil reveries. The specific mutating objects seem to have been unimportant, except in their meandering sequence—and in their chief negative attribute: in that they included nothing at all troubling emotionally or the least bit challenging intellectually (not even on the level of the hobby-like challenge of botanical collecting and cataloging). We are certainly very far from any recorded Socratic experience or from any truly philosophical experience whatsoever (Grace 2019). Most surprising is the silence about any preoccupation with the self, with oneself or with self-consciousness. There is no mention here of the "sentiment of one's own existence." The "thousand confused but delicious reveries" obviously depend on a highly developed and rapidly changing imagination, a capacity that was entirely undeveloped in the self-consciousness or the sentiment of one's own existence attributed by the *Second Discourse* to original, solitary, natural humanity: "the imagination does not speak at all to the savage hearts" (OC 3:158).

Then the Solitary Walker recalls, now without mentioning any reveries, alternative afternoons: when he had the boat glide along the banks and when he often went for a swim; and still other afternoons, when he boated to the smaller island, where he sometimes passed the time in very circumscribed walks amid grasses and shrubs of every sort—without engaging in the botanical classifying and collecting that he pursued in the mornings (the playfully planned catalog was to be, for no good scientific reason, limited to the big island alone).[22] What really caught his attention about the smaller island was the suitability of its vegetation as an abode for rabbits, who he imagined "could multiply there in peace without fearing anything and without doing harm to anything"; and he reports that he proceeded to persuade his host family to introduce breeding rabbits brought from Neuchâtel. This was a source, he says, of great pride for himself as the leading founder of this little colony of rabbits.[23]

When the lake was too rough for boating, he reports, he would spend the afternoon, apparently as a second best, wandering over the main island "seeking for plants right and left." But now he does not speak of the raptures and the ecstasies reported in the morning botanical outings, and he makes clear that this afternoon botanizing lacked the dedication of the morning pursuit. For he sometimes sat down in "nooks that were the most cheerful and the most solitary, in order there to dream";[24] and sometimes he sat up higher "on the terraces and the knolls" in order *not* to dream but simply to let his eyes wander over "the superb and enrapturing view of the lake and especially its shores, crowned on one side by the nearby mountains and, on the other, spreading into rich and fertile plains," leading onto "more distant, bluish mountains" (5:8). So reverie is presented as having been very much an only occasional experience during these solitary afternoon excursions.

In the next or ninth paragraph, he expatiates on the last mentioned alternative: those afternoons when he did not go boating or swimming (and did not experience reveries while lying in the boat contemplating the heavens), and also did not sit down in nooks on the big island in order to dream—when instead, he climbed high on the big island in order simply to look out over the scenery. On such occasions, "when the evening approached," he ceased this gazing, and "descending from the heights of the island," he "went gladly to sit at the edge of the lake, on the beach, in some hidden refuge." There, "the sound of the waves and the agitation of the water [was] fixating my senses [*fixant mes sens*]."[25] This fixation obviated all contemplation of the environment, whether of the heavens or of the earthly surroundings; conversely, he did not speak of any such fixating of his senses during the reveries experienced while drifting in the boat or while sitting in a cheerful and solitary nook. And this fixation of his senses had an extraordinary power. It "chased from my soul every other agitation" and "plunged my soul" (his soul did not plunge by itself) "into a delicious reverie in which the night would often surprise me without my having made myself notice it." These twilight reveries, with his senses fixated, were not only obviously briefer than the purportedly sometimes hours-long, afternoon, thousandfold imaginative reveries in the boat contemplating the sky; unlike those afternoon reveries, these twilight reveries were terminated wrenchingly: "called by the hour and by the agreed-upon signal" for supper, he was compelled by these social demands to "tear himself away with effort" (the Pléiade editor, ad loc., characterizes this as *la rupture*). Yet, it is in regard to these briefer externally caused and externally aborted reveries that the Solitary Walker finally speaks, for the first time, of experiencing the "sentiment of [his own] existence." This was achieved only with the crucial aid of the fixation achieved through the distractive "flux and reflux of that water, its sound continuous but inflated at intervals" and "striking without respite" his fixated ears and eyes. The sight, and especially the sound, but even a kind of feel, of the moving water "took the place of the internal movements that the reverie extinguished" and thereby sufficed to make him "sense with pleasure my existence" (*sentir avec plaisir mon existence*), "without taking the trouble to think" (this last phrase underlines again the totally unphilosophical character of this experience of the sentiment of one's existence[26]). But the next sentence introduces a slight but significant problem, a troubling intrusion of reflective thought into the reverie: "from time to time there was born some feeble and brief reflection on the instability of the things[27] of this world," "of which the surface of the waters offered me the image." Fortunately, however, "soon these light impressions effaced themselves in the uniformity of the continuous movement that was rocking me[28] and that, without any active concurrence of my soul, did not leave off holding me." The intrusion was recurrent, and in order to dissipate the intrusion he depended on the continuous rocking due to the motion outside. This external motion did bring it about that this reverie in which was experienced the sentiment of his own existence was oblivious to all "instability of the things of this world." In this regard, there is a very great dissimilarity to the bittersweet reverie whose content was so meticulously described back in the Second Walk.

In the eleventh paragraph, the Solitary Walker declares that he has completed his account of how he passed his time on the island (not a word has been said about any walks off the island, on the romantic shores). Then, in a remarkable departure from the previous style of almost all of this work,[29] he suddenly enters into a dialogue with his audience, in the here and now (*à present*) of his writing. He asks that someone pose to him (*qu'on me dise*) the following big question: what exactly is so alluring (*assés attrayant*) about all that he has just described so as to excite in his heart such "intense, tender, and durable regrets," with such "surges of desire" (*élans du desir*)?

The Happiness That His Heart Regrets

In what is the very center, by word count, of *The Reveries* as we have it, the Solitary Walker responds to the preceding question by entering into a sustained reflection, from the perspective of "the vicissitudes of a long life," on "the happiness that my heart regrets/yearns for" (recall 3:6: "that happiness for which my heart was avid"). He explains the happiness in question as follows: "a simple and *permanent* state" of being, "which has *nothing* of the intense in it but whose *duration* increases the charm, to the point of finding in it, at last, *the supreme felicity*."[30] So the supreme happiness for which his heart yearns is *constituted* by the achievement of an experience of oneself as existing in permanence of duration. Compared to this experiential state of enduring in permanence through time, "the epochs of the most sweet enjoyments and the most intense pleasures" that the Solitary Walker has experienced (including, it would seem, his rapturous creative reveries)—no matter "how intense they can possibly be"—because they are after all only "short moments of delirium and of passion," because they are experienced as impermanent, are "too rare and too rapid to constitute a state" of supreme felicity (5:12; cf. Grimsley 1972, 446–47).

But is such a state, is such supreme happiness, possible—for mortal, earthly self-conscious existence? At first, the Solitary Walker expresses grave reasons for doubt (switching from the first-person singular to the first-person plural): "everything is in a constant flux on the earth"; "and our affections that attach themselves to external things pass and change necessarily like them"; "there is nothing solid to which the heart can attach itself." Still more profound is the mutability of the restless human heart itself: "there is hardly in our most intense enjoyments an instant in which the heart could truly say to us, '*I would like it for this moment to last forever*'" (italics original). But how, the Solitary Walker asks, "can one call happiness a fleeting state that leaves us still with the heart uneasy and empty, that makes us regret something prior or desire again something after?" (5:13).

Now to this question one can answer—and an Epicurus or a Spinoza would protest[31]—what prevents one finding a hard-won but solid happiness in learning (not an easy lesson, to be sure!) to face and to accept the flux, with a heart that is not uneasy and empty but resolute and full, serene and even (qualifiedly) joyous? And on the other side, why would a thinking being not become rather quickly bored by such passive inertness as the Solitary Walker describes—"an abstract and monotone reverie," as the Solitary Walker will finally characterize it (5:17)? The Solitary Walker seems aware of this last question, of the possibility of boredom, when he insists that he would thus have spent "the whole of eternity without boring myself for an instant."[32]

What exactly is it in the human soul, that (according to Rousseau) makes it impossible to call happiness a state in which one experiences a succession in time of oneself functioning well in satisfying different real needs, especially spiritual needs, that recur for a finite lifetime, ended by death—if or once one achieves, through self-discipline, the greatest possible balance between one's true (naturally limited) needs and one's true capacities to fulfill those needs (consider Aristotle's *Nicomachean Ethics*, bk. 1)? What is it about the human soul, according to Rousseau, that requires a supreme happiness that entails transcendence of the experience of alteration, or of coming into being and passing away?

In struggling to try to understand Rousseau's answers to these questions, we may well be led to compare and to contrast Aristotle's famous and remarkable account of the character of true pleasure (*Nicomachean Ethics* 1174a13–b33). In answering the question "What is, or what sort of thing is" (*ti d'estin ē poion ti*) such pleasure, Aristotle says that we must take our bearings by the experience of seeing: "for seeing seems to be at any time whatsoever complete" (*kath' hontinoun chronon teleia*); for "it is not deficient in anything which, by coming into being at a subsequent time, will complete the form of it—and (Aristotle surprisingly asserts) pleasure is like such." Pleasure "is something whole, and there is no time at which one would be taking pleasure whose form [*eidos*] would be completed by more time coming into being." Our wonder grows as Aristotle continues: pleasure is therefore "not a change/motion [*kinesis*]. For in time is every change/motion, and toward some completion . . . but of pleasure the form is complete at every time." More than that, "it is possible to experience pleasure not in time; for in the now it is something whole"; "for of seeing there is no coming into being, . . . nor is there of pleasure, for it is something whole."

Obviously, Aristotle is not talking about everyday, routine, and especially carnal pleasures. By choosing seeing as his paradigm, the philosopher indicates that he has in mind the pleasure of apprehending reality, by employing the senses in conjunction with the mind (nous). Aristotle has in mind, above all else, the supreme pleasure of philosophical-scientific understanding of the things that are: "for every sense perception there is pleasure, and similarly for discursive reason [*dianoia*] and for theoretical contemplation [*theōria*], and most pleasant is the most perfect, and most perfect is that which is in a good condition in relation to the most serious of the matters it oversees. And the pleasure perfects the being in action [*energeia*] . . . not as an inherent characteristic but as a certain completion that supervenes, like the bloom on those in their prime."

For Aristotle, it seems, the enjoyable sentiment of one's own existence is fully experienced only in joyously self-conscious, sensory-based contemplation of basic aspects of reality—through maximally awakened scientific-philosophical understanding. Thus, the sentiment of one's own existence is not of one's unique self but rather of a self-consciousness similar to, and even to a crucial extent shared with, all other self-conscious contemplators of the same aspects of reality—nous aware of itself, nous of nous.[33]

The Supreme Felicity

"*Here below* one has almost only pleasure that passes; as for the happiness that endures, I doubt" (the Solitary Walker testifies) "that it would be known" (5:13, my italics). The oft-repeated expression "here below" (*ici-bas*) suggests hope for attaining the sought-for happiness in an afterlife—but on a very different basis from that expressed in the Third Walk, and from the basis articulated by the Confession of Faith of the Savoyard vicar,[34] and from the basis articulated by the character "Rousseau" in describing "Jean-Jacques" as the man of nature in *Dialogues* (OC 1:865). In all those writings, the afterlife was hoped for on the basis of moral anguish and a victim's indignation at the injustice of earthly life—a moral experience that cries out for, and therewith gives a hope for, deserved divine judgment, reward, or punishment—what the Savoyard vicar repeatedly calls compensations (*dédommagemens*). Here, instead, we have an amoral yearning for a simple, nonintense, conscious existence in unaltering permanence. Near the end of this Fifth Walk, the Solitary Walker will say (imagining, counterfactually) that if he were enabled to return to the island and there end his days, his "soul would frequently throw itself above this atmosphere and would commune in advance with the celestial intelligences whose number it [now, years later] hopes to augment in a short while."[35]

But in describing the experiences that he claims he actually had at the island years ago, the Solitary Walker proceeds to write as if those experiences did not provoke, nor need, nor seek, any consoling hope for an afterlife. He fully attained perfect happiness, the Solitary Walker proceeds to assert (5:14), in this life here on earth. He now claims that he achieved this often[36] in his "solitary reveries at the island of St. Pierre"—whether lying in his boat, or "sitting on the banks of the agitated lake," or "sitting on the banks of a pretty river or a brook murmuring on its bed." He falls silent about the brief, aborted twilight reveries in which alone he earlier described himself experiencing the sentiment of his own existence; in place of that, he substitutes other experiences some of which would have had to occur off the island and somewhere else, since, as the Pléiade editor notes here, "there is not, on the island, any river or brook." So did these new experiences occur somewhere on the romantic shores? But would the torrents rushing down from the mountains have "murmured on their beds"? However that may be, the Solitary Walker claims that in these three types of situation—lying in the boat, or sitting on the shore of the lake, or sitting on the bank of a murmuring brook or river—he experienced at the island of St. Pierre the following extraordinary (not to say incredible) condition: "a state where the soul finds a base solid enough to rest there in complete entirety [*tout entière*] and to gather there the whole of its being [*tout son être*], without having need to recall the past nor to encroach on the future"; where "time would be nothing [*rien*] for the soul, where the present endures always [*dure toujours*], yet without marking its endurance, and without any trace of succession";[37] "with no other sentiment—of privation or of enjoyment, of pleasure or of pain, of desire or of fear—except that alone of our existence." And "this sentiment alone can fill the soul, in its complete entirety." "So long as this state lasts, whoever finds himself in it can call himself happy," and "not with an imperfect happiness—poor and relative, such as that which one finds in the pleasures of life" but "with a happiness that suffices, is perfect and full, that leaves in the soul no emptiness that the soul feels the need to fill." (Note the "whoever" and the plural "our": as the Pléiade editor stresses, commenting ad loc., the Solitary Walker speaks of an experience that he intends at least some of his readers to aspire to have.)

In this experience, not only do any thoughts of an afterlife or of providential divinity obviously evaporate. There is indicated absolutely no experience, no sentiment of any divine presence or absence.[38] The Solitary Walker delicately highlights this implication in the next paragraph, where he reflects on the relationship between the experience he has just described and the concept of God. He begins with a question about whoever may share in this experience: "In what does one take joy in such a situation?" He answers: "In nothing of what is exterior to oneself, in nothing except one's self and one's own existence; so long as this state lasts, one is sufficient unto oneself like God."[39]

But of course to this last there looms an obvious massive objection: unlike humans, even in this human state of happiness being described, God (or Jesus) is self-consciously immortal and/or is conscious that even if, or when, he does suffer death, he will come back to life (see above all Luke 23:43 and context). So is not Rousseau suggesting that what he and other civilized humans most deeply long for, and can achieve, as self-sufficient self-consciousness and thereby as true happiness, is not self-conscious immortality—not infinitely continued self-conscious existence—but rather self-consciousness minus the consciousness of one's mortality, without the consciousness of one's own inevitable death (cf. Grace 2001, 149–50)? This would be a return, by forgetting, by a kind of nepenthe, to the original, solitary, natural human's blissful lack of awareness of the truth about one's own mortality. Is such self-consciousness the keystone of the Solitary Walker's sentiment of one's own existence?[40]

Descent

The Solitary Walker continues (5:15): "the sentiment of existence, stripped of every other affection, is by itself a precious sentiment of contentment and of peace," which "would suffice alone to render this existence dear and sweet to one who would know how to throw off from himself all the sensual and earthly impressions that come ceaselessly to distract and to trouble the sweetness here below." Why does the Solitary Walker now cease to speak of happiness and instead speak of only contentment and peace and, again, the here below? The answer emerges as we discover that this is the beginning of a descent, from the account of his own vivid experiences of the sentiment of his own existence to the very dim and distant version that is available to most other people, who, he now declares, "have little knowledge of this state" and "have *tasted* it only imperfectly during a *few instants*" so that they "preserve only an obscure and confused idea" of it (my italics: all humans by original and inextirpable nature know, and taste, and preserve some sense and idea of this state, of the sentiment of one's own existence minus awareness of one's mortality). He warns that "it would not even be good, in the present constitution of things," if most people became "avid for these sweet ecstasies" (he speaks of ecstasies only here, when referring to how most people could conceivably yearn for these reveries) and as a consequence "became disgusted with the active life which their always renascent needs prescribe to them as duty" (cf. Meier 2006, 111). We have reentered the realm of duty; and in that realm, the Solitary Walker feels called on to excuse himself for all his preceding statements, which are now to be read as written by "an unfortunate person who has been cut off from human society and who can no longer do here below anything useful and good for another or for oneself"; as such, he is allowed to find, in this state that he has been describing, "*compensations [dédommagemens]* for all the human *felicities,*" which he now claims that he has lost, by being cut off from social duties (5:15). He adds, "It is true that these compensations cannot be felt by all souls, nor in all situations" (5:16; my italics; recall the similar apologia in 1:12–13). As the Pléiade editor puts it, commenting on 5:15, "the 'citizen,' the author of the *Social Contract*, of *Emile*, the organizer of the patriarchal happiness of Clarens, always puts the priority on acting over feeling. Only the exceptional misfortunes authorize this abandonment."

The Solitary Walker proceeds to start to provide a sort of therapeutic manual for his readers (5:16), showing what is necessary for them if they are to put themselves in a condition to share, in some degree, in these "compensations." It is necessary, to begin with, "that the heart be at peace and that no passion come to it to trouble its calm." In addition, it is necessary, in order for one to experience these compensations, that one has dispositions in their favor. Yet again, it is necessary that the "conjunction of surrounding objects" be favorable. Then in the fourth place, it is necessary that in the surroundings there be "neither complete rest nor too much agitation" but "a uniform and moderate movement that has neither jolts nor lapses."

For this last necessity, the Solitary Walker elaborates an explanation, which suddenly affords a major illumination of his earlier stress on the extraordinary power of, and need for, the "fixation" of his senses by the sound and motion of water. Before, he spoke of the sound and motion "chasing from [his] soul every other agitation" and "taking the place of the internal movements that the reverie extinguished" (5:9)—without further specifying what these agitations and internal movements might be. Now (5:16) he informs us that "if the movement is uneven or too strong, it awakens" one, thus "destroying the charm of the reverie" and "wrenching us from within ourselves"; but on the other hand, "an absolute silence leads to sadness."

Why the sadness, precisely?

Because the silence "offers an image of death."

The consciousness of death, with the spiritual agitations that that consciousness entails, is what the soul must be distracted from if the less-than-fully awake sentiment of one's existence is to be fully felt.[41]

But when silence, as image of death, cannot be eliminated by "a uniform and moderate movement that has neither jolts nor lapses," there is, for a privileged few, another remedy—another way to remove the image of death. "Then, the aid of a cheerful [*riant*] imagination is necessary"; and such an imagination "presents itself naturally enough to those whom heaven has gratified with it." Through this cheerful imagination, for the few thus blessed, the needed "movement, which does not come from the outside, generates itself within us." This is indeed only a second best: "the repose is less, it is true." But then again, "it is also more agreeable when light and sweet ideas, without agitating the depth of the soul, do no more than, so to speak, gently touch the surface of it"—"only enough for remembering oneself in forgetting all one's troubles."

This other, distinct or very different species of reverie (*espèce de rêverie*) does not require anything like the sojourn on the island; it "can make itself tasted wherever one can be tranquil"; and suddenly, the Solitary Walker ceases to prescribe for others and puts the spotlight back on himself: "I have often thought that at the Bastille and even in a dungeon where no object would strike my sight, I would have been able to dream agreeably" (5:16).

But if a plurality, and hence a sequence, of light and sweet ideas created by the imagination is constantly touching the soul, even if only gently, and even if only on the surface, then can "time be nothing [*rien*] for the soul?" Can "the present endure always [*dure toujours*], yet without marking its endurance and without any trace of succession"? Apparently yes, in the depth of the soul; apparently, the surface of the soul can be cut off sufficiently from the depth so that the creative motion and succession on the surface, while strong enough to blot out the image of death presented by silence, is not so strong as to be communicated to the uncreative depth of the soul.

In the final paragraph of this walk, the Solitary Walker returns, from thoughts of being imprisoned in a dungeon in the Bastille to his recollection of the much more conducive environment on the island of St. Pierre: "it is necessary to admit that that effected itself much better and more agreeably on a fertile and solitary isle," where "nothing offered itself to me except cheerful images." But then he goes on to characterize himself as a highly imaginative, creative "dreamer who knows how to nourish himself with agreeable chimeras amid the most displeasing objects, who can satisfactorily feed himself at his ease by making everything that in reality strikes his senses cooperate in the chimeras." And at this point, he describes himself, for the first time, as having experienced on the island such imaginatively creative reveries, which he speaks of as if they took him away from himself: "in emerging from a long and sweet reverie, in seeing myself surrounded by verdure, by flowers, by birds, and letting my eyes wander afar over the romantic shores that bordered a vast expanse of clear and crystalline water, I assimilated to my fictions all these aimable objects," and then, "finding myself by degrees finally brought back to myself and to what surrounded me," he nevertheless still "could not mark the point of separation between the fictions and the realities." The Solitary Walker now at the end of the Fifth Walk claims that it is such experiences, of reveries in which he created fictions that blurred reality that were the experiences that "rendered dear the gathered and solitary life that I led during that beautiful sojourn." Then he goes on to assert that if he could return to the island and those experiences, his "soul would frequently commune in advance with the celestial intelligences whose number it hopes to augment in a short while." Suddenly, the recollection of the island reveries takes on an intensely religious cast; suddenly, we are back to the creation of celestial beings that was celebrated in *The Confessions* (OC 1:425–29) and above all in the *Dialogues* (OC 1:814, 819–20, 826–27, 858; recall our chapter 1); and we hear no more about the sentiment of one's own existence in a self-sufficiency like that of God's.

Creative Reveries

At the very end of this Fifth Walk, the Solitary Walker returns emphatically to his beleaguered here and now. Although his fellow humans will not allow him to return to the blessed isle of St. Pierre, they cannot prevent him from transporting himself "there each day on the wings of the imagination and tasting there during several hours the same pleasure as if I were dwelling there again." He asks whether, in now "dreaming that I am there," he doesn't achieve the same dreaming that he would experience if he really were there. Or is the present recollecting not even superior in some sense? For he avers that "to the attraction of an abstract and monotone reverie" he now "joins charming images that enliven it."

Does this not suggest that "the sentiment of existence, stripped of every other affection," in "one who would know how to throw off from himself all the sensual and earthly impressions," may be—in some respects—deficient? He further explains this as follows: in the ecstasies on the island, what he was experiencing often escaped his senses; whereas "now, the more my reverie is profound, the more it paints them vividly. I am often more in the midst of them, and more agreeably still, than when I was really there." This would seem to imply that by having now to employ his imagination in recollecting and re-creating the entire setting and environment, including the island and everything about it, he attends to this setting and environment far more, and more agreeably, than he did when he was actually experiencing the island and the reveries there. He laments: "the unhappiness is that, to the extent that the imagination cools, this comes with more difficulty and does not last so long." Once again, here at the end of the Fifth Walk, the Solitary Walker would seem to be speaking of reveries of *recollection* in the here and now, in which his creative imagination contributes a great deal to the enjoyment—and this even apart from, or in addition to, the creative reveries through which he now says that on the island, way back then, he imaginatively peopled a transfigured reality with the heavenly intelligences. Such imaginatively ecstatic and creative reveries seem very different from the reveries he described as consisting in the tranquil, timeless, simple, and unmanifold experience of the sole sentiment of his own existence. Yet, the latter type of reverie is not specified in, it is missing from, the account in *The Confessions* of the reveries experienced on the island of St. Pierre (OC 1:643–44). Many readers have been provoked to ask in various ways, to what extent is the type of reverie that is the tranquil, timeless, simple and unmanifold experience of the sole sentiment of his own existence an imaginatively created fictive recollection? Did he, does he, really ever undergo such an experience, in actuality?[42] But if not, why would he deceptively pretend that he did? Or why fictively imagine having done so? Could it be that Rousseau the author is here creating a kind of utopia of the self, a utopia whose function has a kind of parallel to the function of imaginative utopian literature in classical political philosophy, beginning with Plato's *Republic*? Could Rousseau be erecting a hopeful vision of what purports to be a rare but possible solution to the human problem, a vision whose deeper aim is to specify implicitly, for the most thoughtful readers, the reasons for its ultimate impossibility, and thus the reasons for the ultimate insolubility, the insuperably problematic character of the human condition? Could Rousseau be indicating the limitations that define and restrict human existence[43]—and that, for Rousseau at any rate, render civilized humans unsatisfiable beings? Could Rousseau be signaling that "a simple and permanent state" of being, "which has nothing of the intense in it, but whose duration increases the charm, to the point of finding in it, at last, the supreme felicity"—where "time would be nothing for the soul, where the present endures always, yet without marking its endurance, and without any trace of succession"—is in truth longed for but in truth not possible for humans having lost the state of nature; and that therefore our earthly existence has become inescapably blighted by the deeply painful consciousness of our mortal mutability? This would indicate the deepest reason why Rousseau finds philosophical thinking too painful, even or especially given the scope and profundity of his own philosophical thinking. This would indicate the reason why in order to achieve such qualified happiness as is available to him, he has a need to distract himself by the hobby of botany and to enchant or to intoxicate himself and others with serious as well as playful imaginative creations. This would not be contradicted by the fact that in most of his writings, Rousseau strives compassionately to protect humanity by convincing his readers that mortality need not so blight their existence: that "the instability of the things of this world" need not so trouble them as it does in fact deeply trouble the philosophical and maximally self-aware Rousseau.

Chapter 6

"Sixth Walk"—Goodness versus Virtue

After two chapters that treated two of the three pillars of his moral thought—first virtue and then (in contrast) happiness—Rousseau next has his Solitary Walker treat the third pillar: goodness, in decided contrast with virtue and as emphatically a source of another, different version of true happiness.[1] Thus, the thematic order and train of thought of the work continue to be reasonably intelligible.

Moreover, the descent that we noted in the last three paragraphs of the previous chapter continues: this sixth chapter no longer speaks either of the supreme felicity achieved through self-absorbed reveries, or of the happiness afforded by rapturously creative reveries; in fact, reveries are never mentioned at all. In striking contrast, the Solitary Walker now proclaims, "I know and I feel[2] that to do good is the truest happiness[3] that the human heart[4] can taste" (6:3). Accordingly, the Solitary Walker reiterates in stronger terms than ever his apologia (recall 5:16) for not being engaged in doing good for others, which he now declares to constitute the truest happiness: "it is a long time since this happiness has been put out of my reach, and it is not in such a miserable lot as mine that one can hope to select with choice, and fruitfully, a single action that is truly good." There were, to be sure, happier times when, "following the movements of my heart, I was sometimes able to render another heart content"; and "I owe to myself the honorable testimony that each time I was able to taste this pleasure I found it more sweet than *any other*; this tendency was lively, true, pure; and *nothing* in my *most secret interior* has *ever* belied it" (my italics). The Solitary Walker traces his exclusion from this truest happiness and sweetest pleasure, of doing good to others, entirely to the actions of his persecutors.[5]

In form, this chapter emphatically continues the previous chapter's address to readers: the first word is *we*, and the first sentence expresses a universal truth about the capacity for self-analysis that the Solitary Walker asserts is shared with his readers: "*we* have scarcely any automatic movement [*mouvement machinal*] of which *we* would not be able to discover the cause in *our* heart, if *we* knew well how to search there."[6] The Solitary Walker thus prompts us readers to join or to imitate him by undertaking our own self-analyses. But in this present case, the Solitary Walker reports that he is continuing a self-analysis that took place on a previous day's walk. So we are back to something like the form of the Fourth Walk, which was devoted to resolving a puzzle of self-understanding caused by events of the previous day. And we are back to the task of that Fourth Walk: the rigorous self-examination as regards his moral character that was announced at the end of the Third Walk and that recurred to the *second*, as well as the *first*, of the five aims for this writing that were set forth in the First Walk. But now the second aim is dropped: the critical self-examination is not said to be a preparation for the afterlife with its divine judgment and compensations. The second aim will never again be referred to. Henceforth, the Solitary Walker's intentionality in this writing will orchestrate only three of the original five distinct aims.

Surveying *The Reveries* as a Whole Thus Far

The complete silence about reveries, which this Sixth Walk shares with the Fourth Walk, prompts us to recognize a remarkable fact about *The Reveries of the Solitary Walker* that has become steadily clearer: despite its title, this work is mostly *not* about reveries.[7] What is more, we will soon hear the Solitary Walker proclaim—in the opening sentence of the next, or Seventh Walk—that although "the collection of my long dreams is scarcely begun," nonetheless "I already feel it touches its end. A different amusement takes its place, absorbs me, and deprives me even of the time for dreaming."

Overall, we can now see emerging a clear trajectory of the work as a whole: an ascent to, followed by a descent from, the Fifth Walk and its relatively brief account of radically solitary, timeless reveries in which the sentiment of one's own existence is experienced as the supreme felicity and pleasure—an account that allows readers to divine what "was this happiness, and in what its enjoyment consisted" (5:6, 13–14; Butterworth 1979, 154). Thus, the work's peak— the allusive, divinatory account in the Fifth Walk—is surrounded and framed by much more manifold and elaborated expositions of the Solitary Walker's unjust and outraged victimhood, his evolving religious beliefs, his virtue of truthfulness as a communicator, his (constrained) goodness toward others, and his solitary botanizing.

What Launched This Self-Examination

The sixth chapter's first three paragraphs tell us what happened on the previous day's walk that initiated the self-analytical reflection that follows. Early on the accustomed route of his peregrination, the Solitary Walker suddenly noticed that he was making a detour and realized that he had "made several times automatically the same detour." Puzzled and "seeking the cause within" himself, he unraveled it as follows (6:1).

He discovered that the cause was his wish to avoid having to encounter a crippled beggar boy to whom, for a while previously, he had regularly enjoyed being chatty and charitable—until, that is, "this pleasure, having become by degrees a habit, found itself, I don't know how, transformed into a species of duty, of which I soon felt the annoyance." From then on, he "passed by that place less voluntarily, and finally" started "automatically taking on the habit of making *most often* a detour" (6:2; my italics). Most often—that is, not always; the Solitary Walker did *not* cease *totally* his encounters, and thus his chatter with, and giving alms to, the crippled beggar boy. It would seem that his active beneficence, no doubt rooted partly in his pity (mentioned for the first time in 6:7), was not entirely cut off by his annoyance at the call of duty.[8]

Prior to this discovery about his motive, he says, "nothing of all this had offered itself *distinctly* to my thought" (6:3; my italics). So the now–fully discovered motive had not previously been simply *un*conscious or *sub*conscious. It had been "offered to his thought" but indistinctly. It had been vaguely or fuzzily in the back, so to speak, of his conscious mind. The Solitary Walker's self-analysis here is therefore not Freudian psychoanalysis, dredging up something from the subconscious or the unconscious; by the same token, it is not Nietzschean-Zarathustrian discovery of "thy body and its great reason" (*dein Leib und seine grosse Vernunft*), the subconscious Self (*das Selbst*).[9] Commentators have imposed on or read into this text a great deal about the unconscious or subconscious for which there is no warrant.

This "observation recalled successively multitudes of other" such observations; the Solitary Walker makes plain that he has previously engaged in multitudinous such discoveries of his semiconscious thinking and motivations. These self-discoveries, all taken together, have confirmed well that "the true and primary motives of most of my actions are not *as clear* to myself as I had for a long time imagined."[10] The Solitary Walker does not say that any of his motives were ever *simply* unclear to him; on the contrary, he speaks of himself as *always* having had some degree of clarity regarding his motives.

The Solitary Walker's Revelation about His Moral Character

We are now ushered into a momentous self-disclosure. The Solitary Walker shares with us his long-standing awareness that he is constitutionally averse to performing any moral *duty* whatsoever and to exercising any moral virtue that requires habitual self-restraint; he is constitutionally impelled to embrace only the beneficence and justice toward others that arises out of a spontaneous benevolence and sense of justice that brings immediate as well as lasting pleasure and even true happiness to the benevolent and benevolently just person himself.[11] And we note that his discovery that his detour was yet another instance of this defining trait prompted in the Solitary Walker the first private laughter we have heard of in this book (6:1 end): he was delightfully amused, he was in no way troubled, at having had so vividly brought to light his totally unvirtuous good character.

There is, however, a complicating and revealing qualification—caused by the Solitary Walker's present miserable fate. His persecutors have manipulated him into a situation in which he must exercise what we learned in the first chapter is a kind of negative duty and thus self-restraint (recall 1:13, "for me to abstain has become my unique duty"; and see 6:7, "as soon as my duty and my heart were in contradiction, the first rarely had the victory, unless only abstaining was required; in that case, I was most often strong"). Since, at the present time of this writing, "the greatest care of those who rule my destiny" has been to "make everything be for me only false and deceptive appearance," any apparent occasion for "virtue is never anything except a lure," and "the sole good that would henceforth be in my power is, to *make* myself *abstain from* action, out of fear of doing harm without willing it and without knowing it" (6:3; my italics). The Solitary Walker finds himself in the uniquely horrible situation where his naturally characteristic impulsion of benevolent goodness, schooled by his prudential reasoning about the trammels of the conspiracy in which he is trapped, motivates him to restrain himself from any active exercise of that natural impulsion. This shows that there is at least a narrow but crucial way in which goodness can spawn virtue. In this limited way, the Solitary Walker is not simply amoral; he is not altogether without a capacity for virtue—for the peculiar virtue of repressing spontaneous goodness, out of goodness, schooled by calculation.

A Moral Autobiography

To provide us with further illumination, the Solitary Walker proceeds to a brief moral autobiography, explaining the experiences that "have procured for me through reflection new enlightenment as regards knowledge of myself and of the true motives of my conduct in a thousand circumstances" (6:6).

He tells us first how, prior to the time of his acquiring fame through his writings, he found that the pleasure he enjoyed in activities of benevolent goodness was sweeter than any other. Yet nevertheless, he often felt from his own beneficial deeds the burden of "the chain of duties" that those deeds "brought in their train," which made "the pleasure disappear," replaced by an "almost insupportable annoyance."[12] (So in assuming the burden of these chains, did he originally follow the call of duty? Or did he accept the burden of these chains only in order to avoid even worse unpleasantness—out of "weakness and shame"? See 6:8 end.) The problem was caused in large part by the indiscriminate, unqualified character of his generosity of heart. For during his brief episodes of prosperity, there were many people who appealed for help, and "never, in *all* the services that" he "could do for them, was *any* of them turned away" (6:4; my italics). Rousseau was effusively generous to all askers, without any exception. He thus certainly did not practice the meticulously selective and prudent, classical virtue of generosity—as laid out above all in Aristotle's *Nicomachean Ethics* (1119b23–22a18; cf. Reisert 2003, 79). Instead, he indulged his heart in what Aristotle labels the vice of thoughtless profligacy. Worse yet, from the classical or Aristotelian perspective, he allowed himself to continue and even to compound this vice. "From these primary beneficial deeds were born chains of successive liabilities that I had not foreseen and whose yoke I was no longer able to shake off." He soft-heartedly allowed himself to become onerously subjected to unfortunate but unreasonably demanding dependents (6:4).

Still, these chains did not seem to him so heavy (it sounds as though he might have remained in his soft-hearted weakness) until he became famous and apparently prosperous through his writings (a fact that, as we saw, was kept pretty well hidden in the spiritual-religious autobiography back in the Third Walk). At that point, his prosperity made him the target of "everyone destitute or so-called such," of "all the adventurers who were looking for dupes" (6:5). Thus, his soft-heartedness grew worse until from this train of cruel experiences, he finally started genuinely to comprehend something of the classical virtue of generosity and of classical virtue altogether: "it was then that I was in a position to understand that all the inclinations of nature, without excepting benevolence itself," when "carried out or followed in society without prudence," and thus without real choice, change their very "nature and become often as harmful as they were useful in their primary directedness."[13] He started to see that for humans in society, the spontaneous goodness of the heart needs to be controlled by prudential utilitarian reason; and we are reminded that this was at the core of the philosophical moral outlook on truth and lie that was highlighted, only to be largely abandoned, in the Fourth Walk. Moreover, the Solitary Walker discovered that his learning from experience gradually changed his primary dispositions—or rather (he corrects himself, sounding yet a bit more Aristotelian-Socratic), "confined them finally within their *true* limits" (my italics); he was "taught to follow less blindly" his "inclination to do good."

Yet, the true limits as conceived by the Solitary Walker seem to be much less strict, much looser, than the limits as defined by classic Aristotelian and Socratic generosity: the Solitary Walker reports that he learned to follow his inclination less blindly *only* in cases where to follow blindly would "serve solely to favor the wickedness of another" (6:5). Otherwise, the Solitary Walker continued to be ruled pretty blindly by his unconfined heart: "sensitive and good, full of pity to the point of weakness, and feeling my soul exalted by everything related to generosity, I was humane, beneficent, helpful by taste, by passion even, so long as it interested *only* my heart" (6:7; my italics). Even now, at the time of this writing, if his reason tells him that something will be bad for himself, but his heart is not aroused, he is tied to his phlegmatic heart against his reason: "I see the harm that menaces me and I let it arrive rather than exert myself to prevent it. I start sometimes, with effort, but this effort very quickly wearies and exhausts me; I don't know how to continue" (6:7). And this accords with the general conclusion to which he has come regarding his own moral character[14]—and also with the anti-classical, anti-Aristotelian, and anti-Socratic analysis he gives of the nature of virtue and of goodness.[15]

He "saw that in order to do good with pleasure, it was necessary that" he "act freely, without constraint, and that to take from" him "all the sweetness of a good deed it was sufficient that it become a duty" (6:6). What is much more, this led him to "modify greatly the opinion that" he had had for a long time of his own virtue. For he contends that "there is nothing whatsoever" of virtue "in following one's inclinations, and in giving oneself the pleasure of doing good when they lead us to do so." Nay, "virtue consists in vanquishing them, when duty commands it, in order to do what it prescribes to us." "And there, that is what I know how to do less than any human being in the world." "To act against my inclination was always impossible for me"; "in everything imaginable, what I do not do with pleasure is soon[16] impossible for me to do" (6:7).

He goes still further in this confession (6:8): even "constraint that accords with my desire suffices to annihilate it, and to change it into repugnance, into aversion even, as soon as it acts too strongly"—"and there, that is what renders distressing for me the good deed that is required and that I was doing on my own as long as it was not required." This last brings out the fact that when he is enacting his goodness, the Solitary Walker finds that the pleasure of seeing others benefited by his actions is not nearly as strong as the pleasure and/or desire of experiencing the beneficial action as done solely out of his own independent and unrequired will, following his own heart. And what of his conscience? It is the voice of his heart; it is *not* the voice that calls to duty: "I reproach myself in my conscience for doing good against the heart [*à contrecoeur*]." This helps us to understand psychologically a fact that seems counterintuitive: the fact that the Solitary Walker's soul feels exalted not by the performance of virtuously dutiful mastery of inclination but by his entirely self-generated beneficence.

This also helps to remind us that Rousseau's goodness, even or especially in its distinction from virtue, is far from being amoral: for it is a powerful source of his passion for justice—corrective-retributive, distributive, and as the common good.[17] At the same time, goodness is also a major contamination or qualification of his concern for justice. It is only in Rousseau's conception of God that pure goodness without virtue is the source of pure and unqualified justice.

The Solitary Walker does not shy from bringing out more problematic implications of goodness for human justice and injustice—in the first place, for his own justice and injustice as a ruling judge: if he had been "the most powerful of humans," in following his heart he "would have been just, without suffering, even against my own interest"; but "against that of persons who were dear to me I would not have been able to resolve to be so" (6:7). In the second place, and more momentously, he draws out the implications for our understanding of justice and injustice in human acts of benefaction generally (6:9): in society, "there is a species of contract, and even the most sacred of all, between the benefactor and the one obligated [*obligé*]"; the "obligated tacitly makes a commitment to gratitude [*reconnaissance*]" while the "benefactor makes a commitment, in the same way, to preserve for the beneficiary, so long as the beneficiary does not render himself undeserving of it, the same goodwill that he has just shown him," and "to renew its acts for him whenever he will be able to, and whenever it will be required." These are "natural consequences of the relationship that has come to be established between them." Here, the Solitary Walker lays out a quasi-natural right and even a beautiful illustration of one aspect of what Rousseau means by natural right altogether (see also Montesquieu, *Spirit of the Laws* 1:1). He who "refuses in a similar case the same grace that he accorded before frustrates a hope that he has authorized the other to conceive"; he "deceives and belies an expectation that he engendered." But for the human species, such injustice is "the consequence of an independence that the heart loves and that it renounces only with effort." And "the pleasure of fulfilling one's duties is one of those that only the habit of virtue engenders," while the pleasures that "come to us immediately from nature do not raise themselves so high as that." In the case of the Solitary Walker, the human heart's natural pleasure in and love of independence excludes the habit-acquired pleasure that is enjoyed in being just, in fulfilling one's contractual duties, as a benefactor (6:9).

If we are to descry the full radical implications of these pronouncements on justice and natural right, we must recognize that the Solitary Walker is speaking here not only of his own heart and not only of his own participation in the justice of giving and receiving. He is speaking more generally.[18] He is indicating that his understanding of the human heart, based on his self-understanding, has led him to the insight that all civilized social interactions of helping and of gift giving establish tacit contractual chains that are deeply contrary to the pleasures and to the natural inclinations of the human heart and its natural goodness and conscience. Since at the instant that any living human gift giver becomes known to his obliged beneficiary, there is fastened on him for an indefinite future a chain of contractual obligation to and from the beneficiary, a human giver can remain free only if he proffers his help and his gifts in strict anonymity. The great advantage of anonymity becomes explicit a bit later, in the seventeenth and eighteenth paragraphs, where the Solitary Walker declares that if his face and features were unknown among humans, then he could live among them without difficulty: "released without constraint" to his natural inclinations, under that condition he "would exercise toward them a universal and perfectly disinterested benevolence," without "ever forming any particular attachment, and without bearing the yoke of any duty." But where anonymity is not possible, then pure goodness of the heart, when guided by rational self-awareness, impels one to avoid acts of generosity in civilized society. Accordingly, at the start of the tenth paragraph, the Solitary Walker confesses, "I have often abstained from a good deed that I had the desire and the power to do, out of fear of the subjection which as a consequence I was going to submit myself to if I yielded to it without reflection." Thus, the Solitary Walker finally reveals that the deepest reason for his failure to express his natural goodness in actual acts of helping others is not the persecution he suffers but rather his good character steered by prudence—away from the chains of obligation, duty, and virtue.

"SIXTH WALK"—GOODNESS VERSUS VIRTUE

The Solitary Walker does of course recognize that "the pleasure of fulfilling one's duties" is a pleasure that (other) humans are capable of acquiring, through the habituation of virtue (6:9). And in the tenth paragraph, he begins to express himself in way that make him sound more like such others—at least formerly, when he was young (thus veiling the previous radical disclosures): "in my youth I did attach myself by my own benefactions, and I often sensed that those whom I made obligated [*ceux que j'obligeois*] were affectionate toward me out of gratitude [*reconnaissance*] more than out of interest." This statement leaves unclear whether or to what extent the Solitary Walker in his youth *himself* accepted the duty (chain) of justice that befalls the giver, toward the recipient, in "that species of contract which is the most sacred of all." But that he felt—and more remarkably, still feels—his own moral *claim* of justice, his *right* to *receive* gratitude and reciprocity from the obligated whom he has benefited, becomes manifest when these memories of his youthful benefactions give way immediately to an indignant tirade[19] against various named beneficiaries and friends (even his votary Paul Moultou![20]) whom he charges with having subsequently betrayed him, out of ingratitude and venality and having joined the universal conspiracy against him. "From true and candid as they were at first, having become what they are, they have done as all the others have." In one case, he speaks of his betrayer (Abbé de Bini) as having "at the expense of his *conscience*" changed from "showing me always the attachment and esteem that my conduct toward him *ought naturally* to inspire" (my italics). In this outburst of righteous indignation, the Solitary Walker blurs or leaves behind important distinctions that were previously indicated.

In the eleventh paragraph, he reiterates his now oft-repeated apologia, blaming his persecutors for his lack of good deeds: "convinced by twenty years of experience that everything nature has put in my heart of happy dispositions is turned to the prejudice of myself or of others by my destiny and by those who dispose of it, I can" (he confesses) "no longer regard the occasion for a good deed as anything but a snare held out to me, and underneath which is hidden some evil." He insists, however, that despite never actually doing any good deeds anymore, he still has "the deserved merit of my good intention." But because he is sure that he is being made a dupe by every apparent occasion to do a good deed, not only does his heart freeze, but "the indignation of the amour propre, joined to reason's disavowal, inspires in me only repugnance and resistance, whereas I would have been full of ardor and of zeal in my natural state." (In this apologia, he no longer admits that the natural state of goodness drives him to avoid all the chains of the tacit contract entailed in helping and giving to others.) As part of his apologia, he now assesses his present abstaining from good deeds as being "innocent *only* because it is *forced*" on him (my italics), though he adds the confession that "this situation does make me find a sort of sweetness in giving myself up completely without reproach to my natural inclination." But he qualifies this by confessing that "I go too far undoubtedly, since I avoid the occasions to act, even where I see only good to do" (6:12).

Because his fellow men have so completely turned against him, he proclaims his disgust with humans (6:13). Yet, he insists that his "repugnance cannot ever go to the point of aversion." In fact, his heart is moved to a real pity for his tormentors when he thinks of "the dependence on me that they have put themselves in, so as to hold me in the same toward them." He is sure that this dependence of theirs makes them unhappy, while his own spiritual removal from them prevents him from suffering the same. Here, the avoidance of psychological dependence on others comes to the fore as essential to avoiding unhappiness. The Solitary Walker admits that in his own case, "pride perhaps mingles itself in these judgments; I sense myself too much above them to hate them"; in short, "I love myself too much to be able to hate anyone." And suddenly, he ascends to a striking self-revelation: "that would be to restrict, to compress my existence, and *I would rather extend it over the entire universe*" (6:14; my italics).

Is this yearning for self-expansiveness not a key to Rousseau's understanding of the psychological source of natural goodness—that source conceived as the human soul's powerful impulse to benefit others, to be the source of the good for others, to shape the lives of others, *so as to make them dependent on oneself*?[21] In the eighteenth paragraph, the Solitary Walker shares with us the imaginative castles in Spain that he has built regarding how he would have behaved if he were the possessor of the famous ring of Gyges (see again Glaucon's speech in Plato's *Republic*). It "would have taken me out of dependence on humans *and put them in dependence on me*." The one thing alone that he would have wished if he had had such power would have been "to see all the hearts content." He goes further: "the appearance of public felicity" brought about by this quasi-divine power of the ring in his sole possession "would *alone* have been able to touch my heart with a *permanent* sentiment"; and "the ardent desire to contribute" to that public felicity would have been "my *most constant* passion" (my italics).

Is such psychic expansiveness, and the sort of reveries that flatter or indulge it, not at a considerable tension with the reveries of complete self-absorption which were stressed in the previous Fifth Walk? Moreover, must not the Solitary Walker be to some extent deeply frustrated, unhappy, inasmuch as he lacks the occasion and power to expand his existence through acts of philanthropic benevolence?[22] Or do we not see here the key to the most important psychological reason why the Solitary Walker is engaged in writing *The Reveries* (Clark

2003, 114), which, we have come to see, is a writing whose eventual publication is very deliberately calculated to have a wide and deep, popular as well as elite, influence? Such philanthropy, as posthumous, enjoys all the advantages of anonymous philanthropy without requiring any anonymity whatsoever: his future beneficiaries will be fully conscious of him as their benefactor. In a sense, his present gratification at this glorious prospect may be even greater than if he had had the ring of Gyges, which requires a considerable degree of anonymity.[23]

Lest we suppose that this moral autobiography casts doubt on the Solitary Walker's concern for justice, he assures us in the sixteenth paragraph that "it would be necessary that my moral being were annihilated for justice to become a matter of indifference to me." But he makes it clear that his passion for justice is nowadays aroused as for "characters in a drama which I would see performed." It is the spectacle of injustice and wickedness that "still makes my blood boil with rage," and it is when he beholds, sitting in the audience as it were, "acts of virtue without boastfulness or ostentation" on the part of others that he always is "made to quiver with joy" and to shed sweet tears.[24]

When he turns in the eighteenth paragraph to imagining his *own* behavior, if he had had the godlike power of the ring of Gyges, he says that he would have been "always just without partiality and always good without weakness"; but he then rephrases this as "perfectly disinterested for myself and having for law only my natural inclinations." He would have been motivated by goodness, not by dutiful virtue. Perhaps, he admits, "I would have had in some moments of gaiety the childishness to perform sometimes some prodigies"; but in general, he would have acted as a responsible adult: "Minister of providence and dispenser of its laws *according to my power*" (my italics; that is, according to goodness, not virtue), "I would have performed miracles more wise and more useful than those of the golden legend and of the tomb of St. Medard."

The Solitary Walker proceeds to confess, however, that the ring of Gyges, endowing its possessor with "the capacity to penetrate everywhere invisibly" might in one sole but overwhelming respect have been able to make him seek temptations that he would have poorly resisted; "sure of myself on every other count, I would have been lost by that one alone." As a consequence, "I believe that I will do better to throw away my magic ring before it has made me commit some folly" (6:19–20). Our author thus delicately alludes to his weakness as regards sexual temptations, which he confesses can lead him to act against his natural goodness. Eros manifests itself as opposed to, not as fueling, natural goodness.[25] And our author provokes us to remark again on how little a role erotic love or intimate friendship (or family) play in his happiness or his goodness as explained in this work. Does this not go with the remarkable absence of music? Insofar as *The Reveries* refer us back to the state of nature and its standard as explained in the *Second Discourse*, the reference is to the solitary state, the true or pure state of nature,[26] not to the familial state of nascent society with its invention or discovery of music (OC 3:167ff.).

The final and concluding paragraph is a boldly forthright statement of the Solitary Walker's profound unsuitability for civil society and of his radically independent conception of liberty: "I have never believed that the liberty of the human being consists in doing what he wishes, but rather in never doing what he does not wish"—and "there, that is what I have always laid claim to, often preserved, and by which I have been most a scandal to my contemporaries." "Their wrong, then, has not been their turning me out of society as a useless member"—he admits that he "has done very little good" and so deserves such expulsion—"but to have proscribed me from it as a pernicious member," since "as regards evil, it has never in my life entered into my will, and I doubt that there is any human being in the world who has really done less of it than me" (see similarly 8:4).

Chapter 7

"Seventh Walk"—Botany as Consuming "Amusement"

The Sixth Walk's elaborate apologia for the Solitary Walker's unvirtuous goodness of character, and his a-civic love of freedom, clears the way for the Seventh Walk's diary-like presentation of his major solitary, self-centered, and even frivolous activity at present.[1] (The thematic order and train of thought of *The Reveries* remain clearly intelligible.) This chapter continues the silence into which the Solitary Walker has fallen concerning divine judgment with its compensations for virtue and vice; there is only the barest hint of a reference to the afterlife (7:21) and to the hand behind nature (7:22), though there is a jesting reference to the Bible's Adam in the Garden of Eden (7:12). God and the afterlife have been evaporating more and more since early in the Fourth Walk.

In form, the beginning of this chapter sounds like the Solitary Walker engaged in a combination of his observational diary and a "sweet conversion with his soul"—the third and fourth of the five aims for this writing that were laid out in the First Walk. But now, in the wake of the previous two chapters, this conversation is more candidly presented with a view to a future readership to whom it signals the approaching end of this writing and, still more surprisingly, the end of reveries altogether. Given the absence of any talk of reveries in the preceding chapter, readers might well expect now a return to them but no. And this is the last chapter of the manuscript that was left in polished form as well as the last that Jean-Jacques Rousseau titled a "Walk." This Seventh

Walk was finished in the summer of 1777, and Rousseau does not seem to have written anything more for the next six months until he wrote the rather rough draft that we have of the chapter titled simply "8" in early 1778, then of that titled simply "9" in March of that year, and finally of "10" on April 12, 1778 (as he says in the text). All this, together with the opening and closing sentences of the present chapter, suggests that this Seventh Walk was put in final form with the original intention of it being the last.[2] The subsequent three chapters thus appear to constitute something of an afterthought, although they make substantial additions to the work's teaching on major themes.

In opening this chapter, the Solitary Walker expresses himself in a way that indicates his expectation of the reader's disappointed and even somewhat disapproving surprise at hearing of the end of this "collection of my long dreams" (which he admits is scarcely begun) and of the end of reverie altogether. Perhaps still more disconcerting for us readers is the seemingly rather frivolous reason given for these terminations: "another amusement replaces it [*un autre amusement lui succède*], absorbs me, and takes from me even the time to dream"; "I give myself up to it with an infatuation that partakes of extravagance and that makes even me laugh when I reflect on it." As if slightly embarrassed, the Solitary Walker at first teasingly delays informing us of what this absorbing amusement is. He defends his unnamed infatuation not on the ground of any intrinsic merit the amusement may have, but "because, in the situation in which I am now, I have no other rule of conduct except to follow in everything my penchant without restraint," without "any other rule except my fantasy." This is what wisdom itself wishes, given that "I have only innocent inclinations" and that all the judgments of humans have become "henceforth nul for me."[3] Only after having laid this rather self-indulgent foundation does he finally reveal what has become "my *entire* occupation": a sort of botany.

The declaration that this is his entire occupation is of course self-referentially absurd. Botanizing cannot be the author's entire occupation since he is occupied in writing a chapter of a book about his occupations, including botanizing. Our author is jesting with us. He pens the disclosure of his botanical amusement in a sentence whose phrasing—"There I am, then . . ." (*Me voilà donc*)—echoes the opening words of the entire writing (J. Scott 2008, 139): here is another subtle signal that this chapter may originally have been intended as the last. Now but back at the opening, with these words our author plunged us into a pit of agonized isolation and gloom; only in the second chapter did he disclose to us his regular experience of delight in botanical observations on his walks. Now, in contrast, botanizing's cheer tinctures his writing of this chapter, bringing reports of the author's delighted laughter, such as has appeared only once before in *The Reveries*;[4] and the botanizing here described includes observing amorous shepherds who are "seeking garlands for shepherd lasses" (17:13, 18): eros gets its first positive mention in *The Reveries*! Although the Solitary Walker is thus much more candid in sharing with us this amusement of his, he does so in a manner that playfully eclipses and draws attention away from his continuing activity as meticulous author (cf. Friedlander 2004, 16).

Our author proceeds immediately to provide a very brief written history of his involvement with botany. He reports that the bug first bit him when he was already old: "in Switzerland with Dr. [Jean-Antoine] D'Ivernois" (this would be in the summer of 1764, when Rousseau was fifty-two).[5] After this, "I had herborized successfully enough during my travels so as to gain a passible familiarity with the plant realm." But "having become more than a sexagenarian, and sedentary in Paris, the strength started to fail me for the grand herborizations," and, "besides, given up to my music copying enough so as not to have need for another occupation, I had abandoned this amusement which was no longer necessary to me."[6] He reports that he had sold his herbarium and all his books on the subject,[7] and with the passage of time, the "little that I knew had almost entirely effaced itself from my memory." So prior to the time of this writing (in his sixty-sixth year), botany does not appear to have ever been more than a (temporary) amusement.[8]

But now "all of a sudden, at the age past sixty-five,[9] deprived of the little memory that I had" and deprived also (he says) of the strength for long excursions in the countryside and of any guide, or books, or garden, or herbarium, "here I am, recaptured by this folly, but with still more ardor than I had when I gave myself to it the first time." In buffo-jocularity (J. Scott 2008, 151), the Solitary Walker lets himself sound carried away with amateur fervor (reminding us of the beginner's craze that he described at the island of St. Pierre back in the Fifth Walk [5:7]): he is now "resolved to reconstruct a herbarium richer than the first one, expecting that I am going to put into it all the plants of the sea and of the alps and all the trees of the Indies!" (7:2).

The Puzzle

The Solitary Walker does not explicitly remind us that he here is in part repeating what he has already told us, back in the Fifth Walk, where he said (speaking of the autumn of 1765) "Doctor D'Ivernois had inspired in me a taste for botany which soon became a passion" (5:7). Curiously and rather conspicuously, this Seventh Walk, though focused on the Solitary Walker's botanizing, is lacking any explicit reference back to the Fifth Walk's vivid portrayal of his initial passionate pursuit of botanical collection. In that earlier account, there was no indication whatsoever that the pursuit of botany (never itself designated reverie) left him without "even the time to dream." All to the contrary! And later in this Seventh Walk (7:25), we will hear the Solitary Walker recall "a botanical excursion that I made one day next to the Robaila mountain farm of Judge Clerc" (this would have been around the time of the sojourn on the island of St. Pierre: CW ad loc.) during which, "insensibly dominated by the strong impression of" the surrounding forest and hills, "I forgot the botany and the plants" and "I set myself to dreaming."

We are thus in several ways provoked by our author to wonder why he has now come to find that his botanizing leaves no time for reverie or dreaming (cf. Gasbarronne 1989, 223, 226–27). Why can he no longer intersperse botanical excursions with reverie, as he describes himself having done long ago, in the reminiscing passage of this Seventh Walk just quoted and as he has previously described himself doing on the island of St. Pierre? In the Fifth Walk, he made the two occupations, botanizing and reverie, sound like two different but compatible and even mutually reinforcing constituents of his *fa niente*: recall especially the long seventh paragraph of the Fifth Walk.

The Solitary Walker at first says only that "I do not seek to justify the course that I am taking in following this fantasy." Then he adds, "I find it very reasonable—being persuaded that, in the position that I am in, giving myself to amusements that gratify me is a great wisdom" (*une grande sagesse* [7:3]). But why is it not part of this great wisdom to include also reverie among these amusements (note the plural)? Besides, would not quiet reveries be a much more suitable occupation for "an old man, doddering, already decrepit and weighed down" and "deprived of the strength for running about the countryside," given the fact that botanizing requires long excursions, which he says here are exertions of youth (*exercises de la jeunesse* [7:2, 4]])?

Clues Pointing to Partial Solutions

He does add that his giving himself to botanizing is not only a great wisdom but even great virtue.[10] In what sense? Surely, this last is a provocatively paradoxical moral claim! He answers: "This is the means to not allow the germination in my heart of any leaven of vengeance or of hatred."[11] Does this imply that if he were to allow himself reverie, then he could not prevent the germination of vengeance and hatred in his heart? Is reverie too susceptible to being overtaken by, or to morphing into, vengeful passions? This seems suggested by his statement four paragraphs later, regarding his attitude toward his reveries after his persecution began: "I even had to fear in my reveries that my imagination, frightened by my miseries, would turn its activity that way"; and so "in this state, an instinct that is natural to me, making me flee every saddening idea, imposed silence on my imagination" (7:7).

But here in the third paragraph, he goes on to make it clear that although he may be able through his botanizing to sustain at present a "nature well purified of all *angry passions*" (my italics), even the botanizing is not sufficient to prevent the pursuit of vengeance—if not in a passionately angry mode, then in a cold mode that is all the crueler. For he adds the confession that "this is how I take vengeance on my persecutors in my manner: I do not know how to punish them more cruelly than to be happy despite them" (7:3; note that he says nothing about expecting or hoping for any punishment of the evildoers by a justly judging God). His inflicting such deserved retributive punishment is an act of justice on his part, and thus of great virtue. Of course, this vengeance requires of *The Reveries* a wide readership so that the infinitely numerous persecutors (see 7:26) can suffer their intended punishment of becoming aware of his happiness from botanizing in his sixty-fifth year. This is something they certainly would not know from his most recent previous writings for publication—the lugubrious "History of the Preceding Writing" and the "Copy of the Circular Note Which Is Spoken of in the Preceding Writing" (OC 1:977–92). Could it be that another reason why our author now wishes to let botanizing eclipse his reveries is because any reveries of which he would now be capable, in this his sixty-sixth year, inasmuch as they lack rapture (not being of the imaginative-creative type), could not so convincingly be portrayed to readers as an entirely joyful amusement but instead would too readily appear to be tinged with mortal melancholy? Recall our analysis of his description of his reveries in 2:5–6 and in 5:7–9, 13–14, 16–17. Recall also that the character "Rousseau," within the fictional *Dialogues*—the character who is the reader of the writings of "J. J."—is convinced that he knows that "an absolute solitude is a sad state and contrary to nature"; that "our most sweet existence is relative and collective, and our true me is not entirely within us," and that "such is the constitution of the human being, in this life, that one never arrives at enjoying well oneself without the cooperation of another." Observing firsthand "J. J.'s" gaiety and serenity on the latter's return from his solitary walks or after "being left alone and tranquil," the character "Rousseau" hypothesized that the reason "J. J." is not made by solitude "somber, taciturn, and always unhappy in life" must be that "J. J.'s" solitude is filled with his visions of imaginary societies of friends.[12] Those visions, that sort of creative social reverie, is never mentioned or even alluded to in this seventh chapter.

Yet, it is doubtful if these considerations suffice to dispel the big puzzle, a part of which the Solitary Walker now proceeds to make explicit: "no doubt, reason permits for me, even prescribes for me, to give myself over to every penchant that attracts me and that nothing prevents me from following"; but reason "does not teach me why this penchant attracts me, and what attraction I can find" in such a vain study. This is a bizarre thing, he exclaims, that "I would like to explain to myself." Once "clarified, it could throw some new light on that knowledge of myself to the acquisition of which I have consecrated my final leisure" (7:4). Thus, gliding back to the first of the five purposes of this writing that he set forth in the First Walk, our author shows yet again that in fact his botanizing amusement is by no means his entire occupation at present. He is also occupied not only with his writing but, in addition, with a third great matter: his continuing quest for further self-knowledge. This last occupation, unlike botanizing, is very serious, even sacred—to this occupation his leisure is consecrated; this occupation is no mere amusement. In the existence and aims of the Solitary Walker, gravity continues to be mingled with levity.

How and Why Reverie Has Been Eclipsed by Botany

Reproducing for us the investigation by which he plumbed the reasons why botanizing now holds such a bizarrely intense attraction for him, the Solitary Walker launches into an autobiographical sketch of his entire life as a thinker, leading up to and providing a kind of genealogy of his mentality at the present time of this writing. He immediately makes plain that he has never experienced himself as a philosopher in anything like the classic sense: as one who "finds his satisfaction, his bliss, in free investigation, in articulating the riddle of being," doing so not through any ecstatic flights of the imagination but through intense and meticulous rational reflection on "all the parts of the whole or the articulation of the whole."[13] On the contrary, the Solitary Walker proclaims, "I have thought sometimes rather profoundly; but rarely with pleasure, almost always against my liking, and as if compelled."[14] Whereas "reverie relaxes me and amuses me, reflection fatigues me and saddens me."[15] He goes still further: "to think was *always* for me an occupation that was painful and without charm" (my italics). He concedes that "sometimes my reveries finish by meditation"; but more often, he insists, "my meditations finish by reverie"; and "during these wanderings, my soul rambles and glides in the universe on the wings of the imagination, in ecstasies which surpass every other enjoyment" (7:5). The Solitary Walker goes on to stress that he is referring here to reveries experienced in his early years, prior to his being "thrown into the literary career by alien impulsions"—that is, prior to the early 1750s (he says not a word here about the political-philosophical contents of his major writings). With the "fatigue of the work of the spirit" that was involved in his writing for publication, "I felt my sweet reveries languish and cool."

Then soon, he continues, he was "forced, despite myself, to concern myself with my sad situation"; and as a consequence, the ecstatic reveries all but ceased: "I could no longer rediscover, except very rarely, those dear ecstasies which during fifty years had for me taken the place of fortune and of glory" and "rendered me in idleness the happiest of mortals" (7:6).[16]

Still worse, in this condition, he even had to fear that in his reveries his imagination would turn toward his sad situation. Therefore, a "natural instinct to flee saddening thoughts" intervened to impose silence on his imagination and fixed his "attention on the environing objects," which led him for the first time to "consider in *detail* the spectacle of nature," which he had "previously hardly ever contemplated except *en masse* and as an *all*" (7:7; my italics).

The Solitary Walker seems to be telling us how, after 1762 or his fiftieth year, reverie was replaced with nonimaginary, protobotanical contemplation of the spectacle of nature in detail: primarily, as he goes on to say, the trees, the shrubs, the plants, as "the attire and the clothing of the earth," which "amid the running of water and the song of birds" offers to humans "the sole spectacle in the world of which" their "eyes and heart never weary" (7:8).

But then the Solitary Walker reminds us once again of the ecstasies, leading to a self-exalting transcendence of nature in detail, to which a contemplator of nature who has a sensitive soul gives himself up (so these ecstasies are not here presented as peculiar to the Solitary Walker)—and which the Solitary Walker has just said he ceased to experience around 1750, when he was "thrown into a literary career."[17] He recollects that when such a "sweet and profound reverie takes possession of one's senses," one "loses oneself, with a delicious drunkenness, in the immensity of this beautiful system with which one feels himself identified." In such ecstatic reverie, "all the particular objects escape one"; one does not contemplate in detail; "one sees and feels nothing except in the all." One's imagination is expansively at work; for, as the Solitary Walker explains, if one is to come down from this semimystical union with the all as all, "in order to enable one to observe by parts this universe that one was urging oneself to embrace," there "has to be some particular circumstance that *constricts* [*resserre*] one's ideas, and *circumscribes* one's imagination."[18]

So we are presented with a profound dichotomy and tension: between (a) what the Solitary Walker shared in his younger days with sensitive souls—an imagination that enables such souls to satisfy their urge to fall into reverie of drunkenness leading to identification with and embrace of the all as all (*tout*); and (b) observant articulation of the particular vegetative beings and their distinct species—an occupation that, for the Solitary Walker, was made possible only by the natural instinct that silenced the imagination which previously propelled him into the aforementioned drunken reveries embracing the all as all (cf. Gasbarronne 1989, 226–28). In his recent observations of natural entities, it naturally happened that his "heart, constricted [*resserré*] by distress, gathered and concentrated all its movements" so as "to preserve that remainder of warmth that was ready to evaporate and to extinguish itself in the despondency" into which he "was falling by degrees." This natural gathering of his constricted heart impelled him to "wander nonchalantly in the woods and in the mountains, not daring to think, for fear of stirring up" his sufferings. In these wanderings, his says, "my imagination," having been "silenced by instinct," then "allowed my senses to give themselves up to the light but sweet impressions of the environing objects." And among his senses, his eyes "put themselves in motion ceaselessly from one object to another" so that "it was not possible that in a variety so great, there weren't found some objects that fixed the eyes and arrested them for a longer time" (7:10).

Such was, according to this autobiographical account by the Solitary Walker, the complex and tension-ridden synthetic-dialectical process—repressing imagination and integrating the forces of instinct and heart—that gave him his peculiar inlet into a sensual-aesthetic botanizing, by which his attention became fixed on particular objects in nature for the first time. This was by no means a philosophical or scientific attention:[19] "I got a taste for this recreation *of the eyes*, which *in misfortune* rests, amuses, *distracts the spirit* and suspends the sentiment of pains" (my italics). Accordingly, this distracting, sensual-aesthetic recreation to which the Solitary Walker gained access, in this unique way, is in itself widely available to others: "it is only necessary to love pleasure in order to give oneself over to sensations so sweet" (7:11). And at this point, the intellectual autobiography is suddenly interrupted by a detour into a rather lengthy explanation of why and how it is, then, that so many other people are prevented from sharing in these sensual botanical joys.

Sensual-Aesthetic versus Philosophical-Scientific Botany

The Solitary Walker judges that some people, even though they are struck sensually by attractive plants, are prevented from enjoying the experience by a "defective natural sensibility." But in the case of most, what prevents them is the fact that "their spirit, too occupied with other ideas, only furtively gives itself to the objects that strike their senses" (7:11). What the Solitary Walker dwells on, however, is the disgusting prejudice (*dégoutant préjugé*) which instills in people of taste (*gens de gout*) "the habit of seeking in plants only drugs and remedies" (7:12). The art of "medicine has to such an extent taken over [the study of] plants, transformed into elements" (*simples*) that "one sees in them only what one does not see at all": one sees the pretended virtues that it pleases this or that practitioner to attribute to them. People "do not conceive that the plant organization could by itself merit some attention."

At this juncture, the Solitary Walker mentions, in contrast, the philosopher Theophrastus, who "went about it otherwise" and "can be regarded as the sole botanist of antiquity." But both here and back in the Fifth Walk, the Solitary Walker seems much more familiar and comfortable with the very different, because rather obsessively species-classifying, modern studies championed by Linnaeus and his rivals.[20] Aristotelian biology, in contrast to Linnaean, shows much, much less interest in such species-classificatory schemes. Aristotelian biology is focused much more on the kindred or analogous parts of organic species and their functioning—as expressing the causality of the "for the sake of which."[21] But the Solitary Walker shows no signs of having considered how Theophrastus, the premier student of Aristotle, conducted his truly philosophical botany, as expressed in the *Inquiry into Plants* and *On Causes of Plants*. These treatises of Theophrastus certainly do not express a study of plants in the sensual-aesthetic manner that is being praised and exemplified and recommended here by the Solitary Walker. Theophrastus instead proceeds in careful parallel with his teacher Aristotle's treatises on animals, the *History of Animals* and above all the *Parts of Animals*, which early on has a famously beautiful defense of the aesthetically unattractive but philosophically truly beautiful investigation of organisms that requires ripping them open to dissect and to analyze causally their most important but disgusting (*duschereias*) inner parts (*Parts of Animals* 645a24–37). By contrast, the Solitary Walker dismisses with revulsion the "necessity to study the dead, to rip them apart, to debone them, to poke at leisure into their palpitating entrails!"—"slavering and livid flesh, blood, disgusting intestines, frightful skeletons, pestilential smells!" (7:20). The Solitary Walker's complaint about his contemporaries is the un-Aristotelian and unphilosophical complaint that their "medicinal ideas are assuredly scarcely suited to render pleasing the study of botany," since they "wither the coloring of the prairie, the impact of the flowers, drying up the freshness of the shrubs, rendering the greenery and the shady spots insipid and disgusting."[22] The Solitary Walker's critique culminates in the romantic expostulation: "one won't go looking for flower garlands for shepherdesses among herbs for purging!" (7:13). All that pharmacology, he assures us, "did not at all sully my pastoral images" (7:14)—"of the greenery and the flowers, of the blue heaven, of the amorous shepherds, and of the robust laborers" (7:18 end).[23] Such romantic criticism would fall hard on Theophrastus, with his prosaic causal investigations of the various types of manures, soils, farmers' practices of crop rotation, and so forth.[24] Still more would this criticism fall on Socrates's own study of plants, which was centered not at all on flowers and greenery (and certainly not on amorous shepherds!) but instead on cereal farming, studied as economically utilitarian as well as theoretically interesting, and only thus as "belonging especially to a philosophical man."[25]

The Solitary Walker broadens and deepens his animadversion by stressing, in un-Socratic and unphilosophical language, that "everything that pertains to the sentiment of my needs saddens and spoils my thoughts." "I have never," he declares, "found any true charm in the spiritual pleasures except by losing sight completely of the interest of my body." If in studying nature he were to concern himself with the body and its needs, the result would be disastrous. He would never find himself occupied with "those delights conferred by a pure and disinterested contemplation"; "my soul would not know how to exalt itself and glide through nature as long as I felt it held to the bonds of my body" (7:15). We are very far from Socrates's study of plants and of farming as dramatized in Xenophon's *Economist*.

Going much further, the Solitary Walker proclaims that nothing personal can "truly occupy my soul": "I never meditate, I never dream, more deliciously than when I forget myself. I feel inexpressible ecstasies, raptures, in blending myself so to speak in the system of beings, in identifying myself with nature entire."[26] Is the Solitary Walker now suddenly suggesting that, after all, he does still experience the ecstasies of self-forgetting, semimystic union with the all—ecstasies that he has previously assigned to a lost youthful vigor of his imagination, before it became troubled by the sad situation in which he has found himself for the past fifteen years? Or is this not a momentary, wistful lapse into a glowing vicarious recollection of those long-ago, and now in fact lost, youthful self-transcending reveries?

A Civic Version of His Intellectual Autobiography

The latter seems indicated by the fact that the Solitary Walker now harks back to the youthful time of his life prior to his alienation from others: a time during which, however, he now presents himself as having been animated not at all by his private reveries, nor indeed by any concern for his own individual happiness, in either the celestial afterlife or in this earthly life. His concern, he claims, was only civic projects on earth: "as long as humans were my brothers, I made for myself projects of *earthly* felicity," which, "being *always* relative to the *whole*,

I could *only* be happy from the *public* felicity, and *the idea of an individual happiness never touched my heart until* I saw my brothers seeking theirs solely from my misery" (my italics). Reverting to apologia, he now claims that it was only in reaction to persecution that, turning for "refuge in the common mother," he "sought in her arms to shield" himself "from the attacks of her children." Only thus did it come to pass that "the most savage solitude seemed to me preferable to the society of the wicked who nourished themselves only on treasons and hatred" (7:16). He now characterizes his turn to nature as having occurred in his mature years and as having had a very different character, a sadly forced or compelled character, from what he depicted a few paragraphs previously as the spontaneously joyous turn to nature in his younger years.

In an emphatic and repeated conclusion to this intellectual autobiography (7:17–18), he describes his situation here and now, at the time of this writing, as one in which he is "forced to abstain from thinking"—"for fear of thinking about my misfortunes"—and "forced to keep in check what's left of a cheerful but languishing imagination." No longer imagining and thinking still less; fleeing humans and seeking solitude; he is "forced to try to forget humans" ("for fear lest the *indignation* finally embitter me"). "I am not able to concentrate myself *entirely within myself*" (my italics). In these last words, we finally get a fleeting and very, very faint reminder of the Fifth Walk's elaborate accounts of those reveries through which, long ago, he plunged into the sentiment of his own existence. Now, however, the Solitary Walker does not speak of self-concentration as intrinsically attractive but rather as another mode of forced retreat from persecution. From this avenue of retreat, he is prevented, however, by a more powerful and contrary spiritual urge: he cannot concentrate himself within himself "because my expansive soul seeks, despite what I have in it, to extend its sentiments and its existence over other beings."

Yet, this expansive psychic urge is now decisively debilitated: "I can no longer, as in other times, throw myself head-first into that vast ocean of nature"; "I no longer sense myself vigorous enough to swim in the chaos of my old ecstasies"; "the sphere of my understanding does not go beyond the objects with which I am immediately surrounded" (7:17); "my soul, dead to all the great movements, can no longer make itself affected by anything except sensible objects; I have nothing but sensations" (7:21).

He is saved by the fact that he is "endowed with a lively temperament" that draws away from "languishing apathy and melancholy." On account of that temperament, along with his instinct for pleasure, he has been able very recently to rediscover, in and by sensual-aesthetic botanizing, a mild and soothing sort of psychic expansiveness into nature that suits his decrepit old age: "I began to occupy myself with everything that surrounded me and by a strongly natural instinct I gave preference to the objects that were most agreeable" (7:18); and he proceeds to explain in some detail why amateur study of minerals, or of animals, unlike the collection of plants and flowers, would not be agreeable to him (7:18–20).

This, then, is the intellectual biography that explains the present attraction, for the Solitary Walker, of botanizing: it is the best available replacement for the no longer accessible or suitable reveries. His passion for botany is "a species of passion that fills the void of all those that I no longer have"; it is "necessary that some object fill the void, and those that my imagination refuses me or that my memory rebuffs are replaced by the spontaneous productions that the earth, not forced by humans, offers to my eyes." In addition, he undertakes botanical excursions "in order to slip away, as much as possible, from the memory of humans and from the attacks of the wicked": "I imagine in my foolishness that in not thinking of" enemies, "they do not at all think of me," and "I find such a great sweetness in this illusion" (7:24).

He does not tire of insisting that in his botanizing "I do not at all seek to instruct myself."[27] This is not only because it is too late. He also reiterates that "besides, I have never seen that such science contributes to happiness of life." Still, he does include, in his description of this idle occupation which in his flagging old age "suffices alone to render life happy and sweet" (7:23), his "seeking sometimes with success" the plants' "general laws, the reason and the end of their diverse structures" (7:22). The Solitary Walker's scientific reasoning mind is not altogether stifled.

But in the final analysis, it is not so much the observation or analysis of the plants themselves as it is the chain of accessory ideas that "attaches me to botany." The "meadows, the waters, the woods, the solitude, the peace above all and the repose that one finds in the midst of all that"; "it recalls to me my youth and my innocent pleasures." It is thus that botany "renders me quite often happy still, in the midst of the saddest lot ever undergone by a mortal."[28]

Chapter 8

"8"—Renewed Self-Exploration

The connection of this eighth chapter (no longer titled a "Walk") to the previous Seventh Walk is like the connection of the Fifth Walk to the Fourth. Once again, the Solitary Walker presents himself in a sweet conversation with his soul that articulates a rather abrupt quasi-dialectical rebound from the previous chapter. Once again, the rebound is from a focus on outward activity of his soul's expansiveness to a focus on his inward self-concentration, and the happiness he thus enjoys—but this time in a more self-querying spirit (thus pursuing the *first*, along with the *third*, and perhaps also the *fourth* of the five aims set forth back in the First Walk).

We have previously limned the Seventh Walk's conspicuous eclipse of the long-ago reveries of intense sentiment of his own existence that the Solitary Walker had described so vividly in the Fifth Walk. This conspicuous eclipse was effected by a stress on sensual-aesthetic botanizing conceived no longer, as it had been in the Fifth Walk, as a complement to those reveries but instead as a replacement for them: as a mild and soothing sort of psychic expansiveness, out into sensible verdant nature that suits the Solitary Walker's enfeebled old age. If, as we have speculated, the Seventh Walk was originally intended by the author to be the last, then, in that case, the second account of botanizing in the Seventh Walk would have been a fitting bottoming out of the descent starting in the last portion of the Fifth Walk that we have discerned as part of the overall organization of the first seven chapters of *The Reveries*. But

137

138   CHAPTER 8

if so, Jean-Jacques Rousseau was not satisfied with the work as a whole in that form; he took up the pen again, after a lapse of about half a year, and began a renewed investigation into himself, his heart and his soul (the word for soul, *âme*, appears more often in this eighth chapter than in any other—the fifth chapter being a close second).

The Puzzle

The Solitary Walker begins with a report of an apparently recent, comprehensive, retrospective reflection on "the dispositions of my soul" in "all the situations of my life." (He does not designate this reflection as a reverie; Davis 1999, 140–41.) Extremely striking to him was his realization that whereas his brief periods of prospering have left him with "almost no agreeable memory" of any "intimate and permanent manner in which they affected" him, he keenly recalls how in all the times of his misfortunes he "felt constantly filled with sentiments that were tender, touching, delicious" and which, "pouring a salutary balm over the wounds" of his broken heart seemed "to convert its suffering into pleasure." He now judges that he has "savored more the sweetness of existence"—indeed, he has really lived more—when his destiny compelled his sentiments to become "constricted so to speak around" his heart (this phrasing dimly reminds, but only dimly reminds, of the "sentiment of one's own existence"). This contrasts, he says, with the times when his sentiments went evaporating outside on "all the objects of men's esteem, which merit so little by themselves" (8:1). But it was not only or mainly the "objects of men's esteem" that drew him "to forget in some way" his very self. When all was going well, his "expansive soul extended itself" and was "ceaselessly drawn out of me" by "the lovable attachments which ceaselessly occupied my heart." It was because he filled the sphere in which he lived with affectionate feelings that (he now sees) "I belonged entirely to what was alien to me" (8:2).[1] The tension between his soul's affectionate expansiveness into actual living and breathing fellow humanity and his deeper need to turn inward, away from such expansiveness, in order to achieve true self-possession and the sweetness of existence has never been so clear.[2]

He goes on to recall a time, years before, when he was "well-received and treated with affection everywhere," when he had not a single enemy and with no one ill-disposed or envious of him, and was surrounded by people being obliging to him, with him being obliging in return. Amid that affectionate social integration, however, he was comfortable nowhere; his heart was agitated, his head spinning; solitude bored him and he had to be in constant motion. "What was I missing, then, to be happy?" He answers, rather surprisingly, "I don't know it; but I know that I was not so."[3]

Today, in contrast, "what am I missing to be the most unfortunate of mortals?"—"Nothing of all that humans have been able to exert" in order to bring him to misery. And yet, "in this deplorable state, I still would not exchange being or destiny with the most fortunate among them" (the rest of humanity). It is true, he concedes, that he nourishes himself only with his own substance, but that substance does not deplete itself: "I am sufficient unto myself even though I ruminate on an empty stomach, so to speak"—even though "my imagination dries up, and my burned-out ideas furnish no more nourishment for my heart" while "my soul sags, clouded, obstructed by my organs" and "no longer has enough vigor to thrust itself, as before, out of its old envelope" (8:3; we are back to a somewhat more decrepit version of the self-description given at the start of the Second Walk, employing some of the same words and phrases: 2:2–3). Yet even or precisely now, in this isolated, and persecuted, and mentally very debilitated condition, he lives happily and serenely—"occupied with flowers, stamens, and childishness" (8:7). Unlike at the start of the Second Walk, he does not mention reveries here or even the recollection of reveries; nor does he speak of the sentiment of his own existence.

How and why, he asks, has this childishness come to pass?

He proceeds to repeat for his readers a new (and, sadly, at least equally paranoid) version of the First Walk's account of how "indignation, fury, delirium, took possession of" him, followed by despair, when he first came to be convinced of the conspiracy against him, involving an entire generation of the human race and in which he "had been entrapped for a long time without having had any awareness of it." And at present, he declares, he remains trapped still, and indeed deeper than ever, without having been able to discover the cause to solve the mystery. There was a time during which he hoped that he would find at least some other humans, a few just souls—even only a single just soul who was an exception, who was not part of the conspiracy. But no: now he sees that "the league is universal, without exception, without return" (8:6–8).

He asks again and more pointedly, what enabled him to find "serenity, tranquility, peace, even happiness" in "this deplorable state"? Evidently the answers suggested in previous chapters no longer fully satisfy the Solitary Walker.

The Yoke of Necessity

The answer that does now satisfy him, he informs us, is "a single thing; this is, that I have learned to bear the yoke of necessity without murmur." This echoes the fourth paragraph of the First Walk. But he now says not a word recalling what the seventh paragraph of that First Walk said about the crucial role played by the previous crucial but mysterious "event as sad as it was unforeseen." Instead, he here adds, "I used to be forcing myself to hold on still to a thousand things, and *all* these having successively escaped me, reduced to myself *alone*, I have *finally* regained my balance"; "I dwell in equilibrium because, no longer attaching myself to *anything*, I depend *only* on myself" (8:9–10; my italics). This formulation makes no exception for dependence on faith in a just God's judgment in the afterlife. Thus the text at this point, in the form in which it has been presented in all printed editions, seems to mark a profound, atheistic break from the First through Third Walks. This would go with what we have seen to be the evaporation of reference to God and to the afterlife in the course of the Fourth through the Seventh Walks.[4]

But the manuscript at this point puts a question mark over this reading and interpretation.

The beginning words of the sentence quoted above—"I used to be forcing myself"—are penned at the bottom of the folio page 8 recto, and the sentence is continued on the next folio page (9 recto). *But* this continuation is written well down on the page, underneath a line drawn across the page, above which line is the following sentence: "That which I do know is that the supreme arbiter is powerful and just, that my soul is innocent and that I have not deserved my lot." Above that, separated by another line drawn across the page, is written, "However sad may be the lot of my last days and whatever humans may be able to do, after I have done what it is that I ought, they will not prevent me living and dying in peace."

So, righteous and mighty (but not *omni*potent) divinity thus reenters the pages of the manuscript containing chapter 8 of *The Reveries*—in an almost explosive eruption (and this is the last time that God is mentioned in the manuscript). Editors and translators have ignored or excised this eruption,[5] in part because the sentence about God reproduces word for word the fourth from the last sentence of "History of the Preceding Writing," whose final sentence resembles the other sentence here, "However sad etc." (which is written in several different forms in the manuscript preparations for that earlier work; see the editorial notes to OC 1:989). Editors have taken these sentences as written here, amid the manuscript of *The Reveries*, to be some sort of vagrant fragments from work on that earlier published writing. But in that earlier, published context, at the end of "History of the Preceding Writing," these two sentences surround sentences that imply a continuing possibility of providential vindication while Rousseau is still alive on earth[6]—something that is excluded by the Solitary Walker's submission here, in this context, to blind necessity for the rest of his earthly life. Plucked by Rousseau out of their original context and placed by him here, amid the manuscript of the eighth chapter of *The Reveries*, as a stand-alone declaration of faith, the sentences on God have a different context and hence a quite different meaning. No doubt, it is impossible to know whether, and if so, how Rousseau might have been thinking to include in the eighth chapter these two sentences or their substance—if he had lived longer and had gotten around to polishing the manuscript (cf. Osmont 1934, 124–25). But we have to wonder, could Rousseau have been indicating, or at least keeping before his mind (and before the mind of anyone who might read this manuscript?) the fact that he has come to know (not merely to believe) that God will bestow on him his deserts in the life after death, compensating for this life on earth—although, or precisely because, Rousseau has come to be persuaded that (as he writes on playing card #26 or OC 1:1171–72; my italics), "providence does not involve itself *in any fashion* in human opinions nor in *all* that depends on reputation, and that it leaves *entirely* to fortune and to humans *everything* that remains *here below* of the human being after his death?" In *Dialogues* OC 1:972, the character "Rousseau" declares that "the moral order, of which nothing here below gives us the idea, has its seat in a different system, for which one will look in vain on earth, but back into which all must one day return." Such a theological conception is of a very austere divine order in which providence plays no discernible role whatsoever—positive or negative—in earthly reputation but eventually compensates in and by a just afterlife for humans in accordance with their deserts. This theology would resolve the contradiction laid out by Pasqualucci (1976, 100–101), while absolving God of the responsibility for the conspiracy and persecution that the Solitary Walker ascribed to God's eternal decrees in the very gloomy theology articulated at the end of the Second Walk.[7] We soon hear the Solitary Walker observing, in what could be taken as an autocriticism of that earlier theology, "when the unfortunate do not know whom to blame for unhappiness, they blame destiny, which they personify and to which they ascribe eyes and an intelligence to torment them intentionally." In contrast, "the wise man who sees, in all the unhappiness that happens to him, only the blows of a blind necessity does not at all have these senseless agitations; he cries out in his suffering but without being carried away, without anger."[8]

Yet in almost the same breath, the Solitary Walker shows that he has not yet entirely achieved the perspective that he here attributes to the wise man. For the Solitary Walker says of his persecutors, "after long and vain researches I see them all still without exception in the most iniquitous and absurd system that *an infernal spirit* could *invent*" (8:12; my italics. Recall "the Demon that inspires" the hatred of him in 1:10 and his assertion in 1:5 that the conspiracy proceeds by "all human power aided by all the ruses of Hell").

Besides, the conception of blind necessity to which the Solitary Walker here says the wise man attributes his suffering proceeds to take on, in the elaboration that the Solitary Walker unfolds, an extremism that is simply irrational, not to say verging on the clinically insane (the latter is suggested by the Pléiade editor ad loc., OC 1:1819). For the Solitary Walker proposes the crazy idea that in their persecution of him, his "contemporaries were in regard to me only mechanical beings who acted only by impulsion and whose action I would be able to calculate only by the laws of motion." And "thus their internal dispositions ceased to exist as something for me"; "I no longer saw in them anything except masses moved differently, deprived in my regard of all morality."[9]

To be sure, as he elaborates further this surreal perspective, it sounds more and more like a kind of fictive-imaginative psychological crutch that the Solitary Walker has concocted to cloud his mind deliberately, as a self-therapeutic device helping him to overcome his otherwise insuperable righteous indignation and to rescue himself from his bewilderment over his paranoid conspiracy theory. For he says that because he realized that he could never figure out an adequate rational explanation of what he conceives to be the human race's universal, unjust conspiracy against him—"my reasoning showing to me only absurdities in all the explications that I sought to give for what was happening to me"—he "understood that the causes, the instruments, the means for all that, being unknown to me and inexplicable, *ought* to be nul for me," and "I *ought* to *regard* all the details of my destiny *as if* so many acts of a pure fatality in which I *ought* to *suppose* neither direction, nor intention, nor moral cause," so as to "submit without reasoning and without resisting" as a purely passive being: "there, *that is what I told myself*" (my italics). His reason, he claims, somehow acquiesced in this "submission, *without* reasoning." (Thus, this acquiescence would seem to belong to a sort of self-healing, self-checking reason, rooted in some awareness of his paranoia?)

Nonetheless, he "sensed this heart murmuring." From where, he wondered, "did this murmuring come?" In searching, he found that "it came from the amour propre which, after having become indignant against humans, rose up also against reason" (8:14).

Amour Propre in the Soul and Heart of the Solitary Walker

Amour propre, the chief source of humanity's psychological pathology in society according to Rousseau and his great system,[10] has not previously been a theme in this work.[11] The Solitary Walker ascribed amour propre to his persecutors in 1:10 and 6:17; he denied that it is a source of his having occasionally lied out of embarrassment in 4:28; and he indicated it as a source of his indignation in 6:11.

Now he intensifies this last self-analysis: indignation generated by amour propre is a weakness that he shares, he says, with all the innocent who are persecuted. This discovery about himself, he confesses, "was not as easy to make as one might believe," because "for a long time a persecuted innocent takes for a pure love of justice the pride of his petty individuality." Still, when such a person comes to realize the true psychological source within him, he finds it easy to dry up that source, or at least to divert it if, that is (a big if), he is a proud soul (as the Solitary Walker has identified himself to be back in 3:19; see also 4:31 and 6:14). The "esteem for oneself is the greatest motive of proud souls," and "amour propre, fertile in illusions, disguises itself and passes itself off as this esteem." "When the fraud finally betrays itself," however, "and amour propre can no longer hide itself; from then on it is no longer to be feared." Even though "one stifles it with difficulty, one can at least easily subjugate it." This makes it sound as if proud self-esteem is altogether different from amour propre.[12] Curiously, however, the Solitary Walker does not quite identify himself here as a proud soul who has undergone the preceding development. In fact, in the manuscript (folio 12 recto, i.e., 8:25), he has crossed out the following ending to this paragraph: "There is the foundation of the recovered tranquility. I feel in me, sounding myself" (with no final punctuation—it looks as if halfway through writing the last sentence, he crossed it out).

Instead, he proceeds to a brief autobiographical retrospective, beginning with the words, "I never had much of a penchant for amour propre." He confesses that amour propre exalted itself in him, prodigiously, when he was *"dans le monde"* and "especially when I was an author." But "the terrible lessons that I received *soon* shut it back up in its former confines" (my italics). At first this makes it sound as if amour propre was stifled and confined by some *other* psychic force—for example, proud self-esteem. But no, the Solitary Walker goes on to say that amour propre "began by revolting against injustice," but it "finished by disdaining it." And by "folding *itself* back into my soul" and by "cutting the external relations that rendered it demanding," and by "renouncing comparisons and preferences," amour propre "contented *itself* with my being good for myself"; what's more, *"becoming again* love of myself, it *returned into* the order of nature and *it delivered me* from the yoke of opinion" (8:16; my italics). So amour propre became a healthy therapeutic force within the soul of the Solitary Walker, using disdain (a certain sense of superiority to others and to their vicious doings, recall 6:14) to support therapeutic reason, and eventually shrinking itself back into a version of the natural self-love out of which it had pervertedly developed.[13] It was only then that he "found peace of soul again and almost felicity" (8:17). At least in the soul of the Solitary Walker, it sounds as though a diverted amour propre took the place of the motive of a proud soul's self-esteem rooted in some other psychic source. Or is not proud self-esteem at bottom nothing but another (healthy) development of amour propre?

Rendered Insensible to Adversity

Yet, the Solitary Walker reiterates that the reasoning, which speaks and consoles him when amour propre silences itself, is a reasoning that expresses the illusionary perspective that views injustices as nothing, because he "sees in these evils only the ill itself and not the intention" (8:17). It is only by this self-imposed blindness to the intentionality of injustice (which is, of course, in reality always present)—it is not by any quasi-Socratic analysis of the incoherence in the opinions concerning retributive justice that are at the heart and basis of the intentionality of indignation—that the Solitary Walker immunizes himself against righteous indignation. We note that this immunization by way of constructing for oneself an illusion about human agency directly contradicts the rule of conscience and of the moral instinct that the Solitary Walker enunciated in the Fourth Walk, where he proclaimed, "it is solely the intention, of the one who discourses, that measures the worth of discourses and determines their degree of malice or of goodness" (4:16; see also 4:18).

The Solitary Walker indicates, however, that he requires more than this self-deluding inoculation. In addition, he now claims that he has been brought to cease not only fearing but even being affected in any way by all future grave harms of any sort that he knows for certain are coming: "I have without effect the knowledge that I will suffer tomorrow; it suffices for me not to be suffering today for me to be tranquil. I do not let myself be affected at all by the harm that I foresee but only by that which I am feeling, and that reduces it to being a very little thing" (8:17). The final sentences of this chapter all but retract this: "the evil that humans have done to me touches me in no way; only the fear of that which they could still do me is capable of agitating me" (8:23). But here, he goes so far as to boast that he has learned to view not only "wealth and misery, glory and defamation" but also "life and death, illness and health, with the same indifference." He admits and even stresses, however, that this is "not the work of my wisdom." It is rather the work of "my enemies" (8:17). What does he mean by this? Apparently, that he has been driven, by the blows of his enemies and especially by what he senses as their outrageous injustice, to shut down somehow his rational awareness: to subjugate, to disconnect from, his emotional and imaginative reaction to all the sufferings that he knows loom for him in the future. His enemies have, he says, "rendered me *insensible to* adversity."[14] Is this fantastic psychological claim rendered more plausible by trying to interpret it as an implicit claim to have recovered something like the lack of awareness of future time that Rousseau attributes to original natural humanity, in its lack of imagination? Recall the *Second Discourse*, OC 3:144: "His imagination portrays nothing to him; . . . his soul, which nothing agitates, gives itself up to the sole sentiment of his own present existence, without any idea of the future, however near it may be."

The Reflowering of Imaginative Creativity

But if we hope or expect that the Solitary Walker is verging on telling us about his return to the experience of "the sole sentiment of his own present existence," that expectation or hope is disappointed.

Nor, it transpires, is the Solitary Walker claiming that his imagination has been subjugated or deadened or even curtailed. Quite the contrary. To our astonishment, he next claims that here at the end of his life he has recovered, as what is natural to him, as the sentiments for which his heart was born, not the return inward to the sentiment of his own existence but instead the enjoyment produced by imaginary societies of comrades that are generated by his reflowering creative imagination (though he does not speak of creative *reveries*): "given over by my penchants to the affections that draw me, my heart nourishes itself again with *the sentiments for which it was born* and I enjoy *them* with the imaginary beings *who produce them* and who *share in them* as if these beings existed really" (my italics). "They exist for me who have created them"; "they will endure" (8:18). We are astounded, not to say incredulous, at this because we were emphatically and repeatedly told in the Second Walk (2:2, 2:6) and reminded here again earlier in this chapter (8:3, "my dried-up imagination") that such creative experience and capacity has flagged at the time of the writing of *The Reveries* and is available only as a matter of recollection; accordingly, such creativity has subsequently not been mentioned or alluded to except when it was very briefly touched on, as a memory, in the last lines of the Fifth Walk. The Solitary Walker does add here (8:19, my italics) that "the happy and sweet life for which I was born" includes also two other ingredients: "I pass three fourths of my life *either* occupied with objects that are instructive as well as agreeable" to which "I deliver with delight my *spirit/mind* (esprit) and my *senses*" (presumably, this refers to his renewed botanizing [8:7], although it is amazing how little note the Solitary Walker takes of botany in the last three chapters) *"or* with the children of my fantasies that I have created according to my *heart* and whose company nourishes my *heart's* sentiments" (botanizing does not so nourish his heart's sentiments), *"or* with myself alone"—"content with myself and already full of the happiness that I sense is owed to me" (this last suggests that his self-contented happiness involves his firm hope for and anticipation of morally deserved compensation in the next life; see Pléiade editor's note ad loc.).

Nonetheless, although "all this is the work of the love of myself (*l'amour de moi-même*), and amour propre does not enter into it at all," the inextinguishable amour propre rears its ugly head in "the sad moments that I spend still amid humans": "the hatred and the animosity that I see in their hearts" not only "tear mine with sorrow" but "the idea of being thus taken for a dupe adds to that sorrow a very childish spite, fruit of a foolish amour propre, of which I sense all the silliness but which I am unable to subjugate." Rousseau added at the end of an insert at this point in the manuscript 14 verso that in this regard, "I have made no progress" and "all my painful but vain efforts have only left me as easy to trouble, to grieve, to render indignant, as before" (8:19). "Convinced of the impossibility to contain these first involuntary motions," he has "ceased all efforts" at that. At each aggression, he allows his "blood to catch fire, the anger and the indignation to take over the senses"—"the eyes flashing, the fire in the visage, trembling limbs, suffocating palpitations"; he "cedes to nature that first explosion." Then he awaits the moment when he can conquer by "letting my reason act"—"what am I saying, alas! My reason! I would commit another great wrong to give it the honor of this triumph, because it plays scarcely any role." His soul is moved as if by the wind—as Rousseau writes in an insert, manuscript 16 verso, "it is my natural ardor that agitates me, and it is my natural indolence that pacifies me" (8:23). The Solitary Walker's practical reason bobs like a boat tossed in the surging swells of natural temperament.

True, these passing affections of righteous indignation "last only so long as the sensation that causes them." The "presence of a hate-filled human affects me violently, but as soon as he has disappeared, the impression ceases" (8:20). So on the days when the Solitary Walker sees no one, he is "happy and content without diversion, without obstacle." But those days are very few. He "rarely escapes some sensed slight"—and "a gesture,[15] a sinister look, that I perceive" is "sufficient to overwhelm me." Since he resides in the middle of Paris, when he leaves his home to seek solitude, he has to go so far to find it that "half the day is passed in anguish before I have reached the refuge for which I was seeking." Sadly, paranoia has generated agoraphobia (see the Pléiade editor's note ad loc.). When, after hours of walking, he finally is away from other humans, his relief from the agoraphobia is so great that "as soon as I see myself under the trees in the midst of the greenery, I believe that I see myself in the terrestrial paradise and I taste an internal pleasure as keen *as if* I were the most happy of mortals" (8:21; my italics). "It is only after having detached myself from social passions and their sad retinue that I have found nature again with all its charms" (8:22; see similarly 9:20–21).

But how does this fit with his immediately previous claim to be now creating intensely social fantasies: his "heart nourishing itself again with the sentiments for which it was born," sentiments "enjoyed with the imaginary beings who produce them and who share in them"; "the children of my fantasies that I have created according to my heart and whose company nourishes my heart's sentiments" (8:18–19)? Was the answer provided at the end of the Fifth Walk, when he recalled his creative fantasizing on the island of St. Pierre—"delivered from all the earthly passions that the tumult of the social life engenders, my soul threw itself frequently above this atmosphere, and communed in advance with the *celestial intelligences* whose number it hopes to augment *in a short while*" (5:17)? Is the hope for the afterlife still crucial?

The Solitary Walker concludes this eighth chapter by abruptly and rather vaguely gesturing back to the peak fifth chapter: "in the first instant of release I become again what nature has wished"; thus he enters, he says, upon "my most constant state, and that through which, despite destiny, I savor a happiness for which I sense myself constituted. I have described that state in one of my reveries" (8:23; note that this seems to imply that what he is now expressing is not one of his reveries). We recall the deep ambiguity at the end of the Fifth Walk as to the relation between (a) the imaginative communing with celestial intelligences said to have occurred frequently while on the island years ago; (b) the elaborately described reveries, while on the island, of the sentiment of his own existence experienced in a solitude of self-sufficiency like that of God but precisely therefore not involving God or other celestial intelligences; and (c) the reveries experienced in the here and now of the time of writing the Fifth Walk, in which the Solitary Walker says he re-creates, and imaginatively paints more vividly, by "adding charming images that enliven," the original reveries experienced years ago on the island.[16]

CHAPTER 9

"9" and "10"—The Solitary Walker's "Truly Loving Heart"

The previous eighth chapter was distinguished from the seven that preceded it in two striking ways. First, the Solitary Walker offered no apology whatsoever for the exclusive "love of myself" (*amour de moi-même*) of his attained happiness (a word used more often in the eighth chapter than in any other). Second, he gave little, if any, hint of a loving and frustrated sociability; when he did speak of his youthful, affectionate integration into society, he characterized those long-ago years as a time of alienated spiritual anguish (8:2, 9, 22).[1] For this twofold self-centeredness, the final two chapters of *The Reveries* constitute a dialectical compensation. In an extended apologia, Jean-Jacques Rousseau strives to leave his readers with the strong closing impression of the Solitary Walker's essentially loving, convivial nature (cf. Butterworth 1979, 221).

The sequentially coherent, if often dialectical, and highly rhetorical ordering of the chapters of *The Reveries* and of the sinuous overall train of thoughts and messages that they develop and unfold, thus continues to the end.

Happiness as Unattainable in Earthly Life

In the eighth chapter, the Solitary Walker spoke no less than eleven times (in the first-person singular) of his having achieved happiness (*le bonheur*) in self-centered solitude.[2] He opens the ninth chapter by stressing the seeming impossibility of any attainment of happiness here below—for humans, on the earth. In doing so, he employs language (in the first-person plural) reminiscent of the language he employed in the thirteenth paragraph of the fifth chapter. But now he stresses more the inner inconstancy of our liking or loving: it is not only that "our affections, that attach to external things, pass and change necessarily like them" (5:13) but that "we ourselves change, and no one can assure himself that he will like/love tomorrow what he likes/loves today"; "therefore all our projects of felicity for this life are chimeras."[3] (There still flickers the hope for felicity in an afterlife.)

Replacing Happiness with Contentment of Spirit

From the preceding, the Solitary Walker draws an emphatically communal lesson as regards the goal that "we" all should pursue in this life. "We" should replace, or at least eclipse, the pursuit of happiness with a pursuit of "contentment of spirit, when it comes" (*du contentement d'esprit, quand il vient*). "Contentment of spirit," in contrast to happiness, is something easily communicated and sharable: "happiness has no exterior sign; in order to recognize it, one would have to read in the heart of a happy human; but contentment lets itself be read in the eyes, in the demeanor, in the accent, in the manner of walking, and seems to communicate itself to him who perceives it." More than that. Contentment has an essentially civic expression: "Is there an enjoyment sweeter than beholding an entire people giving itself over to the joy on a festival day, with all the hearts expanding, through the supreme rays of pleasure that pass rapidly but vividly across the clouds of life?"[4] The Solitary Walker testifies from his own experiences: "I have seldom seen happy humans, perhaps never; but I have often seen *contented* hearts, and of all the objects that have struck me, this is the one that has most *contented* me" (9:1; my italics). We recall that in the sixth chapter, the Solitary Walker shared his imagination of how he would use the ring of Gyges if he were its possessor: having become "master of making *my* desires *contented*," what "would I have been able to desire, with what consequences? A single thing: that would be, to *behold all* the hearts *contented*" (6:18; my italics).

Responding to a Public Accusation of Heartlessness

Abruptly, in the text as Rousseau left it,[5] the Solitary Walker confronts what he imagines, in his paranoid persecution complex,[6] to be a nasty and hurtful, very recent public accusation. He believes that his erstwhile friend D'Alembert has used a eulogy of a certain Mme Geoffrin as a vehicle for implicitly charging Rousseau with being a denatured father and one who hates children. The Solitary Walker reports that he learned of this accusation three days ago, and he now shares with us his ruminations on it (and on the plotting that he imagines brought it to his attention); these ruminations of his took place, he says, the next day, on a long walk that he took in quest of some mosses in full bloom (9:2–3, i.e., in late spring or summer).

Thus, what began in the first paragraph as a recorded sweet conversation with himself (with a view to readers) suddenly shifts to a report of a walk two days previously and a record of his elaboration, during that walk, of a defensive (though confident) self-examination (but with no framing reference to divine judgment in the afterlife).

The Solitary Walker reports first his rebuttal of what he treats as D'Alembert's libel that he hates children: "I do not believe that there was ever a human being who loved more than do I to see the little cherubs frolicking and playing together," and "often in the street and on walks I stop to watch their mischief and their little games with an interest that I see no one sharing." In addition, as evidence that he enjoys *intimacy* with little children, he tells of how, on the very day, and in fact only an hour before the plotters contrived to bring D'Alembert's accusation to his attention, he enjoyed a visit for a few minutes from his landlord's two small sons, the younger of whom "I saw depart with as much regret as if he had belonged to me."[7]

These last words bring the Solitary Walker to the question of his abandonment of his own five children.[8] He has to admit that it is understandable that the reproach of having put his "children in the foundling home has easily degenerated, with a bit of twisting, into that of being a denatured father and of hating children." The defense and rejoinder that he proceeds to offer is worthy of the crueler moments in a W. C. Fields or Aristophanean comedy (e.g., *Acharnians* 731ff.) but is presented without a trace of self-conscious black humor. The Solitary Walker submits that the only alternative for his children (it has been reliably estimated that two of every three children placed in Parisian foundling homes during this epoch died in them) was "a destiny a thousand times worse." And what was that hideous destiny? Being spoiled by their loving mother! And by her family! This solicitude of his for his children's education shows, the Solitary Walker submits, that "no father is more tender than I would have been for them, however little habit might have aided nature."[9]

The Solitary Walker returns from this grotesque proof of his loving paternal devotion to a defense of his attitude toward children in general. He submits that his writings "about the first and true movements of nature," with their enlightenment derived from the study of children, are "the proof that I occupied myself with this research too carefully not to have conducted it with pleasure": "it would assuredly be the most unbelievable thing in the world that *Heloise* and *Emile* were the work of a man who didn't like children!" (9:5). One might rejoin: "Yes, this may prove the absence in you of a *dislike* of children, but does it prove a positive liking for or love of them, especially in their actuality, and not merely in your imagination of them? Might these novels not be understood as the work of a thinker who, rather than *loving*, is only *fascinated* with *actual* children and with what can be learned about human nature by studying them?"

The Solitary Walker admits that for years he has rarely spoken to or interacted with any children. He justifies this on three grounds. In the first place, persecution has made him tongue-tied in general, "and nothing requires a better discernment and a more just choice of expressions than the remarks one makes to children." Second, he is abashed by the onlookers, who would now expect too much from him in his dealing with children, on the basis of his "having written expressly for children" (9:6). Finally, "the sight of decaying nature" in old people is "hideous to children's eyes," and "I prefer to abstain from caressing them rather than make them uneasy or disgusted," which is a motive, he boasts, "that acts only on truly loving hearts" such as his own (9:7).

Perhaps because he recognizes the tepidity of this case he has made thus far for his purported great love of children, he exclaims, "Oh! If only I still had a few moments of pure caresses which come from the heart, were it only from an infant still in a romper"; "if I could behold again in some eyes the joy and contentment, in being with me, that I used to see so often, or of which I were at least the cause!" Of this, he says, he can "judge from examples that are very few but always dear to memory," and he offers a paradigmatic example, from two years ago, in which, while he was kissing a clinging little cherub he had picked up in a sort of transport, he was led to say to himself, "This is how I would have been treated by my own." Rousseau the loving and beloved father is again revealed! But, he reports, he noticed nearby the child's real father, and when he started to approach the father to introduce himself, he believed that he saw the father accosted by "one of those spies that are kept ceaselessly on my trail." The result is that now "there remains of that encounter only a rather lively memory mingling always sweetness and sadness, like all the emotions that still sometimes penetrate to my heart and which a painful reaction always winds up pushing away" (9:8–9).

Still, the Solitary Walker insists that if his pleasures in being together with children "are rare and brief, I also savor them more vividly when they come."

152   CHAPTER 9

And speaking for only a moment in a way that reminds of the previous chapter—sounding, momentarily, as if he could almost attain at least a relative share in happiness—he suddenly declares that "however rare they may be," if the pleasures of children's society "were pure and without adulteration I would be *more* happy, *perhaps*, than during my prosperity" (my italics). One would laugh, he adds, "if one were to see in my soul the impression made there by the smallest pleasures of this kind that I am able to hide from the vigilance of my persecutors." As evidence, he proceeds to relate a rather lengthy example from four or five years ago of how he and his wife contrived to distribute cheap pastries to twenty little girls supervised by a nun, on an "afternoon that was one of those of my life whose memory I recall with the greatest satisfaction" (9:10–14). This is the sole time in *The Reveries* when the Solitary Walker describes his wife as having played an important role. Are we not prompted to wonder whether the wife's presence and participation and encouragement might have been crucial conditions of this little drama of delight in pleasing little girls with gifts?

"This reminds me," the Solitary Walker says, "of another amusement almost of the same species, of which the memory has lasted from much longer ago"—from "the unhappy time when, thrust in among the wealthy and the literary people, I was sometimes reduced to sharing in their sad pleasures." He proceeds to recall a château party, head-spinning instead of amusing, that was followed by an after-dinner walk that turned into a rather cruel mockery of some peasant girls and boys. The Solitary Walker confesses that he participated—like the others, though out of shame, and he did not, he says, "find it as entertaining as they did" (he admits that he did find it somewhat entertaining), so soon he walked away. As he strolled by himself, he ran into five or six penniless urchins looking hungrily at a dozen sorry-looking apples that a poor little girl wanted very much to sell. "This comedy amused me for a long time" (and one might observe, like so much amusement at comedies, it showed a streak of cruelty in the audience). "I finally brought about the comedy's denouement by paying the [impoverished] little girl for the apples and having her distribute them to the [hungry and impoverished] little boys." He then experienced, he relates, "one of the sweetest spectacles that can gratify a person's heart"—that of "seeing joy, united with the innocence of youth, spread all about me," "for even the onlookers shared in it." The Solitary Walker says that he "had in addition the joy of feeling that it was my work" (9:15). He congratulates himself (9:16) on this entertainment of his, as partaking of "healthy tastes and natural pleasures" in contrast to "the pleasures of mockery and the tastes engendered exclusively by contempt" in which his opulent associates on that day indulged (and in which he had for a while partaken).

Taking Pleasure in Healthy Civic Society

Speaking synoptically, the Solitary Walker shares with us his "sustained reflection on the species of pleasure that he savored on these sorts of occasions" (9:17). He "has found that it consists less in a sentiment of beneficence" than in the simple "pleasure of beholding contented visages"—a "charm which, though it penetrates to my heart, seems to be solely one of sensation." He confesses that if he fails to behold directly the satisfaction that he causes, he loses half the enjoyment. But more profoundly and incisively, his is a disinterested pleasure, he submits, in that it does not depend on his having any role in bringing about the satisfaction he beholds others enjoying. Thus it transpires that, on reflection, the Solitary Walker's love consists chiefly of the pleasure of a disinterested onlooking; and this leads him back to reflection on his peculiar enjoyment, not merely of children's society, but of adult citizens' much more profound and rich communal and civic celebrations (recall 9:1 end). "In Geneva and in Switzerland, where the laughter does not evaporate itself in malignant folies, everything breathes contentment and gaiety in the festivals," and "the well-being, the fraternity, the concord dispose the hearts to expand"; "often in the transports of an innocent joy strangers accost one another, embrace, and invite one another to enjoy together the pleasures of the day." In order for the Solitary Walker to enjoy such civic celebrations, it suffices for him to be an onlooker. He need not be a citizen, nor even a welcomed stranger (and certainly not a legislator): "for me to enjoy myself from these amiable celebrations, I have no need to be part of them."

He hastens to add that this detached observer's enjoyment is not without a moral cause. The proof he gives is that when he beholds joy on the faces of the wicked, as a sign of their malignity, he can be "torn with sorrow and indignation," even "though it has no relation to me." It is "innocent joy alone whose signs gratify my heart" (9:18).

Nonetheless, it is an amoral compassion that moves his kind heart most: it is signs of "sorrow and pain that are felt even more, to the point where it is impossible for me to endure them without being agitated myself with emotions perhaps still more intense than those that they reproduce." His "imagination, reinforcing sensation" makes him "identify with the suffering being," apart from moral considerations. Compassion, as Rousseau analyzes it, is understood reductively, as a kind of imaginatively displaced self-love; this is in sharp contrast to the Socratic nonreductive, unselfish understanding of compassion.[10] The Solitary Walker goes on to admit that this compassion is a serious weakness in him, so grave that it contributes substantially to his conviction that he must live alone: *"always* too affected" by signs of "pleasure or pain, friendliness or aversion, I allow myself to be drawn on"; "I belong to myself only when I am alone, otherwise I am the plaything of all who surround me" (9:19; my italics). This has of course been vastly intensified by the imagined universal conspiracy against him of the entire human race: given that, "should one be astonished if I love solitude?" (9:20).

The Solitary Walker does voice a qualification: "I do feel, however—it is necessary to admit it—some pleasure in living amid humans, so long as my face is unknown to them; but this is a pleasure that is scarcely allowed me" (9:21; recall 6:9). Especially painful for him has been the conspiracy's success in alienating the disabled veterans whom he used to enjoy meeting in walks around the École militaire and the Invalides, and who remind him of the Spartan elders as described by Plutarch in his life of Lycurgus. (Thus, *The Reveries* all but ends with the Solitary Walker reminding us of his reverence for Plutarch's Spartans: see Strauss 1953, 294.) "Since my feelings for them do not depend on theirs for me, I never at all behold without respect and without interest these former defenders of their fatherland" despite the fact that "it is very hard on me to see myself so badly paid on their part for the justice rendered to them by" a "soul like mine, into which hatred would not know how to penetrate" (9:23). The sense of just deserving remains very strong in the Solitary Walker.

A memory from last year of an anonymous encounter with a recently arrived disabled veteran, and of the regret that the Solitary Walker initially felt at not having given the poor old fellow some money, leads to a closing reaffirmation of his own principles of charity, which take us into a cosmopolitan moral realm that is a far cry from the closed civic virtue of ancient Sparta: "it is necessary to press oneself to succor those who are in need, but in the ordinary business of life, let us allow natural benevolence and urbanity each to do their work without anything venal and commercial daring to approach such a pure source to corrupt or to adulterate it." In "Holland, it is said, the people require to be paid for telling you the time or showing you the way": this "must be a very contemptible people, who thus traffic in the simplest duties of humanity" (9:23). This is a reminiscence of a striking passage in Montesquieu's *Spirit of the Laws* (20:2): "if the spirit of commerce unites the nations, it does not similarly unite individuals. We see that in countries (Holland) where one is affected only by the spirit of commerce, one traffics in all the human actions, and in all the moral virtues; the smallest things, those that humanity demands, are done or given for money." The Solitary Walker expands this indictment to all of Europe, in contrast to Asia: "I have observed that it is only in Europe alone that hospitality is sold"; "in all Asia they lodge you without a charge." He concedes that "one doesn't find there so well all one's comforts," but "is it nothing to say to oneself, 'I am a human being and welcomed among humans; it is pure humanity that sets a table for me?'" (9:24). This is yet another reminiscence of the same chapter in Montesquieu's *Spirit of the Laws*, which includes this statement: "The spirit of commerce produces among humans a certain sentiment of exact justice, opposed on one side to brigandage, and on the other to those moral virtues that make it so that one does not always discuss one's interests with rigidity, but one can neglect them for those of others." The "total privation of commerce produces on the contrary the brigandage that Aristotle lists in the number of the manners of acquisition." But of brigandage, the "spirit is not at all opposed to certain moral virtues—for example, hospitality, very rare among the countries of commerce, is found admirably present among brigand peoples." Thus here, near the end of his final writing, even as he did in a peak expression of his first philosophical writing,[11] Rousseau uses the words of Montesquieu to make evident the fact that Rousseau's thought as a whole is a rebellion against the political philosophy of that great teacher of his.

Romantic Love as a Peak of the Wise Life

The Solitary Walker concludes *The Reveries* with a recording of an immediately previous sweet conversation with his soul.[12] In the tenth chapter he turns, once again dialectically, from the preceding chapter's closing proclamation of his present-day, anti-commercial, universal charity and humanity back to his intimately personal, youthful love affair with Mme de Warens: "Today, Palm Sunday, it is precisely fifty years since my first introduction to Mme de Warens." The reference to the Christian high holy day makes more conspicuous the silence otherwise about God and about the afterlife, which, we were told in the spiritual autobiography in chapter 3 (3:6), were so important to the young Solitary Walker's Christian (Roman Catholic) spiritual growth under the guidance of Mme de Warens. Although in this final chapter the Solitary Walker expresses deep gratitude to Mme de Warens for her spiritual benefits to him, he includes not a word about the Christian religious instruction she so earnestly bestowed on him. Moreover, here at the end of our study of *The Reveries* is an appropriate place to note, looking back synoptically, that the Solitary Walker's earlier expressions of piety have not foregrounded or made important, let alone central, the sentiment of *gratitude* toward the divine (for an exception, see 7:22 end); here we have another notable and deep contrast with Socrates. Gratitude toward divinity is the chief primary religious emotion inspired by Socrates's teaching on divinity: see especially Xenophon's *Memorabilia* 4.3.15 and context (also 2:2).[13]

So, then, for what spiritual benefits, precisely, does the Solitary Walker express his gratitude to Mme de Warens?

"Without that short but precious time" of the four or five years that he spent with her, he "would have remained perhaps uncertain about myself"; he would have had "difficulty in unraveling what there is of my own in my own conduct." For in all the rest of his life he has been "weak and without resistance," and "so agitated, tossed, caught up in the passions of others" that he has been "almost passive, in a life thus stormy." Through the use that he made of his leisure in her company, "helped by her lessons, and by her example" he "gave to my soul, still simple and new, the form that was advantageous to it and that it has always maintained": the "taste for solitude and for contemplation was born in my heart, along with the expansive and tender sentiments that were made to be its nourishment." "I need to collect myself in order to love."

He goes much further. He now at the end of his life and of all of his writing judges that during the four or five years that he spent enjoying mutual, intimate love with Mme de Warens, he experienced a happiness pure and full (*un bonheur pur et plein*). Through loving and being loved by her for those years, he was fully himself, "without admixture and without obstacle."[14]

Concluding Retrospect

In thus looking back with gratitude to those years of pure and full happiness, when he was fully himself, as an intimately secluded lover and beloved, the Solitary Walker says not a word about his reveries, creative or awed or inebriated or self-centered; nor about the sentiment of his own existence; nor about his enraptured botanizing; nor about his enjoyable acts of goodness toward fellow men in general and in particular; nor about the sweetness of observing and sharing in communal contentment. In retrospect, we see that *The Reveries* portrays each of these, and all of them together—but not in any true whole—as constituting wise flourishing. As for truly philosophical thinking, the bliss that the ancients and above all Socrates found—and that Hegel rediscovered—in progressively articulating the mystery of being through discursive reasoning and nous, it is not among these summits. Such is not part of Rousseau's articulation of the various and evolving peaks of his manifold, tension-ridden, un-Socratic life of wisdom—as "the man of nature enlightened by reason." According to Rousseau, humankind, having departed irretrievably from its original, subrational, harmonious, natural condition, in its historically developed individuality lacks an overarching, unified, architectonic of fulfillment and of flourishing, let alone a single end or telos.

Appendix: The Meaning of the Word *Reverie* before Rousseau

The great literary historian and critic Charles-Augustin Sainte-Beuve famously remarked, "the reverie is Rousseau's innovation, his discovery, his America" (1857–70, 5:93). This is a pardonably dramatic exaggeration. Still more misleading is the recent claim that in previous usage before Jean-Jacques Rousseau, "'reverie' meant idle daydreaming at best and delusion at worst" (Damrosch 2005, 481). In truth, the French word *rêverie*, originally spelled *resverie*, is a "word whose origin remains obscure and whose history announces itself as complex."[1]

In medieval French,[2] *resverie* seems to have connoted either a state of liberated partying of all sorts associated with vagabondage, or else diseased mental delusion (this latter meaning we see in Rousseau's usage at *Confessions* OC 1:293–94). For about a half century starting in 1315, there was a popular genre of nonsense poetry called *resveries* (Kellermann 1969).

Michel de Montaigne in his *Essays* (publ. 1587) employs the word *resverie* to mean "delusions" and "illusions" (1:41, 1:57, 2:12, 2:13, 2:37, 3:5) as well as "dreams" and "daydreams" (3:4, 5) and "follies" or "fancies" (1:8, 1:21, 2:6, 2:8, 2:10, 2:12, 2:18)—sometimes deliberate and pleasing, but usually (though not always) dubious. With ironic self-deprecation, Montaigne characterizes his own writing of the *Essays* as *resverie* a couple of times (1:26, 3:11). Both *The Grand Robert* (2001) and *The Grand Larousse* (1977) dictionaries find some anticipation in Montaigne of the favorable rich meaning bestowed on the term by Rousseau, but both dictionaries adduce unconvincing evidentiary citations in Montaigne; the dictionaries of Huguet (1962) and of Littré (1959) make no such suggestion. Rousseau does say in the First Walk, para. 14, that "I am engaging in the same enterprise as Montaigne," but he does not characterize the latter's essays as reveries.

Something closer to an anticipation of Rousseau's self-absorbed reveries may be seen in a remark on reveries in a 1622 letter of Guez de Balzac to M. de la Motte-Aigron, together with the response this evoked later from René Descartes in letters of April 15 and May 5, 1631, to Guez de Balzac (see the quotations and discussion in Morrissey 1980, 280–83).

An anticipation of Rousseau's creative-romantic reveries may be seen in Mlle. de Scudéry's 1654–61 novel *Clélie* (cited and discussed in Morrissey 1980, 289).

César-Pierre Richelet in his 1680 dictionary qualifies his two primary, pejorative definitions of reverie ("alienation of the spirit caused by suffering of the brain" and "ridiculous visions that one puts into one's spirit") by adding that the word can in some contexts have a favorable meaning, as when applied to poets or *beaux esprits*. Exemplifying this last is the employment of the verb *resver* by the Baroque poets Théophile de Viau[3] (1590–1626) and Marc Antoine Girard de Saint-Amant[4] (1594–1661). Richelet further notes that the word is occasionally used for "the action of a spirit that thinks profoundly." Descartes referred to his *Meditations* as his reveries in letters to Huygens of June 1, 1639, and November 12, 1640 (Raymond 1962a, 162–63). Victor Gourevitch notes that "Sorbière, in the Epistle Dedicatory to his 1649 French translation of Hobbes's *De cive*, had expressed his preference for 'the reveries of Hobbes, Gassendi and Descartes' to the more serious thoughts of some other philosophers" (2012, 489).

In her letters of the 1670s, Mme de Sévigné speaks of dark, feverish or feverlike reveries but also uses the term to designate odd or bizarre ideas and sometimes uses the word as almost equivalent to sustained reflections (see the passages cited in Sommer's lexicon for Mme. de Sévigné, 1866 s.v.).

Philippe Quinault's libretto for Jean-Baptiste Lully's very popular opera *Phaeton* (1686) has the heroine say (Act 1, scene 2, lines 7–8), "one must be in love in order to feel the charm of *la rêverie*"—echoing perhaps Pierre de Ronsard, who in the sixteenth century had used the verb *resver* in such romantic contexts (see Morrissey 1980, 283–84).

Bernard de Fontenelle's widely read, most famous work, *Conversations on the Plurality of Worlds* (1686) has the philosophical interlocutors begin by agreeing on the "sweetness of *la rêverie*" produced by the contemplation of the stars on a clear night. The elderly Fontenelle advised and was much admired by Rousseau (see *Confessions* OC 1:280).

APPENDIX

Maurice comte de Saxe, with irony, titled his famous and rather disjointed book on the art of war *Mes rêveries* (1757).

In the two or three generations prior to the writing and then the first publication (1782) of Rousseau's *Rêveries*, a favorable connotation for the word, as connoting a rich form of sometimes serious, sometimes playful consciousness can be seen in the poetry of Jean-Baptiste-Louis Gresset published in the 1730s and 1740s and in a number of works published, often anonymously, in France as well as in England and elsewhere (e.g., Bar 1745; Champigny 1774; Mountain 1777; Imbert 1778; in at least one case the book is explicitly indebted to Rousseau—Weylar 1770). The fourth edition (1762) of the dictionary of the Académie française has as one of its definitions of *rêverie*: "thought in which one lets one's imagination go"—which can be "profound and continual" (see also ibid., s.v. *rêver*, fourth definition: "to think, to meditate profoundly on something").

Rousseau's America was thus not as undiscovered as Sainte-Beuve suggested: the continent had Indigenous inhabitants.

Notes

Preface

1. The apparent exception (which proves the rule) is Montaigne, who is, however, only ambiguously to be counted among the political philosophers.
2. OC 3:13–14, 29. In *The Confessions*, OC 1:362, Rousseau applies to himself the expression "to walk alone in a new route."
3. "L'homme de la nature éclairé par la raison": *Dialogues*, OC 1:864–65, 935–36, 939.
4. Fragment #10 of *Letter to Beaumont*, OC 4:1019 (see also *Letter to Beaumont*, OC 4:968 and *Emile*, OC 4:524–25, 857–59). Rousseau's vision of the "sage" as dwelling in an unfree political world anticipates Georg Wilhelm Friedrich Hegel's characterization of the sage amid the "unhappiness of the Roman world" as "the age of complete despotism, of the decline of all public or community life" (2016, 265, 317).
5. "When an Author does not wish to repeat himself incessantly. . . . His Writings then explain one another, and the last ones, when there is method, always presuppose the first ones. There, that is what I have always tried to do" (*Letter to Beaumont*, OC 4:950–51).

Introduction

1. Rousseau died July 2, 1778, four days after his sixty-sixth birthday.
2. This will be the form of reference to chapters and paragraphs of *The Reveries*: thus "4:1" means first paragraph of the fourth chapter or "Walk."
3. Jean Starobinski bizarrely comments (1971, 216–17; 1988, 180–81), "For Jean-Jacques, the understanding of self is not a problem: it is a given." The "response to this question is instantaneous." That "is the privilege of the intuitive understanding, which is immediate presence to oneself, and which constitutes itself as an entirety in a unique act of the sentiment." As for "the *Reveries*, where everything is to be begun again," "to the extent that Jean-Jacques encloses himself in his delirium and loses his attachments with humans, the understanding of himself *appears* to him more complex and more difficult" (my italics).
4. Leo Strauss, in his first (1947) major writing on Rousseau, focusing on the *First Discourse*, was led to overestimate Rousseau's deep but ultimately limited overlap with Socrates and the ancients; Strauss corrected this in his subsequent writings on Rousseau (esp. 1953, chap. VI A; also 1959, 37, 50–53, 266; and 1975, 89–95). As Jonathan Marks (2014) has pointed out in a brief essay that is very helpful in understanding Strauss on Rousseau, "on being asked by [Wilmoore] Kendall why he did not include 'On the

Intention of Rousseau' in a collection of his work, Strauss responded this way: 'As for my recent book, I did not include my article on Rousseau because I believe that the chapter on Rousseau in *Natural Right and History* is a more mature and clearer version of the same subject' (Strauss to Kendall, January 19, 1960, in Kendall, 2002, 213; contrast what I believe is the deep misunderstanding of Strauss on Rousseau in Meier 2006, 66–71 and also 110–11—a misunderstanding that is well addressed by Marks).

5. Xenophon, *Memorabilia* 4.2.24ff. (cf. *Education of Cyrus* 7.2.20ff.); Plato, *Apology of Socrates* 21–23, *Alcibiades* 124a, 129a, 132c–d; *Phaedrus* 230a; *Philebus* 48c; *Lovers* 138a. Meier 1984, n42 directs us also to Hobbes's introduction to *Leviathan*, where "nosce te ipsum, read thyself" is interpreted as directing us to "the *similitude* of the thoughts and passions of one man to the thoughts and passions of another" (my italics).

6. For Rousseau's extensive and reflective study of Plato, evidenced not least in his notes on his copy of the works of Plato (British Museum, G.16721–5), in Ficino's (1550) Latin, supplemented by Simon Grynaeus, see Vaughan 1915, 1:2–3; Havens 1946, 68–69; Barker 1951, 388–90; Masters 1968, 14–15, 22–24, 99–106, 233, 443; Grimsley 1973, 53–55; Williams 2012, 110; and above all, Silverthorne 1973, who has observed that Rousseau's markings and signs of approval in his copy indicate that he paid special attention to the death scene in Plato's *Phaedo* and to *Laws* 713, 715c, 738e, 778d, 835c–37a, 856b, 874e–75d, 932d, 942a–43a, 945b, 949e–51a, 952c–d, along with the *Statesman* and *Republic*.

7. As Rousseau has his Savoyard vicar highlight, when the latter says, "the death of Socrates, engaged in philosophizing tranquilly with his friends, is the most sweet that one could desire" (*Emile*, OC 4:626); see similarly the portrait of the avatar of Socrates in Rousseau's unpublished, untitled allegorical fragment on God and revelation, OC 4:1052–53. It is characteristic of Rousseau, and speaks to the difference between him and Socrates, that he ignores or suppresses the fact that Plato has Socrates, just prior to drinking the hemlock poison, leave his friends to their investigative dialogue about the arguments for the immortality of the soul, while the philosopher goes into another room to spend his final hours conversing in private with his family—including his wife with their three sons, Lamprocles, Sophroniscus, and Menexenus, the last a babe in arms (*Apology* 34d6): see *Phaedo* 116b6 and Burnet 1911 ad loc.: "As the conversation recorded in the *Phaedo* began in the morning, and it is now close upon sunset on one of the longest days of the year, it is plain that Socrates spent several hours alone with the women and children. There is no trace of indifference to them." See also Burnet 1911, ad 60a2.

8. The manuscript's lack of capitalization of "reveries" (ignored in most printed editions) has been spotlighted by Crogiez 1997, 28, suggesting that this "indicates that the text is related uniquely to its author, expressing his singularity" and referring to Tripet's entry on *The Reveries* in the *Dictionnaire de Jean-Jacques Rousseau* (Trousson and Eigeldinger 1995, 809). Meier (2016, xiv, 13; 2022, n31) lays even more stress on this point, though he seems unaware of these preceding scholars' work.

9. Butterworth 1979, 151; Davis 1999, 62.

10. The expression "Solitary Walker" never appears in the body of *The Reveries* but only in the title. On the (separate) title page of the polished manuscript of the first seven chapters, Rousseau wrote only the title, at the top of the page, followed by two short drawn lines, one thick and one thin, without any further indication of himself as author. In sharp contrast with his immediately previous work, *Dialogues*, the names "Rousseau" and "Jean-Jacques," or "J. J." are almost never mentioned in *The Reveries*—

the exceptions are 2:18 and 6:3. The title of each of the first seven chapters is usually written at the top of the first page of the manuscript, followed by one or two drawn lines of varying lengths and then usually a short space (the sixth chapter has a sentence inserted later into the space), then the beginning of the text. For Rousseau's painstaking attention to the way his name appears on the title pages of his works, see *Heloise*, second preface (OC 2:27).

11. Marcel Raymond, in his introduction to the Pléiade edition (1:lxxx), protests: *The Reveries* constitute only "in small part, of true reveries"; Rousseau "defines the art of dreaming, rather than engaging in dreams"; "*Meditations*, that is the general subtitle that fits them best." To which Philonenko (1984, 3:344n1) rejoins, "Let's not forget that reveries and meditations (see Senancour [e.g., 1798]) are less separated in the 18th century than in our days." One thing is certain: we do *not* find in *The Reveries* what Starobinski bizarrely claims (1971, 417, 419; 1988, 354–55)—"a voice that, moved by the memory of a first reverie . . . , allows itself to be carried and to drift, on the thread of his descriptive reflection, into a second reverie. . . . To read the *Reveries*, is therefore to immerse oneself in the quasi-continuous current of a *second* reverie."

12. "Preface to a Second Letter to Bordes" (OC 3:105; 106—"a system true but afflicting"); see also preface to *Narcisse* (OC 2:964), "Letter to Philopolis" (OC 3:232), and *Confessions* (OC 1:368). In the second autobiographical letter to Malesherbes (January 12, 1762, OC 1:1136), Rousseau indicates that the system is laid out especially in "my three principal writings," the *First* and *Second Discourses* and *Emile*. The system is stressed in Rousseau's penultimate work, *Dialogues* (OC 1:930–37). For the most helpful overall presentation, see Melzer 1990; see also the pathbreaking Masters 1968, as well as Millet 1966; Goldschmidt 1974 and 1983 (see esp. 1983, 13); Cranston 1982, 242 and 289; Dent 1989; O'Dea 2014; and CW 1:xv–xxvi.

13. Kant 1942, 58–59; see also Staël 1788, 80–82 and Philonenko 1984, 1:8–9 and 3:309–10.

14. Rousseau did refer to his *Second Discourse* as his "sad reveries," disparagingly, in a letter to Voltaire of September 10, 1755 (OC 3:226); Rousseau had spoken of "the more dangerous reveries of such men as Hobbes and Spinoza" in his *First Discourse* (OC 3:28).

15. 1:12 and 1:13; 2:4; see also 4:1 and 4:31.

16. See OC 1:11, 58, 88, 107–8, 123, 165, 169, 176, 243, 245 (recalling 107–8 as a *rêve*), 255, 256; for a couple of similarly light and/or erotic usages in the second part of *The Confessions*, see 1:374 and the very explicit 1:445.

17. In the third autobiographical letter to Malesherbes (January 26, 1762, OC 1:1138), Rousseau writes, "I only began to live on April 9, 1756."

18. OC 1:368; see also the reveries of a philosopher in the unpublished, untitled allegorical fragment on God and revelation, OC 4:1044–54 (date uncertain but after 1750: see the editors' notes, OC 1:1766–67).

19. Meier referring us to *First Discourse* (OC 3:27–28), *Emile* (OC 4:242 and 560), *Letters Written from the Mountain* (OC 3:748), *Letter to Beaumont* (OC 4:1003), as well as *Government of Poland* (OC 3:1041).

20. He does not speak of reveries in these two passages, but later he seems to refer back to these experiences as "reveries" (OC 1:171).

21. See the foreshadowing of this at OC 1:57–58 (speaking of a trip he took at the age of sixteen): "I was in that short but precious moment of life when its expansive

plenitude extends, so to speak, our being by all our sensations, and embellishes in our eyes entire nature with the charm of our existence."

22. See also Rousseau's account of his praying each morning in his mid-twenties (*Confessions* OC 1:236): he asked only, he says, for "an innocent and tranquil life, exempt from vice, from sadness, from painful needs" and "the death of the just"; and he prayed, he says, not only for himself but also for his beloved maman (Mme de Warens). On the other hand, there is a manuscript, carefully written in Rousseau's hand, of a prayer composed not long after this, when he had begun to live apart from Mme de Warens: it is much more conscience stricken and guilt ridden than the preceding would suggest (see Cranston 1982, 135, quoting the Saussure manuscript at the Geneva Public and University Library, pp. 96–98, and commenting, "Rousseau was no longer praying together with *maman*; he was now praying, as he was living, alone").

23. My italics; part 1, letter 23, OC 2:77–79; see also the end of part 1, letter 18, OC 2:69, and contrast the end of part 1, letter 38, OC 2:116.

24. This invented character, despite being given the family name of Rousseau (OC 1:663), is not to be simply identified with the author, who explains his purpose in inventing this character, and in explicitly and emphatically distinguishing him from "J. J." (which is the author, as viewed by the character "Rousseau") as follows: "it was required necessarily that I say from what perspective, *if I had been another*, I would have viewed a person *such as I am*" (*Dialogues*, "On the Subject and Form of This Writing," OC 1:665; my italics. After this preface, Rousseau as author speaks directly only in his footnotes. See the first footnote, 1:680). What most sharply distinguishes the invented character "Rousseau" from "the Author of *Emile* and *Heloise*" (OC 1:673) is that the character "Rousseau" is no writer, no author of any books, but only a reader of them and especially of the books of "J. J." The character "Rousseau" indicates early on his imperfect understanding of the author—by identifying the author as an "inhabitant" of the "ideal world" constructed by "Rousseau" and thereby not as one of the "wise": contrast OC 1:673 with 669–70.

25. OC 1:814, 819–20, 826–27, 858. For a couple of less heavenly elaborations, consider on one hand the fantasy society envisaged by the tutor "Jean-Jacques" in the digression at *Emile* book 4 end, and on the other hand, the "ideal world" envisaged by the character "Rousseau" at the start of the *Dialogues* (OC 1:668–73). In addition, it is to be noted that the *Dialogues* is as a whole a fictive product of Rousseau's creative imagining of friends: see especially the closing paragraph.

26. OC 4:854. Rousseau also refers in a footnote to Homer as "that old dreamer" (*ce vieux rêveur*; OC 4:784); Emile's tutor "Jean-Jacques" confesses at one point late in the novel (OC 4:790) that he is intoxicated to the point of delirium as he imagines the final stages of the courtship of Emile and Sophie.

27. To Paul-Claude Moultou, May 29, 1761 (CC 8:338 or #1423).

28. OC 4:242. For a notable scholarly example of the fulfillment of Rousseau's displeased prediction, see Ravier 1941.

29. OC 4:350–51. See also the third of the (unpublished, so-called) *Lettres morales* #3 (OC 4:1095): "So let us not become astonished to see proud and vain philosophy lose itself in its reveries, and the noblest geniuses waste themselves on puerilities." Cf. Tripet 1979, 28–29: "En un premier temps, le mot est donc négatif, et il sert méraphoriquement et ironiquement à qualifier les idées et les systèmes plus ou moins faux, selon l'usage tout à fait courant d'alors."

30. The Pléiade editors are moved to offer here a Platonic comment (OC 1:1852): "Le désir sans fin (Éros) appelle une autre sorte de jouissance." But Rousseau does not mention eros in this context.

31. The Solitary Walker will recall how "meditation in retreat, the study of nature, the contemplation of the universe, forced" him as "a solitary, to launch himself incessantly toward the author of things and to search *with a sweet anxiety* the end of all he saw and the cause of all he felt" (3:6; my italics). In these two testimonies, there is a possible foreshadowing of Søren Kierkegaard's account of the fundamental experience of primordial humanity: "In the state of innocence the human being is not merely animal, for if at any time in his life he were merely an animal, he never would become a human. So spirit is present, but as immediate, as *dreaming*" (Kierkegaard 2014, 53; my italics). "In this state of innocence there is peace and repose; but at the same time there is something else, something that is not dissension and strife, for there is nothing against which to strive. What, then, is it? Nothing. But what effect does nothing have? It begets angst/anxiety [*Angest*]. This is the profound secret of innocence, that at the same time it is angst. Dreaming, spirit projects its own reality; yet this reality is nothing; but innocence always sees this nothing outside itself.... Angst is a *sympathetic antipathy* and an *antipathetic sympathy*.... We speak of sweet angst, a sweet anxiousness; we speak of a strange anxiety, a shy anxiety, etc" (50).

32. Cf. Vallette 1911, 411–12. The two forms of reverie, the creative and the awed, are somewhat congruent with the two forms of imagination that Jacob Klein (1989, 18–19 and 112ff.) insightfully discerns in the Platonic Socrates's teaching, including not least in the famous image of the divided line in *Republic* 509d–511e: on one hand, *mimnesis*, the faculty by which the imagination playfully fashions, out of the experiences given in the "trusted" empirical world, "unreal" images for itself to enjoy; on the other hand, *eikasia*, the faculty by which the imagination seriously apprehends the given empirical world as itself an image—of a deeper, "higher" realm of reality. But for Plato, the most serious forms of the latter are found in mathematics and in what Klein suggests calling "dianoetic eikasia" (op. cit., 119) centered on *dialectical* "gatherings" (*sunagōgai*) and "distinguishing" (*diaireseis*); in profound contrast to Plato, neither the mathematical nor the dialectical in this sense are ever themes of Rousseau's treatment of imagination.

33. OC 1:816–18. See also Rousseau's letter to the Maréchal of Luxembourg of May 27, 1759 (CC 6:107 or #821): "you know that the Solitary all have the romantic spirit [*l'esprit Romanesque*]. I am full of that spirit; I feel it and it in no way afflicts me. Why would I seek a cure for Such a sweet madness, since it contributes to rendering me happy? People of the world and of the Court, don't go believing yourselves more Wise than me: we differ only by our chimeras."

34. In the *Second Discourse* Rousseau uses this formulation twice for the original solitary state (OC 3:160 and 219), which he also repeatedly terms the "pure state of Nature" (*le pur état de Nature*; OC 3:132, 147, 170, 216, 217) or "the State of Nature in its purity" (*l'État de Nature dans sa pureté*; OC 3:191); he never thus refers to the latter state of "savages" living in primitive society, depicted in the frontispiece. At OC 3:208, he speaks of original solitary individuals as "true savage humans" (*veritable hommes sauvages*); at 3:218, he speaks of "the State of Nature, that is to say, of a state where humans live isolated" (*l'État de Nature, c'est-à-dire, d'un état où les hommes vivoient isolés*). Similarly, when summarizing the core of his thought in the *Letter to Beaumont* (OC

4:936), Rousseau characterizes the human's "original goodness" as that of a being who "has compared nothing, and who has not at all seen his relationships. In that state the human would know only himself," and "limited to only physical instinct, he is nothing, he is beast/stupid [bête]; that is what I have brought to light in my *Discourse on Inequality*." A helpful brief statement of Rousseau's conception of human sociability in his "system" is in the Letter to Philopolis (OC 3:232): "Since you claim to attack through my own system, do not forget, I beg you, that according to me society is natural to the human species like decrepitude is to the individual, and that the arts, the Laws, the Governments are necessary for peoples like crutches are to old men. The whole difference is that the condition of old men follows from only the nature of the human, and that of society follows from the human race not immediately, as you say of it, but only, as I have proven, with the help of certain extrinsic circumstances which could exist or not exist, or at least arrive more soon or more late, and consequently accelerate or retard the progress." Very helpful in clarifying Rousseau's conception of the state of nature is Plattner 1979, esp. 99–101.

35. *Dialogues* OC 1:864–65, 935–36 ("this man of nature who lives a truly human life"), 939; see also Starobinski 1971, 341 (1988, 291); Ancelet 1979; Hoffman 2010, 294.

36. OC 1:850. In the *Second Discourse*, Rousseau identifies the primitive state (*état primitif*) with the originally solitary, prelinguistic state (OC 2:142, 147, 151, 160 [*cette condition primitive*], 170, 208 [*l'état primitif de Nature*]).

37. OC 4:638; quoting Le Beau 1738, 2:69 (the Pléiade edition in a footnote ad loc. mistakenly cites 2:70). Rousseau fails to report what Le Beau goes on to say (about the Canadian natives), "they apply themselves to almost nothing except serious games of chance," "by which they are so animated, that there are some simple enough to prepare themselves by austerities lasting several days, and who spare nothing in order to gain happy luck." Le Beau proceeds to describe in some detail the gambling games of the natives. Rousseau also fails to report that at 2:18 Le Beau tells how the natives ridicule Europeans' penchant for walking, and say, "if this is for thinking, dreaming [*rêver*], seeing or speaking, why don't you sit down?" On natives as daydreamers, see also Le Beau 2:9; but Le Beau never uses the noun *rêverie*, only the verbal form *rêver*. Le Beau's book is repeatedly cited as an authority on natives by Rousseau in *Emile*: OC 4:254, 278–79, 416, 638.

38. OC 1:812–15. A bit earlier (1:827), the character "Rousseau" has spoken of "J. J.'s" hope for human society in the afterlife: "remaining alone on earth, he awaits the moment of leaving it in order to see realized at last his favorite visions, and to find again in a better order of things a fatherland and friends."

39. Part 4, letter 11, OC 2:487; the Pléiade editor Bernard Guyon, noting that Rousseau inserted the word for "reverie" in a marginal addition to the manuscript, complains of Rousseau's having been untrue to the romantic nature of his character St. Preux: "nous aurions préféré un peu moins de vertu et un peu plus d'amour [sic]" (OC 2:1615). See also 2:482 and the foreshadowing back in the striking part 1, letter 23 to Julie, 2:77–80.

1. "First Walk"—Rousseau's Introduction

1. Thérèse le Vasseur (or Levasseur), with whom Rousseau lived, starting in 1745 until his death, and whom he married in 1768. Her love for him is attested in a remark-

ably moving letter she managed to write by herself (she was barely literate) in the middle of the night of June 23, 1762 ("Ce Merquedies a quateur du matin") declining his suggestion, in his letter to her of June 17 (CC 11:95–97 or #1880; see also #1879), that she not follow him into exile, while declaring that her heart had always been his and would never change as long as God allowed them life—and adding that she wished for them to share all their sorrows together: "mon quer a tousgour etés pour vous e quies ne changeraes gamés tan que dieu vous doneuraes des gour e a moi osies. Qule Çatisfasion pour moi deu nous regondre tous les deus e deu pacés tous no douleur ançable" (CC 11:139 or #1904, with a photo of the manuscript).

2. Davis 1999, 62; cf. Kennedy 2014, 417, 419.

3. "About fifteen years before this was written, that is, on June 9, 1762, the Parliament of Paris condemned Rousseau's *Emile* and issued a writ of arrest for him.... During the next twelve years or so, he was forced to flee one place after another." In speaking of "fifteen years and more," Rousseau may have in mind "the events surrounding his bitter quarrel with Mme d'Epinay [and with his erstwhile friends Denis Diderot and Frédéric-Melchior Grimm] in December 1757" (CW ad loc.). In *The Confessions* (OC 1:474), Rousseau speaks of this latter time as "the great revolution in my destiny," the "catastrophe that has divided my life into two such different parts, and that from a very slight cause has drawn such terrible effects."

4. For the "impenetrability of the mystery," see also *Dialogues* OC 1:662–64, 878–79, 883, 990.

5. The brackets are in red in the manuscript p. 3. Osmont 1934, 36–39 insists that the red here and elsewhere, especially on manuscript pp. 3, 11, 81, and 112, is all retouching done by one of the original two editors, Du Peyrou or the Marquis de Girardin, indicating passages to be removed from the printed version in order to tone down manifestations of insanity and to avoid mention of living people's names. The biggest such intervention is on manuscript p. 112, in the Sixth Walk, where some rather feverish marginalia as well as part of the main text is crossed out by red and also dark lines (see OC 1:1054–55 and notes of the editor).

On the other hand, it has been suggested that the interventions in red are by Rousseau himself: Spink 1948, xlvii; see also Eigeldinger 2010, 167–68. If so, the red markings could indicate that Rousseau had some regretful awareness of the extreme of his paranoia at these points in the manuscript of *The Reveries*.

In any case, starting in 1768 and during the last decade of his life, Rousseau insistently believed that the Duke of Choiseul, the prime minister of France (who fell from office in disgrace in December 1770), was working through a worldwide network of secret agents to implicate Rousseau with Robert-François Damiens, who had made a notorious bloody attempt to assassinate Louis XV on January 5, 1757 (see OC 1:xlvi–lv, lx). Rousseau's first written expression of this paranoid delusion is in a long autobiographical letter to Claude Anglancier de St. Germain of February 26, 1770 (in two drafts, CC 37:248–95 or #6673). Although such an elaborate, worldwide plot is incredible, it is true that Choiseul, following Voltaire, was one of the enemies who spread slander against Rousseau.

6. For Rousseau's febrile claim as to the unanimity of the human race in persecuting him, see similarly 3:24, 8:8 (thrice), 8:12, and the long letter to St. Germain of February 26, 1770 (CC 37:248–95 or #6673); only slightly less extreme is Rousseau's introduction to *Dialogues* OC 1:662, where he ascribes the plot to "all Paris, all France,

all Europe . . . this unanimous agreement . . . of an entire generation"; see also OC 1:759, 764, 880–81; but contrast "The Frenchman" at 876 (and context)—"The entire world, whatever you can say, has not joined the plot. I know decent people who do not hate J. J. at all." And the character "Rousseau" at 895 (and context)—"Do you think the entire world really acquiesces in it [the plot]?"; and see similarly 969–70.

7. Attempted retrospective diagnoses of Rousseau's mental illness have been legion and have followed the successive fashions of medical and psychiatric history (for a survey, see Wacjman 1992, 1996). The leading candidate nowadays is intermittent acute porphyria, a genetically based enzyme deficiency; this was submitted most fully by Bensoussan 1974, and more recently "discovered" by Androutsos and Geroulanos 2000 (see Jardin's harsh accompanying comment). As Trousson (1976) justly remarked in a review of Bensoussan's volume, "one remains a bit skeptical about the pertinence of these post mortem diagnostics, always hazardous, even if the analyst is a doctor" (see also Trousson 1977, 349: "psychoanalysis post mortem and autopsy without a cadaver").

8. See O'Dea 2003, 46–47; the plot is referred to in every one of the ten chapters of *The Reveries* (Barguillet 1991, 36; Grace 2006, n33); manifestations of Rousseau's persecution neurosis are also pervasive in the playing cards previously described, especially cards #6, 7, 8, 9, 12, 13, 14, 19, 20, 22, and 24.

9. 1:5; Rousseau does not refer to the threats to his life and limb and household—the stoning, the fleeing and pursuit, the exile: it is the assault on his reputation (the hurt to his amour propre) that he stresses; see similarly *Dialogues* OC 1:926; in the appendix to the *Dialogues*, "History of the Preceding Writing" (OC 1:985), Rousseau criticizes himself for this focus. For a brief account of all the harms that Rousseau did in fact suffer, see Raymond's introduction, OC 1:l–lv. For evidence of the organized persecutions and conspiracies directed against Rousseau especially emanating from Voltaire, see Cranston 1982, 191n, 194n, 254; 1997, 7, 9–10, 32, 55, 85, 100–103 (Voltaire's "most vicious attack"), 108, 122, 126, 147, 157–59 (Walpole), 162–63 (Samuel Johnson), 168–69 (Hume's conniving, though in response to Rousseau's outrageous slanders of Hume), 175. For earlier, milder public persecution, see Cranston 1982, 283–84. For the emergence and growth of Grimm's malicious envy, see Cranston 1982, 310–11 and the evidence assembled from Grimm's writings in his *Correspondance littéraire* (Grimm and Diderot 1829–31) by the Pléiade editors' long note 1 to OC 1:469, rebutting Sainte-Beuve's (1857–70, 7:287–328) defense of Grimm and attack on Rousseau as a liar in regard to Grimm; the Pléiade editors do concede that Rousseau exaggerated and was carried away by his "unhealthy imagination." For evidence that Voltaire began his malicious plotting against Rousseau as early as 1754, see Jean-André De Luc 1798, *Discours preliminaire*, part 4, cxi–cxx—writing about his personal conversations with and observations of both Voltaire and Rousseau in 1754.

10. At the age of twenty-eight, Rousseau wrote of himself that he had "an invincible penchant to melancholy which makes, despite myself, the torment of my soul; temperamentally and habitually being unhappy, I carry within me a source of sadness whose origin I cannot well discern" ("Memoir Presented to M. de Mably on the Education of M. His Son," OC 4:21). But twenty years passed before signs of mental breakdown appeared; the CC editor's notes at 6:66–67 indicate that the first serious manifestation, in Rousseau's surviving epistles, of paranoia about a hidden conspiracy occurs in the missive to Toussaint-Pierre Lenieps of April 5, 1759 (CC 6:57–65 or #795) and became blatant in

1766 and the following years; for the collection of citations of all manifestations of paranoia in the surviving letters, see the index volume of CC 52:332. In the correspondence of the autumn of 1761, one can follow Rousseau's downward spiral as he became obsessed by a paranoid delusion that the printer who was bringing out *Emile* was engaged in a conspiracy with the Jesuits to prevent or to distort the publication: 9:184–85, 213–14, 218, 223, 245–46, 253, 282, 289–90, 301–3, 319–21, 323–28, 341–48 or #1512, 1529, 1532, 1535, 1548, 1554, 1567, 1571, 1580, 1587, 1591, 1602. This obsession eventually rendered Rousseau "prey to a crisis of veritable delirium" (as the Pléiade editors put it, in their notes to the passage in *The Confessions*, OC 1:566, where Rousseau discusses "this madness" that came over him). See also the editors' notes to the letters to Malesherbes, OC 1:1845–54, including this quote (1846) from one of several compassionate letters that Malesherbes wrote to Rousseau in reply, December 25, 1761 (CC 9:355 or #1610; see also Grosclaude 1960, 32–37, 98–99): "This somber melancholy that constitutes the misfortune of your life is prodigiously augmented by the illness and the solitude, but I believe that it is natural to you and that the cause of it is physical." See also Malesherbes's estimate of Rousseau's *passion atrabilaire* in Grosclaude 1960, 94–97. Cranston 1991, 316 does explain that and how "Rousseau's suspicions were not entirely unfounded." For an assemblage of the principal biographical evidence for Rousseau's "undoubtedly suffering from paranoia," of having "certainly fallen victim to delusions of persecution," see Cranston 1997, 129n, 157, 159–60, 162, 165–67 (delusionary fantasies of persecution by Hume), 171–75. See also the firsthand testimony in the recollections of Rousseau's friend De Luc (1798, xcix–c). For a brief survey of alternative ways scholars have treated the expressions of Rousseau's mental illness, see Kelly 1987, 210–15.

11. Cranston 1997, 143–46, citing Rousseau's gratified letters at the time (for which, see CC 27:213–15, 235, 246–47, 255, 259, 261–62, 269, 274–76 or #4788, 4804, 4812, 4817, 4821, 4823, 4829, 4833).

12. Cranston 1997, 176; Coignet 1825 (465, "he cried out, in a moment of enthusiasm, that this was one of the happy days of his life"); but in the *Dialogues* (OC 1:844), the character "Rousseau" speaks bitterly of the way "the musicians in Lyon" treated "J. J's" music—referring to an unsuccessful public performance by a reluctant orchestra of an outdated motet by Rousseau, who was so hurt by this one episode that he then abruptly left Lyon after two happy months (Coignet 1825, 468–69).

13. Cranston 1982, 231; see also Wilson 1957, 275–346 and Kafker 1973, with an epigraph quoting Diderot's foreword to volume 8 of the *Encyclopedia*: "however severely you judge this work, remember that it was begun, continued, and completed by a small number of isolated men who were thwarted in their intentions, viewed in the worst possible light, and slandered and insulted in the most atrocious manner."

14. Regarding Rousseau's early publications, the observation of Cranston (1982, 240) is just: "Rousseau is often spoken of as suffering from persecution mania, but he cannot be accused of regarding the critics of his first *Discours* as enemies, or reacting with excessive emotion to their strictures; his replies were reasoned and reasonable; they were also detailed, taking up—if we include the preface to *Narcisse* among them—something like three times as much space as the *Discours* itself. Admittedly Rousseau's critics were most respectful." Contrast Starobinski's (1971, 19; 1988, 8) very inaccurate assessment: "In the first *Discourse* he plays the role of the accuser, but from the moment he meets with contradiction he finds himself back in the situation of being the accused."

15. OC 1:278; see similarly 1:325, "I am obsessed by the spies"—as well as, again, the long fevered letter to St. Germain of February 26, 1770 (CC 37:248–95 or #6673) and the much earlier letter to the Marquise de Verdelin of September 4, 1762 (CC 13:9–10 or #2131).

16. *"Leur ligue"*—*Confessions* OC 1:381; 383, 386, 491, 575–78.

17. *Confessions* OC 1:585 ("my cruel imagination which ceaselessly torments itself in foreseeing evils, by seeing evils that do not yet exist"); see also 1:219 ("my cruel imagination which always goes ahead of my misfortunes"), 1:566–67 ("this madness"), 1:568 ("the disorder in my poor head"), 1:572 ("imaginary evils, more cruel for me than real evils"), 1:573 ("it must be admitted that these letters did not do great honor to my rationality"). For earlier evidence of Rousseau's cognizance of his own *folie*, see, among others, the letter to Malesherbes of November 20, 1761 (CC 9:253 or #1554) as well as the first autobiographical letter to Malesherbes of January 4, 1762 (OC 1:1131–32): "my disordered imagination"; "such an attack of madness . . . not at all my own will"; and also the letter to Buirette de Darmont de Belloy of March 12, 1770 (CC 37:323–34 or #6686): "the most hideous object never frightened me when I was an infant, but a figure hidden under a white sheet sent me into paroxysms; in this regard as in many others, I will remain an infant until death" (see similarly *Confessions* OC 1:566; *Reveries* 2:13, 22).

18. OC 1:648–56, esp. 651t, "pursued in all my refuges by the subterranean intrigues of my secret persecutors"; see 1:364n, 372n, 389n.

19. Rousseau is (sadly) in earnest; while pitying the extreme of his megalomania here, one cannot help but be reminded, in contrast, of the similar, but deliberately hilarious, boast of Aristophanes in the parabasis of the *Acharnians* (652–54).

20. See similarly 8:6: "indignation, fury, delirium, took possession of me." See also Butterworth 1979, xviii. Garagnon 2010 characterizes the First Walk as "une expression hypertrophiée de l'indignation."

21. According to the character "Rousseau," the *Dialogues* were written largely out of the motive of righteous indignation, and this seems confirmed by the first paragraph of the author's preface (OC 1:836, 661; see also 842). Shklar (1969, 28) characterizes Rousseau's entire oeuvre as an "exercise in indignation."

22. Rousseau's portrait of himself as a wise man convulsed by righteous punitive indignation is in tension with his broad project of trying to heighten compassion or pity and to lessen cruelty in the "bourgeois" civilization that he saw as all too ruthless, heartless, and punitive. (When in the *Second Discourse* Rousseau attacks philosophers for their tranquility in the face of human suffering, he does so in the name not of indignation or of anger but of pity—pace Coleman 2011, 97, who misunderstands this key passage).

23. See especially Plato's *Apology of Socrates* 25c–26a; *Crito* 47b–49e; *Gorgias* 468b–d, 488a, 509e; *Greater Hippias* 296c; *Hipparchus* as a whole; *Meno* 77b–78b; *Phaedo* 68c5–69c2, 82a; *Protagoras* 345d–e, 352b–358d; *Republic* 336d, 381c, 413a, 451b, 505d–e, 517b–c; *Theaetetus* 173a, 176b–77a; *Cratylus* 386b–d, 398b; *Euthydemus* 281; *Sophist* 227d–30; and *Laws* bks. 9–10 as a whole (Silverthorne's [1973] study of Rousseau's marginal notes on Plato's *Laws* found no indication of special attention to the penal code and its discussion of criminal responsibility); Xenophon, *Memorabilia* 1.2.18–24, 3.13.1 and *Apology of Socrates to the Jury* 28; also Aristotle, *Nicomachean Ethics* 1110b and context compared with *Rhetoric* 1386b. For a full exposition, see L. Pangle 2009, 2014, 2020; for Xenophon's presentation, see L. Pangle 2013, 2015. See also Plutarch, *How One Might by Enemies Be Benefited* 90d–e;

On Absence of Anger (Peri Aorgāsias) 455a–b; and Seneca, *On Anger* 3.13. The Socratic thesis does not depend on any thought that "the wicked are punished by their own heart" (as Rousseau contends in *Emile*, OC 4:535). See also Leo Strauss's (1959, 234) eulogy of Kurt Riezler: "he could become angry but he never felt moral indignation.... When I try to see vividly what distinguishes wisdom from cleverness, I think of Riezler" (cf. Riezler 1975, 199–200). For a vivid juxtaposition of the commonsense roots of the contrasting Socratic and anti-Socratic (i.e., Rousseauian) perspectives on retributive justice, see Polybius 5.10.8 versus 5.11.5.

24. *Dialogues*, "History of the Preceding Writing" OC 1:985–86; see similarly *Dialogues* OC 1:937, 938, 896 (in these latter passages, the character "Rousseau" is speaking). For the righteous indignation in the heart of "Jean-Jacques" as "the man of nature"—an indignation that persistently recurs but without leading to lasting hateful feelings toward anyone—see *Dialogues*, OC 1:661, 790, 826, 860, 865, 887, 980, 986; also *Confessions*, e.g., OC 1:20 (and Kelly 2012), 312, 476–77, 585–86, 617; and *Letter to d'Alembert* OC 5:120, author's note (for Rousseau's attributing to indignation the motive for writing the *Letter to d'Alembert*, see his letter to Jacob Vernes of July 4, 1758, CC 5:106 or #664). For the deep and lasting passion of righteous indignation that Rousseau says animated his major political writings, see *Confessions* OC 1:495 as well as 1:327, 365 and *Letter to Beaumont*, OC 4:968b; see also OC 4:983b and 1022b, where Rousseau expresses his hope "to be avenged some day," as well as 1006 ("all my blood is on fire, and tears of indignation flow from my eyes"). On what animated him in writing his articles on music for the *Encyclopedia*, Rousseau wrote the following to Mme de Warens on January 27, 1749 (2:113 or #146): "I am showing my teeth:... I am out to bite back [*je tiens au cu et aux chausses*] people who have done me harm, and the bile gives me strength and similarly spirit/wit and knowledge.... Anger suffices for me and is worth an Apollo" (citing Boileau's *Satires* 1:14). For Rousseau's indignation about the reception of his ideas on music, see also *Confessions* OC 1:333–38. For the intensity with which Rousseau could express his righteous indignation, see the letter to Lenieps of April 5, 1759, and the editor's notes: CC 6:64–67 or #795. For the "unmitigated wickedness," in no degree traceable to ignorance, that Rousseau attributes to his enemy Grimm, see the introduction to volume 5 of CW, xxv–xxvi. Coleman (2011, 1, 97) observes: "Rousseau adopted as his motto a line" from "one of the angriest satires" of a "Roman writer for whom anger was a constant theme." Kelly (2012, 80n20) refers us to the "First Projected Preface" to "Le lévite d'Ephraïm" (OC 2:1205), where Rousseau tells of his inner struggle to transcend an episode of profound indignation that threatened to "devour his heart."

25. OC 4:586; see the Pléiade editors' note a, and Spink's introduction, OC 4:lxviii–lxix: "at the moment of recopying the first version of *Emile*, Rousseau proceeded to incorporate therein a little metaphysical essay independent of the general design of the *Profession of Faith* and in which his opposition to the doctrine of the passivity of judgment plays an essential role." See also Masson 1911, 122; and Rousseau's letter to Grimprel d'Offreville of October 4, 1761 (CC 9:143–47 or #1500).

26. In his earlier drafts, Rousseau wrote instead, "his moral liberty comes exactly from the same source" (OC 4:586, editors' note d).

27. See also the confused anti-Socratic formulations of the vicar at OC 4:589, 591, 592, 602, and above all 604 and 605 (the vicar's "vehement" conclusion).

28. Strauss 1966, 69; see also 76b–77t (and 73t on the normal weakening of righteous indignation in old age). Strauss might well have had in mind his beloved Lessing's *Minna von Barnhelm* Act 4, scene 6 (the wise Minna speaks while laughing at her lover's exaggerated sense of his suffering): "Can one not then while laughing be also very serious? Dear Major, laughing keeps us more rational than does vexation. . . . And am I the one who made it so, that all exaggeration is so easily made laughable?" In the same scene, Minna calls on her lover to stifle his bitter laughter at his being a victim of injustice, which she labels "the terrible laughter of misanthropy."

29. *Letter to d'Alembert* OC 5:24–25; cf. Pagani 2014, 2015. Although there is some mild humor and playfulness in the seventh chapter of *The Reveries* (J. Scott 2008, 139–41, 149–52; Kennedy 2014, 425), there is not a smidgen of the Aristophanean spirit in *The Reveries* (for the Solitary Walker's rare laughter, see 5:10; 6:1; 7.1, 26, 28; 8.7, 23; for very rare instances of Rousseau's laughter in *The Confessions*, see OC 1:243, 355b–56t; in *Dialogues*, see OC 1:905t—see also 984). By the same token, there is not much compassion in Aristophanes. In the *Letters Written from the Mountain*, OC 3:797, Rousseau rather bitterly deplores the ways of thinking by which "the Athenians applauded the impieties of Aristophanes and had Socrates put to death." In the *Letter to D'Alembert*, OC 5:111, he declares that "it was in the theater that the death of Socrates was prepared." But see St. Preux in *Heloise*, OC 2:252.

30. For the primordial root of tears in babies, see *Emile*, OC 4:261, 286–87 and the Favre manuscript, OC 4:76.

31. Strauss 2012, 38: it is "contrary to Plato's explicit meaning" in the *Phaedo* that "Socrates' dying becomes a poignant spectacle"; see also Strauss 1964, 61–62: "the Platonic dialogue brings to its completion what could be thought to have been completed by Aristophanes"; and Strauss 1964, 85, 116; 1989, 105–6, 125–26.

32. Riezler 1975, 176–77; see also Aristotle, *Nicomachean Ethics* 1127a20–b33.

33. See similarly 3:2 end: "the sad truth that time and reason have unveiled for me in making me feel my unhappiness has made me see that there was no remedy for it and there remained for me only to resign myself to it." Guéhenno 1955 speaks of "le dernier progrès dans le désespoir qui conduit à la sérénité." Yet, is it genuine serenity? Launay (1964, 93): "But the very idea of a 'resignation' shows that Jean-Jacques is not liberated from the obsession."

34. Rousseau refers cryptically to "an event as sad as it was unforeseen" that "came finally to efface from" his "heart this feeble ray of hope." For the scholarly disputes over which of several different candidates might be most eligibly identified as this event, see OC 1:lxxxiiiff.; for more recent reports, see Eigeldinger 2010, 9, favoring Osmont 1965 but taking note of Van Staen 2001. All these scholarly investigations obscure the massive and obvious fact that Rousseau intended the event to remain, as Eigeldinger puts it, "mysterious."

35. As Meier (2016, 203n) points out, contrary to what is printed in OC and CW, Rousseau did not capitalize or underline the word *dialogues* here or in 1:15 (manuscript pp. 9, 16), although he did capitalize the word in its subsequent appearance in 1:9 (manuscript p. 10).

36. In the *Dialogues*, see especially the long quote from "Jean-Jacques" at OC 1:952–54, where he rather monomaniacally asserts that the eventual vindication of his good repute is of such world-historical importance for the entire human race that if it fails,

then the way that he has been treated will become a model, and decent society will undergo an unprecedented worldwide collapse—"those who are good, completely handed over to the wicked, would become first their prey, finally their disciples; innocence would have no more asylum, and the earth, having become a hell, would be covered only with demons occupied in tormenting one another. No, Heaven will not at all allow so fatal an example to open for crime a new route, unknown until this day." In contrast to the character "Rousseau," "The Frenchman," stressing his greater knowledge of the facts and thus the insidious power of the plot, is much less confident that "J. J.'s" repute will be redeemed in future generations: OC 1:956–61.

37. For Rousseau's repeated suggestions that Satan or the satanic is behind the plot, see also 3:19—"the traitors silently entwined me with nets forged in the infernal depths"; and *Dialogues* OC 1:927, where Rousseau assimilates himself to Job (as he does also in "History of the Preceding Writing," OC 1:990).

38. The oratorians are a society of secular priests who take no monastic vows. In the *Dialogues* (OC 1:905–6), the character "Rousseau" says the oratorians have "become—I don't know how—the most ardent satellites of the conspiracy." Rousseau as author adds here a footnote in his own name: "Dangerous enemies if there ever were such, not only on account of the body that they compose and the colleges that they govern; but because they know even better than the philosophers how to hide their cruel animosity under a saintly and sweet demeanor." See also *Confessions* OC 1:503–6, 570–71 and Py 1969–71.

39. In the manuscript (p. 11), brackets in red are added at the start and very faintly at the end of this long passage on the doctors and oratorians. For the significance of these red markings in the manuscript, see note 5 above.

40. "To open any of his books, including those written at the very end of his life, is to be reminded that a genius can turn misfortune and neurosis to advantage" (Damrosch 2005, 440); see also Damrosch 2010, 238, as well as Kelly 2003, 141.

41. Lane 2006, 479: "everything we know about the textual history of the work undermines the idea that it was not intended for publication"; and 496: "all ten" chapters "were thoroughly revised, and the first seven were laid out in a fine copy"; see also Leigh 1979, 187–88; Butterworth 1979, 228–29; Crogiez 1997, 38; Davis 1999, 68–69, 90, 127; Todorov 1999, 50–51; Kelly 2003, 141; Friedlander 2004, 17; Meier 2016, 18–19 (but Meier misunderstands the French idiom, I believe, when he takes the use of the first-person plural at 1:12, 2:25, 3:13, 3:18, and 4:7 as "including possible readers in the course of the action"). This is not to deny that, as Ancelet (1979, 55) puts it, "it is a long way from the *Confessions* to the *Reveries*, from the glorification of the singular soul to the anonymity that fascinated the aged Rousseau."

42. See also Cotoni 2001, 297: "The unique narrator of these stories is in them the principal actor." Of course, *The Reveries* is not written to be staged; we do not have here a theatrical soliloquy like those that Rousseau was very fond of putting in the mouths of so many of his dramatic characters—for example, Iphis (OC 2:803–4), Le Cacique (2:822–23), Carime (2:831), Digizé (2:834–35), Dorante (2:850, 915, 919–20), Sophie (2:856), Carlin (2:900, 902, 907–8), Parafaragaramus (2:954–55), Angelique (2:998), Valere (2:1003), Lucinde (2:1007), Sulpitius (2:1031), Brutus (2:1033), Hesiode (2:1058), Ovide (12:063), Erithie (2:1064), Polycrate (2:1072), Themire (2:1073–74), Colette (2:1099–1100), Le Devin (2:1102), Colin (2:1105). Moreover, the Solitary Walker is not here in a quasi-dialogue with the audience of this writing, as is frequently the case in theatrical soliloquies.

43. 1:11; Rousseau first wrote "poor unfortunate mortal," then crossed out "mortal" and reinserted it before "unfortunate" (manuscript p. 12).

44. 1:12; "severe and sincere" are added above the line; and, as is pointed out by Meier 2016, 203n, contrary to what is printed in OC and CW, Rousseau did not capitalize or underline the word *confessions* either here or at 1:13, 1:15, or 2:4 (manuscript pp. 12, 14, 16, 24).

45. Meier (2016, ix, 18, 44) claims that "the *Rêveries* are not part of Rousseau's oeuvre in the demanding sense of that term," that "in a strict sense the *Rêveries* no longer belong to Rousseau's oeuvre"; but Meier does not reconcile this claim with these explicit declarations in the text contradicting his claim.

46. In Kelly's (1987, 241) crisp formulation: "The *Confessions* begins by asking God to assemble an audience for Rousseau. The *Reveries* begins by declaring quasi-divine independence from his audience." But then, of course, this means that *The Reveries* does imply an audience from which independence is being declared.

47. 1:13 end; my italics; see also 3:25; Rousseau characteristically does not, as did Socrates, closely link his hope for an incorporeal afterlife with an insistence on the radical superiority of a life of contemplative theorizing over and above a life of moral/civic virtue: see Plato's *Phaedo* as a whole and especially 68–69 and 82a–c (see Strauss's discussion of this dimension of the Socratic teaching on immortality in 2012, 36–37).

48. Starobinski 1971, 415: "throughout the *Reveries*, the development of the internal relation is accompanied by a reasoned justification for the exclusive relation of the self to itself, a justification that even comes to supplant the intimate dialogue whose advent it announced." See also Françon 1951, 782.

49. Rousseau first wrote and then crossed out "I had been thrown" (*j'aurais été projetté*; manuscript p. 12): By what or by whom? By God? Was this a foreshadowing of the dark theology that he will present at the end of the Second Walk?

50. "It is in any case certain that Rousseau was regarded and loved as a man of sorrows by a very large part of his admirers" (Starobinski 1971, 433; 1988, 367; and see the context). Farrell 2006, 292: "the paranoid element of Rousseau's confessional writings," for "later generations who would encounter Rousseau only in the pages of a book," would "become one of the most attractive elements of the work"; "even for the makers of the Revolution, where Rousseau's authority was cited on every side of the debate, it was his personal story, his heroism as a martyr of liberty, that constituted the source of his appeal" (referencing Blum 1989, 33–35 and McDonald 1965, 155–73). See also Meier 2016, 42, referring us to *Dialogues* OC 1:937 and *Letter to Beaumont* OC 4:1002.

51. See the fragment of the *Letter to Beaumont* (OC 4:1016): "They crucified my master ~~and they gave hemlock to a human who was worth more than me~~" (thus crossed out in the manuscript, according to the Pléiade editor). The Solitary Walker appears unlike Christ, however, in his complete lack of forgiveness of his present enemies. But Pagani (2014, 410) overstates when she claims, "it is hard to dispute that *The Reveries of a* [sic] *Solitary Walker* are characterized by an absolute and emphatic absence of forgiveness." This overlooks or ignores the two elaborate accounts given of young Rousseau's compassionate forgiveness: 4:34–48. One might respond, "But these are accounts of the young Rousseau!"; yes, but the Solitary Walker evokes and honors these accounts as indications of his unaltering nature and suggests that there are many other examples that he could give from throughout his life.

52. Trousson 1967, 99: "For a long time, Rousseau was able to believe himself a reincarnation of Socrates; did he not now believe himself a sort of Christ? When, again in *Emile*, he invokes 'the imaginary just person' of the *Republic* of Plato—that poor fellow 'covered with all the opprobrium of crime, and deserving all the prizes of virtue'—this is Jesus of whom he is thinking, and perhaps of himself." Trousson adds, "One can with reason say that Socrates could not be the hero of Rousseau precisely because he was the hero of the philosophes. To be sure: and the categorical affirmation of *Emile* ought to ring out like a challenge to his old companions. But the rupture between Rousseau and the Socratic myth is not explicable solely by the quarrel between Jean-Jacques and the encyclopedists" (100). See also Cérutti 1791, 17 (#18); Theil 1828; Masson 1916, 2:248; Sage 1951, 242; Burgelin 1952, 42; Seznec 1957, 6–7; Bowman 1966; Gouhier 1968, 416; Voisine 1969; Lecointre and Le Galliot 1971; Rosenberg 1987, 78–80; Pangle and Burns 2015, 342–46. For a very helpful discussion of Rousseau's Socratism, see Orwin 1998.

53. But the Scriptures that Rousseau respected do not include all that is in the epistles of St. Paul, in contrast to the epistle of St. James; see *Letters Written from the Mountain*, OC 3:702–3, on St. James versus St. Paul, as well as 698–700, 754, and 798, author's note; see also *Letter to Beaumont* OC 4:960 together with fragment #5 of *Letter to Beaumont* OC 4:1015–16: "St. Paul appears to me to cover with a figurative language reasonings so sophistic that it must be that someone falsified his books or that he was not always inspired. . . . J. C. said nowhere in the Gospel that St. Paul would be inspired."

54. Written January 15, 1769, and sent with a new covering note March 25, 1769: OC 4:1133–47. The evocation of the Platonic Glaucon's portrait of the just man and the contrast between Jesus and Socrates is at OC 4:1144–47. A major difference between Rousseau's and his vicar's eulogy of Jesus is that Rousseau sees in Jesus a political as well as a religious-cultural revolutionary: "his noble project was to raise up his people again, to make it once more a free people and worthy of being so"; and "in the end, it was only after seeing the impossibility of executing his project that he extended it in his head, and that, not being able to bring about by himself a revolution among his people, he wished to bring about one in the Universe through his disciples." See also Masson 1916, 2:246–61; Jimack 1965; Cotoni 1984, 267–83; Rosenberg 1987, 79–81.

55. My italics; this unfavorable judgment on Socrates's ironic dialectics is given also in a late addition to Rousseau's early "Discourse on This Question: Which Is the Virtue Most Necessary for a Hero and Which Are the Heroes Who Lacked This Virtue?" See OC 2:1274, and the editor's note.

56. OC 4:1052–54; perhaps the most emphatic statement by Rousseau identifying himself as a modern assimilation to Jesus is in his letter to Moultou of February 14, 1769 (CC 37:57 or #6544, quoted in Rosenberg 1987, 80–81). See also Cranston 1994, 17: "Christ was not seen" (by Rousseau) "as the Redeemer, nor even as the object of adoration and prayer. Christ was rather a being in whom" Rousseau "saw himself prefigured, a good man ill used, a victim of society's hostility."

57. *Republic* 598dff. and esp. 603c–606b; consider also *Phaedo* 58e–59a; and Plutarch's *How One Might by Enemies Be Benefited* 90d–e. Farrell (2006, 263) goes so far as to say that Rousseau "licenses and, indeed, justifies each individual in the belief that he or she is the victim of powerful collective forces that have"—with "malicious intent"—"a direct effect upon his or her nature."

58. Published in 1764; composed in 1758 (OC 5:1196–1211, esp. 1200–10; see Letter to Jacob Vernes of January 6, 1759, CC 6:5–6 or #760; Cranston 1991, 150–51; 1997, 80). Unfortunately, the Pléiade editor omits without warning the subtitle: see CW 7:337 (the editor's note ad loc.)—but although the CW note says that the first published edition (Rousseau 1764) bears the subtitle, it does not explain that this is true only in the table of contents at the end of the volume, while in the text itself, first page, there is only the title with no subtitle: see the online photocopy at https://babel.hathitrust.org/cgi/pt?id=uva.x004639387;view=1up;seq=422.

59. 1:12 end. In *The Confessions* (OC 1:243; cf. Manent 2019, 225), Rousseau tells us that in his mid-twenties, studies of Jansenist texts led him at one point to "dreaming on the sad subject" (*rêvant à ce triste sujet*) of damnation and the fear of Hell; but with the help of his kindly Jesuit confessor and of Mme de Warens, and on account of his sanguine "conscience," these "alarms—inseparable, perhaps, from devoutness—were not a permanent state." For Rousseau's sanguinity about the afterlife, see also 1:228, 231; *Dialogues* OC 1:985–86; Letter to Voltaire of August 18, 1756, OC 4:1070: the "eternity of punishments" is something that "neither you nor me, nor ever a human thinking well of God, would ever believe." Contrast Strauss's (2012, 36) characterization of the Enlightenment's "critique of the doctrine of eternal punishments in hell" as "a *softening* of the Platonic sternness" (Strauss's italics) as seen in *Phaedo* 69c, 81d–e, 112–14. Yet in Rousseau's case, the playing card #27 (fragment 1 in Spink 1948, treated as plan of the work) contains as its penultimate line an enigmatic three-word phrase: "eternity of punishments" (*éternité des peines*—not capitalized, as it is misleadingly printed in OC and in Spink); here is evidence that Rousseau never forgot this possibility.

60. I see no textual reason to suppose, as Meier (2016, 15) claims, that here *"réflechir* takes the places of *rêver* and thereby elucidates, sharpens, determines rêveries." The text here immediately stresses the shapeless, foreign, and unconnected character of the thoughts that will be reported. Besides, Meier (2016, 38, 79) soon has to concede that in the *Dialogues* and in the Seventh Walk *"rêverie"* is opposed to *"réflection."*

61. For "the pleasure of writing," see 4:38, 40. Cf. the letter to Voltaire of September 10, 1755 (OC 3:227): "As for me, if I had followed my first vocation, and so that I had neither read nor written, I would doubtless have been more happy. However, if letters were now abolished, I would be derived of the sole pleasure left to me. It is in their bosom that I console myself for all my ills: it is among those who cultivate them that I taste the sweetness of friendship and that I learn to enjoy life without fearing death. I owe them the little that I am." Friedlander 2004, 16 observes (though he is led into some considerable overstatement): "Whatever else he may have been, Rousseau was a writer and his life was a life of writing. Even more, in the *Reveries* Rousseau abandons everything but writing. Everything revolves around this activity of writing and reading what remains of his life, his reveries. . . . Yet in reading the *Reveries* it is easy to miss the fact that writing itself is Rousseau's foremost concern." See also Brand 2013, 67; and Kennedy 2014, 422–23.

62. This is the bizarre characterization of the First Walk by the editor of a recent critical edition: Eigeldinger 2010, 7. For better attempts at a simplifying unification of the manifold five goals set forth in the First Walk, see Butterworth 1979, 145 and Manent 2013, 317. Starobinski (1971, 426; 1988, 361) throws up his hands, declaring, the first chapter "wishes to attain a point that situates itself beyond the reign of goals."

2. "Second Walk"—Nature, Mortality, God

1. Cf. Friedlander 2004, 19; Lee 2008.

2. See Philonenko 1984, 3:292; also Burgelin 1952, 145; Grace 2001, 148; Marks 2005a, 73.

3. Consider here the sequence of reflections that leads to the self-absorbed reverie of St. Preux in *Heloise* part 4, letter 11 (OC 2:486–88).

4. This seems to refer to the years starting around 1762, when *Emile* was published and then was almost immediately condemned, confiscated, and publicly burned at Paris and Geneva, with Rousseau forced to flee into exile.

5. Osmont 1934, 53: "sans doute, ne réalise-t-il la promesse de la *Première Promenade*: 'appliquer le baromètre à son âme' pour en connaître 'l'état journalier.'"

6. "Le récit de la promenade di 24 Octobre 1776 n'illustre pas ce qu'il devait montrer, c'est-à-dire la retombée dans la rêverie rappelèe au détriment de l'écriture, pas plus qu'il ne dit l'affaiblissement de l'imagination" (Bonhôte 1992, 243).

7. This word is added in the margin at this point (manuscript p. 26).

8. Guitton 1997; Swenson 2008, 239.

9. Butterworth 1979, 163: "properly speaking, there is only one account of a recent reverie in this work, the one which precedes the accident."

10. Rousseau presents himself here as "precisely the kind of companion a lonely old person would choose" (Butterworth 1979, 150); Meier (2016, 11) aptly comments: "Rousseau oscillates between the description of an Everyman's existence—replete with experiences and feelings, joys and sufferings of a generally human kind, which invite the reader to share in the suffering and joy, to sympathize and to recognize himself—and the insistence on an exceptional existence."

11. Brand 2013, 69: "the most extreme case of self-estrangement"; Farrugia 2015, 198–200: "the interior echo of a soul subjugated by the integral dissolution into the exteriority . . . this de-personalization and this de-individualization"; see also Swenson 2008, 240; Burkholder 2015, 208–9.

12. There is no Greek or Latin equivalent of the English and French word *existence* or of the verb *to exist* (in contrast to the words for "being" and "to be" and "essence"—the latter coming from essentia, a word coined apparently by Seneca, in *Ad Lucilium* 58.6, in order to translate the Greek *ousia*). "Existence" and "to exist" are words invented by medieval scholastic Latin: first in the form of "existere," meaning "to derive from another"— using the classical Latin verb *exsistere, existere*, composed from *ex* and *sisto*, whose past participle is status, and which in the Latin of Lucretius and Cicero refers to "originating," or "appearing out of." Thus Richard of Saint-Victor asks, in his twelfth-century *On the Trinity* 4.12, "what in fact is it to exist [*existere*]?" And answers, "if not to derive from something else, that is, to be substantially from another?" (*sinon ex aliquo sistere, hoc est substantialiter ex aliquo esse?*). So in medieval Latin, *human* "existentia" connoted the human being's origin from the biblical God. By the seventeenth century, however, "existentia" had come to signify in philosophical writing "the simple and naked being of things without considering any order or rank that they hold among others" (quoted and discussed by Gilson 1948, 13–14, q.v., from Scipion du Pleix, *Metaphysics*, 1617; see also Descartes's title *Meditationes de Prima Philosophia, in qua Dei existentia et animæ immortalitas demonstratur*, 1641). In English, "existence" in the last, postmedieval sense (as opposed to

"nonexistence") may be found as early as Chaucer, according to the *Oxford English Dictionary*. But the original medieval sense, *ex-sistere*, "to originate from," remains important up through Martin Heidegger: see especially Suarez's *Metaphysical Disputations* 31:4n6 as discussed in Heidegger 1961, 2:418.

13. The ending of life—that is, not the process of dying, not the painful throes of death: in sharp contrast with Michel de Montaigne's account of a superficially similar accident, and its alleviation of Montaigne's persistent fear of the painful experience of undergoing dying ("On Exercise," *Essays* 2:6), the Solitary Walker does not present himself as troubled by such fear (another great version of such fear is Thomas Hobbes's axial fear of "violent death")—and accordingly the Solitary Walker does not, as does Montaigne, present himself as taking consolation in discovering the painlessness of the near-death experience.

14. As H. Williams (1983, 170) puts it, "he 'comes to' on the far side of death." See also Farrugia 2015, 191–93, 200–202, 204–5; and Burkholder 2015, 209.

15. The dubiousness of the supposition that such a loss of awareness of self would be in itself pleasing or attractive for a human is vividly portrayed in the otherwise fervently anti-individualist classic of socialist political theory, Edward Bellamy's *Looking Backward 2000–1887*, chap. 8 beginning, where the protagonist undergoes briefly such an experience: "I was no more able to distinguish myself from pure being during those moments than we may suppose a soul in the rough to be before it has received the ear-marks, the individualizing touches which make it a person. Strange that the sense of this inability should be such anguish! There are no words for the mental torture I endured during this helpless, eyeless, groping for myself in a boundless void. No other experience of the mind gives probably anything like the sense of absolute intellectual arrest from the loss of a mental fulcrum, a starting point of thought, which comes during such a momentary obscuration of the sense of one's identity. I trust I may never know what it is again." See also Riezler 1975, 86: "There is, first of all, the love of the I for the I as I, . . . the love of the subject to be a subject. This self-love, alone and isolated, is hardly more than the love of life. I am the one who is alive. . . . It is a necessity of nature."

16. Cf. the Pléiade editor Bernard Guyon's brief but meaty comment "e" (OC 2:1357) on *Heloise* OC 2:31. Rousseau's Savoyard vicar, professing his faith in a divinity that he claims is empirically and rationally evident as having made nature aiming chiefly at moral humanity, confronts mortal finitude and claims to defang it with the following (OC 4:588): "Who is there who would wish to live always? Death is the remedy for the evils that you impose on yourselves; nature has wished that you not suffer always. How the human living in the primitive simplicity is subject to little evils! He lives almost without sicknesses as well as passions, and neither foresees nor feels death; when he does feel it, his miseries render it desirable to him; then it is no longer an evil for him." Nonetheless, a few pages further on we find the same Vicar fervently arguing for faith in a better life, without assignable limit, after death: see similarly Rousseau earlier, at OC 4:306. In the letter to Voltaire of August 18, 1756 (OC 4:1061), Rousseau speaks of death as "almost not an evil except for the preparations one makes preceding it." But by the "evil of death," which of the two very different evils does Rousseau have in mind here: the temporary undergoing of the painful throes of dying *or* the loss forever of continued conscious existence? Has Rousseau sorted this out here?

17. OC 3:143; cf. Farrugia 2015, 203, and also again *Emile* OC 4:588.

18. In the *Second Discourse*, Rousseau's "language is that of conjectural speculation, and everything supernatural is absent from it" (Starobinski 1971, 340; 1988, 290). Or as Cranston (1982, 306) puts it, the *Second Discourse* "seems to depict a universe in which there is no God." We may add that similarly, the *First Discourse* evokes (OC 3:22) "the image of the simplicity of the first times," "shaped by the hands *only* of nature" (my italics).

19. When Starobinski (1971, 241; 1988, 202; see also 1971, 427–28; 1988, 362–63) writes, "the enchanted retreats that Rousseau arranged for himself in dream *would not exist without* his pathological suspicion" (my italics), he exaggerates, fundamentally, the relationship between Rousseau's paranoia and his reveries. Of the circumstances of the period of his greatest happiness, on the isle of St. Pierre with its reveries, the Solitary Walker writes, "nothing offered me anything except smiling images" and "nothing reminded me of saddening memories" (5:17).

20. 2:20; in fact, according to the Pléiade editor (OC 1:1777–78n2), the newspaper had printed an obituary notice on December 20, 1776 in which it had said only that "it pains us not to be able to speak of the talents of this eloquent writer; our readers must feel that the abuse that he made of his talents imposes on us the most strict silence."

21. This is panic but not entirely without some foundation: as Perrin (2011, 275) shows, "Rousseau was not wrong to worry himself about the 'defigurations' that his work would suffer."

22. See the unpublished statement written at about the time Rousseau began to compose *The Reveries* (OC 1:1749): "what is left for me is only to resign myself to the will of heaven which, by a decree whose depths it is not given to me to fathom, seems to favor totally the conspiracies of people for the defamation of my person and of my memory." In *Dialogues*, the character "Rousseau," after quoting at length "J. J." says (OC 1:954), "such are on this point the sentiments of J. J., and such are also mine. By a decree whose depths it is not given to me to fathom, he must pass the rest of his days in scorn and humiliation." Simon Lecointre and Jean Le Galliot (1971, 359) interpret this as a recurrence to Rousseau's youthful Calvinism and its "predestination"; but Rousseau says nothing about being part of the community of the "elect"; and Calvinist theology tends to see manifestations of being elected not in one's worldly suffering or failure but rather in one's worldly success in one's "calling," with a very strong condemnation of "idleness" (this of course is the source of Max Weber's famous thesis on the "Protestant ethic and the spirit of capitalism"; see also Troeltsch 1976, 644–46). Rousseau's lifelong expressions, starting at least from the age of twenty-six, of the view that he was doomed by an inscrutable providence to endure terrible sufferings are manifest in the letters quoted by Rosenberg 1987, 11–14 (see also 87–89): CC #5, 23, 28, 53, 1575, 2040, 2872, 3806, 4345, 6061, 6403, 6478, 6508. For Rousseau's consequent self-identification with Jesus, see Rosenberg 1987, 78–80. And see Rousseau's letter to Saint-Germain of February 26, 1770 (CC 37:267 or #6673): "Although I appear forgotten by providence, I never despair of it. How beautiful must the recompenses for the good people be, since she so neglects them here below!" For numerous other expressions of his hope in providence, see the letters of Rousseau quoted by Rosenberg 1987, 72–73: CC #2040, 2872, 3521, 4948, 5145, 5236, 5549, 5809, 6096, 6185, 6337, 6869, 6997.

23. I see no basis in the text for Meier's (2016, 66) bizarre claim that by this passage Rousseau "means nothing less than an attack on the center of faith in revelation, on

the sovereignty of god" because here "the will of god is bound to justice and subjected to knowledge." I see no sign in the text that Rousseau fell into the mistake of supposing that, as Meier erroneously supposes, and here claims, "faith in revelation affirms" divine "justice or wisdom *while at the same time denying it*" (my italics).

3. "Third Walk"—A Spiritual-Religious Autobiography

1. Rousseau gives no citation for this quotation. In fact, he quotes the line as it appears in Amyot's French translation (15, 65, 61) of Plutarch's life of Solon 33.2 (and, in slightly abbreviated form, 2:2).

2. 3:2; this echoes what we have seen the character "Rousseau" saying in the *Dialogues* about the mentality of "Jean-Jacques": the latter prefers lost comforting illusions to the sad truth (OC 1:819b, 822t, 857b).

3. The word *esprit* occurs more often in this chapter than in any other; the same is true of the word for "heart," *coeur*.

4. OC 1:1779n2 (to 1012), unfortunately with a misprint: for "875" read "857." See also Meier 2016, 60.

5. 3:5; the Pléiade editor in a footnote ad loc. aptly refers us to the Savoyard vicar's diatribe against the philosophers in *Emile*, OC 4:569. One must bear in mind that the word *philosophers* (*philosophes*) became bastardized in the mid-eighteenth-century French Enlightenment. For a good brief account of this bastardization focused on the relation of the so-called philosophes to Rousseau, see Cranston 1982, chaps. 12, 14.

6. 3:5; cf. D. Williams 2012, 119; for the profound philosophical difficulty in which this entraps Rousseau—the problem of subjective certainty (*Gewissheit*)—see the Hegelian Kojève 1991, 148–55 and Strauss's response 1991, 194–202, esp. 200 (the debate is centered on Socrates and dialectic).

7. 3:11; see also *Confessions* OC 1:392; letter to Abbé de Carondelet of March 4, 1764 (CC 19:198 or #3166)—"I never debate, persuaded that each man has his own manner of reasoning which is proper to him regarding something, and which is good for everything to no one else but him"); and Grace 2019. For the emotionally and psychologically fraught character of the refutational dialectic of Socrates, see above all Plato, *Theaetetus* 149a–151d, as well as 157c, 160e–61a, 184a–b, 210b–c (the famous midwifing allegory).

8. In *The Confessions* (OC 1:229), Rousseau stresses that Mme de Warens in her Catholicism made it clear that she did not believe in the existence of Hell but only of purgatory.

9. For a good brief summary of the theological significance of the reference to Fénelon, see CW ad loc. and Masson 1916, 101: "le seul des grands chrétiens du xviie siècle auquel [Rousseau] se soit donné, c'est Fénelon; mais le Fénelon du *Télémaque* et de *l'Education des filles* plutot que celui des *Lettres spirituelles*; le moraliste et le poète sensible . . . chez qui la nature se montrait si belle, si accueillante; . . . le philosophe du *Traité de l'existence de Dieu*, admirateur inépuisable de la noble ordonnance de l'univers." See also St. Preux's qualified assessment of Fénelon in *Heloise* OC 2:685. In *The Confessions* (OC 1:620), Rousseau lists Fénelon as a paragon of true charity who is therefore certainly in Heaven; see also *Heloise* OC 2:259, where it is said that Fénelon is one of the "two greatest, the two most virtuous, of the moderns" (along with Nicolas de Catinat); and similarly *Dialogues* OC 1:863–64 and the Letter to Franquières OC 4:1142. Rousseau

says in *The Confessions* (OC 1:229) that he believes that Fénelon was telling a lie when he spoke as if he believed in the existence of hell in his *Telemachus*; Rousseau adds the comment, "In the end, however truthful one may be, it is certainly necessary to lie when one is a bishop."

10. 3:6; note that here, we do have a reference to, if not exactly final causality, at any rate to a telos of the whole. The precise connection between "the end of all that he sees" and "the cause of all that he feels" is unclear, however.

11. "By my reason" is added above the line (manuscript p. 52).

12. Crossed out at this point are the words "not in speech but in the heart" (manuscript p. 53).

13. The Pléiade editor ad loc. refers us to the use of this word also in *The Confessions* and remarks that in his employment of the term, "Jean-Jacques adds a nuance of voluptuous laziness" (*une nuance de voluptueuse paresse*).

14. Cf. *Confessions* OC 1:363 and the second autobiographical letter to Malesherbes, OC 1:1136–37; see also Guéhenno 1962, 1:253–80; Damrosch 2005, 210–55; Kelly 2016, 3–4; and CW 12:xv. I am perplexed by note 7 appended by CW to the Third Walk, which says that the account given here in *The Reveries* is "very similar" to that in *The Confessions*, adducing as evidence from the latter work OC 1:355–57, 362–64, and 416–19, all of whose passages in fact make vivid the very great dissimilarity between the two works in their accounts of this period in the author's life.

15. In the words of Cranston (1982, 270), plausibly describing Rousseau's outlook at this time in his life, "he said that he desired 'obscurity,' but what he really wanted was to have publicity for his ideas and his writings, not publicity for himself."

16. *Confessions* OC 1:349ff.; Cranston 1982, 169, 209, 236, 270, and esp. 263–64: "In the *Discours sur les arts et les sciences* Rousseau condemned the false values of a sophisticated culture: in *Le devin du village* he demonstrated the aesthetic, and indeed the moral, qualities of a less sophisticated culture—close to nature, to the heart and to the purity of uncorrupted man. The ironical outcome was that the most sophisticated public in the world adored it. . . . The success of the opera was indeed prodigious. . . . It was to help propel music itself into a new direction" (Cranston 1982, 288). "On the musical stage he prepared the way for Mozart, whose *Bastien und Bastienne* is based on *Le Devin de Village*, and for the opera of Gluck," who "wrote: 'all I have tried to accomplish as a musician is to produce the kind of work which Jean-Jacques Rousseau would have produced if he had not forsaken composition in order to write books'" (Cranston 1994, 10–11).

17. For the full philosophical and historical significance of this culture war, see Cranston 1982, chap. 14; and 1997, 191–94.

18. Starobinski 1971, 66 (referring to earlier periods in Rousseau's life): "Epictetus (whom Rousseau studied) counsels us to play out our life as though a role in the theater (*Manual*, 17). . . . The effort of fiction by which the wise man plays out his persona joins the act of humility by which he accepts a role that is imposed on him in advance."

19. Davis 1999, 88: "the whole of the Third Walk proves peculiar in that nowhere does Rousseau really treat the content of his internal reformation."

20. Over the word *ardent*, Rousseau wrote and crossed out *imperious*; and instead of *Atheism*, Rousseau originally wrote *disbelief* (*incrédulité*): manuscript p. 55.

21. 3:11; as we have previously had occasion to note, in speaking of this juncture in his life back in *The Confessions*, Rousseau said (OC 1:392), "The frequentation of the encyclopedists, far from shaking my faith had strengthened it"—on account of his philosophical study of final causality in nature. For Rousseau's extensive studies, prior to the writing of the *First Discourse*, of chemistry (in a spirit rather skeptical of natural teleology), see Kelly 2016 and Bensaude-Vincent 2003.

22. 3:12; in point of fact, at this time of which he is speaking Rousseau was still a close friend and ally of the philosophes, above all of Diderot but also of d'Alembert and of Grimm and even of Voltaire: Cranston 1982, 218–45, 267, 307–8, 348; see also Hobson 2010. In the cultural war over music, the sequel to the *Querelle des Buffons*, "Diderot, d'Alembert and most of the others rallied to Rousseau's side" (Cranston 1982, 287; see also Snyders 1963; for a full account, with bibliography, of the *querelle*, see Sacaluga 1968). In his *Confessions* (OC 1:351–52), Rousseau himself acknowledges the encouragement and help that his writing of the *First Discourse* received from Diderot. In a letter of February 18, 1758, to the Genevese pastor Jacob Vernes, Rousseau writes, "I have passed my life among unbelievers without letting myself be troubled; loving them, esteeming them very much, and being unable to endure their doctrine" (CC 5:32–35 or #616, with an editor's footnote drawing attention to the contradiction with *The Reveries*). As Cranston (1982, 246–47) reports, "In an autobiographical fragment written at the period of life with which we are now concerned" (referring to OC 1.1115), Rousseau refers to Diderot as "this virtuous Philosopher whose friendship, already immortalized in his writings, makes the glory and the happiness of my life"—"this astonishing, universal, and perhaps unique genius." Grimm wrote to Johann Christoph Gottsched on November 25, 1752 (CC 2:202, quoting Danzel 1848, 350, two years after the publication of the *First Discourse*, "What is most singular is that M. Rousseau has converted almost all the philosophers here, who with some reservations all agree that he is right; I might name among others M. d'Alembert and M. Diderot." (D'Alembert did write, in his *Discours préliminaire* to the first volume of the *Encyclopedia*, a friendly rejoinder to Rousseau's attack on the arts and sciences). Cranston comments (1982, 234), "What perhaps rendered Rousseau's *Discours* more acceptable to those two philosophers was its apparent paganism.... It assigned no virtue to the Catholic Church or the Christian tradition." These massive and crucial facts about Rousseau's spiritual biography, attested by himself, are completely eliminated in the *fable convenue* that he is spinning out here in *The Reveries*.

23. In his brief characterization of what "the philosopher" is, in his representation of Plato's critique of poetry in book 10 of the *Republic* ("On Theatrical Imitation: An Essay Drawn from Plato's Dialogues," OC 5:1204), Rousseau writes, "The philosopher does not present himself as knowing the truth: he seeks it, he examines, he discusses, he extends our views, he instructs us even as he errs; he proposes his doubts as doubts, his conjectures as conjectures, and affirms only what he knows. The philosopher who reasons submits his reasonings to our judgment; the poet, and the imitator, puts himself forward as judge."

24. Jean-André de Luc, the famous Genevan geologist (and an earnest Christian), reported years later (1798, xcvii–cxx) about friendly private conversations he had with Rousseau about religion and geology around this time that is being discussed by the Solitary Walker. De Luc says he learned that although Rousseau had "with much heat," defended theism against the atheists he encountered in Paris, "they did shake him as

regards revelation"—on account (Rousseau said in conversing with this Christian geologist) of the scientific evidence of geology, as elaborated by Buffon. "Nevertheless" (De Luc continues) "this man, naturally humane, did not at all abandon the profession of Christianity; because the knowledge that he had acquired of *atheists* had convinced him that a *public religion* was indispensable for the maintenance of society. He therefore went back to Geneva, his fatherland, in order to reconcile himself with the church in which he was born—thinking, that the flag of Christianity, in conciliating a very large part of society, would give to him more influence for maintaining *theism* against the *atheists*. It was at that time that I contracted my first relations with him" (italics in original). Thus, De Luc concludes, although Rousseau "returned, by a formal act, into the Protestant Church, he preserved his incredulity as regards the Mosaic revelation, and thereby as regards every inspiration on the part of our sacred authors." See also in this regard the remarkable letter of Marie-Jeanne Phlipon to Marie-Henriette Cannet, November 29, 1777, CC 40:167–68 or #7141, discussed by Rosenberg 1987, 105–6.

25. Cf. Montaigne *Essays* 3:13: "Oh what a sweet and soft—and healthy—pillow are ignorance and lack of curiosity, for the repose of a well-made head!"

26. 3:15; the Pléiade editor aptly refers us to the pronouncement of the Savoyard vicar in *Emile* (OC 4:568): "Doubt regarding the things that are most important for us to know is a state too violent for the human spirit"; the editor also cites Rousseau's quasi-public letter to Voltaire of August 18, 1756, on the Lisbon earthquake and divine providence (OC 4:1070–71): "I believe in God . . . because the state of doubt is a state too violent for my soul; because, when my reason floats, my faith cannot rest for a long time in suspense and determines itself without her [reason]; that, in short, thousands of subjects of preference draw me to the side that is most consoling, and join the weight of hope to the equilibrium of reason." But to understand Rousseau as a political philosopher, one must bear in mind another passage a bit later in the same letter, addressed to "philosophers" in general (OC 4:1072): "There is a certain inhumanity in troubling the peaceful souls, and in moving people to wasteful despair, when what one wants to teach them is neither certain nor useful. In short, I think, and by your example, that one cannot possibly attack too strongly the superstition that troubles society, nor show too much respect for the religion that sustains it." Bernard Guyon, the Pléiade editor of *Heloise*, relates this latter passage to *Heloise*, pt. 5, letter 5, and comments (OC 2:1700–1701): "Rousseau is thus partisan of religion for the people because it is for them an 'opium.' . . . This is one of the most constant points of his teaching. . . . It is this exigence that explains the secrecy [regarding his atheism] demanded of Wolmar by Julie and accepted by him." Guyon refers us also to Rousseau's letter to Deleyre 1 of October 5, 1758 (CC 5:159 or #699, second para.). See also Rosenberg 1987, 55 and Gourevitch 2000.

27. 3:15 end; the Pléiade editor comments, "It is difficult to believe that Rousseau was not reminding himself here of some elaborations of Pascal, for example" the famous bet, which is expressed, the editors point out, in language taken over here by Rousseau almost word for word. But Rousseau might well have also had in mind the example set by the politic philosopher Locke in his *Essay concerning Human Understanding* 2.21.70.

28. *Sans m'arrêter aux*—the usually reliable translation in CW here blunders, with a reading: "without paying attention to"; Rousseau could hardly have discovered that he could not resolve the objections but that they are in some sense canceled by opposing objections if he failed to pay attention to them.

29. Rousseau crossed out at this point, "There, that is all that depends on us." And before the words "fall into error" in what immediately follows, he wrote and then crossed out "if we deceive ourselves," manuscript p. 59.

30. Shklar 1969, 114; Reisert 2003, 183; Grace 2006, n26; Manent 2019, 225. We will soon point out the major divergences between the Savoyard vicar's profession and the theology being presented in *The Reveries* by the Solitary Walker.

31. Bernard Gagnebin comments, in his introduction to *Heloise* in OC 2:XXI, "Notons le mot 'depuis' . . . le 'résultat' fut acquis avant la rédaction de la *Profession de foi*, dont le premier état date de 1758." Gagnebin refers us to Masson 1916, 2:36ff. See also Gourevitch 2012, 495–96.

32. In the *Letters Written from the Mountain*, Rousseau closely associates the vicar's profession of faith, in *Emile*, with Julie's profession of faith as reported by Wolmar, in *Heloise* (OC 2:714–16; see also *Confessions* OC 1:407). Rousseau adds, "One can presume with some verisimilitude that if the author who published the books in which they are contained does not adopt the one and the other in their entirety, at least he much favors them" (OC 3:694; see also Rousseau's letters to Malesherbes and to Moultou, CC #1303 and 1602). Later, Rousseau discloses in a footnote that "if *Emile* ought to be prohibited, *Heloise* ought to be burned at the least," for "above all the footnotes" in the latter "are of a boldness that the profession of faith of the vicar certainly does not approach" (OC 3:766). See similarly *Letter to Beaumont*, OC 4:933, speaking of the greater reserve of the profession of faith that he put in the mouth of the vicar in contrast to that which he put in the mouth of Julie.

33. OC 3:219 (contrast the *First Discourse* OC 3:22); similarly, Emile reaches puberty an atheist without any religious belief or notion of divinity whatsoever; see Archbishop Beaumont's penetrating animadversions on this aspect of Emile's education, in the "Pastoral Letter of His Grace the Archbishop of Paris" (CW 9:6–8).

34. Rousseau started to indite "writing" but crossed it out and penned "work" above the line (manuscript p. 60). The "Profession of Faith of the Savoyard Vicar" has often been published as a stand-alone work, beginning with a very truncated version published in Leipzig in 1765 (Masson 1914, xcvi); Streckeisen-Moultou reports (Rousseau 1861, ix–xi), on the basis of letters in his possession to his grandfather (Paul Moultou) from Rousseau, that because the latter "feared that the publisher to whom he had sold the rights to *Emile* would be forced to omit or to alter the *profession of faith*, he made a copy, and sent it to his friend, so that the latter could, if needed, re-establish the text in its integrity" and publish it independently.

35. OC 3:730; also 718–21. See in a similar vein the unpublished fragment, "On Proceedings against the Writers," OC 4:1029–30.

36. *Letters Written from the Mountain* (OC 3:695): Rousseau goes on to specify "the fundamental points of the civil religion" as "eternal Providence, love of the neighbor, justice, peace, the happiness of humans, the laws of the society, all the virtues."

37. Reisert 2003, 183–84; Cranston 1994, 11: "The Enlightenment had already poured scorn on religion and traditional political beliefs, but its Baconian empiricism was too dry and utilitarian to offer a satisfying alternative to Catholic spirituality. Rousseau's romanticism, by contrast, was rich enough in emotional intensity to replace lost faith with new excitements." For an instructive study of Rousseau's cultural revolutionary strategy, see Melzer 1996.

38. OC 4:582; here in the Third Walk, the Solitary Walker will soon remind us, in paragraph 12, that he for his part relies theologically on his own system.

39. In his next to final drafts, Rousseau originally had the vicar say, "the king of nature, at least on the earth that he inhabits" (OC 4:582, editors' note d).

40. There is abundant evidence, best assembled by Masson (1911, 1914, 1916) indicating that here and elsewhere in the vicar's profession Rousseau added at the last minute a polemical rejoinder to what he regarded as the shockingly dangerous, as well as erroneous, *De L'Esprit* (1758) of Helvétius, published while Rousseau was putting the finishing touches to his vicar's profession. But this must not obscure the more incisive fact: Rousseau here puts in the mouth of his vicar an excoriating assault also on the foundation of Rousseau's own philosophical system. As Masson (1911, 124) says, "Ce n'est point pour réfuter Helvétius que Rousseau s'est mise à écrire La Profession du Vicaire. Les intentions de l'oeuvre sont plus profondes, plus générales et moins conditionnées par l'actualité immédiate." For another major issue—the existence or nonexistence of spiritual (nonmaterial) substance—on which Rousseau's own views differ from those expressed by his Savoyard vicar, see CW 13, xxix–xxxi.

41. Rousseau as author does interject (OC 4:591) a footnote quoting the opening of Psalm 115 (CW, following Bloom, erroneously comment that the quotation differs radically from the original Bible, whereas in fact Rousseau quotes accurately the standard Genevan-Calvinist translation: see, e.g., among countless editions, *Les psaumes de David* 1801).

42. Wolmar, the noble rationalist husband of Julie, is a (secret) atheist because "he lacks the interior or sentimental proof" (*Heloise* pt. 5, letter 5, from St. Preux to Milord Edward, OC 2:592, 594). In an earlier draft, Rousseau here added to St. Preux's letter, "and the path of reasoning alone furnishes no rigorous demonstration of the [important] [consoling] truths that he rejects" (Pléiade editor's note a to OC 2:594). In his unpublished, so-called Moral Letters, Rousseau begins the sixth letter by asking the addressee, as regards the conscience, "if it speaks to all the hearts, oh Sophie, why then are there so few who listen to it? Alas, it speaks to us the language of nature, which everything makes us forget" (OC 4:1112).

43. In a late change, Rousseau replaced the following phrase: "because to live according to one's nature is not to deserve recompense" (see OC 4:1547). It would appear that Rousseau glimpsed but then sailed on past the basic Socratic insight—that it simply makes no sense to say that true virtue, as human excellence and thus the core of human flourishing, deserves compensation of any kind, any more than vice, as the diseased alienation from flourishing, deserves retributive punishment.

44. The closest thing to an echo of the Solitary Walker's dark view of Demon and of persecuting God is the vicar's striking statement about the source of ancient paganism's "abominable Gods": "*vice armed with sacred authority descended in vain from the eternal abode*, the moral instinct repulsed it from the heart of humans" (my italics)—suggesting that the pagan gods came not from the human imagination but from the eternal abode: does the vicar think that God sent the "abominable Gods" as His terrible testing of humans and their conscience?

45. OC 4:606: note that here again, Rousseau implies that until rather late in human development, there was no cult of divinity. Somewhat earlier in *Emile*, Rousseau contends that the first development of religion was animism: "the human began by

animating all the beings whose action he felt" on account of being "afraid of everything during the first ages" (OC 4:552); this can perhaps be made consistent with the *Second Discourse* if we presume that by "the first ages" Rousseau refers to a period late in the development of what he calls savage peoples (OC 3:168–72). In the less mature *First Discourse* (OC 3:22), Rousseau evokes "the image of the simplicity of the first times," "shaped by the hands only of nature" (not of God): "When humans innocent and virtuous loved to have the gods for witnesses of their actions, they dwelled together under the same huts; but soon become wicked, they got rid of these discomfiting spectators and relegated them to magnificent temples."

46. Rousseau 1762; Dufour 1925, 1:149ff., esp. 156.

47. The Pléiade editors have failed to include this very thought-provoking engraving (CW does reproduce the engraving, inserted at the proper original place in the text). The Pléiade editors have a vague footnote reference to the engraving, with an expression of their surprise at "the intervention in this place of the divine Orpheus" (OC 4:1569–70). It is to be noted that whereas Rousseau has the "author of this paper" speak of Orpheus as divine, when Rousseau speaks in his own name in his brief explanation, he does not speak of Orpheus as divine (OC 4:869). Most sources of the classical period make Orpheus the son of one of the Muses, hence a demigod; but the later geographer Strabo (bk. 7, frag. 18) reports that Orpheus was said to be only a human magician (*andra goēta*) and even a charlatan (*agurteuonta*); see similarly Pausanias 6.20.18. It is relevant to note that Archbishop Beaumont, in his intelligent pastoral letter condemning the profession of faith of the Savoyard vicar, alertly insists that "it implies, then, that there are several gods" (CW 9:9).

48. See St. Preux's similarly shallow dismissal of testimonies to experiences of inspired grace in *Heloise* pt. 5, letter 7, OC 2:684–85. In *Letters Written from the Mountain*, OC 3:727–29, Rousseau lays down what he claims are the three criteria for valid prophecy coming from God and omits grace or inspiration by the holy spirit! (In general, in the *Letters*, Rousseau obscures and fails to meet the serious challenge to reason from purported revelation.)

49. This passage was repeatedly rewritten in the last drafts. For the different versions, see OC 4:625, and editor's note a (4:1584).

50. The ingenuously earnest Pléiade editor Pierre Burgelin remarks ad loc. that this "rings curious after all that we have been able to read" but insists that this is testimony to Rousseau's personal proto-Kierkegaardian (!) acceptance of the Christian revelation in the New Testament (relying also on Rousseau's highly defensive *Letter to Beaumont* OC 4:964, 996).

51. Rousseau added this word above the line (manuscript p. 61).

52. Rousseau first wrote "harmony," then inserted above the line "universal," then crossed both words out and wrote above the line "physical order" (manuscript p. 61).

53. Rousseau first wrote "resources," which he crossed out, and wrote "the props" (*les appuis*) above the line (manuscript p. 61).

54. OC 4:590: as the Pléiade editor Burgelin points out (OC 4:1546), in the vicar's doctrine strictly speaking, "morality implies a survival, but not exactly the immortality" of the soul; the editor then opines, "The latter implies an incomprehensible infinity, it is only a presumption"—"this has to do with consoling beliefs to which the vicar accommodates himself."

55. It is noteworthy, however, that in the Platonic Glaucon's original portrait, there is no indication of any moral indignation in the heart or in the expression of the tormented just man.

56. The Pléiade editor Raymond (OC 1:1785) judges this passage to be a "new usage of vocabulary that is excessive, hyperbolic, of a delirious anguish."

57. "In the exposition of the results of his reform, Rousseau puts the accent, in a strangely repetitive and insistent manner, on the objections that he ceaselessly encounters against the conclusions to which he has come" (Manent 2019, 225). See also MacLean 2013, 138–41.

58. 3:22; the Pléiade editor Raymond refers us here to Rousseau's letter to Franquières (OC 4:138): "All the peoples of the earth recognize and adore God, and although each clothes him according to its custom, under all the diverse costumes one nevertheless always finds God." Raymond adds what he seems to think is the Savoyard vicar's similar statement (4:597–98): "Among so many inhuman and bizarre cults, among this prodigious diversity of mores and characters, you will find everywhere the same ideas of justice and honesty, everywhere the same notions of good and evil"; but Raymond fails to note that the vicar immediately follows this with the profoundly complicating statement, "Ancient paganism gave birth to abominable Gods. . . . The most contemptible divinities were served by the greatest men."

59. Condorcet 1971, 216–17 (originally published 1795): "There formed soon in Europe a class of men occupied less in discovering or deepening the truth than in spreading it; . . . in France Bayle, Fontenelle, Voltaire, Montesquieu, and the schools formed by these celebrated men, fought in favor of the truth, employing by turns all the arms that erudition, philosophy, wit, literary talent can furnish to reason; using every tone, employing every form, from humor to pathos, from the most learned and vast compilation to the novel or the pamphlet of the day; *covering the truth with a veil to spare eyes too weak, and leaving the pleasure of divining it; skillfully caressing prejudices, the more effectively to attack them; almost never threatening them, and then never several at one time, nor ever one in its entirety*" (my italics).

60. On the other hand, he does not criticize the duplicity of such a dual teaching; this is not surprising, given that this entire Third Walk exhibits a wonderfully artful benevolent version of such duplicity. According to Rousseau, the distinction between exoteric (public, masking) and esoteric (secret) doctrines, especially as regards religion, is intrinsic to philosophizing: "What shall we say of the distinction of the two doctrines, so avidly received among all the philosophers, and by which they profess in secret sentiments contrary to those that they teach publicly? Pythagoras was the first who made use of the interior teaching; he revealed it to his disciples only after long tests and with the greatest mystery: he gave them, in secret, teachings of atheism, and solemnly offered Hecatombs to Jupiter. The philosophers found this method so suitable to themselves that it spread rapidly in Greece, and from there to Rome, as one sees from the works of Cicero . . . [and] *was also born in China along with philosophy*" ("Observations on the Reply [to the *First Discourse* by Stanislas]" OC 3:46; my italics).

61. "The final argument is a little strange, since if Rousseau has forgotten his former arguments, it would be enough to refer to the Profession of Faith in order to remind himself of them" (Manent 2019, 226).

62. For accounts elsewhere in Rousseau of the overwhelming experience of God's presence, see *Heloise* OC 2:353–56 (contrast 685); also 358–59, 593–94, 716; see also *Emile* OC 4:792t (and Bloom 1993, 129–30).

63. *Confessions* OC 1:121 and CW note ad loc.; Letter to Father Claude Boudet, April 19, 1742 (CC 1:146–51 or #45); Cranston 1982, 83 and 153. By deceptively claiming in *The Confessions* that the memo was written and sent when he was nineteen, Rousseau avoids having to confess either of the two mutually exclusive necessary alternatives: either that he wrote the memo not in good faith but deceptively (perhaps to flatter the good bishop's memory?) or that he did write it in good faith and thus continued to be a believer in the miracle at the age of twenty-nine.

64. Plato *Apology* 33c; for Socrates being guided by divinely inspired dreams see also especially *Crito* 44a–b and *Phaedo* 60d–61b. For Rousseau's recognition of Socrates's "belief that he had a familiar spirit," see *Letter to Beaumont*, OC 4:977.

4. "Fourth Walk"—The Virtue of Truthfulness

1. Butterworth 1979, 180–81; Gourevitch 2012, 496; O'Dea 2014, 176; Manent 2019, 226.

2. Butterworth 1979, 181; Rosenberg 1987, 99n; Meier 2016, 62–63.

3. The Greek title is literally, *How One Might by Enemies Be Benefited*; Jacques Amyot (1572) translated this as *Comment on pourra receuoir vtilité de ses ennemis* (How one will be able to receive utility from one's enemies); Rousseau writes, with slightly wavy underlining, manuscript 70, "comment on pourra tirer utilité de ses enemis" (how one will be able to *draw* utility from one's enemies).

4. In the passage of Xenophon's *Economist* (1:15) to which Plutarch refers, Socrates is presented saying, in a refutation of his young interlocutor Critobulus, "and then even the enemies, according to your argument, are riches, for one who is capable of being benefited from enemies."

5. This was first announced by Rousseau in the (September) 1758 *Letter to D'Alembert* OC 5:120n; see also the editor's notes in CC 4:446 and 5:193, 216–17. The original context in Juvenal is a description (*Satires* 4:81–91) of one Crispus Placentinus, an "agreeable old fellow" (*iucunda senectus*) who would have been a "rather useful" minister to another emperor but who felt that he had to be a toady to the tyrannical emperor Domitian—and by doing so, managed to live to the ripe old age of eighty: "That one, therefore, never attempted to swim against the stream, nor was he a citizen who was able freely to express the words in his soul, and to dedicate/consecrate life to truth" (*illa igitur numquam derexit bracchia contra torrrentum, nec civis erat qui libera posset verba animai proferre et vitam impendere vero*). The translation "to risk his life for truth" in the Loeb (Braund 2004, which prints in*pendere* instead of *impendere*) and employed by scholars such as Coleman (2011, 1, 97–98) does not fit Rousseau's appropriation of the phrase, and what is more is not, I judge, really accurate as a rendering of the Latin: see the assemblage of uses of this verb in classical Latin literature in Lewis and Short 1879, s.v. *impendo, impensus*; see also the assemblage of the way this word was used by Augustine in Berchtold 2006. But Berchtold goes astray in suggesting that Rousseau has in mind Augustine's reflections on Christian martyrdom, and consecrating life to the truth of the City of God; for Rousseau is invoking Juvenal's pagan wisdom and Roman civic virtue; Crispus is described by Juve-

nal as a "citizen" (*civis*); and when Rousseau placed this motto as the epigraph to his work *Letters Written from the Mountain*, he insisted that it be printed surrounded by the device of "the civic crown" (*la couronne civique*)—letter to the printer Marc-Michel Rey, August 1, 1764 and reply of September 28, 1764 in CC 21:2 and 200 or #3437 and 3536. See also Villaverde 1990. Unfortunately, Coleman (2011, 1, 97–98) confuses Crispus Placentinus with Crispinus, who is Juvenal's principal target in this same fourth satire: Crispinus is labeled "a monster, without any virtue to redeem his vices" (4:2–3).

6. Meier 2016, 147n: "It is quite possible, not to say highly probable, that Rozier's dedication was not intended as an attack, was free from irony, and was an expression of his admiration for Rousseau." Osmont 1934, 14n20: "C'est donc sur un ancien ami que pese le soupçon de Jean-Jacques; il n'en est que plus maladif." See also Eigeldinger 2010, 71n5. Friedlander 2004, 42 does not realize that the Latin *impendenti* is in the dative case and on the basis of this misunderstanding of the Latin grammar contends that Rousseau was correct to interpret Rosier's dedication as an imperative and thus an insulting sarcasm.

7. See especially Plutarch's page 90 (my translation): "So when something is said that is untrue, one ought not, because it is false, hold it in contempt and disregard it, but investigate what words or acts or serious pursuits or associations have given some color to the slander, and take care to avoid that." For "there are many things that an enemy perceives better than does a friend (for 'blinded is friendly love [*to philoun*], concerning the one loved [*to philoumenon*],' as Plato says" [quoting *Laws* 731e: in the context, preceded immediately by "the excessive friendship for oneself is the cause of all of each man's wrongdoing on every occasion"]). Plutarch concludes, "silence in the midst of reviling is dignified *and Socratic*" (my italics). Amyot's translation is rather loose and reads as follows: "Quand doncques on aura dit quelque chose qui ne sera pas veritable, il ne le faudra pas mespriser ny contemner, pour ce que lon sçaura bien qu'il fera faux, ains faudra examiner & enquerir, que c'est que nous aurons dit out fait, ou nous, ou quelqu'un de ceaux que nous aimós, ou avec qui nous hantons, qui ait peu bailler aucune verisimilitude à la calomnie controuuee ... car un ennemy sent beaucoup de choses plus promptement que ne fait un amy, pourautant que l'amant, ainsi que dit Platon, est aveugle à l'endroit de ce qu'il aime ... mais quie plus est en tolerance d'iniures, y a ne sçay quoy de la gravité de Socrates."

8. The Pléiade editor Raymond is seduced by Starobinski 1971, 216 (1988, 180) into making the following bizarre comment ad loc. (OC 1:1788n3): "For Rousseau, the knowledge of oneself is not a problem, but a given. From an existential contact with oneself is born an immediate intuition of self."

9. Hypocrisy is a principal charge against which Rousseau defends himself in the *Dialogues*: see especially OC 1:667, 686, 688–89, 702–3, 755, 760, 860, 947–48, 958. As regards hypocrisy, not only in Rousseau but also in other great thinkers throughout history, Nietzsche's statement *"On the 'Intellectual Conscience'"* (*Zum "intellektuellen Gewissen"*) is apt: "Nothing seems to me today rarer than the genuine hypocrisy [*die echte Heuchelei*] ... when a man does not, on account of being constrained to wear, for the sake of appearance, another faith, lose the faith that he has" (*Twilight of the Idols*, "Skirmishes of an Untimely Man," #18).

10. *Letters Written from the Mountain* OC 3:692; see also *Letter to Beaumont* OC 4:939–40n.

11. Cotoni 2001, 301: "Les conséquences de ce mensonge sur Marion étant ignorées, ce sont ses effets sur lui-même que le narratuer relève . . . au fil de la lecture le coupable se change en victime."

12. Rousseau first wrote "passions," then crossed that out and (continuing on the next line) wrote "interests" (manuscript p. 73); thus, as he was writing, he made it clearer (not only to his readers but even to himself?) that he had in mind at this point the conscience as opining, and thereby allowing itself to be corrupted by persuasion, in a process of deliberation, and not the conscience as instinct being overwhelmed by the sheer force of passions.

13. Rousseau first wrote "force," then crossed that out and (continuing on the next line) wrote "rectitude" (*droiture*). On the next line, he first wrote "penchants," then crossed that out and (continuing on the same line) wrote "passions" (manuscript p. 73); thus, as he wrote, he made it clearer (not only to his readers but even to himself?) that he had in mind at this point the conscience being overwhelmed by the force of passions while itself remaining unaltered and uncorrupted, as instinctual.

14. Summarizing the teaching of the *Second Discourse*, Rousseau writes in the *Letter to Beaumont* (OC 4:936), "the love of order when developed and rendered active carries the name of conscience; but the conscience does not develop itself nor act except with the enlightenment of the human being [*les lumières de l'homme*]. It is only by this enlightenment that he arrives at knowing the order, and it is only when he knows it that his conscience carries him to love it." On "the order of the Universe," see also 951 and 939n.

15. 4:4; Yasuda 2018, 127: "Rousseau s'étonne (ou bien feint l'étonnement) d'avoir découvert un aspect de soi dont il n'avait pas conscience. . . . Rousseau prend un risque en révélant qu'il lui arrive de mentir en dépit de sa devise 'vitam impendere vero'; cela veut dire que même légèrement et avec prudence, il modifie son principe de la vérité affiché dans ses œuvres précédentes."

16. "No true" is written above the line, over a crossed-out "not the least" (manuscript p. 72): Rousseau here has the Solitary Walker quietly confess that he may have felt some untrue (histrionic) repenting.

17. Manent 2019, 227: "One is not sure that this book is in the library, but one understands that such a proposition suits Jean-Jacques extremely well. I am, to be sure, mocking, but I believe that I am doing so with his authorization, since his sales pitch here is too ostensibly weak to be avowed by him. He feigns to excuse his lies while lying."

18. See the article "Mensonge" (Lie) by the Chevalier Louis de Jaucourt in Diderot and d'Alembert's *Encyclopédie* (1751–72), 10:336—whose page is curiously (deceptively playfully?) numbered falsely as 338: "The lie consists in expressing oneself, deliberately, in words or in figures, in a false manner, with the intention of doing bad, or of causing damage, provided that the one to whom one speaks has a right to know our thoughts, and that one is obligated to furnish him with the means, as much as depends on us. From this it follows that one does not *lie* all the times when one speaks in a manner that does not conform, either to things, or to our own thoughts; . . . It further follows that those deceive themselves very badly, who make no distinction between *to lie* and *to speak a falsehood*. To lie is a dishonest and condemnable action, but one can say an indifferent falsehood; one can say a falsehood that is permitted, praiseworthy and even necessary: . . . There are, in discoursing, innocent falsehoods, that prudence requires or authorizes; . . . the usage of this faculty ought to be submitted

to the lights of our reason, to which it belongs to decide which things it is necessary to reveal or not. Finally, in order to be held to declare candidly what one has in one's spirit, it is necessary that those to whom one speaks have a right to know our thoughts" (original italics). See Montaigne, *Essays* 3:13; Grotius, *On the Law of War and Peace* 3.1.6ff., especially 3.1.9.3 (see also 3.1.14.2 and 3.1.17.1–3): "Among the philosophers there stand openly on this side [holding that lying is sometimes permissible] Socrates and his pupils Plato and Xenophon; at times, Cicero; if we may trust Plutarch and Quintilian, also the Stoics, who among the endowments of the wise man include ability to lie in the proper place and manner. In some places Aristotle too." Perrin 1997, following Deprun 1989 (see also Marshall 1984, 328n), traces the source of this definition to Rousseau's critical marginalia (OC 4:1126) inserted in his copy of *De L'esprit* by Helvétius, who had written on p. 79, note c: "M. de Fontenelle defined the lie: To keep silent a truth that one owes [*Taire une vérité qu'on doit*]"; but Perrin and Depru fail to give due weight to the fact that the philosophical definition on which Rousseau focuses is one that specifies not merely keeping silent about but instead *actively concealing* the truth—and makes the former only an entailment of the definition, not the defining characteristic (cf. Manent 2019). The difference, with a view to eternal punishment, may be not inconsiderable: see Thomas Aquinas, *Summa Theologica* 2a 2ae ques. 111, art. 1 and Augustine, *On Lying* 1.1.3, 4, 17.

19. To Fontenelle was widely attributed (by Helvétius among others) the famous or notorious statement, uttered in company, "If I had my hand full of truth, I would take good care how I opened it." Marvick 1993, 75: "Fontenelle was given to sugarcoating the bitter truths of science and philosophy," citing also Sainte-Beuve, "Fontenelle," in 1857–70, 3:315. Rousseau met Fontenelle when the latter was eighty-five (he lived to be one hundred) and tells us that Fontenelle "until his death never ceased to show me friendship and to give me, in our tete-à-tetes, advice from which I should have better profited" (*Confessions* OC 1:280).

20. 4:9; cf. *Letter to Beaumont* OC 4:967: "For myself, I have promised to speak the truth in every useful matter, to the extent that I can; this is a commitment that I have had to fulfill according to my talent."

21. See Plutarch's life of Solon 8 and then his "Comparative Judgment of Solon and Publicola," 4.1–2.

22. "Preface to a Second Letter to Bordes" (OC 1:106): "It is only gradually and always for few readers, that I have developed my ideas. It is not at all myself that I have cared for, but the truth, so as to make it pass more surely and to render it useful. . . . Often most of my readers will have found my discourses badly connected and almost entirely disjointed, out of failure to perceive the trunk of which I have shown them only the branches. But this was enough for those who know how to understand, and I have never wished to speak to the rest."

23. 4:14; my italics; Neidleman 2013, 824: "Rousseau seems to be implicitly establishing a defence of something like Plato's noble lie."

24. "The proof of" is written above the line, over a crossed-out "its" (manuscript p. 77).

25. First published in 1725; for many years Montesquieu denied authorship, but he had a new edition published anonymously in 1743. I doubt that he would have approved of the notorious engravings that Paul-Emile Bécat designed for the 1954 Editions Eryx

publication. As Gourevitch (1980; see also Kelly 2003, 12) points out, Rousseau is scrupulous in not naming Montesquieu as author: Rousseau shows he can help keep a secret.

26. 4:19; my italics; Rousseau takes the word *poison* from Montesquieu's text, where the philosopher writes (*Le temple de Gnide*, chant premier), "It was in this temple that Venus saw for the first time Adonis: the poison coursed to the heart of the goddess."

27. See Diderot and d'Alembert's *Encyclopédie* (1751–72, 6:273–74), the entry "Exoteric and Esoteric [*Exotérique et Esotérique*]" (by Johann Heinrich Samuel Formey; see also Formey 1779, especially 353–54): "The ancient philosophers had a double doctrine; the one external, public or exoteric; the other internal, secret or esoteric. The first was a teaching open to all the world, the second was reserved for a small number of chosen disciples." See also the entry "Soul [*Âme*]" (1:339, by Abbé Claude Yvon, who had to flee into exile in 1752 and supported himself partly by correcting page proofs of Rousseau [Kafker 1973, 124–25]): "In fact the most enlightened ancients regarded what this Philosopher [Plato] said about the penalties and recompenses of another life as things of an exoteric genre, that is to say, as opinions designed for the populace, and of which he himself believed nothing." In the second half of the eighteenth century, there was intense discussion of the proper role and nature of exoteric/esoteric writing, especially as regards religion; for lists of major publications, see Crocker 1953 and Melzer 2014, 275–76. Twenty-some entries in the *Encyclopédie* refer to exoteric/esoteric communication, almost always favorably: in addition to the entries "Exoteric and Esoteric" and "Soul," see especially "Asiatics, Philosophy of" (1:754); "Encyclopedia" (5:635ff., by d'Alembert; the key passage is translated in Melzer 2014, 250–51); "Egyptians, Philosophy of," 5:438; "Esoteric [*Esotérique*]," 5:953; "Japanese, Philosophy of," 8:456; "Jew," 9:44; "Pythagorism, or Philosophy of Pythagoras," 13:615 and 617; see also d'Alembert 1967 and 1821, 450–53; Diderot's letter to François Hemsterhuis, summer 1773, in 1955–70, 13:25–27; Condorcet 1971, 216–17; Holbach 1772, secs. 203–5 (pp. 309–14); *Dictionary of the Academy Française*, 5th ed. (1798), s.v. "exotérique." For Rousseau's employment of exoteric/esoteric writing, see Lovejoy 1948, 18–19; Crocker 1954, 311; Fellows 1960, 192; Masters 1968, 106–11; Mortier 1969; Smith 1971; Marshall 1978, 1984; Plattner 1979, 19–31, 37–38; Margel 2000, 11; Kelly 2003, chap. 6. For general discussions of this phenomenon in France during the Enlightenment, see especially Morel 1909, 135; Wade 1938; Havens 1961, esp. 231, 233, 261; Plattner 1979, 19–21; Canziani 1994; Prat and Servet 2005; Pilaud 2005; Hummel-Israel 2010; and Fumaroli 2014. Unfortunately, Perrin (1997) exhibits a complete ignorance of this crucial dimension of the French historical context in his attempt to present that context.

28. In the manuscript (81), the sentence starting "If it involves an imaginary being" has a red vertical line at the start and end, and the phrase in it that begins "at least, if one does not judge falsely" is written above an earlier crossed-out version which reads: "even if he praises ["blames" written as an alternative] the being unjustly for a blamable ["praiseworthy" written as an alternative] act, because he alone then errs without deceiving anyone since each can see the falsity of his judgment and redress it."

29. For Rousseau's repeated discussions of how "all" philosophers ("ancient and modern") communicate (not always in writing), above all as regards religious issues, on two levels ("la distinction des deux doctrines"): exoteric-popular (for "tout le monde," or "le public," or "tout un peuple," or "les hommes vulgaires" or "le peuple, incapable de raisonnemens suivis, d'observations lentes et sûres"; but also for the "tout

Gentilhomme" and "les bons"), versus esoteric (*la doctrine intérieure*) directed to the few ("le petit nombre," "les sages," "les bons raisonneurs," "les initiés" who "se reconnoisent entre eux"), and which the philosophers "teach in public only while hiding," see especially Rousseau's polemical writings defending his *First Discourse*, OC 3:46, 102, 105–7; then Letter to Voltaire, August 18, 1756, OC 4:1072; *Heloise* (Wolmar's exoteric worship and esoteric "atheism": OC 2:592 and the Pléiade editor Guyon's notes); Letter to Deleyre of October 5, 1758 (CC 5:159 or #699); *Confessions*, OC 1:46, 229, 408, 468 (the Pléiade editors comment, evidently in wonder: "cette doctrine 'intérieure' ou 'secrète' semble avoir beaucoup préoccupé Rousseau"); preface to the *Letter to D'Alembert*, OC 5:6; *Letters Written from the Mountain*, OC 3:727–31, 766n; *Letter to Beaumont*, OC 4:933, 955, 967–69; *Dialogues*, OC 1:672, 695; Letter to Franquières of January 15, 1769, OC 4:1146–47; *Reveries* 3:22. See also Melzer 2014, esp. xi, 16, 19, 112–14, 118, 123, 141, 213–14, 220, 242, 255, 272, 301, as well as Rosenberg 1987, 55, 96–99 ("in the fourth Promenade, he comes the closest to disclosing the extent of his duplicity"), 102–3, 105–6 (quoting the remarkable letter of Marie-Jeanne Phlipon to Marie-Henriette Cannet of November 29, 1777, CC 40:167–68 or #7141); Gourevitch 2000; Kelly 2003, esp. chap. 6; Meier 2016, 154–57; the Pléiade editor Guyon's note 2 to *Heloise*, OC 2:11. It is truly amazing how little any of the biographers of Rousseau seem aware of this massive and crucial dimension of his historical context, with all its far-reaching implications, historical and philosophical as well as biographical: the authentic intellectual biography of Rousseau—as well as of his contemporaries—thus remains to be written by scholars who will wake up to these facts about the historical context.

30. Not, however, "the only cases of underlining in the *Reveries*," as Manent (2019, 227) mistakenly believes.

31. Here for the first time, the Solitary Walker evokes the kind of passion that Plato designates as eros in its high reach: self-sacrificing, devotional love of something viewed as transcendent.

32. "The good and upright people" are those "who see the truth wherever they see justice" (*Letters Written from the Mountain*, OC 3:728). Meier 2016, 20n refers us also to OC 3:45–46. The ingenuous Starobinski (1971, 220; 1988, 183) mistakenly takes Rousseau to be speaking about himself. In *The Confessions* (OC 1:369), speaking of his attempts to act the part of a man of virtue, Rousseau confesses, "It is certain that in private I always sustained poorly my impersonation."

33. See also Rousseau's letter to Saint-Germain of February 26, 1770 (CC 37:294 or #6673): "I hope that some day people will judge what kind of man I was by what I knew how to endure. . . . No, I find nothing so great, so noble, as to suffer for the truth. I envy the glory of the martyrs." And see the footnote to the *Letter to d'Alembert* in which Rousseau announces his motto (OC 5:120): "If my writings inspire in me some pride, this is by the purity of intention which dictates them; this is by a disinterestedness of which few authors have given me an example, and which very few will wish to imitate. . . . I have almost always written against my own interest. *Vitam impendere vero*. There is the motto that I have chosen and of which I sense myself worthy. . . . The love of the public good is the sole passion that has made me speak to the public, so I know how to forget myself." See the discussion in Meier 2016, 22–24.

34. Kelly (1987, 243) goes so far as to suggest that here "Rousseau drops his normal motto," and "adopts the new motto" of these lines. They are spoken by Tasso in

194   NOTES TO PAGES 94–96

praise of Sophronia, a Christian maiden who steps forward to take responsibility deceitfully for the theft and destruction of an image of the Virgin Mary that a Muslim tyrant had sacrilegiously taken for himself from a Christian shrine. She thus succeeds in averting the tyrant's wrath from the Christian populace, which the tyrant had intended to exterminate as collective punishment for the theft. The identity of the true thief is left a mystery, but the poet concludes that it is more pious to give the credit to God Himself performing a miracle.

35. See again *Letter to Beaumont* (OC 4:967): "As for me, I have promised to say the truth in everything useful, as much as is in my power."

5. "Fifth Walk"—Happiness

1. 5:5, "le plus heureux": the words *heureux* and *bonheur* originally meant or connoted "good luck" (as at 1:9, 2:12, 4:29) rather than "felicity" or "happiness"; the latter, "the modern sense, Rousseau contributed mightily to impose," and "notably in the Fifth Walk" (Deloffre 1985, 26).

2. Charles Taylor's (1991, 27, 63) reference to this walk as showing that "le sentiment de l'existence would make me a perfectly moral creature if I were but in full contact with it" is thus very wide of the mark (see Marks 2005a, 2005b, 122–23; Spector 2014, 352n3). Perhaps Taylor has in mind the contrasting account given in *The Confessions*, especially OC 1:639–40, or the passage on the conscience in *Moral Letters* 6, OC 4:1112–13.

3. 5:6; cf. Butterworth 1979, 190–91, 228–29 and Yasuda 2018.

4. This "extension of the usage" of the term *circumscribe* "appears unique to Rousseau, and reveals itself to be full of psychological significance" (Deloffre 1985, 26).

5. See also the third autobiographical letter to Malesherbes (OC 1:1138), on Rousseau's wish that others would share his joy in reverie: "Oh that the fortune that I have enjoyed were known by all the universe! Each would wish to make himself a similar fortune; peace would reign on the earth; humans would no longer think of harming themselves." See again Rousseau's portrait of the character "Rousseau" as idealized reader in *Dialogues*, especially OC 1:727–29.

6. One of the first appearances in French of this subsequently momentous word: "on peut le considérer comme à peu près francisé à partir de *Rêveries* de Rousseau" (Spink 1948, 236). The word was introduced from its usage in English by the first translator of Shakespeare, Le Tourneur, whose text Rousseau may have become familiar with at Ermenonville, when he was with the Marquis de Girardin. In the latter's work *De la composition des paysages* (1777, 128), he had written that he used this word in preference to "our French word *romanesque* because that designates more the fable of a novel," while "this [English] word" designates "the situation and the touching impression that we receive." See Mercier 1801 s.v.; François 1909; and Deloffre 1985. Commenting on *Emile* OC 4:559, the Pléiade editor notes, "*Romanesque* est l'épithète qu'emploie Rousseau pour désigner les notions qui lui sont venues par les romans (*Confessions*, O. C. t. 1, p. 8), mais le mot revient pour désigner cette période de sa vie (*ibid.*, pp. 77 et 89; *2e Dialogue*, p. 819)."

7. Marks 2005b, 73; see also Rousseau's letters of October 1, 1765, to the Marquise de Verdelin and to Pierre Guy (CC 27:51–56 or #4692 and #4693).

8. 5:7; Reisert 2003, 116; Cranston 1997, 137—"all the evidence shows that he had a constant stream of visitors."

9. Only in *The Confessions* does Rousseau explain the economic basis of his and his wife's subsistence at this time: OC 1:638–39; Cranston 1997, 134.

10. After the publication of Rousseau's *Letters Written from the Mountain*, the inhabitants of Môtiers, where Rousseau had found refuge after having been expelled from Bern, became hostile, and his house was attacked in the middle of the night of September 6, 1765, by people throwing rocks. The damage was so extensive and the hostile intention so evident that he left Môtiers as soon as possible: *Confessions* OC 1:634–35 and Cranston 1997, 129–33.

11. The Solitary Walker thus gently recalls that after receiving the official notice of his expulsion from the island, Rousseau sent a letter to the bailiff asking to be permanently imprisoned there and offering to live without paper and pen: letter of October 20, 1765, to Emmanuel de Graffenreid, Bailiff of Nidau (CC 27:147–49 or #4740; *Confessions* OC 1:647–48).

12. 5:17; this is certainly not the case in the description given in *The Confessions*: "the ardent desire to end my days on this isle was inseparable from the fear of being forced to leave it.... This anxiety went to the point of altering the sweetness. I felt my situation to be so precarious that I did not dare to count on it.... How could I expect that my persecutors, seeing me happy here, would allow me to continue to be so.... Finally, abandoning myself to these reflections and to disquieting presentiments about new storms always ready to burst upon me [etc.]" (OC 1:643b–46); a bit later he adds, "pursued in all my refuges by the subterranean intrigues of my secret persecutors ... I had always suspected M. de Choiseul of being the hidden author of all the persecutions that I experienced in Switzerland.... I saw that France was secretly influencing everything that happened to me in Berne, in Geneva, in Neufchâtel, and I believed that I had in France no powerful enemy except only the Duke of Choiseul" (OC 1:651).

13. 5:6; my italics; see also *Confessions* OC 1:641; idleness is of course a civic and moral vice in the eyes of Rousseau and of the classical republican tradition: see *First Discourse* OC 3:18, Plato, *Laws* 807ff., Montesquieu, *Spirit of the Laws* 4:8 and context; Nietzsche, *Twilight of Idols*, "Maxims and Arrows," #1.

14. *Second Discourse* OC 3:140, 145. In the account of his stay on the island of St. Pierre that he gives in *The Confessions*, Rousseau characterizes the island as like La Fontaine's and Rabelais's "Papimania, that very happy country where one sleeps" and then says, "I have always hardly missed sleep; idleness suffices for me, and provided that I am doing nothing, I like much better to dream awake than in sleep."

15. An illuminating contrast is to be found in Diderot's article "Delicious" in the *Encyclopedia* (1751–72, 4:784): "Repose also has its deliciousness; but what is this delicious repose? He alone has known the inexpressible charm of it" who "has the spirit troubled by no cloud, the soul agitated by no emotion that is too lively"; who "has come from a sweet and light fatigue" and who "has experienced in all the parts of his body a pleasure so equally spread that he cannot make himself distinguish it in any one." There "remains for him in this moment of enchantment and of weakness neither memory of the past, nor desire for the future, nor worry about the present. Time has ceased to run for him, because he exists entirely within himself; the sentiment of his happiness weakens only with that of his existence." He "passes, by an imperceptible movement, from wakefulness to sleep; but during this imperceptible passage, in the midst of the loss of all his faculties, he awakes again enough, if not to think about

anything distinct, at least to feel all the sweetness of his existence"; "but he enjoys a joy totally passive, without being attached to it, without reflecting on it, without rejoicing in it, without congratulating himself upon it. If one could fix by thought this situation of pure sentiment, where all the faculties of the body and of the soul are alive without being agitated," and "could attach to this delicious quietism the idea of immutability, one would form for oneself the notion of the happiness that is the greatest and the purest that the human could imagine." Rousseau's sentiment of one's own existence is not such; it is, rather, a sentiment of awakeness.

16. See similarly *Confessions* OC 1:641; letter to Malesherbes, November 11, 1764 (CC 22:44 or #3638); Starobinski 1971, 279; 1988, 235–36 ("Jean-Jacques botanized as a collector, and not as a naturalist. It was for him an occupation, an amusement, rather than a true activity"); Grimsley 1972, 459; and D. Scott 1979, 82–83: "although the contemplation of the flowers in nature or subsequently in the herbarium stimulated Rousseau's imagination to a certain degree it was never allowed to initiate profound meditation"; "the mind is not allowed to make excursions into broader areas of significance." We note that the word *esprit* (mind) never occurs in the Fifth Walk.

17. In *The Confessions* (OC 1:641–42), Rousseau explains that in his botanizing he could "observe thousands of times the same things, and always with the same interest, because" he "always forgot them"; "my defect of memory ought to hold me always in that happy point of knowing so little about the matters, that everything was new to me, and knowing enough, so that everything made sense to me."

18. The Pléiade erroneously reports that in the manuscript "'old' replaces 'good'"; in fact, "good" is simply crossed out; originally, Rousseau wrote "good old song."

19. Contrast *Dialogues*, where the character "Rousseau," speaking of "J. J.," says, "I have never seen anyone as passionate for music as he is, but only for that which speaks to his heart. . . . He sings with a voice that is feeble and cracked but still animated and sweet; . . . [and] has given himself to this amusement for several years now with more ardor than ever" (OC 1:872–73, as well as 677–86, 831–32, 869–71).

20. Marks 2005, 73–74. Contrast the letter to Voltaire of September 10, 1755 (OC 3:227): "if writings were now annihilated, I would be deprived of the sole pleasure left to me. It is in their bosom that I console myself for all my ills: it is among people who cultivate letters that I taste the sweetness of friendship and that I learn to enjoy life without fearing death. I owe to them the little that I am."

21. The Solitary Walker erases from the picture something remarkable that we learn from Rousseau's account in *The Confessions* (OC 1:644): that he had his "poor dog" with him, "who did not like such long stays on the water" and required him "ordinarily" to avoid a lengthy stay in the boat and instead to go straight to the smaller island. Concerning this dog (named Sultan) as "my friend, not my slave—we had always the same will, but he never obeyed me," see also the third letter to Malesherbes, OC 1:1141 and Cranston 1997, 133, 136, 140. Was Rousseau ever entirely alone on the island? This was not the only time in his life when Rousseau had a pet dog: see *Confessions* OC 1:556–57 ("Duke" was "this dog, not handsome, but rare among his species, of whom I had made my companion, my friend, and who certainly deserved this title better than the majority of those who had taken it"). See also the editors' notes at OC 1:1348–49 and 1546 on Rousseau's earlier dog, whom he named after the companion of Aeneas. Socrates has a remarkable statement indicating his disinterest in animal pets and why—yet another not insignificant

contrast with Rousseau: "even as another is pleased by a good horse or a dog or a bird, so I myself am even more pleased by good friends." And "reading collectively with my friends, I go through the treasures of the wise men of old which they wrote and left behind in their books" (Xenophon, *Memorabilia* 1.6.14). What you are doing now, dear reader, is much more a Socratic than a Rousseauian employment of leisure.

22. In the parallel account in *The Confessions* (OC 1:644), Rousseau reports that he "stretched out on the grass at the summit of the mound" on the smaller island "to satiate" himself "with the pleasure of admiring this lake and its surroundings" and then also "built for himself, like another Robinson, an imaginary domicile on this little isle."

23. 5:7: Orwin (1997, 320n59) comments mordantly, "Rousseau as the benefactor not of human beings but of rabbits." The problems likely to be caused by pullulating rabbit overpopulation, not least for the vegetation of the confined little island, do not seem to have occurred to our amateur botanist with his proud founder's vision of an insulated rabbit utopia (Lane 2006, 486).

24. In manuscript p. 99, the word *sometimes* as well as the phrase "and the most solitary, in order there to dream" are inserted above a line crossed out that, as originally written, made no reference to solitude or to dreaming; the words *at my ease* went with simply gazing at the countryside; in other words, this "dreaming" alternative was missing from the final draft until the last revision.

25. In manuscript p. 99, the important words "fixant mes sens et" (fixing my senses and) are inserted above a line.

26. See similarly *The Confessions* OC 1:641, 643–44. Jean Wahl (1946, 94–95) has justly remarked, "'I think, therefore I am,' said Descartes. But in these states that Rousseau describes to us, 'I am because I scarcely think'; one could say, 'because I do not think.'" And "how distant we are from Pascal, since we experience pleasure in this feeling!" Consider also Rousseau's letter to Voltaire of August 18, 1756 (OC 4:1063): "the philosophers, in the comparison of the goods and the ills, always forget the sweet sentiment of existence, independent of every other sensation."

27. In manuscript p. 99, the word *human* was originally written modifying "things" (*choses humaines*) and is crossed out.

28. In manuscript p. 99, Rousseau originally wrote, "the uniformity of the continuous movement of the sentiment that was dominating me." He crossed out "of the sentiment" (*du sentiment*) and "was dominating me" (*me dominoit*) and wrote over the latter "was rocking me" (*me berçoit*); the rocking would presumably be internal, spiritual? Or does he mean that he started rocking his body in time with the water? But if so, it would seem to have been involuntarily, since he says that the rocking occurred "without any active concurrence of my soul."

29. But consider Friedlander 2004, 17 and Yasuda 2018, 125n33.

30. 5:12; my italics; the word *félicité* has not previously been used in this work; the Solitary Walker will later speak once of having achieved "almost felicity" (8:17); see also 5:15 ("felicities"), 6:18 ("public felicity"), 7:16 (making "projects of earthly felicity for myself"), and 9:1 ("our projects of felicity for this life are chimeras"). The Pléiade editor points out (OC 1:1080n2) that the word "carries often a religious nuance" and quotes the fourth edition (1762) of the *Dictionary of the Académie Française*: "*félicité*—béatitude, grand bonheur." See also *Moral Letters* 2 beginning, OC 4:1087: "the object of human life is the felicity of the h[uman], but who among us knows how to arrive at it?"

31. Spinoza, *Ethics* bk. 4, prop. 67 and bk. 5, prop. 6. Lucretius *De Rerum Natura* 3.830ff. The *Second Discourse* shows that Rousseau was an intent student of Lucretius's poem (Morel 1909, 155, 163–64 and especially 164–65n4; see also Nichols 1976, 198–201; Brook 2010, 45–47; for Rousseau's crucial departure from Lucretius, see Strauss 1953, 271n37).

32. See also *The Confessions* (OC 1:641) on his botanizing: it was only because he always forgot everything, he says, that he could "spend eternity" on botany "without boring myself for an instant."

33. Cf. Reisert 2003, 79; see *On Soul* 429b27ff.; and similarly Hegel 2019, 82–83—#24, Zusatz 1: when I say *"I,"* in rational thinking, I may "mean myself as this singular, thoroughly determinate person." But "I do not in fact express anything particular about myself. *I* is also anyone else"; "I express straightaway something completely universal." Although it is true that "what I in my consciousness have, that is for me," at the same time my rationally thinking I, like everyone's, is a universalizing "receptacle for anything and everything, that for which everything is and which preserves everything within itself." When rationally "considering anything, the human always considers it" in universal terms, even when "fixing on something singular." But since "language expresses only what is universal, then I cannot say what I only *mean*," in trying to express my *feeling* of uniqueness. "And the *unsayable*—feeling, sensation"—while certainly not totally false or unimportant, "is not what is most important, most true, but what is most insignificant, most untrue" (2019, 74—#20). In rational "thinking there immediately lies *freedom*, because it is the activity of the universal"—a "being-with-self that is undetermined in its subjectivity, and is in its *content* [*Inhalte*] only the *subject matter* [*Sache*] and its determinations"—a self-consciousness that is "immersed in the *subject matter*" and is thus "not a *particular* being or doing of the subject," but "the consciousness which conducts itself as abstract 'I,' as *freed* from all *particularity* of peculiar properties, states, etc., and does only what is universal, in which it is identical with all individuals." Hegel adds, "When Aristotle summons one to consider oneself *worthy* of comportment of this sort [e.g., at the close of the *Nicomachean Ethics* and opening of the *Metaphysics*], then the worthiness that consciousness ascribes to itself consists precisely in the giving up of *particular* opinions and beliefs and in allowing the *subject matter* to hold sway over oneself" (2019, 80—#23). "That is just what freedom is: being by oneself in one's other, depending upon oneself, and being one's own determinant." In "all drives I begin with an other, with what is for me something external. So here we speak of dependence." The "natural man, who is determined only through his drives, is not by himself; however self-willed he may be, the *content* of his willing and opining is not his own, and his freedom is only a *formal* one." But when I truly think rationally, "I give up my subjective particularity, sink myself in the subject-matter, let thought follow its own course; and I think badly whenever I add something of my own" (2019, 84–85—#24, Zusatz 2).

34. The Pléiade editor here helpfully reminds us of the words of the Savoyard vicar (OC 4:604): "I aspire to the moment when, delivered from the shackles of the body, I will be me without contradiction, without division, and will have need of only me to be happy."

35. 5:16; see the more pious formulation in the account of the sojourn on the island in *The Confessions* (OC 1:640): "there remained as my last hope only that of living without trouble in an eternal leisure. This is the life of the happy in the other world, and I made it henceforth my supreme happiness in this one."

36. In manuscript p. 101, the words "often [*souvent*] at the isle of St. Pierre" are written above an original, crossed-out "sometimes" (*quelquefois*) with an insert sign below the line.

37. The lack of "any trace of succession" in the consciousness entails the absence of discursive reasoning and, it would seem, of any sequence of imaginations.

38. The Pléiade editor comments, ad loc., "To experience in oneself the absolute sufficiency, this is certainly to do without God." As Rosenberg (1987, 99) stresses, a profound and remarkable contrast between the account given here in *The Reveries* and the account of the same island sojourn given in *The Confessions* is that in the latter account, prayer—to "nature, my mother" and to nature's God—plays a prominent role, while it is entirely absent from the account here in *The Reveries*: see OC 1:642 and 644, and our quotations from *The Confessions* in the section titled "Reverie in Awe of Nature" in our introduction. See also Grimsley 1972, 447; Butterworth 1979, 197; Cranston 1997, 136; contrast Starobinski 1971, 312; 1988, 263, who rather characteristically smooths over the tension.

39. 5:15; Farrell 2006, 305–6; Eigeldinger 2010, 97 comments, "Comparaison étonnante sous la plume de l'auteur de la 'Profession de foi du vicaire savoyard.'" The Pléiade editor reminds us, ad loc., that in 1:11, Rousseau described himself as "impassive even like God." In *Heloise* OC 2:466–67, St. Preux writes to Milord Edward, "A father of a family who takes pleasure in his house is rewarded for the continual cares he bestows on it by the continual enjoyment of the sweetest sentiments of nature. He alone among all mortals is master of his own felicity, because he is happy like God Himself, without desiring anything more than what he enjoys: like that immense Being, he does not dream of amplifying his possessions but of rendering them truly his by the most perfect relations and the most extended direction." The contrast between the Solitary Walker in *The Reveries* and St. Preux in *Heloise* is nowhere clearer. Still, St. Preux's account of human "felicity" also includes no reference to any need for assistance from, or any felt presence of, God.

40. Contrary to Grimsley's (1972, 447) reading, the text does not speak in a *"higher* and *more* spiritual key" of a *"higher* state of consciousness" (as does Aristotle, in the passage cited previously) nor does Rousseau's text speak of what Grimsley calls an *"eternal* 'present'" or of "allowing man's *higher* consciousness to exist in all its purity."

41. This account by the Solitary Walker of the need in himself that necessitates the external, fixating motion takes us much deeper into the nature of the most profound reveries than the character "Rousseau" was able to reach in *Dialogues*; in that text, the (somewhat obtuse) character "Rousseau" is presented as trying to understand, on the basis of his own and other people's experiences, this need in "J.-J."—by interpreting it as a form of "relaxation" (*delassement*) and of needed "rest" (*repos*). These are his words (OC 1:816–17): "The reverie, however sweet it may be, exhausts and tires after a while; it has need of *relaxation*." The "most indifferent spectacle has its sweetness by the *relaxation* that it procures *us*"; "the light movement with which it agitates *us* suffices to preserve *us* from a lethargic torpor and nourishes in *us* the pleasure of existing without giving any exercise to *our* faculties" (my italics). Like "us," the character "Rousseau" goes on to explain, the "contemplative J. J., who is at all other times so little attentive to the objects that surround him, often has a great need for this *rest*, and savors it with a sensuality of a child, which our sages scarcely suspect." J. J. "even stops himself at spectacles without movement, as long as they have variety"; "that all

arrests him and amuses him when his *fatigued* imagination has need of *rest.*" The character "Rousseau" is very pleased with this interpretation he has worked out of Jean-Jacques's reveries: "there, sir" (he says to his interlocutor, "The Frenchman") "is a great discovery and one on which I very much congratulate myself, because I regard it as the key of the other singularities of that person."

42. Cf. Grimsley 1969, 296; H. Williams 1983, 171–72; Kelly 1987, 234n36; Crogiez 1997, 86–87; Cooper 1999, 193; Davis 1999, 116, 164; Grace 2001, 150–51; Lane 2006, 495; J. Scott 2008, 145; Farrugia 2015, 190–91.

43. Consider the parallel in Riezler 1975, 268: "What in an elated moment suddenly overtakes the solitary being and makes it still? It matters little whether we speak of the senses or the soul, of pleasure or of joy, of the presence of a god or of a union with nature, or in some other mysterious or romantic way. Man, though alone, needs no one and nothing. . . . Time itself stands still—for a moment." Those "who know this joy" can "remember a felicity that for the moment rests in itself." Yet "no matter what language we use, the words never capture the elated moment. . . . I may have trespassed on the boundaries of what an ordinary man should try to say, or perhaps could even pretend to feel. I may have said only what man in an ideal of an elated moment would like to feel; thinking of the felicity he covets, man eagerly transcends all reality."

6. "Sixth Walk"—Goodness versus Virtue

1. For the contrast, see also especially *Second Discourse* OC 3:156, 170b; *Emile* OC 4:467, 817–18, 858; *Confessions* OC 1:47, 56, 416; *Dialogues* OC 1:670–71, 823–26, 851, 863–64, 892.

2. "And I feel" is inserted above the line, manuscript, p. 106.

3. On true happiness, contrast 2:3, 3:10, and the third letter to Malesherbes (OC 1:1142), as well as the preceding Walk; recall that on the island of St. Pierre, the greatest good for others that the Solitary Walker was proud of having done was for rabbits, not fellow humans: see again, Orwin 1997, 320n59.

4. In this Sixth Walk (of about 3,836 words), the word *heart* (*coeur*) occurs eighteen times, the word *soul* (*âme*) only twice; in the Fifth Walk (of about 3,766 words), the word *heart* occurred seven times, the term *soul* eight times. The supreme happiness described in the Fifth Walk was a "state of soul" (5:9 and 5:14), which was "regretted or longed for" by the "heart" (5:12–13)—a state in which the "heart must be at peace" (5:16); the peak happiness indicated in this Sixth Walk is "the truest that the human heart can savor" (6:3)—"pouring itself out" to "make another's heart content" (6:4), an expansiveness that makes the soul feel "exalted" (6:7); furthermore, in this Sixth Walk the soul is said to be elevated and strengthened by adversity (6:12). "Heart" comes more to the fore in the company of generous expansiveness and active goodness toward others, confronting adversity and feeling pity (the greatest number of mentions of "heart," twenty-six, is in the Third Walk, on religion, a chapter of about 5,094 words); "soul" comes more to the fore along with self-absorbed fulfillment (the greatest number of mentions of "soul," nine, is in the eighth chapter, of 4,190 words). The word *esprit* (spirit, wit, mind) is never mentioned in either the Fifth or the Sixth Walk.

5. 6:3 recall similarly 1:13; see Butterworth 1979, 200.

6. My italics; in the manuscript 105, this first sentence is inserted between the title and the original first sentence, which thus became the second sentence: "Yesterday, crossing etc."

7. Cf. again Raymond, in his introduction to the Pléiade edition (OC 1:lxxx); Tripet 1979, 95–96; H. Williams 1983, 167–68; Friedlander 2004, 123n4.

8. Unfortunately, the usually quite accurate Butterworth translation unaccountably omits the crucial qualifying words *most often* (*le plus souvent*).

9. *Thus Spoke Zarathustra*, "On the Despisers of the Body"; see, too, and also in contrast with Rousseau, *Daybreak: Thoughts on the Prejudices of Morality*, #115, "The So-called 'Ego'" and #116, "The Unknown World of the 'Subject,'" as well as *Twilight of the Idols*, "The Four Great Errors," #3–#5.

10. 6:3 (my italics); the words "and primary" are inserted above the line, manuscript p. 106.

11. 6:6; see also Meier 2016, 43, who quotes the character "Rousseau" in *Dialogues*, characterizing "J. J.": "according to me, he is not a virtuous man"; "he is a person without malice, more than good, a soul healthy but feeble, who adores virtue without practicing it, who ardently loves acting well [*le bien*] and who scarcely does any of it" (OC 1:773–74, 823, 829; see also 670 as well as 812, 818, 851, 859, 864).

12. 6:4; "almost" is inserted above the line, manuscript p. 106—removing what would seem otherwise a contradiction with the start of the next paragraph.

13. There is an echo here of Aristotle's teaching on the relation between what Aristotle calls "natural virtue" (*aretē phusikē*, which belongs "even to children and wild animals")—and "virtue in the sovereign sense" (*aretē kuriōs*), which comes into being when the natural virtue "takes on intelligence" (*labēi* noun): *Nicomachean Ethics* 1144b1–21.

14. In profound contrast to the Solitary Walker, Socrates was "self-controlled so that he never chose the more pleasant instead of the better, and prudent so that he did not err in judging the better and the worse, nor did he need another, but was self-sufficient as regards recognition of these matters" (Xenophon, *Memorabilia* 4.8.11).

15. Clark (2003, 112–13) has brought out well the gulf between the Solitary Walker's perspective and a perspective (that of Wordsworth) much closer to Aristotle and to the classical conception of virtue and goodness: "Where'er the aged beggar takes his rounds,/ The mild necessity of use compels/ To acts of love; and habit does the work/ Of reason: yet prepares that after-joy/ Which reason cherishes. And thus the soul/ By that sweet taste of pleasure unpursued,/ Doth find herself insensibly disposed/ To virtue and true goodness" ("The Old Cumberland Beggar," lines 98–105). Clark comments, "Wordsworth sees no conflict between inclination and duty, or between natural and societal compassion. For Wordsworth, what Rousseau sees as 'chains' of obligation strengthen—rather than pervert—natural sympathy. Further, in Wordsworth's account, virtue does not consist in subordinating one's inclinations to one's duties."

16. Originally, Rousseau wrote "always" (*toujours*), which is crossed out with "soon" (*bientôt*) written above the line: manuscript p. 110.

17. See especially *Dialogues* OC 1:798, 803, 825b, 850t, 952–54 ("Rousseau" quoting "Jean-Jacques") 968.

18. "The nature of this contract and its implications for sympathy and the larger question of moral virtue is the real center" of "Rousseau's Walk": Clark 2003, 112.

19. 6:10; here, the manuscript (p. 112) consists partly of marginalia and interlinear overwriting, in Rousseau's hand—seeming to testify to agitation on the writer's part; Osmont (1934, 36) comments, "we see, in effect, Rousseau getting himself enflamed in writing this phrase." These marginal and interlinear additions are bracketed and crossed out with red and dark lines: see the discussion in Osmont 1934, 36–39.

20. The attack on poor Moultou is inserted above a line in the marginalia, indicating a sort of final paroxysm of moral outrage.

21. For the importance of the human soul's natural expansiveness, see especially *Dialogues* OC 1:805–6 (the character "Rousseau" speaking): "positive or attractive action is the simple work of nature which seeks to extend and to reinforce the sentiment of our being"; from it "are born all the loving and sweet passions"; "it is very natural that he who loves himself should seek to extend his being and his enjoyments and to appropriate for himself through attachment what he feels ought to be a good for him"; also 827b ("J. J." reported speaking of his "expansive soul"); 864 ("expansive and sweet passions"); *Emile* OC 4:289, 304, 307, 312, 330, 359, 419, 421, 427, 430, 494, 501, 502, 506, 514, 543–44; *Confessions* OC 1:57, 426 (otherwise, curiously, expansiveness of soul is unemphasized in *Confessions*); *Heloise* OC 2:231, 559, 592, 689; and fragment #21 in OC 2:1324–25. Applied to the psyche, the adjective *expansif* (and the verb *s'épanouir*) is a Rousseauian neologism, derived from terminology in chemistry (Deloffre 1985, 26; and see Spink 1948, 224).

22. I do not find convincing Melzer's (1997, 291, 295n39) suggestion that what Rousseau designates as his soul's "expansiveness" can be fully satisfied by "a caring voyeurism"; and in general, Melzer's account of "sincerity" in Rousseau ("Rousseau is the first to define the good as being oneself, regardless of what one may be. . . . Liberated from shame and guilt, . . . I must be 'myself' regardless of *what* I may be . . . the only true sin is insincerity" [286, 290, 295n36]) fails to reckon with the potentially indignant, but also forgiving, intense righteousness, and the generous and affectionate or charitable concern for the well-being of others that are essential to Rousseau's conception of "goodness" (which includes but goes well beyond compassion and pity). I am speaking, of course, of goodness as it is experienced in historically developed humanity, as found above all in Rousseau himself, not least as writer. See also Bloom 1993, 260 on the fundamental difference between Rousseau's "sincerity" and twentieth-century "authenticity."

23. For Rousseau's love of glory, see above all the fragment #12 of *Letter to Beaumont*, OC 4:1021–22. Cf. Still 1993, 128–29. Consider the famous remark of Diderot (1875–77, 18:101): "posterity is for the philosopher what the other world is for the religious person." See also Rosenberg 1987, 89–90.

24. Clark 2003, 114: "Is this attitude coldly selfish and irresponsible? Perhaps. But we should also consider what comes out of this apparently 'useless' stance: the freely given, spontaneously charitable gift of Rousseau's own reflective poetry of sensibility." Rousseau's soul and its intended "afterlife" as that of an overwhelmingly influential writer is powerfully, world-historically, expansive and "spontaneously charitable" (cf. also Friedlander 2004).

25. See Still 1993, 122, referring us to the Letter to Franquières, OC 4:1143–44.

26. OC 3:132, 147, 160, 170, 191, 208, 216, 217, 218, 219.

7. "Seventh Walk"—Botany as Consuming "Amusement"

1. When he first took up botany, Rousseau wrote of it as an activity that would not only be amusing, and forestall serious thinking, but would fill the place of, and would help to prevent his being punished for, his lack of morally and civically virtuous activity; see the letter to Malesherbes of November 11, 1764 (CC 22:44, #3638): "I've been tempted to try botany, not like you, sir, in a grand way and as a branch of natural history; but entirely as an apothecary's assistant, to know how to brew my tea and my bullions. This is the true amusement of a solitary who takes walks and does not wish to think about anything. There never comes to me a virtuous and useful idea that doesn't make me see next to me the gallows or the scaffold; with a Linnaeus in the pocket and hay in the head, I hope not to be hanged. . . . I have no wish to know, but to study, and this study, so in conformity with my ambulatory life, will amuse me a lot and will be healthy for me." See also Crogiez 1997, 95–96.

2. Spink 1948, xl; Crogiez 1997, 20–21, 39; Meier 2016, 47–48.

3. In the manuscript p. 120, inserted above the line is the phrase, "I can do nothing about my lot": was this perhaps added after he had written the next and rather fatalistically gloomy chapter?

4. Cf. 6:1 with 7:1, 26, 28; Davis 1999, 138n1; J. Scott 2008, 139–41, 149–52; Kennedy 2014, 425; Meier 2016, 76; but it is going overboard to say, as does J. Scott (2008, 152), that this walk is "devoted to laughter" in the spirit of Cervantes's *Don Quixote*.

5. Cranston 1997, 89, 106–7: "the death in January of his instructor, Jean-Antoine d'Ivernois, did not interrupt the pursuit of his hobby, for his interest was aesthetic rather than scientific."

6. See similarly the report by the character "Rousseau" about "J.-J." (*Dialogues* 1:793): the striking point is well expressed by Starobinski 1971, 279 (1988, 235): "curiously, Rousseau equates his interest in botany with his work as a copyist."

7. The Pléiade editor ad loc. refers us to Rousseau's letter to the Duchess of Portland, July 11, 1776 (CC 40:77, #7093)—one year previous to this writing: declining an herbal gift from her, he writes, "I've gotten rid of all my books of botany, I've quit the agreeable amusement, which became too fatiguing for my age." See also the author's footnote to *Dialogues* OC 1:832.

8. Scholars have accused Rousseau of considerable prevarication in the account of his botanizing provided in this walk: Ambrus 2011, 568n5, "En réalité, Rousseau recommence à s'intéresser à la botanique dès l'automne 1771, comme le montrent sa correspondance et différents témoignages. Pour la chronologie, voir Gagnebin 1962 et OC 4.CXCIV–CCII, ainsi que Trousson et Eigeldinger 1998." See also Cook 2008; 2012, 7.

9. Rousseau's birthday was June 28, so this seems to have been written after that day in 1777.

10. *Grande vertu*: as the Pléiade editor stresses ad loc., Rousseau first wrote "a great virtue" (*une grande vertu*) and then crossed out "a" (*une*); could it be that the Solitary Walker, tongue in cheek, conceives his giving himself to botanizing as constituting the *entirety* of his "great virtue?" On "great virtues," see "Observations on the Reply Made to His [First] Discourse" OC 3:39 and "Last Response" OC 3:72 (on Socrates).

11. 7:3; in *Dialogues* (OC 1:839) the character "Rousseau" quotes "J. J." as having told him, "I have always found it very good to arm my heart against hating, employing all the enjoyments that I have been able to procure for myself."

12. OC 1:812–15; a bit earlier (1:827), the character "Rousseau" has spoken of "J. J.'s" hope for human society in the afterlife: "remaining alone on earth, he awaits the moment of leaving it in order to see realized at last his favorite visions, and to find again in a better order of things a fatherland and friends."

13. Strauss 1953, 75, 122–23; Xenophon *Memorabilia* 4.6.1: Socrates "never left off investigating, amid his companions, what *each* of the beings might be." There is no sign that Socrates ever experienced the quasi-pantheistic, semimystical, cosmic "ecstasies" that Rousseau reports himself having experienced (or that Meier 2006, 42–43 attributes to "the philosopher" as such—e.g., Socrates—and to philosophical "eros"). As Kelly puts it (2003, 181), for Rousseau, "philosophic understanding in the more traditional attempt to understand the truth about the whole is important only to the extent that it can provide the solid basis for fulfilling but nonphilosophic experiences."

14. In *Dialogues*, the character "Rousseau" describes the thinking of "J. J." thus: "An active heart and a natural laziness ought to inspire the taste for reverie" (the first mention of reverie in the book); "he does not elevate himself without pain to meditations that are purely abstract, and he does not maintain himself in them for long. But this feebleness of understanding is perhaps more advantageous to him than would be a more philosophical head. The concourse of sensed objects renders his meditations less dry, more sweet, more illusory, more appropriate to him in every way" (OC 1:816); "given by taste to his sweet reveries, thinking profoundly sometimes, but always with more fatigue than pleasure, and liking better to let himself be governed by a cheerful imagination than to govern with effort his head by reason" (OC 1:865). Cf. Butterworth 1979, 210.

15. My italics; and see again "Rousseau's" quotation from "J. J." himself at *Dialogues* (OC 1:839): "Thinking is for me a very painful labor that fatigues me, torments me and displeases me.... If I like sometimes to think, it is freely and without trouble, in letting my ideas flow as they will without subjecting them to anything." See also again the description by the character "Rousseau" of "J. J.'s" thinking at *Dialogues* OC 1:845: in his "reverie there is nothing active at all. The images trace themselves in the brain, combining themselves as in sleep, without the concourse of the will; all that is allowed to follow its pace, and one enjoys without being active." But "as soon as reasoning and reflection mix themselves in, the meditation is no longer a repose; it is a very painful activity, and that is the pain that horrifies J. J. and of which the mere idea floors him and renders him lazy."

16. 7:6: "in idleness" is added above the line; the CW editor plausibly suggests that the "sad situation" to which this refers is "when *Emile* was condemned by the French Parliament on June 9, 1762," and "he was forced to flee"—if so, the "fifty years" would encompass Rousseau's entire life, from birth; but perhaps the Solitary Walker is presented as speaking loosely here.

17. Swenson 2008, 237 (also 238): "a careful reading of the 'Septième promenade' shows that, for the author of the *Rêveries*, this experience is decidedly in the past." See also Terrasse 1979.

18. 7:9; my italics: the Pléiade editor comments ad loc.: "il y a ici un appauvrissement vital."

19. Cf. *Dialogues* OC 1:808: "The sensual human is the human of nature; the reflecting human is the one of opinion; it is he who is dangerous."

20. 7:12; recall the classificatory book project that the Solitary Walker says he conceived on the island of Bienne (5:7). In *The Confessions* (OC 1:643), Rousseau speaks of his "study of the system of Linnaeus, for which I conceived a passion that I have never been able to cure myself of, even when I sensed the emptiness of it. This great observer is in my judgment the sole, with Ludwig, who has up until now viewed botany as a naturalist and philosopher." See Cook 2012, 131–34 (also 7): "Eighteenth-century botany did not concern itself with internal plant systems such as reproduction, respiration, and nutrition; this was the preserve of 'physiologie végétale.' . . . Rousseau elected to study botany, which was synonymous with taxonomy, . . . Rousseau was in fact a careful student of systems and methods." But "Rousseau's preoccupation with the 'parties sexuelles' of plants continued his long-standing interest in reproduction" (170). There is no evidence that Rousseau studied the works of the truly philosophical botanist Theophrastus (though see the reference to him in OC 4:1215): see Cook's appendix 1, "Rousseau's Botanical Sources."

21. *Parts of Animals* 642b5–44b22; 645a24–26. For a good introduction to the crucial question of classification in Aristotelian biology, see Balme 1987.

22. In fragment #4 on botany (OC 4:1252), Rousseau writes, "I will contemplate, I will gather, I will uproot, I will divide, I will dissect perhaps, but I will never crush with a stupid and brutal hand and destroy the fragile beauties I admire." Commenting on Rousseau's instructions for examining a plant in his letters to Mme Delessert (OC 4:1162–63), Kuhn (2006, 6) comments, "Each act of dissection is qualified by an adverb that moderates its intrusive quality; each act of taking apart is accompanied by a concern for keeping the plant (or least its parts) whole." See also Gasbarronne 1989, 222.

23. See the beginning of the entry "Flowers" in Rousseau's *Fragments for a Dictionary of the Terms of Usage in Botany* (OC 4:1220–21): "If I gave my imagination over to the sweet sensations that this word seems to call up, I could make an agreeable article perhaps on shepherds but a very bad one for botanists. Let us then set aside for a moment the lively colors, the fragrant odors, the elegant forms, in order to seek first to understand well the organized being that assembles them." Gasbarrone comments on this as "the vacillation between poetry and natural history" but adds, "at no other moment in the dictionary will the shepherd's voice be heard"; "Rousseau's botanical dictionary, in remarkable contrast to his better-known works, attempts to fix the writer's gaze and to hold off the wandering vision of the shepherd *or of the promeneur solitaire*" (1986, 12, 14, 16; my italics). See also D. Scott 1979, 72: these lines "illustrate the ambivalence of Rousseau's attitude toward botany." But it is to be noted that recently a strong argument has been made questioning the authenticity of the *Fragments for a Dictionary* (no manuscript exists): Cook 2012, 298–308, suggesting that what we have here may be only notes that Rousseau took down on his reading of various botanical texts.

24. In Theophrastus's botanical works, we find a rich compendium of previous Greek natural science's understanding of soils as well as of the other aspects of farming. We see from these writings of Theophrastus that the classical scientific-philosophical study of the nature of plant life-forms is combined with, and dependent on, the scientific study of farming—mainly insofar as farming is plant, rather than animal, husbandry, though the analysis of manure remains important. See especially *On Causes of Plants* book 3 beginning: "theorizing about plants comprises two inquiries and is in

two ranges: one about the coming into being of the spontaneous, of which the principle is nature, the other about the coming into being from thought and preparation, which we declare indeed to work with nature toward the end."

25. See Xenophon's *Economist* 16, and T. Pangle 2020, chapter 6 as well as Strauss 1970, 185: "A philosopher, we gather, is not a man who unqualifiedly wishes to get the richest harvest of crops; nor is he a man who wishes to know how to get the richest harvest of crops merely for the sake of knowing this (or of teaching it); but he is a man who wishes to know it because he might wish to get such a harvest. The philosopher, it would seem, is a man characterized by a conditional or qualified love of lucre."

26. 7:16; the Solitary Walker seems now to erase from his life story the reveries of intense sentiment of his own existence described so vividly in the fifth chapter—which chapter thus continues to be rather conspicuously eclipsed throughout this seventh chapter.

27. Cf. Starobinski 1971, 280; 1988, 236–37; Kelly 2003, 179–80.

28. 7:30, end; D. Scott 1979, 75–78; Saint-Amand 1983, 159–60, 167—"C'est contre le même destin, contre la mort, que botanique et écriture luttent ensemble."

8. "8"—Renewed Self-Exploration

1. At this point and continuing on the next page, the manuscript becomes quite complicated, with crossed-out lines, a long indicated insertion that completes the second paragraph, and two chunks of writing, separated by long lines drawn across the page, that lack indication of their relation to the rest and which we will discuss presently.

2. Recall also 2:1 and our discussion of that passage. Cf. Poulet 1950, 169–76; Burgelin 1952, 149–52; Farrugia 2015, 189–90.

3. 8:2; see also 8:9 ("lengthy anguish," *longues angoisses*, inserted above the line, folio 8 recto) and 8:2; and recall 3:6. Consider also St. Preux's letter to Julie, *Heloise* OC 2:231–36. One cannot help but remark here a strong anticipation of what Martin Heidegger characterizes as the crux, ontological-existential phenomena that are experienced within the social world of "the Falling Prey" (*das Verfallen*) in "Everydayness" (*Alltaglichkeit*): "Angst" that faces and expresses one's "thrownness" (*Geworfenheit*) with its implicated "alienation" (*Entfremdung*), "plunge" (*Absturz*), and "eddying" (*Wirbel*). See *Being and Time* secs. 29, 35–38, 40, 68.

4. Cf. Butterworth 1979, 217; Perrin 1999, 332.

5. These two important sentences are not even noted in Frédéric Eigeldinger's critical edition (2010, 137).

6. "Whatever the humans do, the Heaven in its turn will do its work. *I do not know the time, the means, the species of it*" (OC 1:989; my italics). Similarly, "J. J." is quoted in *Dialogues* declaring, as regards the danger that his posthumous fame will be sullied, "No, Heaven will never permit it at all, and to whatever condition destiny has reduced me, I will never despair of providence, knowing well that it chooses its time and not ours, and that it likes to strike its blow at the moment when one expects it no longer" (OC 1:953; see what follows in the same quotation as well as the final sentences of the book and "History of the Preceding Writing" as a whole).

7. Alain Grosrichard comments (1978, 340), "Voilà sa façon d'anéantir le Malin Génie" (of Descartes). Rousseau reports at OC 1:980 a moment in which "I believed I

saw Heaven itself concur in the iniquitous work of humans." Cf. the Pléiade editor's comment ad loc., OC 1:1818n2.

8. 8:13; in the manuscript (folio 11 recto), the paragraph has another sentence that is crossed out: "I was very far from being that man but I have learned to become him, my persecutors have been my teachers I have learned to become him."

9. 8:12; see similarly playing card #12, in which Rousseau writes that he regards all fellow humans now as somewhat below the level of suffering dogs: "I would help similarly and with a warmer heart a dog who is suffering.... A dog is much closer to me than a human of this generation." An adumbration of this outlook is in the much earlier letter to Belloy of March 12, 1770 (CC 37:326, #6686): "my heart inflames itself much more at the injustices of which I am the witness than at those of which I am the victim.... I view the wicked one who persecutes me and defames me as I would view a rock detaching itself from a mountain and coming to crush me: I would repel it if I had the force, but without anger, and then I would leave it there without thinking more of it."

10. As the Solitary Walker soon declares, "in whatever situation one finds oneself, it is only by it [amour propre] that one is constantly unhappy" (8:17 beginning).

11. See the *Second Discourse*, note XV or O (OC 3:219–20): "The amour propre is only a relative, factitious sentiment born in society, which carries each individual to make more of oneself than of any other, which inspires in humans all the evils that they mutually do one another, and which is the veritable source of honor." And *Emile* OC 4:493 (see also 523, 534): "The love of oneself, which regards only ourselves, is content when our true needs are satisfied; but the amour propre, which compares oneself, is never content and would not know how to be, because this sentiment, in preferring ourselves to others, demands also that the others prefer us to themselves, which is impossible." And *Dialogues* OC 1:669 (the character "Rousseau" speaking): "amour propre—that is to say, a relative sentiment by which one compares oneself, which demands preferences, whose enjoyment is purely negative, and which no longer seeks to satisfy itself by our own well-being, but only by the harm of another." See also the same character at 805–7; note that amour propre is not quite the same as vanity, inasmuch as the latter can lack jealousy—"very often fools are vain [*vains*], but rarely are they jealous [*jaloux*], because believing themselves ensconced in the first place, they are always very content with their lot."

12. Cf. similarly Nietzsche's *Beyond Good and Evil* #261.

13. For this "degenerative" development, see *Dialogues* OC 1:806 and *Emile* OC 4:322 (see also 356): "The sole passion natural to the human is the love of oneself [*l'amour de soi-même*] or amour propre taken in an extended sense. This amour propre in itself or relative to us is good and useful, and since it has no necessary relation at all to others, it is in this regard naturally indifferent; it only becomes good or bad by the application that one makes of it and the relations that one gives to it." In *Heloise*, the term *amour de soi* never appears and Wolmar seems to collapse it into what he terms amour propre (OC 2:491). See similarly Montesquieu's treatment of amour propre: *Considerations on the Causes of the Greatness of the Romans and of Their Decline*, chap. 12 end.

14. 8:17; that the Solitary Walker continues to think within the framework of retributive justice, with its stress on deserved "compensation" of reward and of punishment, is evident in his characterizing the good his enemies have inadvertently done

him as his "compensation": "Let us learn to take, then, these advantages as compensation for the evils that they do me."

15. The words *a gesture* (*un geste*) are omitted in OC.

16. I see no textual basis here for Meier's (2016, 17) claim that at this point "rêverie becomes synonymous with promenade."

9. "9" and "10"—The Solitary Walker's "Truly Loving Heart"

1. For paragraphs #22 and #23 of the Ninth Walk, I follow the manuscript rather than OC 1:1095, which fails to indent #22, at the words "Une de mes promenades favorites" (cf. Meier 2016, xiv).

2. In paras. 7 (twice), 9, 19 (twice), 21 (four times), 22, and 23.

3. 9:1; my italics. Davis (1999, 149) comments, "Given what has just preceded it, the Ninth Walk begins strangely. The same Rousseau who claims in the Eighth Walk that after a long period of anguish he has finally regained 'serenity, tranquility, peace, even happiness' (VIII.9) here makes it a universal feature of human nature that happiness is not available to us. . . . The new reason is the permanence of flux or change, and what is perhaps most striking is our inclusion within this constant flux—nous changeons nous-mêmes."

4. The Pléiade editor Raymond at the same place aptly refers us to "the pages of the *Letter to D'Alembert* on the public festivals" but expresses bewilderment at "this distinction between contentment and happiness," which Raymond finds "astonishing from the pen of Jean-Jacques."

5. It appears that Rousseau added the first paragraph (folio 17 verso) after having originally begun the ninth chapter with what is now the second paragraph (folio 18 recto): the title "9" is at the top of *both* pages (contrary to the impression given in CW ad loc.).

6. The Pléiade editor at the place notes that in the passage that provoked Rousseau, "D'Alembert, himself a foundling child, would have been thinking of himself much more than of Rousseau."

7. 9.3; Davis 1999, 152 comments, "It may be that 'never had a man loved more than [Rousseau] to see little bambinos frolic and play together' (IX.3), but watching children play shows no concern whatsoever for what they will become. When Rousseau says of the little du Soussois that he was 'more child than they,' it is very clear that he does not think of them as a parent would. His pleasure comes from being able to feel with them, not from taking care of them or overseeing any change in them. He is delighted by them, wishes them well, and certainly longs to be loved by them, but he does not presume to care for them. His relation to them is, in small, the same as his relation to the children he abandoned."

8. Recall 4:29–30. For an informative brief account of what is known and has been opined and judged about Rousseau's abandonment of his five successive offspring—"one of the most controversial problems that his biography poses"—see the editor's long note in OC 1:1416–22. See also Cranston 1982, 208–9 ("the deed which most shocked the world after he became famous and that deed became known"), 238–39, 244–46. On April 20, 1751, Rousseau wrote an unrepentant letter about his child abandonment to Mme de Francueil (CW 5:551–52), appealing to Plato's *Republic* for part of

his (labored and tendentious, and indeed cruel) justification. But a decade later, at a time when Rousseau thought that he was dying, he wrote as follows to the Duchess of Luxembourg (June 12, 1761, CC 9:14–15, #1430): "From these liaisons [with Marie-Thérèse] there came five children, who all were put into a foundling-home, and with so little precaution to recognize them someday, that I have not even kept the date of their birth. For several years the remorse for this negligence has troubled my repose, and I am dying without being able to repair it, to the great regret of the mother and of myself. . . . The ideas with which my fault have filled my mind have contributed in great part to making me meditate the Treatise on Education, and you will find there, in the first book, a passage that can indicate to you that disposition." (For the passage in question, see *Emile*, OC 4:262–63.) Contrast Xenophon's depiction of Socrates's educative involvement with his teenage son: *Memorabilia* 2.2 (cf. T. Pangle 2018, 80–85).

9. 9.4; Rousseau had abandoned all his children when he penned the famous passage in the *Second Discourse* (OC 3:168) in which he speaks of humanity's first epoch of familial society as having given "birth to the sweetest sentiments that are known among humans, conjugal love, and paternal love." In *Confessions* OC 1:558, Rousseau observes that as regards paternal love, "all the charm" of "the true sentiment of nature needs, in order to sustain itself, at least during infancy, to lean on habit." This is an appropriate place to remark that neither here nor anywhere else in *The Reveries* does the Solitary Walker ever speak of his conjugal love for his wife and bosom companion of many years; compare the note that Rousseau added to *Confessions* OC 1:281, where he contrasts favorably his own marriage with that of Socrates to Xanthippe, and also *Confessions* OC 1:330–33, 352–55, 413–21.

10. See above all *Second Discourse* (OC 3:155–56) and *Emile* (OC 4:504–12, as well as 559b); contrast Socrates in Xenophon's *Memorabilia* 2.6.21; see Orwin 1980.

11. *First Discourse* (OC 3:19): "the ancient political thinkers spoke ceaselessly of morals and of virtue; ours speak only of commerce and money"; Montesquieu, *Spirit of the Laws* 3:3: "the Greek political thinkers, who lived in popular government, recognized no other force that could sustain it except that of virtue. Today's speak to us only of manufactures, of commerce, of finances, of riches and even of luxury."

12. I see no good reason to consider the tenth chapter unfinished; see Clément 1978; Davis 1999, 160. Contrast Butterworth 1979, vii, 226.

13. See T. Pangle 2020 ad loci; see also Xenophon, *Education of Cyrus* 8.7.3; and Nietzsche, *Beyond Good and Evil* #49: "That, which in the religiosity of the ancient Greeks produces astonishment, is the unlimited sentiment of gratitude that streams out from it—it is a very noble kind of human being who stands *thus* before nature and before life!"

14. Recall the similar language, but in reference to solitude, at 2:1; Meier (2016, 3) characterizes *The Reveries* as a "work, whose alpha and omega is solitude"; while this is true of the "alpha," it certainly does not hold of the "omega."

Appendix

1. Morrissey 1980, 261; see also Raymond 1962b, 358–61 and above all Forestier 1988 and Orwat 2006.

2. See Godefroy 1881–1902 s.v. *resver* and *resverie*; Bloch 1932 s.v. *resver*; Jud 1936.

3. In Théophile's poem "A une dame," we find the following remarkable anticipation of Rousseau (1856, 1:219; my italics):

Je veux faire des vers qui ne soient pas contraints,
Promener mon esprit par des petits desseins,
Chercher des lieux secrets où rien ne me desplaise,
Mediter à loisir. *resver*; tout à mon aise,
Employer toute une heure à me mirer dans l'eau,
Ouyr, comme en songeant, la course d'un ruisseau,
Escrire dans le bois, m'interrompre, me taire,
Composer un quatrain sans songer à le faire.

See also "Satyre premiere," 1:238.

4. 1855, 1:9 and 1:258 as well as 2.47; see the discussion in Morrissey 1980, 284–87.

Works Cited

Alembert, Jean le Rond d'. 1821. "Éloge de Montesquieu." In *Oeuvres complètes*. Vol. 5. Paris: Belin.
Alembert, Jean le Rond d'. 1967. Letter to Voltaire of July 21, 1757. In *Oeuvres et correspondances inédites de D'Alembert*, 51. Geneva: Slatkine.
Ambrus, Gauthier. 2011. "Une rêverie matérialiste: La septième promenade dans la correspondance de Jean-Jacques Rousseau." *Revue d'histoire littéraire de la France* 111:567–75.
Amyot, Jacques, ed. and trans. 1565. *Les vies des hommes illustres grecs et romains, comparé l'une avec l'autre par Plutarch de Cheronee*. Paris: Vascosan.
Amyot, Jacques, ed. and trans. 1572. *Les oeuvres morales et meslees de Plutarque*. Paris: Vascosan.
Ancelet, Christian. 1979. "Des *Confessions* aux *Rêveries*: Le retour à l'existence primitive." *French Studies in Southern Africa* 8:49–59.
Androutsos, Georges, and Stéphane Geroulanos. 2000. "La porphyrie aigüe intermittente: Une nouvelle hypothèse pour expliquer les troubles urinaires de Jean-Jacques Rousseau (1712–1788)." With a [harsh] "Commentaire" by Alain Jardin. *Progrès en urologie* 10:1282–89.
Balme, David M. 1987. "Aristotle's Use of Division and Differentiae." In *Philosophical Issues in Aristotle's Biology*, edited by Allan Gotthelf and James G. Lennox, 69–89. Cambridge: Cambridge University Press.
Bar, Georges-Louis de. 1745. *Rêveries poetiques sur des sujets différens*. Vol. 3 of *Epitres diverses sur des sujets différens*. 2nd ed. 3 vols. London: Changuion.
Barguillet, Françoise. 1991. *Rousseau ou l'illusion passionnée: Les rêveries du promeneur solitaire*. Paris: Presses Universitaires.
Barker, Ernest. 1918. *Greek Political Theory: Plato and His Predecessors*. London: Methuen.
Barker, Ernest. 1951. *Principles of Social and Political Theory*. New York: Oxford University Press.
Bensaude-Vincent, Bernadette. 2003. "La nature laboratoire." In *Rousseau et les sciences*, edited by Bernadette Bensaude-Vincent and Bruno Bernardi, 155–74. Paris: Harmattan.
Bensoussan, David. 1974. *La maladie de Rousseau*. Paris: Klincksieck.
Berchtold, Jacques. 2006. "*Vitam impendere vero*. Dépense, dette et dédommagement: Autour de la devise de Rousseau." *Europe: Revue littéraire mensuelle* 84, no. 930:141–60.

Bloch, Oscar, with Walther von Wartburg. 1932. *Dictionnaire étymologique de la langue française*. 2 vols. Paris: Presses Universitaires.
Bloom, Allan. 1993. *Love and Friendship*. New York: Simon & Schuster.
Blum, Carol. 1989. *Rousseau and the Republic of Virtue: The Language of Politics in the French Revolution*. Ithaca, NY: Cornell University Press.
Bolotin, David. 1999. "Aristotle on the Question of Evil." In *Action and Contemplation: Studies in the Moral and Political Thought of Aristotle*, edited by Robert C. Bartlett and Susan D. Collins, 159–70. Albany: State University of New York Press.
Bonhôte, Nicolas. 1992. *Jean Jacques Rousseau. Vision de l'histoire et autobiographie: Etude de sociologie de la littérature*. Lausanne: L'Age d'Homme.
Bowman, Frank-Paul. 1966. "La 'Confirmatio christianorum per Socratica' dans le romantisme français." *Revue des sciences humaines*, 2nd ser., fasc. 122–23:217–26.
Brand, Roy. 2013. *Love Knowledge: The Life of Philosophy from Socrates to Derrida*. New York: Columbia University Press.
Braund, Susanna Morton, ed. and trans. 2004. *Juvenal and Persius*. Cambridge, MA: Harvard University Press.
Brook, Christopher. 2010. "Rousseau's *Second Discourse*: Between Epicureanism and Stoicism." In *Rousseau and Freedom*, edited by Christie McDonald and Stanley Hoffman, 44–57. Cambridge: Cambridge University Press.
Burgelin, Pierre. 1952. *La philosophie de l'existence de Jean-Jacques Rousseau*. Paris: Slatkine.
Burkholder, Jeff. 2015. "La nature chez Rousseau: Une poétique négative?" In *L'Accident de Ménilmontant*, edited by Anouchka Vasak, 207–16. Paris: Garnier.
Burnet, John. 1911. *Plato's Phaedo*. Oxford: Clarendon.
Butterworth, Charles E. 1979. *The Reveries of the Solitary Walker*. New York: Harper & Row.
Canziani, Guido, ed. 1994. *Filosofia e religione nella letteratura clandestina: Secoli XVII e XVIII*. Milan: FrancoAngeli.
Cérutti, Joseph-Antoine-Joachim. 1791. *Bréviaire philosophique, ou histoire du judaisme, du christianisme, et du déisme en trentetrois vers par le feu roi de Prusse, et en trente-trois notes par un célèbre géomètre*. N.p.
Champigny, Jean Bochart, chevalier de. 1774. *Rêveries d'un habitant de Lillyput*. London: Mesplet.
Clark, Lorraine J. 2003. "Sympathy and Sensibility in Rousseau's Sixth Walk and Wordsworth's 'The Old Cumberland Beggar.'" In *Approaches to Teaching Rousseau's Confessions and Reveries of the Solitary Walker*, edited by John C. O'Neal and Ourida Mostefai, 110–14. New York: Modern Language Association.
Clarke, Samuel. 1998 (orig. 1704–5). *A Demonstration of the Being and Attributes of God and Other Writings*. Edited by Ezio Vailati. Cambridge: Cambridge University Press.
Clément, Pierre-Paul. 1978. "*Les reveries du promeneur solitaire*: Dixième promenade." In *Rousseau et Voltaire en 1978: Actes du Colloque internationale de Nice*. Geneva: Slatkine.
Coignet, Horace. 1825. "Particularités sur J. J. Rousseau, pendant le séjour qu'il fait à Lyon en 1770." In *Oeuvres inédites de J. J. Rousseau suivies d'un supplément à l'histoire de sa vie et de ses ouvrages*, edited by Victor-Donatien de Musset-Pathay. 2 vols., vol. 1 #9. Paris: Peytieux.

Coleman, Patrick. 2011. *Anger, Gratitude, and the Enlightenment Writer*. Oxford: Oxford University Press.
Condorcet, Antoine-Nicolas de. 1971. *Esquisse d'un tableau historique des progrès de l'esprit humain*. Edited by Monique Hinker and François Hinker. Paris: Editions Sociales.
Cook, Alexandra. 2008. "The 'Septième promenade' of the *Rêveries*: A Peculiar Account of Rousseau's Botany?" In *The Nature of Rousseau's Rêveries: Physical, Human, Aesthetic*, edited by John C. O'Neal, 11–34. Oxford: Voltaire Foundation.
Cook, Alexandra. 2012. *Jean-Jacques Rousseau and Botany: The Salutary Science*. Oxford: Voltaire Foundation.
Cooper, Laurence D. 1999. *Rousseau, Nature, and the Problem of the Good Life*. University Park: Pennsylvania State University Press.
Cotoni, Marie-Hélène. 1984. *L'Exégèse du nouveau testament dans la philosophie française du dix-huitième siècle*. Vol. 220 of *Studies on Voltaire and the Eighteenth Century*. Geneva: Institut de Musée Voltaire.
Cotoni, Marie-Hélène. 2001. "La voix narrative dans les *Rêveries du promeneur solitaire*." *Cahiers de narratologie* 10, no. 1:297–306.
Cranston, Maurice. 1982. *Jean-Jacques: The Early Life and Work of Jean-Jacques Rousseau 1712–1754*. Chicago: University of Chicago Press.
Cranston, Maurice. 1991. *The Noble Savage: Jean-Jacques Rousseau 1754–1762*. Chicago: University of Chicago Press.
Cranston, Maurice. 1994. *The Romantic Movement*. Oxford: Blackwell.
Cranston, Maurice. 1997. *The Solitary Self: Jean-Jacques Rousseau in Exile and Adversity*. Chicago: University of Chicago Press.
Crocker, Lester G. 1953. "The Problem of Truth and Falsehood in the Age of Enlightenment." *Journal of the History of Ideas* 14:575–603.
Crocker, Lester G. 1954. *Diderot: The Embattled Philosopher*. New York: Free Press.
Crogiez, Michèle. 1997. *Solitude et méditation: Etude sur les Rêveries de Jean-Jacques Rousseau*. Paris: Champion.
Damrosch, Leo. 2005. *Jean-Jacques Rousseau: Restless Genius*. Boston: Houghton Mifflin.
Damrosch, Leo. 2010. "Paranoia and Freedom in Rousseau's Final Decade." In *Rousseau and Freedom*, edited by Christie McDonald and Stanley Hoffman, 231–44. Cambridge: Cambridge University Press.
Danzel, Theodor Wilhelm. 1848. *Gottsched und seine Zeit: Auszüge Aus Seinem Briefwechsel*. Leipzig: Dyk.
Davis, Michael. 1999. *The Autobiography of Philosophy: Rousseau's* The Reveries of the Solitary Walker. Lanham, MD: Rowman & Littlefield.
Deloffre, Frédéric. 1985. "Sur le vocabulaire de Rousseau: *Rêveries du promeneur solitaire* (V–X)." *L'Information grammaticale* 25:23–27.
De Luc, Jean-André. 1798. *Lettres sur l'histoire physique de la terre addressées a M. le professeur Blumenbach, renfermant de nouvelles preuves géologiques et historiques de la mission divine de Moyse*. Paris: Nyon.
Deman, Thomas. 1944. *Socrate et Jésus*. Paris: L'Artisan du Livre.
Dent, Nicholas J. H. 1989. *Rousseau: An Introduction to His Psychological, Social and Political Theory*. Oxford: Blackwell.

Deprun, Jean. 1989. "Fontenelle, Helvétius, Rousseau et la casuistique du mensonge." In *Colloque Fontenelle Rouen Octobre 1987*, 423–31. Paris: Presses Universitaires.

Diderot, Denis. 1875–77. *Oeuvres complètes*. 20 vols. Edited by Jules Assézat and Maurice Tourneux. Paris: Garnier.

Diderot, Denis, and Jean le Rond d'Alembert, eds. 1751–72. *Encyclopédie, ou dictionnaire raisonné des sciences, des arts et des métiers*. 17 vols. Paris: Briasson et al.

Dufour, Théophile. 1925. *Recherches bibliographiques sur les oeuvres imprimées de J.-J. Rousseau: Suivies de l'inventaire des papiers de Rousseau conservés à la bibliothèque de Neuchâtel*. 2 vols. Paris: Giraud-Badin.

Eigeldinger, Frédéric S. 2010. *Jean-Jacques Rousseau*, Les rêveries du promeneur solitaire. Paris: Champion. [A critical edition (but unfortunately not always in conformity with Rousseau's manuscript, especially in the eighth chapter), with photographic copies of the notes Rousseau wrote on the backs of playing cards.]

Farrell, John. 2006. *Paranoia and Modernity: Cervantes and Rousseau*. Ithaca, NY: Cornell University Press.

Farrugia, Guilhem. 2015. "L'Épérience du bonheur dans *Les rêveries du promeneur solitaire*." In *L'Accident de Ménilmontant*, edited by Anouchka Vasak, 185–205. Paris: Garnier.

Fellows, Otis. 1960. "Buffon and Rousseau: Aspects of a Relationship." *Publications of the Modern Language Association of America* 75:184–96.

Ficino, Marsilio. 1550. *Divini Platonis operum*. Omnia emendatione et ad Graecum codicem collatione Simon Grynaeus. Lugduni: Tornaesius. [The original edition of the Latin translation of Plato's works that Rousseau studied and annotated.]

Fomey, Johann Heinrich Samuel. 1779. "Examen de la question: Si toutes les vérités sont bonnes à dire?" In *Nouveaux mémoires de l'Academie royale des sciences et belles-lettres 1777*, 333–54. Berlin: Decker.

Fontenelle, Bernard le Bovier de. 1686. *Entretiens sur la pluralité des mondes*. Paris: Blageart. [Three subsequent and enlarged editions were published by Fontenelle, in 1687, 1724, and 1742—the last in his *Oeuvres complètes*, Paris: Brunet.]

Forestier, Georges. 1988. "Le rêve littéraire du baroque au classicisme: Réflexes typologiques et enjeux esthétiques." *Revue des sciences humaines* 211:213–35.

François, Alexis. 1909. "Romantique." *Annales de la Société Jean-Jacques Rousseau* 5:199–236.

Françon, Marcel. 1951. "Sur les dates mentionnées dans les *Rêveries d'un* [sic] *promeneur solitaire*." *Studies in Philology* 48:779–82.

Friedlander, Eli. 2004. *J. J. Rousseau: An Afterlife of Words*. Cambridge, MA: Harvard University Press.

Froidefond, Dominique. 1997. "Rousseau, le trop-plein et le non-dit dans la première Promenade." *Annales de la Société Jean-Jacques Rousseau* 41:109–129.

Fumaroli, Marc. 2014. "*Les contes* de Perrault et leur sens second: L'Éloge de la modernité du siècle de Louis le Grand," *Revue d'histoire littéraire* 1124:775–96.

Gagnebin, Bernard. 1962. Introduction to *Lettres de J.-J. Rousseau sur la botanique*. Paris: Club des libraires de France.

Gagnebin, Bernard, and Marcel Raymond, eds. 1959–95. *Jean-Jacques Rousseau, oeuvres complètes*. 5 vols. Paris: Gallimard, Bibliothèque de la Pléiade.
Garagnon, Anne-Marie. 2010. "Etude stylistique de la première Promenade." *La gazette des délices* 27. http://institutions.ville-geneve.ch/fileadmin/user_upload/bge/sites_html/bge-gazette/27/pdf_27/27_a_propos.pdf.
Gasbarrone, Lisa. 1986. "Blindness or Oversight? A Closer Look at Rousseau's *Dictionnaire de botanique*." *French Forum* 11:5–17.
Gasbarrone, Lisa. 1989. "From the Part to the Whole: Nature and Machine in Rousseau's *Rêveries*." *Studies on Voltaire and the Eighteenth Century* 267:217–29.
Gilson, Etienne. 1948. *L'Être et l'essence*. Paris: Vrin.
Girardin [aka Gérardin], René Louis de, Marquis de Vauvray. 1777. *De la composition des paysages, ou Des moyens d'embellir la nature autour des habitations, en joignant l'agréable à l'utile*. Geneva: Delaguette.
Godefroy, Frédérich. 1881–1902. *Dictionnaire de l'ancienne langue française et de tous ses dialectes du IX au XV siècle*. 9 vols. Paris: Vieweg.
Goldschmidt, Georges-Arthur. 1978. *Rousseau ou l'esprit de solitude*. Paris: Phébus.
Goldschmidt, Victor. 1974 and 1983 reprint. *Anthropologie et politique: Les principes du système de Rousseau*. Paris: Vrin.
Gossman, Lionel. 1978. "The Innocent Art of Confession and Reverie." *Daedalus* 107:59–77.
Gouhier, Henri. 1968. "Socrate et Caton vus par Jean-Jacques." *Studi francesi* 36:412–18.
Gourevitch, Victor. 1980. "Rousseau on Lying: A Provisional Reading of the Fourth *Rêverie*. *Berkshire Review* 15:93–107.
Gourevitch, Victor. 2000. "Rousseau on Providence." *Review of Metaphysics* 53:565–611.
Gourevitch, Victor. 2012. "A Provisional Reading of Rousseau's *Reveries of the Solitary Walker*." *Review of Politics* 74:489–518.
Grace, Eve. 2001. "The Unbearable Restlessness of 'Being': Rousseau's Protean Sentiment of Existence." *History of European Ideas* 27:133–51.
Grace, Eve. 2006. "Portraying Nature: Rousseau's *Reveries* as Philosophy." In *Autobiography as Philosophy: The Philosophical Uses of Self-presentation*, edited by Thomas Mathien and David G. Wright, 151–77 London: Routledge.
Grace, Eve. 2019. "Rousseau's Socratic Sentimentalism." In *The Rousseauian Mind*, edited by Eve Grace and Christopher Kelly, 13–22. New York: Routledge.
Grand Larousse de la langue française. 1977. 7 vols. Paris: Larousse.
Grand Robert de la langue française. 2nd ed. 2001. 6 vols. Paris: Le Robert.
Greig, John Young Thomson, ed. 1932. *The Letters of David Hume*. 2 vols. Oxford: Oxford University Press.
Gresset, Jean-Baptiste-Louis. 1765. *Oeuvres*. London: Kelmarneck.
Grimm, Friedrich Melchior, Baron von, and Denis Diderot. 1829–31. *Correspondance littéraire, philosophique et critique*. 16 vols. Edited by Jules-Antoine Taschereau and A. Chaudé. Paris: Furne. [A journal, originally published 1753–90.]
Grimsley, Ronald. 1969. *Jean-Jacques Rousseau: A Study in Self-Awareness*. Cardiff: University of Wales Press.

Grimsley, Ronald. 1972. "Rousseau and the Problem of Happiness." In *Hobbes and Rousseau: A Collection of Critical Essays*, edited by Maurice Cranston and Richard S. Peters, 437–61. Garden City, NY: Doubleday.
Grimsley, Ronald. 1973. *The Philosophy of Rousseau*. London: Oxford University Press.
Grosclaude, Pierre. 1960. *Jean-Jacques Rousseau et Malesherbes: Documents inédits*. Paris: Fischbacher.
Grosrichard, Alain. 1978. "'Ou suis-je?' 'Que suis-je?' (Réflexions sur la question de la place dans l'oeuvre de J.-J. Rousseau, à partir d'un texte des *Rêveries*)." In *Rousseau et Voltaire en 1978: Actes du Colloque internationale de Nice*, 338–65 Geneva: Slatkine.
Guéhenno, Jean. 1955. "La dernière Confession de Jean-Jacques." *La nouvelle revue française* 35:855–66.
Guéhenno, Jean. 1962. *Jean-Jacques: Histoire d'une conscience*. 2 vols. Paris: Gallimard.
Guitton, Edouard. 1997. "À propos du projet 'descriptif' de Rousseau." In *Rêveries sans fin: Autour des Rêveries du promeneur solitaire*, edited by Michel Coz and François Jacob, 89–97. Orléans: Paradigme.
Hadot, Pierre. 1995. *Philosophy as a Way of Life: Spiritual Exercises from Socrates to Foucault*. Oxford: Blackwell.
Havens, George R. 1946. *Jean-Jacques Rousseau: Discours sur les sciences et les arts*. London: Oxford University Press.
Havens, George R. 1961. "Diderot, Rousseau, and the *Discours sur l'inégalité*." *Diderot Studies* 3:219–62.
Hegel, G. W. F. 2016. *Lectures on the History of Philosophy 1825–6*. Vol. 2: *Greek Philosophy*. Translated by Robert F. Brown. Oxford: Clarendon.
Hegel, G. W. F. 2019. *Enzyklopädie der philosophischen Wissenschaften im Grundrisse 1830*: Erster Teil, *Die Wissenschaft der Logik*, mit den mündlichen Zusätzen. Frankfurt am Main: Suhrkamp.
Hegel, G. W. F. 2021. *Enzyklopädie der philosophischen Wissenschaften im Grundrisse 1830*: Zweiter Teil, *Die Naturphilosophie*. Frankfurt am Main: Suhrkamp.
Heidegger, Martin. 1961. *Nietzsche*. 2 vols. Pfullingen: Neske.
Helvétius, Claude Adrien. 1758. *De L'Esprit*. Paris: Durand.
Hobson, Marion. 2010. "Jean-Jacques Rousseau and Diderot in the Late 1740s: Satire, Friendship, and Freedom." In *Rousseau and Freedom*, edited by Christie McDonald and Stanley Hoffman, 58–76. Cambridge: Cambridge University Press.
Hoffman, Stanley. 2010. "Postface: Rousseau and Freedom." In *Rousseau and Freedom*, edited by Christie McDonald and Stanley Hoffman, 292–94. Cambridge: Cambridge University Press.
Holbach, Paul Henri Thiry, Baron d'. 1772. *Le bon-sens ou idées naturelles opposées aux idées surnaturelles*. London [a mask; actually Amsterdam]: n.p.
Huguet, Edmond. 1962. *Dictionnaire de la langue française du seizième siècle*. Paris: Didier.
Hummel-Israel, Pascale Catherine, ed. 2010. *Paralangues: Etudes sur la parole oblique*. Paris: Philologicum.
Hunter, Josiah. 1780. *A Review of an Exposition of Some Late Reveries, concerning the Sonship of Christ, &c*. Edinburgh: Churnside and Wilson.

Imbert, Barthélemy. 1778. *Rêveries philosophiques*. The Hague: Gosse.
Jimack, Peter D. 1965. "Rousseau and 'La beauté de l'Evangile.'" *French Studies* 19:16–28.
Jud, Jakob. 1936. "Resver et desver." *Romania* 62:145–57.
Kafker, Frank A. 1973. "The Risks of Contributing to Diderot's Encyclopedia." *Diderot Studies* 16:119–43.
Kant, Immanuel. 1942. *Gesammelte Schriften*. Vol. 20, *Handschriftlicher Nachlaß*. Edited by Gerhard Lehmann. Berlin: de Gruyter.
Kellermann, Wilhelm. 1969. "Ein Sprachspiel des französischen Mittelalters: Die Resveries." In *Mélanges offerts à Rita Lejeune*, 1331–46. Gembloux: Duculot.
Kelly, Christopher. 1987. *Rousseau's Exemplary Life: The "Confessions" as Political Philosophy*. Ithaca, NY: Cornell University Press.
Kelly, Christopher. 2003. *Rousseau as Author: Consecrating One's Life to the Truth*. Chicago: University of Chicago Press.
Kelly, Christopher. 2012. "On the Naturalness of the Sentiment of Justice." *Esprit créateur* 52:67–79.
Kelly, Christopher. 2016. "Rousseau's Chemical Apprenticeship." In *Rousseau and the Dilemmas of Modernity*, edited by Mark Hulliung, 3–28. New Brunswick, NJ: Transaction.
Kendall, Wilmoore. 2002. *Wilmoore Kendall: Maverick of American Conservatives*. Edited by John A. Murley and John E. Alvis. Lanham, MD: Lexington.
Kennedy, Rosanne. 2014. "Rêver de politique: Les *Rêveries du promeneur solitaire*." In *Philosophie de Rousseau*, edited by Blaise Bachofen, Bruno Bernardi, André Charrak, and Florent Guénard, 413–26. Paris: Garnier.
Kierkegaard, Søren. 2014. *The Concept of Anxiety*. Translated by Alastair Hannay. New York: Liveright.
Klein, Jacob. 1989. *A Commentary on Plato's Meno*. Chicago: University of Chicago Press.
Kojève, Alexandre. 1991. "Tyranny and Wisdom." In Leo Strauss, *On Tyranny, Revised and Expanded Edition, Including the Strauss-Kojève Correspondence*, 135–76 New York: Free Press.
Kuhn, Bernhard. 2006. "'A Chain of Marvels': Botany and Autobiography in Rousseau." *European Romantic Review* 17:1–20.
Lane, Joseph H., Jr. 2006. "Reverie and the Return to Nature: Rousseau's Experience of Convergence." *Review of Politics* 68:474–99.
Launay, Michel. 1964. "Vocabulaire politique et vocabulaire religieux dans les 'Rêveries.'" *Cahiers de lexicologie* 5:85–100.
Le Beau, Claude. 1738. *Avantures du sieur Claude Le Beau, avocat en parlement: Voyage curieux et nouveau parmi les sauvages de l'amerique septentrionale*. Amsterdam: Uytwere.
Lecointre, Simone, and Jean Le Galliot. 1971. "Essai sur la structure d'un mythe personnel dans les *Rêveries du promeneur solitaire*." *Semiotica* 4:339–64.
Lee, Natasha. 2008. "A Dream of Human Nature." In *The Nature of Rousseau's Rêveries: Physical, Human, Aesthetic*, edited by John C. O'Neal, 99–110. Oxford: Voltaire Foundation.
Leigh, Ralph A. 1965–98. *Correspondance complète de Jean Jacques Rousseau*. Vol. 52. Geneva: Institut et Musée Voltaire.

Leigh, Ralph A. 1979. "La mort de J.-J. Rousseau: Images d'Epinal et roman policier." *Revue d'histoire littéraire de la France* 79:187–98.
Les psaumes de David. 1801. Translated by Valentin Conrart, completed by Marc-Antoine Crozat, and retouched by Bénédict Pictet. Lausanne: Fischer & Vincent. [The standard Calvinist translation in Rousseau's time, quoted by him.]
Lewis, Charlton T., and Charles Short. 1879. *A Latin Dictionary, Founded on Andrews' Edition of Freund's Latin Dictionary*. Oxford: Clarendon.
Littré, Emile. 1959–60. *Dictionnaire de la langue française*. 7 vols. Paris: Gallimard.
Lovejoy, Arthur O. 1948. "The Supposed Primitivism of Rousseau's *Discourse on Inequality*." In *Essays in the History of Ideas*, 14–37. Baltimore: Johns Hopkins University Press.
MacLean, Lee. 2013. "The Quality of Rousseau's Intention and the *Reveries of the Solitary Walker*." In *The Free Animal: Rousseau on Free Will and Human Nature*, 131–50. Toronto: University of Toronto Press.
Manent, Pierre. 2013. "Montaigne and Rousseau: Some Reflections." In *The Challenge of Rousseau*, edited by Eve Grace and Christopher Kelly, 312–24. Cambridge: Cambridge University Press.
Manent, Pierre. 2019. "To Walk, to Dream, to Philosophize." In *The Rousseauian Mind*, edited by Eve Grace and Christopher Kelly, 312–24. London: Routledge.
Margel, Serge. 2000. "'*Mendacium est fabula*' ou le droit de mentir par aveu d'innocence. J.-J. Rousseau: De la IVe Promenade à l'exergue des *Confessions*." *Archives de philosophie* 63:5–29.
Marks, Jonathan. 2005a. "Misreading One's Sources: Charles Taylor's Rousseau." *American Journal of Political Science* 49:119–34.
Marks, Jonathan. 2005b. *Perfection and Disharmony in the Thought of Jean-Jacques Rousseau*. Cambridge: Cambridge University Press.
Marks, Jonathan. 2014. "Strauss's Rousseau: A Preface to Strauss's 1962 Seminar on Rousseau at the University of Chicago." Leo Strauss Transcripts. The Leo Strauss Center at the University of Chicago. http://leostrausstranscripts.uchicago.edu/navigate/5/1/3/.
Marshall, Terence. 1978. "Rousseau and Enlightenment." *Political Theory* 6:421–55.
Marshall, Terence. 1979. "Perception politique et théorie de la connaissance dans l'oeuvre de Jean-Jacques Rousseau." *Revue française de science politique* 29:605–64.
Marshall, Terence. 1984. "Art d'écrire et pratique politique de Jean-Jacques Rousseau (I et II)." *Revue de métaphysique et de morale* 89:232–261, 322–347.
Martin, Carole. 2008. "De rêveries en promenades: Essai d'étude générique à partir des *Rêveries du promeneur solitaire*." In *The Nature of Rousseau's Rêveries: Physical, Human, Aesthetic*, edited by John C. O'Neal, 245–60. Oxford: Voltaire Foundation.
Marvick, Louis W. 1993, "Fontenelle and the Truth of Masks." *Modern Language Studies* 23:70–78.
Masson, Pierre Maurice. 1911. "Rousseau contra Helvétius." *Revue d'histoire littéraire de la France* 18:103–24.
Masson, Pierre Maurice. 1914. *La "profession de foi du vicaire savoyard" de Jean-Jacques Rousseau; édition critique d'après les manuscrits de Genève, Neuchâtel et Paris, avec une introduction et un commentaire historique*. Paris: Hachette.

Masson, Pierre Maurice. 1916. *La religion de Rousseau*. 3 vols. Paris: Hachette.
Masters, Roger. 1968. *The Political Philosophy of Rousseau*. Princeton, NJ: Princeton University Press.
Masters, Roger, and Christopher Kelly, eds. 1990–2010. *The Collected Writings of Rousseau*. 13 vols. Hanover, NH: University Press of New England.
McDonald, Joan. 1965. *Rousseau and the French Revolution, 1762–1791*. London: Athlone.
Meier, Heinrich. 1984. *Jean-Jacques Rousseau, Diskurs über die Ungleichheit/Discours sur l'inégalité*. Kritische Ausgabe des integralen Textes. Paderborn: Ferdinand Schöningh.
Meier, Heinrich. 2006. *Leo Strauss and the Theologico-Political Problem*. Cambridge: Cambridge University Press.
Meier, Heinrich. 2016. *On the Happiness of the Philosophic Life: Reflections on Rousseau's Rêveries in Two Books*. Chicago: University of Chicago Press.
Meier, Heinrich. 2022. *"Les rêveries du promeneur solitaire": Rousseau über das philosophische Leben*. 3rd ed. Munich: Siemens Stiftung.
Melzer, Arthur M. 1990. *The Natural Goodness of Man: On the System of Rousseau's Thought*. Chicago: University of Chicago Press.
Melzer, Arthur M. 1996. "The Origin of the Counter-Enlightenment: Rousseau and the New Religion of Sincerity." *American Political Science Review* 90:344–60.
Melzer, Arthur M. 1997. "Rousseau and the Modern Cult of Sincerity." In *The Legacy of Rousseau*, edited by Clifford Orwin and Nathan Tarcov, 274–95. Chicago: University of Chicago Press.
Melzer, Arthur M. 2014. *Philosophy between the Lines: The Lost History of Esoteric Writing*. Chicago: University of Chicago Press.
Mercier, Louis Sébastien. 1801. *Néologie, ou Vocabulaire de mots nouveaux, à renouveler, ou pris dans des acceptions nouvelles*. Paris: Moussard and Maradan.
Millet, Louis. 1966. *La pensée de Rousseau*. Paris: Bordas.
Morel, Jean. 1909. "Recherches sur les sources du discours de l'inégalité." *Annales de la Société Jean-Jacques Rousseau* 5:119–98.
Morrissey, Robert. 1980. "Vers un topos littéraire: La préhistoire de la rêverie." *Modern Philology* 77:261–90.
Mortier, Roland. 1969. "Esotéricisme et lumières: Un dilemme de la pensée du XVIIIe siècle." In *Clartés et ombres du siècle des lumières: Etudes sur le 18e siècle littéraire*, 60–103. Geneva: Droz.
Mountain, Jacob. 1777. *Poetical Reveries*. London: Dodsley.
Neidleman, Jason. 2013. "The Sublime Science of Simple Souls: Rousseau's Philosophy of Truth." *History of European Ideas* 39:815–34.
Newell, Waller. 2022. *Tyranny and Revolution: Rousseau to Heidegger*. Cambridge: Cambridge University Press.
Nichols, James H., Jr. 1976. *Epicurean Political Philosophy: The* De Rerum Natura *of Lucretius*. Ithaca, NY: Cornell University Press.
O'Dea, Michael. 2003. "'Tout le monde se tut': Problems of Rhetoric in Rousseau's Autobiographical Works." In *Approaches to Teaching Rousseau's* Confessions *and* Reveries of the Solitary Walker, edited by John C. O'Neal and Ourida Mostefai, 44–49. New York: Modern Language Association of America.

O'Dea, Michael. 2014. "Les méditations d'un solitaire: Un approche chronologique." In *Philosophie de Rousseau*, edited by Blaise Bachofen, Bruno Bernardi, André Charrak, and Florent Guénard, 268–78. Paris: Garnier.

Orwat, Florence. 2006. *L'Invention de la rêverie, une conquête pacifique du grand siècle.* Paris: Champion.

Orwin, Cifford. 1980. "Compassion." *American Scholar* 49:309–33.

Orwin, Cifford. 1997. "Rousseau and the Discovery of Political Compassion." In *The Legacy of Rousseau*, edited by Clifford Orwin and Nathan Tarcov, 296–320. Chicago: University of Chicago Press.

Orwin, Cifford. 1998. "Rousseau's Socratism." *Journal of Politics* 60:174–87.

Osmont, Robert. 1934. "Contribution à l'étude psychologique des *Rêveries du promeneur solitaire*. La vie du souvenir—le rhythme lyrique." *Annales de la Société Jean-Jacques Rousseau* 23:7–134.

Osmont, Robert. 1965. "Un événement aussi triste qu'imprévu." *Revue d'histoire littéraire de la France* 65:614–28.

Pagani, Karen. 2014. "Living Well Is the Best Revenge: Rousseau's 'Reveries' and the (Non)problem of Forgiveness." *Eighteenth-Century Studies* 47:407–23.

Pagani, Karen. 2015. *Man or Citizen: Anger, Forgiveness, and Authenticity in Rousseau.* University Park: Pennsylvania State University Press.

Pangle, Lorraine Smith. 1999. "Friendship and Self-Love in Aristotle's *Nicomachean Ethics*." In *Action and Contemplation: Studies in the Moral and Political Thought of Aristotle*, edited by Susan Collins and Robert Bartlett, 171–202. Albany: State University of New York Press.

Pangle, Lorraine Smith. 2001. "Friendship and Human Neediness in Plato's *Lysis*." *Ancient Philosophy* 21:305–23.

Pangle, Lorraine Smith. 2003. *Aristotle and the Philosophy of Friendship*. Cambridge: Cambridge University Press.

Pangle, Lorraine Smith. 2009. "Moral and Criminal Responsibility in Plato's *Laws*." *American Political Science Review* 103:456–73.

Pangle, Lorraine Smith. 2013. "Virtue and Self-Control in Xenophon's Socratic Thought." In *Natural Right and Political Philosophy: Essays in Honor of Catherine and Michael Zuckert*, edited by Lee Ward and Ann Ward, 15–35. Notre Dame, IN: University of Notre Dame Press.

Pangle, Lorraine Smith. 2014. *Virtue Is Knowledge: The Moral Foundations of Socratic Political Philosophy*. Chicago: University of Chicago Press.

Pangle, Lorraine Smith. 2015. "Moral Indignation, Magnanimity, and Philosophy in the Trial of the Armenian King." In *In Search of Humanity: Essays in Honor of Clifford Orwin*, edited by Andrea Radasanu, 101–13. Lanham, MD: Lexington.

Pangle, Lorraine Smith. 2020. *Reason and Character: The Moral Foundations of Aristotelian Political Philosophy*. Chicago: University of Chicago Press.

Pangle, Thomas L. 2018. *The Socratic Way of Life: Xenophon's* Memorabilia. Chicago: University of Chicago Press.

Pangle, Thomas L. 2020. *Socrates Founding Political Philosophy in Xenophon's* Economist, Symposium, *and* Apology. Chicago: University of Chicago Press.

Pangle, Thomas L., and Peter J. Ahrensdorf. 1999. "The Rousseauian Revolt." In *Justice among Nations: On the Moral Basis of Power and Peace*, 185–90 Lawrence: University Press of Kansas.

Pangle, Thomas L., and Timothy Burns. 2015. "Rousseau's *First* and *Second Discourses*." In *The Key Texts of Political Philosophy: An Introduction*, 331–64 Cambridge: Cambridge University Press.

Pasqualucci, Paolo. 1976. *Rousseau e Kant*, Vol. 2: *Immanenza e trascendentalità dell'ordine*. Milan: Giuffré.

Pernot, Laurent. 2021. *The Subtle Subtext: Hidden Meanings in Literature and Life*. Translated by W. E. Higgins. University Park, PA.: Pennsylvania State University Press.

Perrin, Jean-François. 1997. "Du droit de taire la vérité au mensonge magnanime: Sur quelques arrière-plans théoriques et littéraires de la quatrième Promenade." *Littératures* 37:115–30.

Perrin, Jean-François. 1999. "Vie automate et quête de soi dans les *Rêveries du promeneur solitaire*." *Romanistische Zeitschrift für Literaturgeschichte* 23:331–39.

Perrin, Jean-François. 2011. *Politique du renonçant: Le dernier Rousseau: Des* Dialogues *aux* Rêveries. Paris: Kimé.

Philonenko, Alexis. 1984. *Jean-Jacques Rousseau et la pensée du malheur*. 3 vols. Paris: Vrin.

Pilaud, Christiane. 2005. "La Rochefoucauld: La duplicité de l'écriture des *Mémoires*." *Les Cahiers du GADGES* 2:185–97.

Plattner, Marc. 1979. *Rousseau's State of Nature: An Interpretation of the* Discourse on Inequality. DeKalb: Northern Illinois University Press.

Poulet, Georges. 1950. *Etudes sur le temps humain 1*. Paris: Plon.

Prat, Marie-Hélène, and Pierre Servet, eds. 2005. *La parole masqué*. Geneva: Droz.

Py, Gilbert. 1969–71. "Jean-Jacques Rousseau et la Congrégation des Prêtres de l'Oratoire de Jésus." *Annales de la Société Jean-Jacques Rousseau* 38:127–53.

Ravier, André. 1941. *L'Éducation de l'homme nouveau: Essai historique et critique sur le livre de l'Emile de J.-J. Rousseau*. 2 vols. Issoudun: Spès.

Raymond, Marcel. 1948. *Les rêveries du promeneur solitaire*. Édition critique. Geneva: Droz.

Raymond, Marcel. 1962a. *Jean-Jacques Rousseau: La quête de soi et la rêverie*. Paris: Corti.

Raymond, Marcel. 1962b. "Rêver à la Suisse." *Les cahiers du sud* 367:358–73.

Reisert, Joseph. 2003. *Jean-Jacques Rousseau, a Friend of Virtue*. Ithaca, NY: Cornell University Press.

Ricatte, Robert. 1959–62. "Un nouvel examen des cartes à jouer." *Annales de la Société Jean Jacques Rousseau* 35:239–62.

Ricatte, Robert. 1965. *Réflexions sur les "Rêveries."* Paris: Corti.

Richelet, Pierre. 1680. *Dictionnaire français contenant les mots et les choses, etc.* 2 vols. Geneva: Widerhold.

Riezler, Kurt. 1975. *Man Mutable and Immutable: The Fundamental Structure of Social Life*. Westport, CT: Greenwood.

Roddier, Henri. 1960. Introduction to *Les rêveries du promeneur solitaire*. Paris: Garnier.

Rosenberg, Aubrey. 1987. *Jean-Jacques Rousseau and Providence: An Interpretive Essay*. Sherbrooke, QC: Naaman.

Rousseau, J. J. ("Citizen of Geneva"). 1762. *Émile, ou De l'éducation*. 4 vols. The Hague [a mask; really, Paris]: Jean Néaulme [a mask; really, Duchesne; but the second edition was indeed from Néaulme at The Hague—see Dufour 1925, 1:149].

Rousseau, J. J. 1764. *Oeuvres de M. Rousseau de Genève*. Vol. 5. Neuchatel: Duchesne.

Rousseau, J. J. 1861. *Oeuvres et correspondance inédites*. Edited by George Streckeisen-Moultou. Paris: Lévy.

Sacaluga, Servando. 1968. "Diderot, Rousseau, et la querelle musicale de 1752. Nouvelle mise au point." *Diderot Studies* 10:133–73.

Sage, Pierre. 1951. *Le "bon prêtre" dans la littérature française: D'Amadis de Gaule au génie du christianisme*. Geneva: Droz.

Saint-Amand, Pierre. 1983. "Rousseau contre la science: L'Exemple de la botanique dans les textes autobiographiques." *Studies on Voltaire and the Eighteenth Century* 219:159–68.

Saint-Amand, Pierre. 2010. "Freedom and the Project of Laziness." In *Rousseau and Freedom*, edited by Christie McDonald and Stanley Hoffman, 245–56. Cambridge: Cambridge University Press.

Saint-Amant, Marc Antoine Gérard. 1855. *Oeuvres complètes*. 2 vols. Paris: Jannet.

Sainte-Beuve, Charles-Augustin. 1857–70. *Causeries de lundi*. 3rd ed. 15 vols. Paris: Garnier.

Saxe, Maurice comte de. 1757. *Mes rêveries*. 2 vols. Amsterdam: Arestée and Merkus.

Schaub, Diana J. 2009. "The Education of the Sentiments in Montesquieu's *The Temple of Gnidus*." In *The Arts of Rule: Essays in Honor of Harvey C. Mansfeld*, edited by Sharon R. Krause and Mary A. McGrail, 125–46. New York: Lexington Books.

Scott, David. 1979. "Rousseau and Flowers: The Poetry of Botany." *Studies on Voltaire and the Eighteenth Century* 182:73–86.

Scott, John T. 2008. "Rousseau's Quixotic Quest in the *Rêveries du promeneur solitaire*." In *The Nature of Rousseau's* Rêveries: *Physical, Human, Aesthetic*, edited by John C. O'Neal, 139–52. Oxford: Voltaire Foundation.

Senancour, Etienne Pivert de. Germinal, an VI [1798]. *Rêveries sur la nature de l'homme: Sur ses sensations, sur les moyens de bonheur quelles lui indiquent, sur la mode social qui conserveroit le plus de ses formes primodiales*. Paris: De La Tenna.

Seznec, Jean. 1957. *Essais sur Diderot et l'antiquité*. Oxford: Clarendon.

Shklar, Judith. 1969. *Men and Citizens: A Study of Rousseau's Social Theory*. Cambridge: Cambridge University Press.

Silverthorne, M. J. 1973. "Rousseau's Plato." *Studies on Voltaire and the Eighteenth Century* 116:235–50.

Smith, David Warner. 1971. "The 'Useful Lie' in Helvétius and Diderot." *Diderot Studies* 14:185–95.

Snyders, Georges. 1963. "Une révolution dans le goût musical au XVIII siècle: l'apport de Diderot et Jean-Jacques Rousseau." *Annales. Economies Sociétés Civilisations* 18:20–43.

Sommer, Edouard. 1866. *Lexique de la langue de Madame de Sévigné*. 2 vols. Paris: Hachette.

Spector, Céline. 2014. "De Rousseau à Charles Taylor: Autonomie, authenticité, reconnaisance." In *Philosophie de Rousseau*, edited by Blaise Bachofen, Bruno Bernardi, André Charrak, and Florent Guénard, 349–61. Paris: Garnier.

Spink, John Stephenson. 1948. *Les rêveries du promeneur solitaire*. Édition critique publiée d'après les manuscripts autographes. Paris: Didier.
Staël, Germaine de. 1788. *Lettres sur les ouvrages et le caractère de J. J. Rousseau*. Lausanne: Mourer.
Starobinski, Jean. 1957. *Jean-Jacques Rousseau: La transparence et l'obstacle*. Paris: Plon.
Starobinski, Jean. 1971. *Jean-Jacques Rousseau: La transparence et l'obstacle* [rev. ed.], *suivi de Sept essais sur Rousseau*. Paris: Gallimard.
Starobinski, Jean. 1988. *Jean-Jacques Rousseau: Transparency and Obstruction*. Revised and with seven essays. Translated by Arthur Goldhammer. Chicago: University of Chicago Press. [A somewhat loose translation, especially of passages cited here.]
Still, Judith. 1993. "Gyges' Ring: A Reading of Rousseau's 6e Promenade." In *Justice and Difference in the Works of Rousseau*, 108–30. Cambridge: Cambridge University Press.
Strauss, Leo. 1947. "On the Intention of Rousseau." *Social Research* 14:455–87.
Strauss, Leo. 1953. *Natural Right and History*. Chicago: University of Chicago Press.
Strauss, Leo. 1959. *What Is Political Philosophy and Other Studies*. Glencoe, IL: Free Press.
Strauss, Leo. 1964. *The City and Man*. Chicago: Rand McNally.
Strauss, Leo. 1966. *Socrates and Aristophanes*. New York: Basic Books.
Strauss, Leo. 1970. *Xenophon's Socratic Discourse: An Interpretation of the Oeconomicus*. Ithaca, NY: Cornell University Press.
Strauss, Leo. 1975. "The Three Waves of Modernity." In *Political Philosophy: Six Essays*, edited by Hilail Gilden, 81–98. Indianapolis: Bobbs-Merrill.
Strauss, Leo. 1989. *The Rebirth of Classical Political Rationalism*. Edited by Thomas L. Pangle. Chicago: University of Chicago Press.
Strauss, Leo. 1991. *On Tyranny, Revised and Expanded Edition, Including the Strauss-Kojève Correspondence*. New York: Free Press.
Strauss, Leo. 2012. *Leo Strauss on Moses Mendelssohn*. Translated and edited by Martin D. Yaffe. Chicago: University of Chicago Press.
Strauss, Leo. 2014. Transcript of 1962 Seminar on Rousseau at the University of Chicago. Leo Strauss Transcripts. The Leo Strauss Center at the University of Chicago. http://leostrausstranscripts.uchicago.edu/navigate/5/1/3/.
Swenson, James. 2008. "The Solitary Walker and the Invention of Lyric Prose." In *The Nature of Rousseau's Rêveries: Physical, Human, Aesthetic*, edited by John C. O'Neal, 225–44. Oxford: Voltaire Foundation.
Taylor, Charles. 1991. *The Ethics of Authenticity*. Cambridge, MA: Harvard University Press.
Terrasse, Jean. 1979. "Dieu, la nature, les fleurs: Sur une page des *Rêveries*." In *Index des "Fragments autobiographiques" et de la "Lettre à Voltaire"; précédé d'une édition critique de la "Lettre à Voltaire sur la Providence"; et suivi des Actes du Colloque de Nice (28–30 juin 1978) sur Jean-Jacques Rousseau et Voltaire*, edited by Gilles Fauconnier, 593–615. Paris: Champion.
Theil, Martin du. 1828. *Jean-Jacques Rousseau, apologiste de la religion chrétienne*. Paris: Belin-Mandar et Devaux.
Todorov, Tzevetan. 1999. *Frail Happiness: An Essay on Rousseau*. University Park: Pennsylvania State University Press.

Tripet, Arnaud. 1979. *La rêverie littéraire: Essai sur Rousseau*. Geneva: Droz.
Troeltsch, Ernst. 1976. *The Social Teaching of the Christian Churches*. Translated by Olive Wyon. Chicago: University of Chicago Press.
Trousson, Raymond. 1967. *Socrate devant Voltaire, Diderot et Rousseau: La conscience en face du mythe*. Paris: Minard.
Trousson, Raymond. 1976. Review note on David Bensoussan, *La maladie de Rousseau*. *Dix-huitième siècle* 8:498.
Trousson, Raymond. 1977. "Quinze années d'études rousseauistes." *Dix-huitième siècle* 9:343–86.
Trousson, Raymond. 1988. *Jean-Jacques Rousseau*. 2 vols. Paris: Tallandier.
Trousson, Raymond. 1992. "Quinze années d'études rousseauistes (II)." *Dix-huitième siècle* 24:421–89.
Trousson, Raymond, and Frédéric S. Eigeldinger. 1995. *Dictionnaire de Jean-Jacques Rousseau*. Paris: Champion.
Vallette, Gaspard. 1911. *Jean-Jacques Rousseau Genevois*. Paris: Plon.
Van Staen, Christophe. 2001. "De l'espoir et du désespoir: La 'folle tentative' du billet circulaire et la genèse des *Rêveries*." *Bulletin de l'Association Jean-Jacques Rousseau* 58:3–24.
Vaughan, Charles Edwyn. 1915. *The Political Writings of Jean-Jacques Rousseau*. 2 vols. Cambridge: Cambridge University Press.
Viau, Théophile de. 1856. *Oeuvres complètes de Theophile [sic]*. 2 vols. Paris: Jannet.
Villaverde, Maria-José. 1990. "*Vitam impendere vero* de Juvénal à Rousseau." *Etudes Jean-Jacques Rousseau* 4:53–70.
Voisine, Jacques. 1969. "Rousseau ou le Socrate moderne." In *Modern Miscellany Presented to E. Vinaver by Pupils, Colleagues, and Friends*, edited by Thomas Edward Lawrenson et al., 276–93. Manchester, UK: Manchester University Press.
Wacjman, Claude. 1992. *Fous de Rousseau: Le cas Rousseau dans l'histoire de la psychopathologie*. Paris: Harmattan.
Wacjman, Claude. 1996. *Les jugements de le critique sur le "folie" de J.-J. Rousseau: Représentations et interprétations, 1760–1990*. Vol. 337 of *Studies on Voltaire and the Eighteenth Century*. Geneva: Institut de Musée Voltaire.
Wade, Ira. 1938. *The Clandestine Organization and Diffusion of Philosophic Ideas in France from 1700 to 1750*. Princeton, NJ: Princeton University Press.
Wahl, Jean. 1946. *Tableau de la philosophie française*. Paris: Revue Fontaine.
Weylar, Maria. 1770. *Reveries du coeur, or, Feelings of the Heart*. London: Dodsley.
Williams, David Lay. 2012. "The Platonic Soul of the 'Reveries': The Role of Solitude in Rousseau's Democratic Politics." *History of Political Thought* 33:87–123.
Williams, Huntington. 1983. *Rousseau and Romantic Autobiography*. Oxford: Oxford University Press.
Wilson, Arthur M. 1957. *Diderot: The Testing Years, 1713–1759*. New York: Oxford University Press.
Yasuda, Yurie. 2018. "*Rêveries du promeneur solitaire*, texte sans destinaire?" *Revue de langue et littérature françaises* 50:115–31.

Index

Adam, 125
Adonis, 192n26
Aeneas, 196–97n21
Alembert, Jean Le Rond d', 150, 171n24, 172n29, 182n2, 208n6; *Encyclopedia, Discours préliminaire,* 182n22, 190–91n8, 192n27, "Encyclopedia," 192n27; "Éloge de Montesquieu," 192n27
Alfarabi, ix
amour-propre (vanity), 84, 85, 121, 142–46, 168n9, 207nn10–11, 207n13
Apollo, 1, 75
Aristophanes, 24, 150, 170n19, 172n29, 172n31; *Acharnians,* 150, 170n19
Aristotle, ix, 3, 118, 155, 190–91n18, 201n15; *History of Animals,* 133; *Metaphysics,* 105–6, 198n33; *Nicomachean Ethics,* 22, 105–6, 117, 170n23, 172n32, 198n33, 199n40, 201n13; *Parts of Animals,* 133, 205n21; *On Soul,* 198n33; *Rhetoric,* 170n23
atheism, 55–57, 59, 68, 140, 181n20, 182–83n24, 183n26, 184n33, 185n42, 187n60, 192–93n29
Augustine, Saint, 45, 188n5; *On Lying,* 190–91n18

Bacon, Francis, 184n37
Bayle, Pierre: Condorcet on Bayle's esoteric writing, 187n59
Beaumont, Christophe de: "Pastoral Letter of His Grace the Archbishop of Paris," 184n33, 186n47
beauty, x, 9, 10, 31, 55, 93, 100, 110, 119–20, 131, 133, 179n22, 205n22
Bellamy, Edward: *Looking backward 2000–1887,* 178n15
Bible, 24, 55, 64–65, 74–75, 85, 100, 125, 175n53, 177n12, 185n41. *See also* Jesus Christ
Bloom, Allan, 185n41, 188n62, 202n22

Bolotin, David, 22
bourgeois (as corrupt, vs citizen), 53, 85, 170n22
Buffon, Georges-Louis Leclerc De, 182–83n24
Burgelin, Pierre, 175n52, 177n2, 186n50, 186n54, 206n2
Butterworth, Charles E., 39, 54, 60, 114, 148, 176n62, 177n9, 201n8, 209n12

Calvinism, 179n22, 185n41
Cannet, Marie-Henriette, 182–83n24, 192–93n29
Canziani, Guido, 192n27
Catinat, Nicolas de, 180–81n9
Cato the Elder, 51
Cérutti, Joseph-Antoine-Joachim, 175n52
chance. *See* fortune
charity, 17–18, 115, 117–18, 120, 154–55, 180n9, 202n22, 202n24
Chateaubriand, François-René de, 30
Chaucer, 177–78n12
children, 16, 48, 135, 146–47, 150–53, 162n7, 201n13, 208n7, 208–9n8, 209n9. *See also* family
Choiseul, Étienne François, Duke of, 167n5, 195n12
Christianity, 51–57 passim, 64–65, 155, 182n22, 182–83n24, 186n50, 188–89n5, 193–94n34. *See also* Bible; Jesus Christ
Cicero, ix, 177n12, 187n60, 190–91n18
citizenship, citizen, x, 3, 55, 60, 81, 84–85, 89, 108, 153, 188–89n5
Clark, Lorraine J., 122–23, 201n15, 201n18, 202n24
Clarke, Samuel, 61
Coignet, Horace, 19, 169n12
Coleman, Patrick, 170n22, 171n24, 188n5
comedy, 24, 150, 152. *See also* Aristophanes; laughter
commerce, 154–55, 209n11

226   INDEX

compassion, 26, 29, 31, 41, 93, 112, 115, 118, 122, 153, 170nn, 172n29, 174n51, 200n4, 201n15, 201–2n18, 202n22. *See also* goodness
Condorcet, Antoine-Nicolas de: *Esquisse d'un tableau historique des progrès de l'esprit humain*, 187n57, 192n27
conscience, 61–64, 69, 71, 77–95 passim, 119–21, 144, 185nn42–44, 189n9, 190nn12–16. *See also* duty; instinct (moral); virtue
consciousness, x–xi, 2, 4–5, 8, 31, 35–43 passim, 64, 76–77, 101–9 passim, 112, 115, 123, 150, 159, 198n33, 199n40
contentment (vs happiness), 40, 62, 108, 149, 151, 153, 156, 208n4. *See also* happiness
contract, 119–22, 201n18
Cook, Alexandra, 203n8, 205n20, 205n23
cosmopolitanism, 154
Cotoni, Marie-Hélène, 173n42, 175n54, 190n11
courage and cowardice, 51. *See also* virtue
Cranston, Maurice: atheism of *Second Discourse*, 179n18; conspiracy against Rousseau, 168n9, 168–69n10; D'Alembert, 182n22; Diderot, 19, 169n13, 182n22; 18th cent. bastardization of word "philosophers," 180n5; Grimm, 182n22; paganism of *First Discourse*, 182n22; Querelle des Buffons, 181n17; Romanticism, 29–30, 184n37; Rousseau's abandonment of his children, 208–9n8; Rousseau's botany unscientific, 203n5; Rousseau's celebrity, 53; Rousseau's influence in music, 181n16; Rousseau's paranoia, 168–69n10; Rousseau's pet dogs, 196–97n21; Rousseau's praying, 164n22; Rousseau's "system," 163n12; Rousseau's view of Christ, 175n56; Voltaire, 182n22
Critobulus, 188n4
Crocker, Lester G.: exoteric and esoteric writing, 192n27
Crogiez, Michèle, 51, 162n8
Cyrus. *See* Xenophon: *Education of Cyrus*

Damiens, Robert-François, 167n5
Damrosch, Leo, x, 157, 173n40, 181n14
Davis, Michael, 50, 138, 181n19, 208n3, 208n7, 209n12
De Luc, Jean-André, 168n9, 168–69n10, 182–83n23
Descartes, René, 7, 158, 206–7n7; *Meditationes de Prima Philosophia, in qua Dei existentia et animae immortalitas demonstratur*, 158, 177n12
dialogic refutation, xi–xii, 2–3, 22–31 passim, 50–51, 56, 64–65, 70–71, 103–4, 175n55, 180
Dickinson, Emily, 9
Diderot, Denis, 19, 27, 167n3, 168n9, 169n13, 182n22, 190–91n18, 192n27, 202n23; *Encyclopedia*, 13, 19, 53, 86, 171n24, 175n52, 182nn21–22, 195n15; articles "Delicious," 195n15; and "Mensonges officieux," 86
Dufour, Théophile, 4, 186n46
duty, 10, 28–29, 52, 54–55, 73, 95, 108, 115–23, 154, 201n15. *See also* conscience; instinct (moral); virtue

education, xi, 11, 49–50, 150, 184n33, 208–9n8
Eigeldinger, Frédéric, ix, 4, 167n5, 172n34, 176n62, 199n39, 206n5
Eisen, Charles, 63
Eleatic Stranger, 3
Emile, 11, 16, 87, 164n26
The Enlightenment, ix, 68, 85, 176n59, 180n5, 184n37, 192n27
Ephraim, 171n24
Epictetus, 181n18; *Manual*, 181n18
Epicurus, 104–5
Epinay, Louise d', 167n3
eros, the erotic, xi, 5, 10–11, 54, 84–85, 89, 123–24, 127, 165n30, 193n31, 204n13. *See also* Plato
eternity, 13, 25, 45, 55, 57, 63, 66, 68, 105, 141, 176n59, 184n36, 198n32
exoteric and esoteric communication, 60, 68, 82, 87, 187n60, 192n37, 192–93n29. *See also* hypocrisy; lying

Fabricius, 75
family, 16–18, 30, 54–55, 84–85, 97, 102–2, 123–24, 150–52, 162n7, 199n39. *See also* children; marriage
Farrell, John, popular attractiveness of Rousseau's paranoia, 174n50, 175n57
Farrugia, Guilhem, 177n11, 178n14
felicity and bliss. *See* happiness
Fénelon, François, 51–52, 57, 180–81n9; *l'Education des filles*, 180–81n9; *Lettres spirituelles*, 180–81n9; *Télémaque*, 180–81n9; *Traité de l'existence de Dieu*, 180–81n9
Ficino, Marsilio, 162n6

INDEX

Fields, W. C., 150
Formey, Johann Heinrich Samuel: Encyclopedia article "Exoteric and Esoteric," 192n27; "Examen de la question: Si toutes les vérités sont bonnes à dire?" 192n27
Fontanelle, Bernard le Bovier de, 158, 190–91n18, 191n19; *Conversations on the Plurality of Worlds*, 158; Condorcet on Fontanelle's esoteric writing, 187n59
fortune (chance, luck), 14, 23, 32, 44, 50, 52, 57, 109, 131–32, 135, 138, 141, 166n37, 194n1
Foucault, Michel, xi
France, 44, 159, 167n5, 167–68n6, 187n59, 192n27, 195n12
Francueil, Marie-Aurore de Saxe, Madame Dupin de, 208–9n8
Franquières, Laurent Amyon de, 180–81n9, 187n58, 192–93n29
freedom (liberty), 10, 22–24, 43, 124–25, 171n26, 174n50, 198n33. *See also* independence
"The Frenchman" (interlocutor in *Dialogues*), 14–16, 21, 30, 87, 167–68n6, 172–73n36, 199–200n41
Freud, Sigmund, 115
Friedlander, Eli, x–xi, 176n61, 189n6, 197n29
friendship, 3, 9–11, 16–20, 33, 41, 48–49, 53, 62, 65, 71, 93, 101, 121, 123, 129, 150, 154. *See also* eros; Plato

Gagnebin, Bernard, 184n31, 203n8
Garagnon, Anne-Marie, 170n20
Gasbarrone, Lisa, 128, 132, 205nn22–23
Gassendi, Pierre, 158
generosity. *See* charity
Geneva, 3, 5, 55, 85, 96, 153, 164n22, 177n4, 182–83n24, 185n41, 195n12
Gilson, Etienne, 177n12
Girardin, René Louis de, Marquis de Vouvray, 167n5, 194n6; *De la composition des paysages*, 194n6
Glaucon, 30, 66, 122–23, 175n54, 187n55
Gluck, Christoph Willibald Ritter von, 181n16
Goethe, Johann Wolfgang von, 13, 30
goodness (vs. virtue), 23, 62, 70, 83, 93, 94, 113–25, 144, 156, 166, 200–2. *See also* charity; compassion; instinct (moral); virtue
Gospel. *See* Bible
Gossman, Lionel, x, 27

Gourevitch, Victor, 158, 191–92n25
Grace, Eve, 101, 108, 168n8
Graffenreid, Emmanuel de, Bailiff of Nidau, 195n11
Greig, John Young Thomson, 71–72
Gresset, Jean-Baptiste-Louis, 159
Grimm, Frédéric-Melchior, 167n3, 168n9, 171n24, 182n22
Grimsley, Ronald, 41, 70, 104, 199n40
Grosclaude, Pierre, 168–69n10
Grosrichard, Alain, 206–7n7
Grotius, Hugo, *On the Law of War and Peace*, 190–91n18
Grynaeus, Simon, 162n6
Guéhenno, Jean, 172n33, 181n14
guilt, 22–24, 58, 77–78, 89–90, 94, 164n22, 202n22. *See also* indignation; sin
Guyon, Bernard, 166n39, 178n16, 183n26, 192–93n29
Gyges, ring of, 122–23, 149

Habakkuk, 100
Hadot, Pierre, xi
happiness (vs contentment), 12–14, 21, 38, 43, 46, 49, 52, 62–116 passim, 122–23, 129–30, 134–56 passim
Hegel, Georg Wilhelm Friedrich, 156, 180n6; *Encyclopedia of Philosophic Sciences*, 13, 198n33; *Lectures on the History of Philosophy 1825–6*, 161n4
Heidegger, Martin, 177–78n12; *Being and Time*, 206n3
Helvétius, Claude Adrien, 191n19; *De L'Esprit*, 185n40, 190–91n18
history, 2, 5, 20, 25, 127, 129, 140, 157
Hobbes, Thomas, 55, 162n5, 163n14, 178n13; *De Cive*, 158
Holbach, Paul Henri Thiry, Baron d': *Le bon-sens ou idées naturelles opposées aux idées surnaturelles*, 192n27
Homer, 31, 164n26
Hume, David, 71–72, 168n9, 168–69n10
Huygens, Christiaan, 158
hypocrisy, 76, 94, 189n9. *See also* exoteric and esoteric communication; lying; sincerity; truth

idleness (vs virtue, and labor), 97–99, 128, 131, 179n22, 195nn13–14, 204n17
independence, 120, 174n46. *See also* freedom
indignation, 21–29, 62, 75, 84, 106, 121, 135, 139, 142–46, 153, 170n20–22, 171n24, 187n55. *See also* guilt; sin

instinct (amoral), 129, 131–32, 135–36, 165–66n34. *See also* goodness
instinct (moral), 77–90 passim, 144, 185n44, 190nn12–13. *See also* conscience; virtue
irony (Socratic or classic), 25, 51, 159
Ivernois, Jean-Antoine d', 127, 128, 203n5

James, Saint, 175n53
Jaucourt, Chevalier Louis de, article "Lie" in *Encyclopedia*, 190–91n18
Jesus Christ, 24, 30–31, 63–66, 107, 174n51, 175nn52–54, 175n56, 179n22. *See also* Bible
Job, 173n37
Johnson, Samuel, 168n9
Julie (d'Étange), 9, 16, 59, 87, 183n26, 184n32, 185n42, 206n3
Juvenal, 188n5; *Satires*, 75, 188n5

Kant, Immanuel, 4, 65, 90, 163n13
Kelly, Christopher, 7, 59, 171n24, 174n46, 181n14, 191–92n25, 193–94n34, 204n13
Kierkegaard, Søren, 165n31, 186n50
Klein, Jacob, Plato's conception of imagination in relation to Rousseau's, 165n32
Kojève, Alexandre: problem of subjective certainty, 180n6

labor, hard work (vs idleness), 5–7, 15–16, 32–33, 39, 48–49, 62, 97–100, 131, 133
La Fontaine, Jean de: fables, 100, 195n14
Lamprocles (son of Socrates), 162n7
Lane, Joseph H., Jr.: *Reveries* intended by Rousseau for publication, 173n41
laughter, 24–25, 101, 116, 126–27, 152–53, 172n28–29, 203n4. *See also* Aristophanes; comedy; weeping
Launay, Michel, x, 172n33
law, 7, 23, 55, 96, 123, 136, 142, 165–66n34, 184n36. *See also* Grotius's *On the Law of War and Peace*; Montesquieu's *Spirit of the Laws*; Plato's *Laws*
Le Beau, Claude: *Avantures du sieur Claude Le Beau, avocat en parlement: Voyage curieux, et nouveau parmi les sauvages de l'amerique septentrionale*, 16, 166n37
legislator, lawgiver, 47, 87, 153
Leibniz, Gottfried Wilhelm, 7
Lessing, Gotthold Ephraim, *Minna von Barnhelm*, on laughter and indignation, 172n28
liberty. *See* freedom
Linnaeus, Carl, 133, 203n1, 205n20

Locke, John, 7, 68; *Essay Concerning Human Understanding*, 183n27
Louis XV, 167n5
Lucretius, 177n12; *De Rerum Natura*, 198n31
Lully, Jean-Baptiste: *Phaeton*, 158
lying, deceiving, 26, 45, 62, 73–94, 118, 120, 143, 180–81n10, 190–91n18, 191n23, 193–94n34. *See also* exoteric and esoteric communication; hypocrisy; sincerity; truth

Machiavell, ix
Malebranche, Nicolas, 7
Malesherbes, Chrétien-Guillaume de Lamoignon de: crucial letters to and about Rousseau, 168–69n10
Manent, Pierre, 2, 47–48, 77, 93, 176n62, 187n57, 187n61, 190n17, 193n30
Marion, 90
Marks, Jonathan, 161–62n4, 194n2, 194n7, 196n20
marriage, 18, 42, 85, 87, 97, 100, 152, 162n7, 195n9, 209n9. *See also* children; family
Mars (the god), 8
Masson, Pierre Maurice: Rousseau and Fénelon, 180–81n9, 184n34, 185n40
Medard, Saint, 123
medicine and doctors, 26, 127, 133, 168n7, 173n39
medieval, ix, 157, 177–78n12
Meier, Heinrich, 7, 89, 94, 108, 161–62n4, 174n45, 176n60, 177n10, 179–80n23, 204n13, 208n16
Melzer, Arthur: Rousseau's cultural revolutionary strategy, 184n37; Rousseau's "system", 163n12; exoteric and esoteric communication, 192n27, 192–93n29; soul in Rousseau, 202n22
Menexenus (son of Socrates), 162n7
miracle, 71, 123, 188n63, 193–94n34
misanthropy, 19–20, 25–26, 172n28
moderation, 50–51. *See also* virtue
modernity and moderns (vs ancients), ix, 11, 54–58, 85, 87, 133, 180n9, 192–93n29, 209n11
Montaigne, Michel de, 61, 161n1; *Essays*, 157–58, 178n13, 183n25, 190–91n18
Montesquieu, ix, 68, 84–8, 89–90, 191–92n25; D'Alembert on Montesquieu's esoteric writing, 192n27; Condorcet on Montesquieu's esoteric writing, 187n59; *Considerations on the Causes of the Greatness of the Romans and of Their Decline*, 207n13;

Le temple de Gnide, 84–8, 89–90, 192n26; *Spirit of the Laws*, 120, 154–55, 195n13, 209n11
moral responsibility. *See* guilt and indignation
Moultou, Paul-Claude, 121, 164n27, 175n56, 184n32, 184n34
Mozart, Wolfgang Amadeus, 181n16; *Bastien und Bastienne*, 181n16
The Muses, 186n47
music, x, 19, 53–54, 63, 100–101, 123–24, 127, 169n12, 171n24, 181n16, 182n22, 196n19

natural right or natural law, 55, 119–20
nature, man of, 16, 106, 156, 166n35, 171n24, 205n19
nature, state of, 59, 61, 70, 99, 112, 124, 165–66n34
necessity, 23, 25, 78, 109, 133, 139–42, 178n15, 199n41, 201n15
Newton, Isaac, 4
Nietzsche, Friedrich: *Beyond Good and Evil*, 207n12, 209n13; *Daybreak*, 201n9; *Thus Spoke Zarathustra*, 115, 201n9; *Twilight of the Idols*, 189n9, 195n13, 201n9
the noble, 7, 22, 50, 86, 87, 99, 175n54, 191n23, 193n33, 209n13. *See also* virtue

Orpheus, 63, 186n47
Orwin, Clifford: Rousseau's Socratism, 175n52, 209n10; Rousseau and his founding of a rabbit colony, 197n23, 200n3
Osmont, Robert, 177n5, 189n6; manuscript of *Reveries*, 141, 167n5, 172n34

Pagani, Karen, Rousseau's vengefulness, 22, 172n29, 174n51
paganism, 47, 54, 63, 74–75, 85, 182n22, 185n44, 187n58, 188–89n5
Pangle, Lorraine, Socrates's critique of retributive justice, 22, 101, 170n23
Paris, 6, 19, 39, 53, 127, 146, 150
Pascal, 183n27, 197n26
Paul, Saint, 175n53
Pausanias, 186n47
Perrin, Jean-François, 179n21, 190–91n18, 192n27
Persia, 75. *See also* Xenophon: *Education of Cyrus*
Philonenko, Alexis, 163n11, 163n13, 177n2
Phlipon, Marie-Jeanne, Mme de Roland: letter on Rousseau's religious belief, 182–83n24, 192–93n29

pity. *See* compassion
Placentius, Crispus, 188n5
Plato, ix, xi, 2–3, 22–23, 30–31, 41, 61, 65–66, 71; *Alcibiades*, 162n5; *Apology of Socrates*, 3, 51, 71, 162n5, 162n7, 170n23, 188n64; *Cratylus*, 3, 170n23; *Crito*, 3, 170n23, 188n64; *Euthydemus*, 170n23; *Euthyphro*, 3; *Gorgias*, 170n23; *Greater Hippias*, 170n23; *Hipparchus*, 170n23; *Laws*, 22–24, 56, 162n6, 170n23, 189n7, 195n13; *Lovers*, 162n5; *Meno*, 170n23; *Phaedo*, 2–3, 19, 23–25, 65, 70–71, 162nn6–7, 172n31, 174n47, 176n59; *Phaedrus*, 3, 33, 162n5; *Philebus*, 162n5; *Protagoras*, 170n23; *Republic*, 24–25, 30–31, 55, 66, 87, 112, 122–23, 162n6, 175n52, 182n23; *Sophist*, 3, 51, 170n23; *Statesman*, 162n6; *Symposium*, 3; *Theaetetus*, 3, 170n23, 180n7
Plattner, Marc, 59, 166n34, 192n27
Pleix, Scipion du, *Metaphysics*, 177n12
Plutarch, xi, 55, 74–76, 81–82, 94, 190–91n18; "Comparative Judgment of Solon and Publicola," 191n21; *How One Might by Enemies Be Benefited*, 74–76, 170n23, 175n57, 188nn3–4, 189n7; Life of Lycurgus, 154; Life of Solon, 74–76, 94, 180n1, 191n21; *On Absence of Anger*, 170n23
Polybius, 170–71n23
pride, 5, 6, 78, 92, 102, 122, 143–44, 164n29, 193n33, 197n23, 200n3
prudence, 116, 117, 118, 120, 190n15, 190–91n18, 201n14
Pythagoras, 187n60, 192n27

Quintilian, 190–91n18

Rabelais, François, 195n14
Raymond, Marcel, 52, 163n11, 168n9, 187nn, 189n8, 201n7, 208n4
revelation, 61–66 passim, 71, 80, 88, 162n7, 163n18, 180–81n23, 182–83n24, 186n48, 186n50. *See also* Bible
revolution, cultural and political, 29, 53, 54, 60, 174n50, 175n54, 184n37
Riezler, Kurt, 172n32, 200n43; Leo Strauss's eulogy of, 170–71n23; self-love, 178n15; Socratic irony, 25
Robinson Crusoe, 197n22
Romanticism, 29–30, 53–54, 96–97, 103, 107, 110, 133–34, 155–58, 165n33, 184n37
Rome, Romans, 51–53, 75, 155, 161n4, 171n24, 188–89n5

230   INDEX

Rosenberg, Aubrey, 182–83n24, 183n26, 202n23; prayer missing in *Reveries*, 199n38; Rousseau's esoteric writing, 192–93n29; Rousseau's identification with Jesus, 179n22
Rosier (aka Rozier), François, Abbé, 75, 94, 189n6
"Rousseau," a character in *Dialogues*, 14–16, 20–21, 24, 37, 53, 60, 87, 106, 129, 141, 164n24
Rousseau, other writings of, *Confessions*, passim; conspiracy against, 18–29 passim, 44–48 passim, 62–63, 66, 116, 121, 139–42, 149–51, 154, 164–69 passim, 172–73; "Copy of the Circular Note Which Is Spoken of in the Preceding Writing," 129; *Dialogues*, passim; "Discourse on This Question: Which Is the Virtue Most Necessary for a Hero and Which Are the Heroes Who Lacked This Virtue?" 175n55; *Emile*, passim; *First Discourse*, passim; "Four Letters to Malesherbes," 12, 39, 46, 51, 168–69n10; *Fragments for a Dictionary of the Terms of Usage in Botany*, 205n23; *Government of Poland*, 19, 163n19; *Heloise*, passim; "Le lévite d'Ephraim," 171n24, 180–81n9; *Letter on French Music*, 53; *Letter to Beaumont*, passim; *Letter to D'Alembert*, 171n24, 172n29, 188n5, 192–93n29, 193n33, 208n4; "Letter to Franquières," 30, 180–81n9, 187n58, 192–93n29, 202n25; "Letter to Philopolis," 163n12, 166n34; *Letters Written from the Mountain*, 22, 59, 163n19, 172n29, 175n53, 184n32, 188–89n5, 195n10; *Lucretia*, 5; *Moral Letters*, 185n42, 194n2, 197n30; "Observations on the Reply Made [to the First Discourse by Stanislas]," 187n60, 203n10, "On Theatrical Imitation: An Essay Drawn from Plato's Dialogues," 31, 61, 182n23; "Preface" to *Narcisse*, 53, 163n12, 169n14; "Preface to a Second Letter to Bordes," 163n12, 191n22; *Pygmalion*, 19; *Second Discourse*, passim; *Social Contract*, 5, 87, 108–9; *The Village Soothsayer (Le devin du village)*, 19, 53, 181n16

Sainte-Beuve, Charles-Augustin, *Causeries de lundi*, 157, 159, 168n9, 191n19
Saint-Victor, Richard of: *On the Trinity*, 177n12
Satan, 173n37

Savoyard vicar, 11, 23–24, 30, 45, 58–66, 87–88, 106, 162n7, 171n27, 178n16, 184nn32–34, 186n47, 186n54
Schaub, Diana, 85, 90
Scott, David, Rousseau's botanizing not a scientific pursuit, 196n16, 205n23
Scott, John T., 126–27, 172n29, 203n4
Scudéry, Madeleine de: *Clélie*, 158
Senancour, Etienne Pivert de, 163n11
Seneca: *Ad Lucilium*, 177n12; *On Anger*, 170n23
sentiment of existence, 43, 101–14 passim, 135–39, 145–47, 156, 194n2, 195–96n15, 197n26, 206n26
Sévigné, Marie de Rabutin-Chantal, marquise de, 158
Shakespeare, 194n6
shame, 20, 31, 51, 76, 91, 93, 117, 152, 202n22
Shelley, Percy Bysshe, 30
Shklar, Judith: Rousseau's entire oeuvre an "exercise in indignation," 170n21
Silverthorne, M. J.: Rousseau's annotations on his copy of Plato, 162n6, 170n23
sin, 58, 202n22. *See also* guilt; indignation
sincerity, 2, 57–58, 60, 202n22. *See also* exoteric and esoteric communication; hypocrisy; lying; truth
socialism, 178n15
Socrates ix, xi, 2, 3, 19–20, 22–25, 30–33, 41, 50–51, 54, 64–66, 70–72, 75–77, 89, 92, 101, 118, 134, 144, 153–56
Solon, 47, 69, 74–76, 81, 94, 180n1, 191n21
Sophie, 11, 87, 164n26
Sophronia, 193–94n34
Sophroniscus (father of Socrates), 30
Sophroniscus (son of Socrates), 162n7
Sorbière, Samuel de, 158
Sparta, 75, 154
Spink, John Stephenson, 3, 176n59, 194n6, 202n21; manuscript of *Reveries*, 167n5, 171n25
Spinoza, Baruch, 55, 104–5, 163n14; *Ethics*, 198n31
Staël, Germaine de, 163n13
Starobinski, Jean, 27, 174n48, 174n50, 179n18, 181n18, 193n32, 199n38; bizarre comments on *Reveries*, 161n3, 163n11, 169n14, 176n62, 179n19, 189n8; lack of seriousness in Rousseau's botanizing, 196n16, 203n6
Still, Judith: Rousseau's love of glory, 202n23, 202n25

Stoics, ix, 190–91n18
St. Preux, 9, 16, 29–30, 87, 166n39, 177n3, 186n48, 199n39
Strabo, 186n47
Strauss, Leo, 24, 154, 161–62n4, 170–71n23, 172n31, 206n25
Suarez, Francisco, *Metaphysical Disputations*, 177–78n12
sympathy. *See* compassion
system, Rousseau's "sad and grand system," 4, 6, 15, 41, 48, 53, 59, 61, 65–67, 142

Tasso, Torquato, 93, 193–94n34; *Jerusalem Delivered*, 93
Théophile de Viau, 210n3
Theophrastus, 133–34, 205n20, 205–6n24; *Inquiry into Plants*, 133; *On Causes of Plants*, 133, 205–6n24
Thomas Aquinas, *Summa Theologica*, 190–91n18
Tripet, Arnaud, 5, 162n8, 164n29, 201n7
Trousson, Raymond, x, 162n8, 168n7, 175n52, 203n8
truth, truthfulness, 2, 59–95 passim, 108, 112–18 passim, 182n23, 187n59, 188–89n5, 190–91n18, 191, 193nn32–33, 194n35, 204n13. *See also* exoteric and esoteric communication; hypocrisy; lying; sincerity

vanity. *See* amour-propre
Vasseur, Marie-Thérèse le (Rousseau's wife), 18, 41, 97, 100, 150, 152, 166–67n1, 208–9n8, 209n9
Venus, 85–87, 192n26
Vernes, Jacob, 171n24, 176n58, 182n22
Virgin Mary, 30, 193–94n34
virtue (vs goodness), x, 10–11, 15, 22, 24, 30–31, 53–55, 60–62, 70–95 passim, 114–25 passim, 128–29, 133, 154–55. *See also* charity; citizenship, citizen; courage; conscience; duty; indignation; moderation; the noble; prudence; sincerity; truth
Voltaire, 19, 87; *Candide, ou l'Optimisme*, 87; Condorcet on Voltaire's esoteric writing, 187n59; organizer of conspiracy against Rousseau, 167n5, 168n9; originally a friend of Rousseau, 182n22

Wacjman, Claude: history of diagnoses of Rousseau's mental illness, 168n7
Wade, Ira, esoteric writing in France before Rousseau, 192n27
Wahl, Jean: Rousseau's "sentiment of existence" as opposed to thinking, 197n26
Warens, Françoise-Louise Madame de (Rousseau's "Maman"), 12, 51, 71, 155–56, 164n22, 171n24, 176n59, 180n8
weeping, tears, 10, 24, 123, 171n24, 172n30. *See also* laughter
Wittgenstein, Ludwig, x
Wolmar, 87, 183n26, 184n32, 185n42, 192–93n29, 207n13
Wordsworth, William, 201n15

Xanthippe, 162n7, 209n9
Xenocrates, 3
Xenophon, ix, xi, 22, 41, 71, 170n23, 190–91n18; *Apology of Socrates to the Jury*, 24–25, 170n23; *Economist*, 75, 82, 134, 188n4, 206n25; *Education of Cyrus*, 75, 162n5, 209n13; *Memorabilia*, 50–51, 92, 155, 196–97n21, 204n13, 208–9n8, 209n10; *Symposium*, 3

Yvon, Abbé Claude, article "Soul" for *Encyclopedia*, discussing Plato's esoteric writing, 192n27

zoology, 133, 136